Rewriting Saints and Ancestors

THE MIDDLE AGES SERIES

Ruth Mazo Karras, Series Editor
Edward Peters, Founding Editor

Rewriting Saints and Ancestors

Memory and Forgetting in France, 500–1200

Constance Brittain Bouchard

PENN

UNIVERSITY OF PENNSYLVANIA PRESS

PHILADELPHIA

Published by
University of Pennsylvania Press
Philadelphia, Pennsylvania 19104-4112
www.upenn.edu/pennpress

Printed in the United States of America on acid-free paper
10 9 8 7 6 5 4 3 2 1

Library of Congress Cataloging-in-Publication Data
Bouchard, Constance Brittain.
    Rewriting saints and ancestors : memory and forgetting in France, 500-1200 / Constance Brittain Bouchard. — 1st ed.
        p. cm. — (Middle Ages series)
    Includes bibliographical references and index.
    ISBN 978-0-8122-4636-0 (hardcover : alk. paper)
    1. Historiography—France—History—To 1500. 2. France—History—To 987—Historiography. 3. France—History—Medieval period, 987-1515—Historiography. 4. France—History—To 987—Sources. 5. France—History—Medieval period, 987-1515—Sources. 6. Christian hagiography—History—To 1500. 7. Genealogical literature—France—History—To 1500. 8. Middle Ages—Historiography. 9. Memory—History. I. Title. II. Series: Middle Ages series.
    D13.5.F8B68 2014
    944'.01072—dc23
                                                                    2014007757

To my mother, Harriet Ann Beckwith Brittain

Contents

List of Illustrations   ix

Preface   xi

Notes on Terminology   xiii

Introduction   1

1. Cartularies: Remembering the Documentary Past   9

2. The Composition and Purpose of Cartularies   22

3. Twelfth-Century Narratives of the Past   38

4. Polyptyques: Twelfth-Century Monks Face the Ninth Century   53

5. An Age of Forgery   63

6. Remembering the Carolingians   87

7. Creation of a Carolingian Dynasty   106

8. Western Monasteries and the Carolingians   126

9. Eighth-Century Transitions: The Evidence from Burgundy   152

10. Great Noble Families in the Early Middle Ages   176

11. Early Frankish Monasticism   193

12. Remembering Martyrs and Relics in Sixth-Century Gaul   213

Conclusion   228

Appendix I. Monasteries in Burgundy and Southern Champagne   233

Appendix II. Churches in Auxerre   245

List of Abbreviations   251

Notes   253

Bibliography   327

Index   353

Acknowledgments   361

llustrations

Map. Early medieval France   xvi

Figure 1. The Merovingian dynasty   101

Figure 2. The Carolingian dynasty   107

Figure 3. The Carolingian dynasty according to Einhard, Paul the Deacon, and the Annals of Metz   111

Figure 4. The Etichonids   181

Figure 5. The Robertians   186

Figure 6. Seventh- and eighth-century men named Robert   189

Preface

In medieval France thinkers constantly reconceptualized their past. The proper interpretation of past events could give validity to the present and help control the future. The saints that now presided over churches and the ancestors that had first established a dynasty were an especially crucial part of creative memory. Scholars have long known that many of our primary sources for the period were written well after the events they describe, so that, for example, the reign of Clovis is known principally from the *Historia* of Gregory of Tours, composed nearly a century later. Such post facto accounts form the heart of this book, including twelfth-century scribes contemplating the ninth-century documents they copied into cartularies; ninth-century churchmen considering their sixth-century predecessors; and sixth-century writers in Gaul coming to terms with the Christianity of the fourth and fifth centuries. The changes and upheavals of the period 500–1200 were met by rewriting and re-remembering. Memory was always malleable, as each generation decided which events of the past were worth remembering and which were to be reinterpreted or else quietly forgotten.

Memory is a potentially enormous subject, and this book has constantly sought to become the thousand-page wonder that makes academic publishers of the twenty-first century recoil in horror. To keep it manageable in size, I have omitted many interesting topics—some of which were spun off as articles, summarized only briefly here—and tried (not always successfully) to pare down the endnotes to the most recent or most influential works. I urge those seeking a fuller historiography to consult the notes to the books and articles cited. References are generally given in short form; full details are reserved for the bibliography.

Notes on Terminology

Royal lineages had no official names in the period covered by this book. Members of these lineages did, however, clearly recognize their relatives, and it has not therefore seemed an undue stretch for modern scholars to give collective names to those related in the male line. The Merovingians were those descended according to legend from Meroveus, offspring of a fifth-century sea serpent. The Carolingians, the family of Charlemagne (d. 814), are here the Arnulfings (or occasionally the Pippinids) before Charlemagne's time.[1] The Capetians are the kings related in the male line to Hugh Capet, who replaced the last Carolingian on the French throne in 987, even though he was not in fact the first king in his family, a distinction that goes to his great-uncle. Before Hugh, the lineage is usually called Robertians, after his great-grandfather Robert the Strong.

Most of the people who appear in the book have names that could be spelled three or four or even more different ways: in modern English, French, or German (or occasionally Italian), or in medieval Latin. Thus Hugo, Ugo, Huo, Hugh, and Hughes are all possible ways to refer to the same person. If I have not always been completely consistent in choosing which version of a name to give someone (e.g., Charlemagne rather than Karl der Grosse, but Theoderic rather than Thierri), at least I have always called the same person the same thing. For clarity, I make a distinction in how I refer to a saint and how I refer to a church dedicated to that saint: Saint Martin indicates the person himself, St.-Martin a church dedicated to him.

Most of the examples in this book are from the regions now called France and Belgium, plus the westernmost edge of Germany (although the French-German border was not then where it is now, and Belgium did not exist as a country until the nineteenth century). In late antiquity this region is Gaul. In the Carolingian age it is Francia. In the eleventh and twelfth centuries it is simply France (although the French kingdom of the high Middle Ages did not include the lower Rhône, which had been part of Roman Gaul but in the twelfth century was part of the Holy Roman Empire). Although I take my examples from a broad geographic area, especially for the earlier period when the records are much sparser, the heart of my discussion is Burgundy-Champagne, the region stretching roughly from Châlons and Langres to Chalon and Mâcon, including Auxerre and Autun, the quintessential region "between the Rhine and the Loire." Place-names are given according to their modern French spelling (Reims instead of Rheims, Lyon instead of Lyons), except for those located in modern Germany (Aachen, not Aix-la-Chapelle). The few exceptions are for places much better known to an English-speaking audience by a different version of the name (Cologne, not Köln, and Burgundy, not Bourgogne).

Rewriting Saints and Ancestors

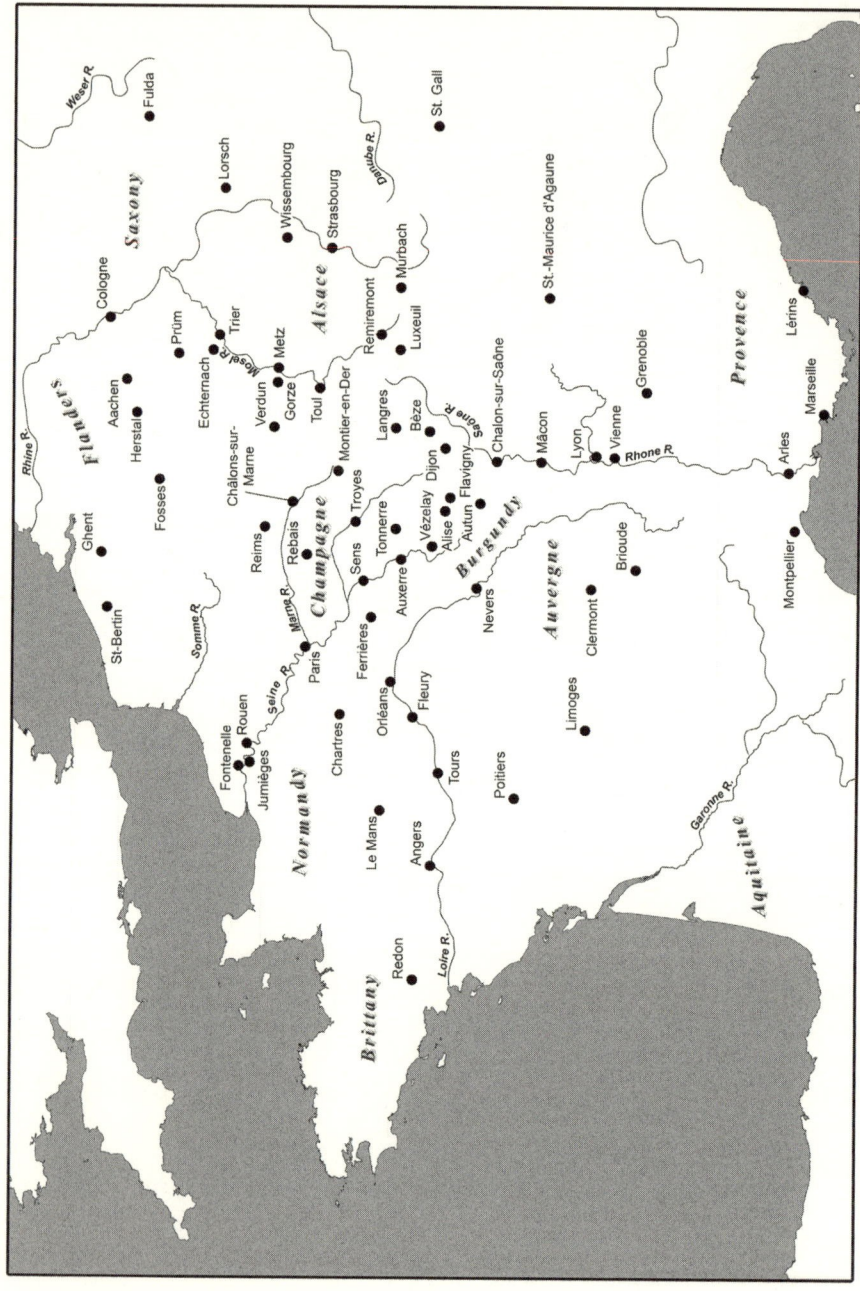

Early medieval France. By Gordon Thompson.

Introduction

The past is never dead. It's not even past.
—William Faulkner, *Requiem for a Nun*

Time's arrow moves in one direction only: forward. But memory moves backward. The past does not stand still but rather is in constant flux as it is remembered, remembered differently, or forgotten. In this book I examine, through the lens of memory, the sources from which modern scholars have constructed the church history and family history of France in the early and high Middle Ages in order to give the sources their full due as efforts to remember—or to create—a useful past for those who wrote them.

Medieval authors wanted above all to make sure that the events they recorded were *remembered*. Anselm of St.-Remy, giving the history of the 1049 dedication of his monastery and the great council at Reims, mentions memory three times in succession in his prologue. He wrote, he said, so that the events would not be "obliterated by silence." He wanted to be sure that the deeds of Leo IX, "of blessed recollection," be recorded, as worthy of *memoria*. And he wished to have the "memorable conclusion" to his monastery's rebuilding program preserved. At almost exactly the same time, a scribe at the monastery of Bèze began a charter recording a nobleman's gift to his monastery by saying, "The human mind is changeable, and what has been done is soon lost to memory, unless recorded in charters."[1] Sources thus should be seen as written so that certain events be properly remembered—or that those events *not* recorded be allowed to pass into oblivion. The past was malleable, and writing itself became an act of power, an effort to use the past to make sense of the present.

Medieval society was a "traditional" society—not in the sense that society was unchanging, because in fact society and culture were highly dynamic. But it was traditional in that tradition legitimized: "We have always done so" carried enormous moral and legal weight.[2] But the exercise of memory allows one to alter—or at least be selective with—tradition. The "old ways" provided validity even when those ways were being changed as they were invoked.[3] By changing what was "always done" in the past, one could change the present. Historical writing involved a conversation with the records of the past, at least some of which would have seemed disturbingly strange. Yet the past was the source of present custom and even identity, so writers had to be creative. Hence I shall discuss how medieval thinkers reconceptualized their pasts, sometimes altering tradition quite consciously but more commonly trying to interpret a past that seemed highly foreign in order to make it comprehensible to their own time.

Medievalists have always realized that the primary sources do not give a transparent window into the Middle Ages.[4] These sources were rarely written at the same time as the events they described. For example, even the essentially contemporary documents detailing property transactions between monks and laymen tended to be drawn up once the event was over, after all the negotiations had been completed, after the various people whose involvement was deemed necessary had been sought out and their consent given. Narrative composition was even further removed from the events recorded. Even in year-by-year "Annals," a selection was still made of which events, perhaps many months in the past, were significant enough to merit a record. Indeed, most surviving "Annals" were written substantially later, with a single author telling a continuous story even if he broke it down year by year. An additional distance is put between event and surviving record because, in the majority of cases, we have not the original manuscript but rather a later copy of it, which itself might have been reworked to serve the needs of its own time.

Forgeries are also a key element of the study of creative memory.[5] Yet their study has been primarily restricted to German-speaking scholars and diplomaticists and to the question of whether particular charters should be considered false or authentic.[6] But false charters, like narrative sources, could reflect the past their composers would have liked to remember. Monks creating forged charters may sometimes have convinced themselves that they were only writing down what would or should have been written originally, or in other cases they may have knowingly tried to pass off blatant confections as genuine. They did at any rate often fool their own successors.

Merely to ask if a charter is "true" or "false" is not enough. I would certainly not suggest that medieval authors failed to understand the difference between real or imaginary. When medieval authors forged, they knew it. Both late imperial and early medieval law codes took forgery very seriously, and penalties were severe.[7] But one could not merely conclude that these authors hypocritically committed forgery behind a pious facade. To re-remember the past, even to the extent of creating documents that *should* have existed, was to engage in activities that, for them, were true.

Given the relative sparsity of sources in the first place, their unreliability (in a positivist sense) can cast something of a pall over efforts to write history. But medievalists have been asking not "what really happened" but "what did contemporaries find significant" or "what were the authors' attitudes toward the events they described" long before postmodern theory became established within the historical discipline.[8] This is not to cast doubt on the possibility of studying early medieval history at all or to flog the gap between document and reality, already too well understood. Rather, it emphasizes the need to study the ways that medieval chroniclers and cartulary compilers used, understood, and reworked their own sources for the history of their past.

Recently a number of scholars have decided to make a virtue rather than liability out of the gap between event and record. "Memory" has rather abruptly become one of the more exciting ways of approaching medieval history.[9] If von Rankian positivism has not been completely abandoned, then the question has still certainly shifted. Three scholars essentially began the current study of memory in the Middle Ages, two historians and a literary specialist: Walter Goffart, Patrick Geary, and Mary Carruthers. Goffart studied the great "national" narratives of the early Middle Ages, not to mine them for nuggets of information but rather to ask about the meaning of the past they portrayed for their own contemporaries. Geary argued that the modern vision of the tenth century as a rather dark and chaotic period is based not on tenth-century sources but rather on sources written by eleventh-century authors, who deliberately created such a vision in order to draw a contrast with their own period. Carruthers focused on how medieval thinkers conceptualized the process of memory itself, including their methods for remembering complicated texts and the importance of preserving the *memoria* of sacred events.[10]

Initial scholarly doubts as to whether there could be anything useful to be learned by the study of memory were quickly cast aside, as growing numbers of historians have found it much more worthwhile to ask how medieval authors thought of their own pasts than to pursue a rather fruitless search for historical "truth."[11] Modern psychology has also made clear how flexible human memory is, with remembered events continually subject to change, shuffled and altered to make emotional or intellectual sense.

Medieval people's memory and the shaping of that memory for present needs have thus become a focus of study in their own right. The study of medieval memory has also begun to merge with hagiographic studies, which have shaken off the old label of "history of superstition."[12] Because a saint's life was often written long after the saint herself had lived or was rewritten a century or two later even if there was a roughly contemporary *vita*, such lives were long considered useless as sources of accurate history. But they have more recently been recognized as extremely useful sources for discovering how medieval people conceptualized their own pasts.[13] Patrick Geary, a pioneer in treating saints' lives as a fit subject for study just as he was later a pioneer in memory studies, at first received strong discouragement in this area as well.[14] But almost immediately a number of other medieval scholars began treating saints' lives as a new, previously undiscovered source with which to ask questions about everything from gender to power relationships, and by the 1990s the need to justify the use of hagiographic materials was over.[15] Merovingian studies especially, once nearly moribund, have been revived by the new interest in the *vitae* of Merovingian-era saints, especially women saints.[16]

In this book I take the study of medieval memory one step further, using it as a tool to ask questions about both the political and ecclesiastical history of France in the early and high Middle Ages. Here I address the ways that the past was creatively remembered, not simply as an exercise in memory but as part of self-definition and the creation of identity. I shall provide close examinations of how clerical authors viewed, tried to come to terms with, and often reworked the histories of their churches and of how noble families sought to define their authority and their ancestors. Representations of a family's past could serve as a bulwark for their political and social position in the present.[17]

The most important ecclesiastical sources for the present study are cartularies, chronicles, saints' *vitae*, and "Gesta," the latter being histories of the abbots or bishops who headed a particular church. Secular sources include the family histories and royal chronicles that served a similar function as "Gesta," although for different sorts of rulers. In addition, sources include forged documents, which deserve to be analyzed much more broadly than they often have been.

By focusing on the creation of written works, forged or authentic, I am of course privileging literacy over orality, but this should not be taken as any a priori judgment on the worth of the literate. After all, the line between literary and oral is not the same as the line between elite and popular, for many authors wrote down accounts they said they had heard orally, and even the illiterate could and did have stories read aloud to them. Literacy was also (relatively) common in the Middle Ages, scholars now agree, at least as much so as before the origins of modern schooling in the eighteenth century. Recent studies of medieval memory have thus discarded the artificial distinction between oral memory, assumed to be flexible, and written memory, assumed to be invariable. A study of records necessarily focuses on the written word, but one must always recall that words were generally spoken before they were written and that oral comments upon the completed page would have been part of the written page's uses.[18]

In addition, the written word was used to validate nonwritten sources and vice versa. Abbot Bovo's eleventh-century account of the discovery (*inventio*) of the relics of Saint Bertin, the patron of his monastery, justified his own authority and the spiritual power of his house, but his written text would not have sufficed without the relics themselves, and the relics would have had little value without his account validating their identity.[19] Hence, although the following discussion focuses on the creation of the written word, it must always be kept in mind that the present silence of the surviving parchment and the words written on it masks an original context of doubtless noisy conversation.

The monks, bishops, and kings who reworked the received memories of their own pasts, of ancient saints and ancestors, creatively reworked memory so powerfully that the paradigms they created have persisted in modern historical memory. That is, the modern conception of Roman Gaul is heavily influenced by the historians of the sixth and seventh centuries, and the modern view of the Merovingian period is still that shaped by their Carolingian-era successors. Carolingian history itself tends to be studied with an eye toward the tenth and eleventh centuries, when supposedly it all came apart, or even (sometimes) toward the European Union, when supposedly it all came together again.[20] Even when we still have the sources on which medieval chroniclers drew to create an account of their past—which we do in a surprising number of cases—scholars tend to accept medieval authors' perspective on what these sources mean.

Here I am not so much interested in creating new paradigms to replace the ones that have held sway from the early Middle Ages until now—although to some extent that is the result—as in examining how those paradigms were created in the first place. I want to emphasize that my central purpose is *not* to create a more "accurate" version of early medieval history. Rather, this book explores how the version that writers of the Middle Ages wanted to be remembered was constructed and how elements that did not fit into that vision were reworked, reexplained, or quite deliberately forgotten.

Thus the contrasts between what one period remembered and what the sources of an earlier period suggest may in fact have happened indicate that cartularies were far more than transcriptions of a church's archives; that monasticism became well established in Gaul only in the seventh century, not the fifth; that the Merovingian church was not in decline when the Arnulfings rose to power; that Pippin the Short's ancestors were not a straight line of mayors of the palace leading inevitably to the Frankish throne; and that monasteries of the high Middle Ages had very different records, rules, and patrons than those in late antiquity. Though these will not be novel insights to modern historians, the point is that all of these issues were seen quite differently by medieval people themselves, looking back at their own pasts. Throughout, even if I cast doubt on the accuracy of medieval memories, I strive not to denigrate the integrity and dignity of those whose memories they were. They remembered in a certain way for certain reasons, and their reasons are this book's true focus.

This study spans a broad period, from the sixth century to the twelfth, from the establishment of what one might term the medieval form of Christianity, to the rise and decline of Carolingian hegemony, to the broadest flourishing of monasticism. Or rather this study spans the period from the twelfth century to the sixth, because for a study of looking backward I have structured the book to move chronologically backward. The reverse chronology was chosen in order to emphasize that my central concern is not particular events but rather the memory of those events. If a chapter (say) on ninth-century records were followed rather than preceded by one on the use of such records in the twelfth century, it would be too easy to make the principal question whether the twelfth century got it right. The chief geographic focus is the region of Burgundy-Champagne, but for earlier centuries, with a much smaller number of surviving sources, the territory from which materials have been selected expands.

This book builds on yet goes well beyond my earlier work on the medieval church and noble families. The organization here, starting in the twelfth century and then moving back toward the sixth, mirrors my own scholarly career. Previously I tended to focus on the new, on reformation of the old or the creation of entirely novel forms of thought and religious life.[21] Here, however,

I examine how monks in houses with long histories tried to understand the documents in their archives, many of which made little sense for contemporary purposes, and to come to terms with the events of earlier centuries as reflected in those documents. In my previous work on Carolingian-era family trees, I tried to work out what family connections really existed, as well as what these family connections can tell us about contemporary family structure,[22] but here my main interest is how some relatives were deliberately added to family genealogies—and which ones just as deliberately left out.

In taking the story of memory back into the Merovingian era, I am entering a new field of study. Scholars of the early Middle Ages have for years been trying to persuade those of us primarily focused on the twelfth century that "our" century did not invent religious reform, literacy, government, or family consciousness, and it thus seems appropriate for someone who began with twelfth-century studies to go back to the first medieval centuries for a good look.

Many other extremely able scholars have of course worked with early medieval sources before me. Because of the relative scarcity of those records (and also somewhat ironically, given these scholars' zeal for informing others of the importance of the period), historians studying the era often become highly protective of their sources and contentious over what they tell us. Some could thus be irritated at a historian entering their territory from a twelfth-century perspective. Perhaps because it has been so difficult to answer the basic questions about the narrative of events in the sixth through eighth centuries, those studying the period are still trying to address them, but these are not the only questions worth asking.

If I do not always appear properly appreciative of the historiography of a modern dispute (for example, over the functions of a Merovingian royal official), it is not because I am dismissive of such scholarship but because I believe it crucial to include the beginnings of the Middle Ages within broader medieval history. Gaul's saints were the principal saints revered in medieval France, and the Merovingian kings were the original model for what the Carolingians and later the Capetians either had to adopt or react against. The memory of late antiquity needs to be kept alive even among scholars who have not spent half their lives studying it, so that it shall not be forgotten in the twenty-first century any more than it was in the ninth century or the twelfth.

The first chapters of this book focus on chronicles and charter collections from the high Middle Ages, as compositions intended to order the past and make it useful. I begin with cartularies, which were, in the form they acquired in the twelfth century, a way of making sense of the Carolingian past. I also study chronicle sources that put the histories of the authors' own monasteries at the center of global history, as constructed by monks trying to be true to the records they found but also trying to create something useful for their own present.

Next I turn to the Carolingian era, when polyptyques were compiled to order both the more recent and the more distant past, when forged documents took the creation of memory to new levels, and when noble families reorganized themselves around the imperial center. Crucial to this section is the Carolingian royal family themselves: how they justified their position by reworking the memory of their family, with the assistance of clerical authors at court, and how the monks of the Carolingian empire reacted to them. The transitional period between the Merovingian and Carolingian eras, I shall argue, was to a large extent a true time of forgetting.

Finally I turn to the Merovingian period, for even an age that may now appear long forgotten looked at its own forgotten past and tried to revive it. Here I reexamine the rise of the cult of the saints through the lens of memory, specifically the way that hagiographers of the sixth century tried to deal with the almost complete gap in veneration between the time when martyrs lived and died and their own time, when those martyrs were honored and their bodies dispersed among the churches—a gap which, from the hagiographers' point of view, should not have existed. When people lived in times of long ago, they never thought they lived long ago. They thought they lived Now.

Chapter 1

Cartularies: Remembering the Documentary Past

In the first decade of the twelfth century, Warin, cantor of the cathedral of Châlons-sur-Marne, set out to create a cartulary for his church, a book into which he copied old charters. He began, "Here are the documents (*precepta*) of the church of St.-Etienne of Châlons, which were scattered (*dispersa*) and nearly destroyed by age. Warin the cantor collected them and copied them with his own hand." On the following pages he transcribed charters from kings and bishops, as well as a few from powerful laymen, dating between 565 and 1107.[1]

This cartulary, composed of forty-eight parchment folios, is the only source for the documents Warin copied, for all of the originals have disappeared.[2] Since he was already concerned about the ravages of time, and since the earliest of the documents he copied was already some 550 years old when he worked and doubtless written on papyrus, this disappearance is unsurprising. The cartulary has been little noted by scholars, other than those editing the charters of Charles the Bald, who issued a large number of *precepta* for the bishopric of Châlons. There is nothing particularly remarkable about Warin's cartulary, other than our knowing the scribe's name and his stated purpose for creating it. Dozens of scribes at other monasteries and cathedrals across the neighboring regions of Champagne and Burgundy created cartularies within a generation on either side of Warin's enterprise. But this modest cartulary underlines something far too easy to overlook: we would know *substantially* less about the Merovingian and Carolingian periods were it not for obscure scribes of the high Middle Ages.

The majority of earlier documents are now available only because later scribes believed they were worth copying and preserving. It has been estimated that, for all the regions contained within modern-day France, fewer than five hundred original charters survive from before the year 900,[3] meaning that our knowledge of the early Middle Ages depends on high medieval cartularies. Thus, although the study of cartularies might be considered diplomatic history, it is also an example of memory studies. We remember what the monks, nuns, or cathedral canons of the high Middle Ages wanted posterity to remember.

Ecclesiastical and Secular Cartularies

To give the simplest definition, a cartulary is a codex into which were copied charters that had been collected over a period of years or even centuries. The term *cartularium* originally just meant a collection of charters, probably kept in a box.[4] Codexes containing copies of charters became common in the high Middle Ages, but such a volume was rarely called a *cartularium* before the seventeenth century; in the Middle Ages it was most commonly called simply a *liber*.[5]

Cartularies remain surprisingly little studied; it is not even possible to create an accurate list of the French cartularies that still survive.[6] Treating a cartulary as an unproblematic window into a monastery's archival holdings, as has too often been done, can make the cartulary itself invisible, thus preventing proper appreciation of this kind of record.[7] My purpose here is to give visibility to cartularies as an expression of memory: not just witnesses to what might have been written down at an earlier time but as evidence of medieval people making conscientious efforts to order and renew their memory of the past.

To the modern medievalist, French cartularies may seem a normal and unambiguous source. One goes to the library or to interlibrary loan, and there they are: edited by conscientious scholars, perhaps dusty and a bit yellow but still perfectly serviceable. Like Warin eight centuries before them, editors have prepared useful copies of documents they feared would otherwise be lost or made inaccessible. Cartularies' familiarity may, however, obscure a crucial aspect of their composition: they were novel, even revolutionary when they were first put together and represented a new way of organizing and thinking about both a monastery's past and its possessions.[8]

Modern edited cartularies are themselves the product of reconsidering the past. A well-done edition is a boon for the scholar, obviating the need for every person using the same cartulary to try to sort out the identification of the same persons or places or to decipher the same obscure readings. But a printed edition is a commentary, not just a form of transmittal, and medieval cartularies were themselves much more than transmittals of earlier documents.

Most eleventh- and twelfth-century French cartularies were produced by ecclesiastics for their churches, whether monastery or cathedral. In addition, a handful of great nobles (usually king or count) produced cartularies, beginning in the 1180s, although most secular cartularies, always rarer than ecclesiastical cartularies, date from the late Middle Ages.[9] Secular cartularies were generally composed not primarily of donation charters but rather of fiscal accounts and the records of oaths of fidelity and the settlement of disputes. These secular cartularies were often drawn up in response to specific crises—in Champagne, for example, the rebellions and difficulties that accompanied the regency of Countess Blanche at the beginning of the thirteenth century.[10] In the following pages I shall focus almost entirely on ecclesiastical cartularies, but secular cartularies, too, served to organize and perpetuate memory.

The Origin of Cartularies

Copying charters was already an old practice when the cantor Warin worked at Châlons. The first cartularies, the first volumes composed of integral copies of documents, were composed in the Rhineland.[11] Fulda's cartulary, begun under Abbot Hrabanus Maurus in the early ninth century, was a collection of small books, one for each region where the monks owned property, with charters arranged roughly chronologically within each booklet. Although only fragments remain of these original booklets, they were recopied into a single codex in the twelfth century.[12] The future of cartularies was as a codex, not booklets. The monastery of Wissembourg, a seventh-century foundation, put its cartulary together a generation or two after Fulda's, in the 860s.[13] At Lorsch, a monastery founded in 764, almost all the documents in the existing twelfth-century cartulary are organized by early medieval *pagus* and indeed date from before the final decades of the ninth century, so it seems likely that the cartulary was originally put together in the 870s, and the monks of the twelfth century, like their contemporaries at Fulda, recopied it.[14]

A key role in the creation of these ninth-century cartularies may have been played by the late eighth-century *Codex Carolinus*. This volume was originally put together by the Frankish royal chancery in 791, when Charlemagne feared that the letters on papyrus that he and his predecessors, Charles Martel and Pippin the Short, had received from the popes over the previous three-quarters of a century would be lost if not recopied.[15] Short headings were added to each charter in the codex, summarizing the contents, just as later cartulary scribes typically used short headings (rubrics, commonly written in red ink). The original, eighth-century version of the *Codex Carolinus* was copied in Cologne in the second half of the ninth century and thus may well have been the inspiration for other cartularies composed in the Rhineland.

If the *Codex Carolinus* gave the format for early cartularies, then the need for such a book came from the large number of charters, which by the ninth century must have become very unwieldy. At Fulda, for example, there are some five hundred documents in its cartulary dating from before the year 800, which may well have been why the organization and copying of these documents seemed necessary. Large numbers of charters did not necessarily lead to cartulary creation, however. Cartularies remained unusual in the Carolingian era. St.-Gall, with as many documents as Fulda, managed very well without one.[16] Sometimes documents might just be paraphrased briefly in *libri traditioni* (*Traditionsbücher* in modern German) or listed even more summarily in a register.[17]

In contrast to the Rhineland, there were essentially no French, English, or Italian cartularies before the eleventh century.[18] Individual charters might be recopied or a few related charters copied together into a dossier for a specific purpose,[19] but for the most part the original documents in the archives were considered sufficient before the year 1000. Ecclesiastics could be acutely aware of what their archives contained and be determined to preserve the memory of the events recorded in those archives, without requiring integral transcriptions.

At the monastery of St.-Wandrille of Fontenelle, for example, a chronicle from the early ninth century related the history of the house and its abbots since its seventh-century foundation. The chronicler spoke proudly of royal charters in the archives (*in scriniis*, the same term he used for reliquaries) and paraphrased a number to illustrate his points, but he saw no need to make complete copies.[20] Similarly, a contemporary monk at St.-Denis wrote the "Gesta Dagoberti," fleshing out the *vita* of the Merovingian king with short paraphrases of royal documents given to his monastery, where Dagobert was buried.[21]

In the tenth century one occasionally sees a transitional form between ninth-century paraphrases within a chronicle and eleventh-century cartularies. For example, at the Flemish monasteries of St.-Bertin and of St.-Peter's of Ghent, the monks wrote *gesta* of the abbots of their houses (the version at Ghent modeled directly on that of Fontenelle), including a full transcription of some of their charters.[22] In all these cases, the authors knew their archives, knew that they were special, even sacred, but the chroniclers at Fontenelle and St.-Denis, unlike the later monks of St.-Bertin and Ghent, did not see copying entire texts as a necessary part of preserving what was already so precious.

One possible reason why eastern Francia developed its cartularies so much earlier than did the West, it has been suggested, is that western estates were larger and better organized, whereas eastern monasteries had received a great many small gifts in many places, requiring a cartulary to keep track of them.[23] It has also been suggested that, because public notaries were never found in eastern Francia as they had been in the West, churches there took charge of their own records sooner and found the cartulary form a convenient tool.[24] The problem with this explanation is that public notaries were also gone from western Francia by 800, and western churches hence took responsibility for their records at least two centuries before the appearance of cartularies.[25]

Another proposed explanation is that eastern churches felt threatened by the Carolingians and created first dossiers of property holdings and then cartularies to help defend these holdings from the king.[26] The difficulty here is that western churches were just as threatened by royal seizure of property, as discussed in Chapter 8. Perhaps the explanation should be found rather in the difficulties western monasteries faced in the ninth century from Vikings, lay abbots, and royal depredations, difficulties that left few with a regular life. Only with monastic reform and renewal did houses look back over the records of their history and seek to retell that doubtless glorious past through ordering those records in cartularies.[27]

Cartularies in the Eleventh to Thirteenth Centuries

One hundred and fifty years after the first Rhineland cartularies, ecclesiastical records began to be copied into cartularies in the French heartland.[28] Cartularies first appeared there in the eleventh century and became common only in the early decades of the twelfth. They appear to have been composed in the context of reform and increased order; the cartulary of St.-Etienne of Dijon, for example, was put together just after this house of secular canons was reformed to the Augustinian rule in 1113.[29]

Perhaps the earliest existing codex from the Burgundy-Champagne region that could now be considered a cartulary is that of St.-Pierre-le-Vif of Sens, from the opening years of the eleventh century.[30] It took the form of a lectionary into which, at several points, documents from St.-Pierre's archives were copied.[31] This cartulary, a volume that included prayers, sermons, and charters all copied together, was clearly not modeled on the very differently organized Rhineland cartularies. Rather, in an effort to organize and preserve important material, the St.-Pierre scribe joined liturgy and charters in an act of conscious memory.

If we know, because it still survives, that the monks of St.-Pierre-le-Vif were creating a cartulary at the beginning of the eleventh century, then we can infer that at roughly the same time another one of the earliest Burgundian cartularies was being created at the monastery of Flavigny. Here, however, the earlier compilation is suggested only by the much better known cartulary of the twelfth century. The dates of the charters range from 717 to 1113, but virtually all date from before the second quarter of the eleventh century. Although it is known from the *Chronicon* of Hugh of Flavigny, abbot at the end of the eleventh century, that the monks received a large number of gifts from the local laity after about 1050, none of these are recorded in the cartulary. Thus it seems most likely that the cartulary was initially put together in the early eleventh century, shortly after the monastery was reformed under Abbot Heldric (992–1009), and that Hugh of Flavigny listed gifts in his *Chronicon* as a supplement.[32]

The cartulary of Flavigny doubtless achieved its final form shortly after 1113, when a scribe recopied the early eleventh-century compilation, incorporating the records of the half-dozen gifts that had been made since the cartulary was originally put together but that had eluded Abbot Hugh. The twelfth-century scribe seems also to have physically attached the original charters recording the house's eighth-century foundation to the back of his codex. There they were copied by a late medieval scribe, who made a duplicate of the cartulary, and there they were seen by Jean Mabillon in the seventeenth century.[33]

When Flavigny's 1113 cartulary was composed, cartularies had become much more common than they had been a century earlier. The real impetus for cartularies in Burgundy had come in the middle of the eleventh century, with their composition at Cluny. It is surely significant that Cluny was founded after the era of Viking attacks and had always observed a regular life. There scribes tried, not always successfully, to group the charters from their voluminous archives by abbot. Cluny's first cartulary (Cluny A) includes documents dating to the monastery's early decades; other cartularies were then composed using the same organizational system.[34] St.-Bénigne of Dijon, which had been reformed to Cluny's *ordo* two generations earlier, quickly produced its own cartulary.[35]

Cluny's cartularies proved highly influential, and in the first decades of the twelfth century a number of older monasteries also produced their first (relatively comprehensive) collections of charters. As well as Warin's cartulary at Châlons and the final version of the cartulary of Flavigny, examples from the same region include the cartularies of St.-Etienne of Dijon, St.-Marcel-lès-Chalon, Bèze, Montier-en-Der, Vézelay, and the Cluniac nunnery of Marcigny.[36] The rapid multiplication of cartularies suggests that scribes at one church were inspired by hearing about the new cartulary at another. Some older houses waited to produce cartularies, but most late twelfth-century cartularies were composed at houses that had been founded only recently. Among the Cistercians of Burgundy, for example, Pontigny and Theuley put together their first cartularies at the very end of the twelfth century.[37]

Many churches that had not created a cartulary in the twelfth century composed one in the thirteenth. The houses that did so included both new foundations of the twelfth century and small, older houses that did not have enough accumulated documents to require a cartulary before the thirteenth century. For example, Cîteaux, Clairvaux, and the old Benedictine house of St.-Seine all composed cartularies in the 1220s.[38] The cathedral chapter of Langres, whose archives dated back only to the late eleventh century, waited until the early 1230s to create their first cartulary, although by then they had accumulated so many documents in their archives that they needed five scribes to work simultaneously on the project.[39] The monastery of St.-Germain of Auxerre, though founded in the Merovingian era, had few enough early documents that there was nothing like the same urgency in cartulary compilation. But even this house composed a cartulary in 1266, which was then added to in the following decades and indeed as late as the seventeenth century.[40]

Churches with an eleventh- or early twelfth-century cartulary might create an additional one in the late twelfth or thirteenth century, incorporating the charters that had been collecting since the original codex was put together. The monks of St.-Serge of Angers composed their first cartulary at the beginning of the twelfth century, including documents dating back to the house's foundation, and then, some two generations later, composed a second, including documents issued during the intervening years and some concerning the house's priories.[41] The monks of both Montier-en-Der and Molesme, who had composed their first cartularies in the 1120s, waited until the end of the thirteenth century to compose their second.[42] Similarly, monks with an early thirteenth-century cartulary generally waited to compile a second. The Cistercian monks of Cîteaux, Longué, Fontenay, and Pontigny, for example, who had composed their first cartularies early in the thirteenth century (in the 1190s for Pontigny), created their second cartularies only in the final years of that century.[43]

Forging the Past at St.-Denis

Cartulary scribes rarely attempted to improve what they found in their archives. Although most cartularies ended up with at least a few forgeries in them, generally these were created well before the cartulary itself. At Montier-en-Der, for example, which has an unusually large number of forged papal bulls, the forgeries were all created in the eleventh century, a good fifty years before a cartulary scribe incorporated them as authentic. Here the eleventh-century monks used the recent rise to preeminence of the papacy for their own purposes.[44] A forgery was confected to address a particular challenge to a monastery's rights or possessions, but the twelfth-century cartulary scribe, in assuming the forgery's authenticity, made its memory part of the house's ongoing present.

St.-Denis provides an unusual exception, in that the monks of the high Middle Ages repeatedly changed what they found in their records. They carried out a wholesale reworking of their history in the eleventh century, with the deliberate effort to deceive, to create a falsified past that would help them maintain their lands.[45] Their initial forgeries were created at the same time as the monks of Montier-en-Der were composing false papal charters, but the St.-Denis monks preferentially forged Merovingian-era documents.

More papyrus documents survive from St.-Denis than from any other monastery north of the Alps, and the reason is that they took on a new life, and hence a new value, when the monks turned them over so that forgeries could be written on the backs.[46] The monks were well aware that ancient records had been written on papyrus; their own archives told them so. But papyrus had not been imported into western Europe for centuries. Therefore, in order to give their forgeries a specious air of authenticity, they reused what they had. Although this reuse has been labeled a "destruction" of the memory of the past,[47] they actually ended up doing a better job than any other French monastery of preserving their Merovingian-era papyri. For that matter, the same monks of St.-Denis were very careful to preserve, unaltered, their earliest parchment charters. It thus seems more appropriate to see their activities not as destruction but rather as the re-creation of the past in a more comprehensible (to them) and useful form.

At about the same time or a few years later, these monks also confected a small cartulary full of forged documents, supposedly dating from the seventh through ninth centuries, plus a few privileges from eleventh-century popes. Although the documents in the cartulary are not precisely the same as the forgeries on papyrus—indeed, two of the cartulary's Merovingian-era documents are considered authentic—the texts are close enough that it seems most likely that efforts were coordinated.[48] By the 1060s the composition of cartularies was considered normal enough that the monks believed that displaying copies of their "privileges" written in such a cartulary would give an additional air of plausibility to the papyri. In order to claim property for their monastery, the monks turned to the past, a past that was mediated through the production of cartularies. Antiquity provided validity, both they and their contemporaries would have agreed. Thus they forged documents of those who had supposedly been generous to the house in its earliest days.

Especially important to the eleventh-century monks was King Dagobert I (d. 639). Dagobert had been buried at St.-Denis, as already noted. St.-Denis's ninth-century vita of Dagobert had transformed him into a virtual saint, and it seemed entirely appropriate that their cartulary begin with gifts from him. But the monks had no necessary preference for one dynasty over another; their cartulary also included gifts and privileges from Charlemagne, Charles the Bald, and Philip I, their contemporary, whom they asked to confirm everything recorded in the cartulary. Popes were equally important; included were many (supposed) charters from the time of Popes Zacharias and Stephen II in the middle of the eighth century, up through the monks' contemporaries Nicholas II and Alexander II. The eighth-century popes were identified as the same ones who helped establish the Carolingians on the Frankish throne,[49] which further validated the monastery's status. In addition, the monks referred to the Pseudo-Isidorian decretals (discussed further in Chapter 5) under the name of the "*Decretum* of Pope Gregory"; the decretals, by stressing the pope's eminence, reduced the authority of bishops over monasteries. The whole cartulary was thus intended to create a memory of their house and its possessions: beloved by kings and popes, not subject to the whims of the bishops of Paris, it was wealthy and holy and deserved every bit of its preeminence.[50]

Cartularies and the Written Word

Composition in the high Middle Ages has sometimes been seen not merely as an effort to shape memory through writing but as a symptom of a new attitude toward record keeping, an increase in what is termed the "literate mode."[51] The first cartularies, it has been argued, were a response to a new way of looking at the written word: indeed, a "mutation" of the year 1000 as significant as those that have been postulated for political and social structures.[52] But as I shall argue, this is too simple a way to look at cartularies.

Certainly the administration of power in the high Middle Ages became increasingly focused on written documents. Orders and commands were communicated in writing, as were judicial decisions, and the maintenance and organization of written records became the task of professionals at the papal and royal courts. The late antique distinctions between public and private charters, or between judicial decisions given in writing and documents that merely recalled a judicial action (*subjectif* versus *objectif* in modern French), were long gone, and scribes and chanceries felt free to develop their own models.[53] At roughly the same time, nonroyal laymen began sealing charters as kings had done for centuries, and bishops routinely sealed the charters that they witnessed. The seal, which normally carried a stereotyped image of the bishop or the lord, became a projection of authority and by association of the sealed charter. By the late twelfth century an unsealed charter was rare.[54]

Here it is worth stressing something that should be obvious: even when the cartulary preserves the text of charters whose originals are now long lost, at the time that cartularies were composed all the originals must have existed, or else copies could not have been made of them. A cartulary thus cannot be assumed to be a response to a new interest in keeping records in writing, for ecclesiastics had been doing so all along.[55] Even if monks felt the need to have a written record when no such formal charter was produced, they could jot down notes, often combining multiple transactions on a single piece of parchment. For St.-Rigaud, for example, an eleventh-century foundation in the diocese of Mâcon, there still exist three large sheets of parchment on which a whole series of different gifts were recorded in multiple hands during the 1060s and 1070s.[56] Such notes were not a substitute for a cartulary; they rather were one of the sorts of sources that were copied into a cartulary.

A cartulary scribe was thus not *creating* a written record of his church's history. He or she was instead reworking and reconceptualizing those records by the very act of organizing and copying them. Monasteries had always valued the written record. Cartularies may have been created in part as a response to the multiplication of archival documents but not to a new attitude toward writing. Rather, they represented a new approach to organizing the monks' collective memory. It should not be surprising that the great era of cartularies was the twelfth and thirteenth centuries, during the Renaissance of the Twelfth Century and Henry Adams's Greatest Century. The impulse that led to the systematic treatment of both canon law and theology also led monks to work out exactly what their monastery owned and how they had obtained it. They ordered their archives and copied them into codexes as part of a broader effort, involving everything from making lists of books in the library to writing universal chronicles, intended to create a coherent documentary record of their history and possessions. In the high Middle Ages, memory was supposed to be organized.[57]

Even before they began composing cartularies, Frankish monks had known the relationship between memory and property and known that memory was dependent on written documents. The attacks of Saracens and Vikings, fires, or other destruction meant that churches often felt obliged to try to re-create the lost records of their patrimony and privileges. In the ninth century they generally went to the kings. Kings were, as a group, extremely obliging, willing to take the churchmen's word for what they had owned, even if the records confirming that ownership were lost. That the Carolingian kings often mentioned that their royal predecessors had given grants and privileges to the bereft churches indicates that they could proclaim their position by their generosity: to be those who granted, as their predecessors had, meant that they shared in their authority.[58]

For example, in 814, almost immediately after succeeding his father, Louis the Pious was approached by Betto, bishop of Langres. Betto told him that during the Saracen incursions all the *instrumenta* issued to the bishops of his see had been burned or lost, including royal privileges and immunities.[59] Louis readily agreed to confirm the bishop's authority.[60] Both Betto and Louis recognized that an orderly exercise of power depended at least in part on the written word but that a lack of a charter from the past could be compensated for by a new, impeccably authoritative document.

Cartulary scribes, like Betto several centuries earlier, knew that memory was preserved best when in writing. But cartularies were a special kind of writing, for they did not originate a written record but rather rewrote and reorganized what already existed, as can further be demonstrated in comparing them to pancartes.

Pancartes and Cartularies

Cartularies were not the only way to inscribe together a number of different transactions. If a gift or quarrel settlement was not recorded in writing when it occurred, the most common response in the twelfth century, especially for the monks of the Cistercian order, was to have the bishop draw up a pancarte.[61] A pancarte, most simply, is a single piece of parchment on which numerous transactions, taking place at different times and involving different people, are all recorded together. This form of record keeping first appeared in the middle of the eleventh century and became common in the twelfth century.

The term *pancarta* had been in occasional use earlier but in a different sense: as registers of a church's property acquisitions, brief summaries of donations that might also be recorded on other pieces of parchment, or sometimes as recapitulations of everything a church owned.[62] But once a church started composing cartularies, integral copies of documents from its archives, they stopped, at least in the high Middle Ages, composing such summary registers. Instead, the term *pancarta* came to be used exclusively for collected paraphrases of donations and other actions that had not already been recorded in writing.[63]

Although at first glance a pancarte might thus be seen as a handy economy-sized version of a cartulary,[64] the composition and purpose of pancartes and cartularies were thus quite different. A pancarte was drawn up in order to make the transition from *living* memory to *written* memory. Gifts and privileges from the wealthy were generally recorded on parchment when they took place, thus immediately becoming part of written memory. Pancartes created a similar written record for donations from the less powerful.[65] Occasionally a pancarte would include a transcription of an original charter (especially a monastery's foundation charter), but these transcriptions were unusual, even when such originals existed.[66] For example, the Cistercian house of La Ferté, which produced pancartes but no cartulary, copied a few complete documents into pancartes, but most of its surviving originals were not so copied.[67] The occasional inclusion in a pancarte of a previously written document should not therefore obscure a pancarte's real purpose: to put in writing small transactions that might otherwise be "recorded" only in human memory.

A cartulary, in contrast to a pancarte, copied together transactions that had *already* been preserved in writing. Thus the records copied into a cartulary had previously made the transition from living to written memory, even before the cartulary was composed. Indeed, at Cistercian houses the twelfth-century pancartes generally fill the first few dozen folios of the cartulary.[68] A pancarte was thus not considered to serve the same purpose as a cartulary; rather it was something to be incorporated into one.

Such pancartes would typically be a detailed listing, written and sealed at the bishop's direction, of a number of gifts that had been received in the previous few years.[69] So many of them might be included that an episcopal pancarte from the twelfth century could easily reach three-quarters of a meter in length.[70] A pancarte was much more than an episcopal confirmation, such as would refer only very generally to a monastery's possessions. When a pancarte was drawn up, the memory of the gifts it recorded would still be fresh; in addition, the monks had usually made brief notes that they could present to the episcopal chancery.[71] These notes had little importance other than as an *aide-mémoire*, for once the pancarte was drawn up the notes seem frequently to have been cut into slices, to be frugally recycled as the strips that attached a wax seal to a charter. Although to a modern eye a sealed pancarte and a list of transactions that might be used as the basis for such a pancarte might look very similar, they thus served quite different functions.

The only exception in Burgundy to episcopally produced and sealed pancartes is that of the Cistercian house of La Bussière. There the monks had composed so many lists of donations—each entry being nothing more than a quick note on who had given what and where—that the bishop, rather than having his chancery rewrite the lists into a pancarte, merely sealed all the lists.[72] These were much less detailed than the pancartes at contemporary Cistercian houses, where living memory could supplement the material in the brief notes.[73] This example shows the importance of having the bishop seal a pancarte. Cartularies, in contrast, were never sealed, indeed not even presented to the bishop for confirmation or approval.

Cartularies, then, whose origins lay in the ninth century and whose tentative beginnings in France included chronicles that might incorporate some copies of charters, came into their own in the eleventh through thirteenth centuries. Determinedly focused on the written word, they did not *create* written accounts, as did pancartes, but rather reorganized the documentary memory of their past. In the next chapter I shall examine more closely the purpose and functions of these cartularies.

Chapter 2

The Composition and Purpose of Cartularies

Those who created cartularies did so with the purpose of creating a history of their church that was both coherent and complete. Cartularies were intended as part of the broader history of an ecclesiastical community. The documents in the archives were voices from a church's past, and for that past to be incorporated into the present they had to be copied out, made new again. An eleventh-century biography of a bishop of Auxerre praised the bishop for "renovating" the *Gesta* of his predecessors, having them copied out cleanly, ready for new entries—this bishop, according to his biographer, also restored tapestries to his church's walls and suitable vestments to his chapter clergy.[1] "Renovation," like restoration, made the best of the past a part of the present. The same impetus motivated those who composed cartularies.

Cartulary Composition

Cartulary scribes generally intended to give a fairly complete overview of their monasteries' records, but "complete" could vary considerably. Cartularies were not, as has sometimes been assumed, simply a transcription of everything in the archives. In the case of the cartulary of Châlons discussed in Chapter 1, the cathedral chapter would certainly have preserved more mundane charters as well as the royal and episcopal charters that the cantor Warin selected for inclusion. The cartulary of Pontigny does not include any of the dozens of papal bulls that still exist as originals; presumably these were copied instead into a separate bullarium—or were intended for one.[2] Any documents that were located elsewhere would of course not be copied. The twelfth-century cartulary of Montier-en-Der, for example, does not include several existing charters that were issued for the monastery's priories, charters that were presumably housed at those priories rather than the mother-house, or the privileges issued to the monks when they fled to St.-Chef in the Jura at the end of the ninth century, privileges that stayed at that house when the monks returned home.[3]

In addition, many a cartulary scribe, like a nineteenth-century editor, appears to have felt flagging enthusiasm as he progressed deep into his project and began to abbreviate heavily. Following many of the charters copied into the thirteenth-century cartulary of the bishopric of Auxerre are brief, one-line summaries of other charters dealing with the same subject.[4] Paul, the cartulary scribe for St.-Père of Chartres, expressed more explicitly than most the tedium of copying redundant or irrelevant charters: about halfway through his cartulary, Paul, who had so far been assiduously telling his readers that he had transcribed every charter he could find, instead commented, "I have decided to leave out those charters in which it appears there is nothing worth remembering now."[5]

Scribes, of course, did not include documents that no longer existed when they worked. This may seem self-evident, yet it is common for modern editions to include references to *perdita*, "lost charters" (use of the Latin giving a spurious suggestion that medieval scribes made annotations about such missing entries). For example, if a document of Louis the Pious refers to a privilege from his grandfather Pippin, then an editor may insert an entry, with document number even if no actual text, into the mid-eighth-century section of his edition. But cartularies of the high Middle Ages included only those charters currently in existence—and one cannot know whether, in this particular example, there had ever been a charter from Pippin the Short, or whether there was just an oral memory (or assertion) of such a privilege in the ninth century.

Cartulary scribes appreciated the aspects of the documents before them that gave the originals dignity and authority. They were well aware of the importance of such signs of validation as seals and monograms and sought to copy those symbols into their cartularies; if an original document were sealed, they might write *sigillum* in the margin.[6] At Cluny, for example, a comparison of the surviving charters with copies made for the eleventh-century cartularies shows that the scribes went out of their way to draw accurate reproductions of the graphic elements of the charters they copied.[7] The cartulary scribe at Auxerre carefully copied royal monograms and papal *rota* into his cartulary.

Not all documents copied into high medieval cartularies were originals, for it is possible that some recopying of charters had taken place in the Frankish heartland before the year 1000, as this would explain an apparent anomaly in Merovingian-era documents. Cartularies often include charters from the sixth and seventh centuries that differ enough from what modern scholars consider normal Merovingian protocols that they have been labeled forgeries. And yet many of these same charters contain elements arguing for authenticity, such as the correct names of contemporary bishops, spelling that is nonclassical in the same way that the spelling in surviving original documents is nonclassical, and a total silence on topics that would have been crucial when the cartularies were composed. Diplomatic studies have now passed beyond the former hypercriticism in which a document was considered either authentic or else a forgery—and most likely a forgery at that.[8] "Reworking" or "interpolation" is now often suggested as an alternative to assuming that twelfth-century scribes, without any Merovingian originals, were still able to create texts that look remarkably like authentic Merovingian originals. The question of *when* these reworkings took place, however, is rarely asked.

Here I would hypothesize that in at least some cases the monks of the ninth and tenth centuries were responsible: not out of an effort to forge but out of a desire to preserve. Although the use of parchment was just becoming common in the seventh century, it was still considered inferior to papyrus, which meant that most Merovingian-era originals were written on a material that proved highly fragile in northern Europe's climate.[9] Monks of the ninth century are well known for copying manuscripts of literature, theology, and law from late antiquity; indeed, were it not for their efforts, major portions of what we know of Roman history and culture would now be lost. The monks' own archival records, like the codexes they copied, would have been written on a material already showing signs of disintegration and in a script that few knew how to read. It would thus have seemed entirely appropriate to copy their most precious charters, in some cases "correcting" what they saw as errors in protocol—or simply filling in difficult passages with their best guesses. Most twelfth-century scribes, in turn, would not have appreciated that these (to them) ancient parchments from the ninth century were not originals and would have proudly copied them with the rest of their documents.

This is the case, for example, with the royal documents confirming the foundation of Montier-en-Der. Abbot Bercharius founded the monastery in 666, with the assistance of Bishop Nivard of Reims and of King Childeric II. In the following decades, in 675 and 685, King Childeric and his brother, King Theoderic III, confirmed the monastery's foundation and property and issued privileges of immunity.[10] These royal privileges were once treated as forgeries, owing to such anomalies as King Childeric being referred to as "Chilperic" in his brother's charter (at least in the cartulary copy, the earliest version we have); the absence of the kings' names at the very beginning of their charters; a reference to the bishop of Reims as an archbishop (a title that did not yet exist); and the inclusion of the name of the palace where the act was given, the last a relatively unusual element in Merovingian-era charters.[11] And yet there is also much to suggest the authenticity of Montier-en-Der's Merovingian privileges.

The names of the contemporary bishops and the mayor of the palace are all given correctly. The property listed, located as much as two hundred kilometers distant, bears no relationship to property the monks later owned and thus was unlikely to be a later confection. There is a good deal of overlap with a *vita* of Bercharius composed in the tenth century, although the property lists were radically shortened in the latter, suggesting that the hagiographer had read and used the Merovingian-era founding documents; it thus seems most likely that these documents were recopied at the same time as the *vita* was written.[12]

Everything from the protocols to the handwriting to the papyrus would have seemed strange to a tenth-century scribe, who might not even have recognized the king's name in the first line of a Merovingian charter, written in elaborate, elongated letters, and could easily have mistaken Childeric for Chilperic and decided to call the bishop of Reims an archbishop, the correct title in the Carolingian if not Merovingian era. The anomalies in these charters, in the only manuscript where they are now found—the twelfth-century cartulary—thus suggest a recopying some three centuries after they were originally issued.

Similarly, at the Benedictine monastery of Bèze, the monk who composed the cartulary-chronicle in the twelfth century included the semi-apocryphal story of his house's seventh-century foundation by Duke Amalgarius, with the support of King Clothar II. But the cartulary scribe had not created this story. It was already in circulation around 830, when the bishop of Langres referred to it as he restored the house and received royal confirmation of its possessions.[13] A twelfth-century chronicler, faced with such unimpeachable evidence, could not have raised doubts.

Cartulary scribes of the high Middle Ages sought accuracy. When a nun of St.-Julien of Auxerre was putting together a cartulary in the thirteenth century, she paused every document or two to recheck what she had transcribed, making corrections if necessary and writing in the margin, "Facta est collatio cum originali."[14] It may be hard to judge how truly accurate a cartulary transcription was, given the small number of cases in which both original and cartulary versions of the same charter survive, but when comparisons are possible the medieval scribe can generally be shown to be very conscientious—more so than many a nineteenth-century editor.[15]

For example, a number of original documents survive from the archives of the cathedral chapter of Langres, as well as the thirteenth-century cartulary, and when they are compared it is clear that the team of copyists creating the cartulary tried to transcribe as accurately as possible. Three randomly chosen documents from this cartulary serve as indications that the scribes followed their originals closely, including witnesses and dating formulae.

In 1159, Count Henry of Champagne granted the chapter of Langres an annual income to compensate for the damages his vassal Simon of Sexfontaines had done. The cartulary version of the attesting charter is nearly identical to the original; it substituted "Dominus Symon de Sansonis Fontis" for "Simon dominus Sansonis Fontis," spelled Ronca (the surname of one of the witnesses) as Ranca, and changed *Auctum* in the dating formula to the more standard *Actum*, but these are very small changes.[16] For a crucial 1179 document in which Count Henry of Bar gave the church the county of Langres, the only changes between the original and the cartulary copy are spelling; one of the witnesses' names is given as Simon in the original and Symon in the cartulary, and twice the cartulary spelled *ecclesie* without the cedilla on the final -*e*- as in the original.[17] The 1182 charter in which Simon, lord of Clefmont, settled a quarrel between the bishop of Langres and his own brother again was modified only minimally in the cartulary. The cartulary scribe spelled Simon as Symon; spelled Wichardus once as Wiardus and once (mistakenly) as Willermus; and skipped two words that did not materially affect the sense of the charter, but was otherwise perfect. As all these examples indicate, cartulary scribes sought to be as accurate as possible.[18]

But a cartulary was more than copies of old charters. It had an inherent structure imposed upon the charters and thus was a form of created memory. A cartulary's composition needs to be seen as a transitional—even liminal—activity. Before the cartulary scribe worked, a monastery's archives might have been kept in a single box or perhaps been "scattered," as were the documents of Châlons before Warin set to work. Thus before a scribe began copying charters into a cartulary, it was necessary to do a certain amount of organization.

Cartulary Organization

The ordering of contents always visible in a cartulary, whether by geographic location, by abbot, or by sender, suggests a prior ordering of the archives. Such ordering may have been done by the same person who copied out the codex or may have been done earlier, sometimes quite a bit earlier. Indeed, the documents in the archives might be ordered and annotated without necessarily recopying them; most original documents have a few words on the back summarizing the contents, generally in a hand later than that of the document itself. The monks of both Redon and St.-Gall, for example, organized their archives into dossiers in the ninth century, even though Redon did not create a cartulary for another two hundred years—and St.-Gall never did.[19] At the Cistercian monastery of Fontenay in the thirteenth century, the documents copied into the cartulary were first grouped geographically, and even today those documents that survive as originals are still in the same order in their *liasses* as in the cartulary.[20]

Every cartulary was arranged somewhat differently. No bishop or chapter general ever called for all churches to compose cartularies or imposed a single model. It is possible, however, to perceive three major types of organization, frequently combined: roughly chronological, with the grouping by abbot or bishop; roughly geographical, so that all property grants in one area were grouped together; or roughly by grantor, so that gifts from kings were grouped with gifts from other kings, and so on.[21] The late thirteenth-century cartulary of the bishopric of Auxerre adopted its own, unusual organization, based on which particular rights were supported by the documents in each section; the cartulary scribe labeled each section with a letter, A, B, C, and so on, and said that these letters corresponded with the boxes in which the original documents were kept.

Most commonly cartularies began with a foundation charter (if there was one) or other great privileges from popes or kings, followed by an organization by place, probably reflecting the order of the archives.[22] Another option was to arrange the cartulary by where the principal actors fit into the human hierarchy. Thus the twelfth-century cartulary of the northern French house of Homblières began with papal privileges, followed by the monastery's earliest documents, then charters of bishops, charters of local laymen, and finally acts of the abbots. Similarly, the thirteenth-century monks of St.-Germain began their cartulary with charters of popes, then emperors and kings, and stated that these would be followed by counts, bishops, magnates, and "other Catholics." The scribes at St.-Germain organized roughly chronologically within each category and left several blank folios at the end of each, for later additions. In practice they found the last category, "other Catholics," rather unwieldy and further broke it down as the cartulary was composed.[23]

Similarly, the cartulary of the chapter of Langres gave in order charters from popes, bishops, kings, dukes, counts, other powerful lay lords, and finally a mixed group of ecclesiastics and other laymen. The monks of Montier-la-Celle, near Troyes, also arranged their contemporary cartulary by status of issuer of the document but chose a quite different order: counts, abbots and ecclesiastical officials, secular lords of the region, kings, popes, and bishops. Here, as at Homblières, Langres, and St.-Germain, the organization suggests the way that cartulary scribes made groupings—mental and physical.[24] When organizing charters geographically, a careful cartulary scribe would copy all of the charters that pertained to one area, starting with the earliest and working roughly chronologically up to the most recent, before moving on to the next place. The late thirteenth-century scribe at Longué, more meticulous than most, added an extra slip of parchment to record a transaction if he discovered he had accidentally left it out.[25] At Marmoutier the archives contained so many different documents that the late eleventh- and twelfth-century monks felt obliged to create at least half a dozen cartularies, one for each region.[26]

Interestingly, no medieval cartulary followed what modern editors consider the most logical plan, that of strict chronology. The original organization is often lost in printed editions, where the editors have reorganized the charters by date. Even individual donations that were made over several years but were all confirmed at once may be divided in a modern edition into separate entries, thus giving each a distinction never intended in a medieval cartulary. The essentially chronological arrangement of some cartularies was due to an effort to arrange by abbot, not by year.[27]

For medievalists of the nineteenth and twentieth centuries, the past was to be organized as a series of events that all took place in order, and a privilege of Pippin the Short or a donation charter from a twelfth-century castellan needed to be correctly placed within that order. For cartulary scribes of the high Middle Ages, on the other hand, the past was not a chain of events disappearing backward in time. Rather, all such events had a very present and ongoing significance for the monastery, and that significance was far more important than the order of their occurrence. The privileges of popes and emperors had validity whether they had been issued a few years or a few centuries earlier, and it was more important that repeated donations had been made in one place than that such donations covered a four-hundred-year span.

The foundation charters that began many cartularies, or were inserted immediately after great papal or imperial privileges,[28] similarly listed property that was still very much a present concern for the monks. When scribes organized donation charters by geographic location, the first gift of property in a certain villa would continue to be as important to the monks as the most recent. The property was theirs, given to them by benefactors for whom they prayed. Both the property itself and the long-dead benefactors continued as living presences, despite any separation in time.[29]

Thus the ordering of the material in a cartulary codex deliberately took the charters out of time. A community of donors would be created, whose names were inscribed in the cartulary with what they gave. If the scribe abbreviated lists of witnesses—which in fact medieval scribes did less frequently than nineteenth-century editors—the reason was that the names of these witnesses, a marker for a charter's legal validity, were not needed in a cartulary copy. A cartulary's purpose then should be seen as more commemorative than combative, less a legal brief than another form of a *liber memorialis*. Just as in late medieval art a donor, the monastery's patron saint, and the magi might all join together in adoration of the Christ child, an event that was considered to be happening *now* as well as in A.D. 1, so five centuries of gifts and privileges would bind together a monastery's friends in the eternal present.[30]

It was certainly because of this perception of the past and present as part of a seamless Now that the scribes would make their single biggest change in the body of a charter, altering the spelling of place-names to correspond to the contemporary spelling. The orthography of proper names varied enormously anyway, with someone called "Vlricus" at the beginning of a charter often becoming "Hulricus" by the end. But if the scribe came across a Carolingian charter that spelled a place-name somewhat differently than it was normally spelled in the twelfth century, he would unhesitatingly give the name in what he considered the correct form. The same impulse that made eleventh- and twelfth-century scribes improve the spelling and grammar of four-hundred-year-old charters was the same impulse that made them gather, organize, and copy all the charters they could find into a cartulary in the first place.

Documents from the ninth through eleventh centuries could be dealt with fairly easily by twelfth- and thirteenth-century scribes, requiring little more than a regularization of spelling. But Merovingian-era charters were different. The protocols were foreign, the spelling strange, the handwriting, even the customary abbreviations, difficult to interpret. Documents from the time of Charlemagne on were copied into cartularies essentially unchanged, but the same cannot be said of documents from before his time. A seventh-century privilege for Montier-en-Der, issued by the bishop of Châlons, was copied into both the cartulary of the cathedral of Châlons and the cartulary of Montier-en-Der. Although the two cartularies were composed within just a few years of each other, the two scribes reached very different conclusions on a number of words as to what the seventh-century original actually said. Both were confused by some of the abbreviations and made their own best guesses. In addition, the scribe at Montier-en-Der easily recognized "Putiolos," the original name of his monastery, but Cantor Warin of Châlons, stumped, put "pociolus."[31]

Here the creation of cartularies reveals a seeming discrepancy in medieval views of the past: chroniclers sought to assign events such as the accessions of kings and popes to their proper years, but events from different epochs were treated as comparable, as having taken place at different times but without any sense of fundamental change over the intervening period. In biblical illuminations, Roman soldiers were routinely shown wearing medieval armor, and Caesar, Charlemagne, and Otto I could all be portrayed as exactly the same.[32] Temporal change was not a concern, even though medieval thinkers operated within a theological context in which certain events that happened at certain times—the Incarnation and Crucifixion—shaped both human history and the cosmos. A cartulary needed to be ordered because order was a part of the divine plan, but temporal ordering was only one of several options.

The rather timeless nature of the events that a monastery recorded was doubtless responsible for one aspect of cartularies that is extremely irritating to modern scholars: the scribes were notoriously careless about dating. Cartulary copies often do have dating formulae, but in many cases the scribes simply did not bother with the date. The date had a diplomatic significance when a charter was drawn up, but this ceased to be relevant once the charter was copied into a cartulary intended for an internal rather than external audience. But it would be wrong to see this as an indication of sloppiness or of valuing speed over accuracy, for the detailing of donated property, and the explanation of how the donor was related to the other people for whom he intended the monks to pray, would be copied conscientiously and accurately. But the cartulary scribe, organizing his monastery's archives and copying into his codex the charters that detailed how the monastery had acquired its now timeless possessions, might find irrelevant that part of a charter that located it at a certain time and place.

The Purposes of Cartularies

The composition of cartularies thus needs to be seen as a new stage in how churches thought about their past and organized and preserved those memories. Certainly cartularies served a utilitarian as well as memorial function, but it would be a mistake to separate the quotidian and the liturgical functions too sharply. After all, medieval monks considered all their activities in the cloister a form of prayer. Creating well-ordered records of a church's property acquisitions for management purposes was as much an act of pious memory as was making a well-ordered list of the dead.

The purpose that cartulary scribes expected their volumes to serve was rarely stated explicitly. Most cartularies have no prologue, and those that do generally have a laconic statement such as, "In this volume are collected the privileges of our saint and the record of transfers of property in various locations," with at most some comment about the role of preserving memories against loss or forgetfulness;[33] such was the stated motivation of Warin of Châlons. The first, eleventh-century cartulary of Cluny has a preface with a somewhat more aggressive tone: the cartulary was drawn up, it says, "to eliminate the malicious misrepresentations of those who would overthrow the sanctuary of God in their perversity and who foolishly dare to seize the alms piously given to the mother church." The monks' defense was to be found in "the perusal of many written records."[34] Three generations later, the preface to the cartulary of Cluny's daughter-house of Marcigny similarly spoke darkly of "false claimants" and of an "undisciplined posterity" who might dare to go against what their predecessors had granted but who could be stopped with the written word.[35]

The monk Paul, who composed the cartulary of St.-Père of Chartres in the 1080s, said that he compiled his "little book," in spite of a professed weakness in Latin, because of the fire that had swept the abbey in 1078, from which a number of archival documents had barely escaped. If such documents were copied into a book, Paul said, "they could more easily be saved from fire or other dangers." To this eminently practical purpose Paul added that if a question arose about the house's property, the answer could quickly be found in such an organized volume, *per ordinem colligendo*. The monks would also have ready to hand, together with the details of their property holdings, the names of those who had given the property and who were thus included among the "heavenly flocks of most holy sheep." Paul did mention that his cartulary might be used "to repel the ambitions of the sacrilegious," but only after he had explained its use for the house's internal purposes.[36]

And the chief internal purpose was to remember St.-Père's glorious past. Paul knew that kings must have been generous, but none of their charters existed. Missing, too, were donation charters spelling out how the monastery had acquired its possessions. As Paul said, "the gifts of the faithful either were not recorded, due to a lack of scribes, or if they were written down they were lost, due to the negligence of those in charge of the archives (*archiscrinorum*)."[37] He did not attempt to forge replacement charters for those that were lost but rather set out to create a more durable form for those that had escaped the recent fire. Like the writers of the sixth century who found it inexplicable that their predecessors had forgotten the tombs of the martyrs (see Chapter 12), Paul could not understand why his predecessors had so neglected the archives.

Here the cartulary's purpose was explicitly tied to memory. An organized volume would make it easier for the monks to recall what they owned and for whom they were offering prayers. Its existence would ensure that that memory was not lost. A cartulary was thus intended primarily for those inside the religious community, not those outside, even if its information could be used against outsiders. It became a continuing reference book for the monastery, as indicated by the well-thumbed nature of all cartularies and their many marginal notes, in handwritings that span six hundred years.

Although cartularies sometimes functioned as legal proof in the seventeenth century, these codexes can rarely have been used for this purpose in the high Middle Ages, in spite of the scribes' concern for repelling the sacrilegious. Greater validity was assigned to living witnesses in the twelfth and thirteenth centuries than to written charters, and a charter's veracity was considered to be found in its seals,[38] which of course did not exist in a cartulary. If the monks still had their original donation charters, the cartulary would have had *less* legal authority than these originals. Indeed, it has been argued that a distinction between original and copy, with only the former serving as valid proof, developed in the eleventh century,[39] suggesting that French cartularies, first developed then, could not have been primarily intended for proving claims.

The inadequacy of cartularies as legal proof is vividly demonstrated by an example from thirteenth-century Langres. In 1200, the cathedral chapter reached an agreement with the abbot of Cluny to divide some tithes between the two churches, and two identical original charters detailing the agreement were produced, one sealed by the dean and chapter of Langres and intended for Cluny's archives, and the other sealed by the abbot of Cluny and intended for the capitular archives at Langres. A scribe for the chapter carefully transcribed the version in their archives into the cartulary in the 1230s.[40]

However, the original document became lost during the next half century. When during the 1280s the abbot of Cluny began keeping all of the tithes that he had formerly shared, the Langres chapter's cartulary copy of the agreement was inadequate to deter him (and the original in Cluny's own archives was understandably not produced). A scribe at Langres wrote rather forlornly in the cartulary margin, "I once saw this *littera*, sealed with the seal of Abbot Hugh of Cluny, but when we looked for it we could not find it anywhere, even though we searched from 1283 to 1286." Finally the canons of Langres had to take the case to court and have a new agreement drawn up with the current abbot of Cluny. Clearly a cartulary copy might serve as a record of a transaction; the canons of Langres knew about their earlier agreement with the abbot of Cluny precisely because of its presence in the cartulary. But it could not be produced as proof the way that an original, sealed document would have been.

Cartularies were thus intended more for internal record keeping than external validation. And even their administrative function should not be assumed to be simple. A cartulary, after all, was not the only administrative text in the monastery. All houses would have had at least some records of income and expenditures in the high Middle Ages. The Benedictine Rule, letters of discipline from bishops or (for Cistercian houses) the chapter general, calendars and lists of popes or bishops, as well as liturgical volumes were all works that concerned the daily life of the monastery and the material base on which that life was built, perhaps even more so than the charters in the cartulary.[41] Liturgical books and obituaries might themselves include a few copied charters.[42]

The memory at the heart of a cartulary's purpose was thus more than potential legal proof and more than record keeping. As already suggested, cartularies were also a form of commemoration, recalling and celebrating the most important events in a monastery's history. The monks of Homblières began their cartulary with a papal privilege from 1169—and indeed this privilege was probably responsible for the decision to draw up their cartulary the following year. In the same way, the monks of St.-Marcel began their own cartulary with a papal privilege and two imperial privileges—two of the three of which were forged.[43] This active act of memory was in many ways similar to contemporary *libri memoriales*,[44] which served as a record that an individual—and in many cases a whole family—had entered into a spiritual relationship with that church.

Cartularies' commemorative aspect was present from the beginning. It is surely significant that in the ninth century Abbot Hrabanus Maurus of Fulda first ordered a necrology of his monastery be compiled, then a commemorative listing of the living monks, and then the copying of his monastery's charters into booklets.[45] Similarly, the thirteenth-century cartulary of Langres was part of a two-volume set; the other volume contained a rule for canons and a martyrology and necrology.[46] This cartulary, then, for those who composed it, was intended to be part of what its modern editor, Hubert Flammarion, has called an "ideologically coherent ensemble," a group of texts that helped define the status and position of the church and those who served it.[47]

The cartulary and its legal texts were not separate from liturgical or narrative texts; they were an integral part of a church's corporate and spiritual identity. In a cartulary a royal privilege was treated as more than a list of rights; it was an indication that the highest secular power in the land had recognized the continuing spiritual power of the church's saint and the worth of the monks or clerics serving that saint. One should thus be careful not to draw too sharp a distinction between cartularies and other forms of records that might also preserve and organize the memory of the past. The line has often been blurred by editors who call any printed collection of medieval charters a cartulary, even if the texts are drawn from many different sources, but the response should not be to erect an artificial wall between cartularies and other sorts of record keeping.

Cartularies and Original Charters

If a cartulary's initial purpose was to create an orderly memory of what the monastery owned and how the monks had acquired it, supplementing rather than replacing their archival collection, then its purpose was modified once it existed. It quickly became in essence a substitute for the documents from which it was copied. Monks with a cartulary became much less concerned about their original charters. Only a tiny fraction of the originals survive from which cartulary copies were made. Indeed, it is probably significant that St.-Gall, the monastery with the most existing early medieval originals north of the Alps, never produced a cartulary.[48] This tendency to devalue charters once copied into the cartulary may be responsible for the loss at Langres of the charter of their agreement with Cluny. An original document was precious and unique, but its value declined when a clean, useful copy had been made.

In times of trouble, a cartulary could be snatched up and carried to safety much more easily than could an armful of documents. A book that could be chained in place, as was the cartulary of the cathedral of Mâcon,[49] was more secure than an untidy pile of individual parchments. Although it is well-known that enormous numbers of medieval charters were lost at the time of the French Revolution, for a number of monasteries the charters that had been copied into a cartulary were lost well before then. For example, *none* of the over one hundred charters copied into the cartulary of the bishopric of Auxerre in the thirteenth century still survives as an original, and indeed all but one were already lost in the seventeenth century.[50] At St.-Marcel of Chalon, all the monastery's original documents, except for one privilege from Charlemagne, were also long gone in the seventeenth century when Mabillon looked for them.[51]

Such carelessness with original documents was possible only when the cartulary itself had taken on an iconic quality that it never would have had for the scribe who put it together in the first place. The monks who created cartularies in the high Middle Ages had succeeded so thoroughly in organizing and regularizing the record of their monasteries' possessions that their productions were, in future centuries, seen not as a guide to those possessions but as a proof of their legitimacy. Monks carrying out efforts to organize and regularize in the early modern period thus felt no need to look back any further than the high medieval cartulary.

As this suggests, it is important not to essentialize the original charter. Of course a cartulary copy was always further from the events described than was a charter drawn up more or less at the time, but the existence of an original piece of parchment tells us little about how those events were later remembered—although a later copy does. And after all, the true prototype for any charter, whether the original or a copy, was not the parchment on which an act was first described but rather the act itself.[52]

The details of a particular act could be written down multiple times, but that did not mean that the versions transcribed later were necessarily considered inferior to the earliest transcription. For example, when Heraclius, papal legate and archbishop of Lyon, settled a quarrel in 1157 between the bishop of Langres and his chapter, he had two originals made detailing the settlement—and the two originals were later copied separately into the chapter's cartulary.[53] The first was drawn up by Heraclius's own chancery at Lyon and sealed with his seal; the other was drawn up slightly later by the chancery of Langres and sealed with both the archbishop's and the bishop of Langres's seals.[54] The archbishop's sealing of the document penned in Langres shows that he considered it valuable; to him it was not an inferior because later copy.

Indeed, in some ways the second "original," transcribed in Langres, is superior although later than the archiepiscopal chancery version. The archbishop's scribe had had trouble with the spellings of the names of some of the places near Langres, which the Langres scribe of course corrected, and the former apparently could not remember the names of all the abbots who witnessed the quarrel settlement (although he recalled the names of their houses) because he left blanks where their names should go, and again the Langres scribe filled in the blanks. As these examples suggest, copying a charter, as in the composition of a cartulary, should not be seen as necessarily the creation of an inferior version.

Cartularies' Subsequent Uses

There was thus a complex relationship between the original pieces of parchment (or sometimes papyrus) from which the cartulary scribes worked and the codexes of transcribed charters that resulted from their efforts, codexes that could take on functions the scribes might never have expected. Throughout the tribulations of late medieval and early modern war, famine, and fire, monks, nuns, and priests did their best to hold onto their cartularies. After the cartulary was created, the original documents became much less important. Not only was the cartulary codex more comprehensive and better organized than a perhaps untidy heap of disintegrating originals, but it also took over the iconic element that original charters had once enjoyed. This does not mean that the monks rejected their original documents. After all, in speaking of monks "conserving" their documentary past by copying charters into cartularies, one could draw a contrast between *neglect* of original documents and outright *destruction* of original documents.[55] There is no sign of deliberate destruction of monastic archives (at least by the monks themselves), but there are plenty of indications of neglect, once there was an easily referenced and easily portable version.

Once the idea of a cartulary was established, monks of subsequent generations might take up the idea repeatedly. At Montier-en-Der, for example, there still exist some half-dozen codexes all titled "Cartularies," composed between the twelfth century and the mid-seventeenth century. The second cartulary was composed at the end of the thirteenth century in order to collect the documents that the monastery had acquired since the first cartulary was put together in the 1120s. The third, fourth, and fifth, from the sixteenth and seventeenth centuries, do not contain any medieval documents but do indicate the continuing interest in the model of a cartulary. The sixth cartulary, compiled in 1658, included a number of documents copied directly out of the first two cartularies, not from the originals, even when those still existed.[56] Here the purpose seems to have been to organize the legal "titles" to the monastery's landholdings, and indeed Simon Berquin, the compiler of Montier-en-Der's sixth cartulary, insisted that the very antiquity of the cartulary from which he copied a number of charters conveyed legal authority.[57]

Also in 1658, the monks of Flavigny had their cartulary verified and sealed by a royal councilor.[58] Although no explicit statement was made here of cartularies' legal value, such a statement was in fact made in 1670, when the legal status of the cartulary of St.-Serge of Angers was officially confirmed.

> It has been the practice at all chapters and especially at Benedictine abbeys to record in books called cartularies . . . all records of donations, to avoid the loss of original title-deeds through disappearance or decay over the course of years . . . this cartulary is to be accepted at all times by the presiding judges of Angers, who order that it serve as sufficient proof, without contestation.[59]

During the ancien régime, then, cartularies' purpose and function underwent a final transformation. From a way to order a monastery's records for internal purposes or to help prepare a response to its enemies, to an evocation of the timeless community between monks, patron saint, and donors, to legal proof in provincial courts, a cartulary served many functions over the centuries. In the twenty-first century their use has changed again, as they are routinely mined for information on medieval lordship, political networks, family structure, and economic organization. In all these cases cartularies served as a way to remember the past. In the next chapter I shall turn to the chronicles composed at the same time as the cartularies—often at the same houses—for another aspect of creative memory in the high Middle Ages.

Chapter 3

Twelfth-Century Narratives of the Past

To write was to create a record for posterity. As Gregory the Great said, "What we speak is transitory, but what we write remains."[1] A twelfth-century bishop of Chalon put it just as clearly if not as elegantly: "Since, in this world, unless things are corroborated in writing, they are often lost to negligence or oblivion, therefore . . ."[2] Thus anyone putting pen to parchment, an activity both difficult and expensive, did so because the words were important enough to need to be read again.

At the same time as churchmen created cartularies to order their past, they also wrote universal chronicles, in which recent events in their regions figured prominently. Chroniclers since the third century had been starting their accounts with Creation,[3] but they saw no difficulty in concentrating on their own period after a quick trip through the Bible and early medieval history. The twelfth-century chronicler of St.-Pierre-le-Vif of Sens, for example, began with a universal chronicle, proceeding from the year 1 to the sixth century, when he believed his house was founded, and then continued seamlessly with events—both local and international—down to his own time.[4] The chronicle of Alberic of Trois-Fontaines begins with Adam but is primarily concerned with twelfth- and early thirteenth-century Burgundy and Champagne.[5]

A number of chroniclers of the high Middle Ages, intent on placing their abbeys into their appropriate place in history, combined what would now be considered narrative history with integral copies of charters—what the French now call *pièces justificatives*. Such accounts reveal that both cartularies and chronicles were efforts to order and retain the memory of the past. Most chroniclers appear to have tried conscientiously to be what would now be considered scholarly, consulting earlier annals, saints' lives, and charters. The twelfth-century chronicler of St.-Pierre-le-Vif, for example, relied in part on the account by Odorannus, also a monk at St.-Pierre, written nearly a century earlier.[6] But the past the chroniclers re-created was not the same as the story that modern historians can now re-create using essentially the same sources. Monastic chroniclers especially tended to make their houses older and more prestigious than their sources might support because their standing in the past increased their authority in the present.

Cartularies and Chronicles

Although to the modern medievalist cartularies are collections of legal documents, thus very different from narrative sources (indeed, in most French *départements* a deliberate if not completely successful effort has been made to put legal documents, including cartularies, into the Archives, and narrative sources into the Bibliothèques), to medieval monks the distinction was not as sharp.[7] Several houses produced what are now known as cartulary-chronicles, where a narrative history of the house is interspersed with copies of documents from the house's archives. Most of the early records of both St.-Bénigne of Dijon and St.-Pierre of Bèze, for example, are known only from such a chronicle.[8]

The first cartulary of St.-Père of Chartres, compiled in the 1080s, also mixes chronicle and document, although Paul, the compiler, attempted to distinguish the two forms for the reader. He began his work with a prologue (which Paul, proud of his scraps of Greek, calls an *epilogus*), in which he touched on highlights of his house's history, an account that also called for documentary evidence. For the earliest documents he copied (dating from the tenth century), he followed each with a brief discussion of the subsequent fate of the relevant property. Sometimes it had been lost to the house, sometimes it had been augmented. In some cases he recorded more recent gifts in the same area by subsequent donors. At one point he mentioned that he tried to find out about a certain church by inquiring of the "oldest monks."[9] Or sometimes, more prosaically, the road that had marked the boundary a century and a half before Paul wrote had been shifted, and Paul explained the shift to be sure his readers were not confused.

Chroniclers continued to include copies of charters along with other materials in twelfth-century manuscripts. The monastery of Flavigny produced a chronicle around the year 1100 that included copies of a number of charters.[10] Flavigny's chronicle was not intended as a substitute for a cartulary, any more than was the contemporary chronicle of St.-Pierre-le-Vif, for both houses already had a cartulary, as noted in Chapter 1. Rather, both chroniclers used the material from the cartularies to help develop their own narratives and made copies of additional charters to validate their points. The chronicle of St.-Pierre, in fact, also includes such miscellany as decisions of councils, a hymn, and a brief Latin-Greek list of phrases handy for the traveler.

At Vézelay the formats of chronicle and cartulary were not so intermingled, but a codex from the second half of the twelfth century, its contents all written at the same time, combines brief annals, a short history of the counts of nearby Nevers, the cartulary itself, and a chronicle of the abbey's history, indicating that the scribe saw no fundamental distinction between different sorts of records of his house's past.[11] Earlier in the twelfth century the monks had already copied out some of their documents—including ones from Count Girard, their ninth-century founder, that showed how he had acquired the property he gave his new foundation—but again had not separated these charters from other materials but copied them within a larger, rather miscellaneous manuscript.[12] The charters, then, were not treated as a distinct form of record but were part of what a monastery wanted to preserve in writing and hence in memory.

Early Monasticism Remembered

Crucial for all monastic chroniclers from the eleventh and twelfth centuries was, not surprisingly, the original foundation of their houses. Few had genuine foundation charters—both because foundation charters were unusual for most of the Merovingian period and because five centuries of fire, upheaval, disintegration, and carelessness had destroyed most of their earliest charters—so the chroniclers had to be imaginative. The past they sought to construct was in many cases quite different from that seen by modern historians of the Merovingian era, but that is not the point. Rather, chroniclers of the high Middle Ages should be seen as making the best of whatever sources they had to create a coherent account of their predecessors: long established, well endowed, and admirably religious.[13]

Early monasticism in Gaul was sparse and ad hoc by twelfth-century standards. There were still very few monasteries in the sixth century, most formed around a hermit or recluse, as discussed in more detail in Chapter 11. Although a number of basilicas could be found in most Gallo-Roman cities, some erected where saints' bones were found, others built so that newly discovered relics could be brought in from outside of town, the evidence is skimpy at best that more than a handful of these basilicas supported a community of monks before the final decades of the sixth century. Only at the end of the sixth and in the seventh centuries did monasteries begin to be founded in some numbers. This was not, however, how later monks conceptualized their early years.

Monasteries in the twelfth century all sought to celebrate their origins in late antiquity, supported by royal benefactors from the beginning. They preferred to have been founded during the century from the baptism of Clovis around the year 500 down through the time of Columbanus and his foundations and reformations in the decades on either side of the year 600. Although many bishoprics in the high Middle Ages asserted apostolic origins,[14] the monasteries were generally content to claim origins coinciding with the beginning of Christian kings in Gaul.[15]

Since many Frankish monasteries had not in fact been founded until the seventh through ninth centuries, monastic memory clearly dealt creatively with the sources. For example, at St.-Pierre-le-Vif, the monks had a genuine episcopal charter from the seventh century, doubtless issued within a fairly short time after the establishment of a community of monks, which noted that one *Teodechildis regina* was buried at the house.[16] Later chroniclers were able to use this mention of a queen to create a story of the house's being founded shortly after the year 500. Supposedly Theuchildis, daughter of Clovis, was baptized at the same time as her father, decided to remain a virgin perpetually, and undertook to found the monastery outside of Sens. Although modern scholars, quite rightly, cast doubt on this account, from a twelfth-century perspective the Queen Theuchildis in St.-Pierre's crypt *must* have been their founder and most logically would have been closely connected to the first Merovingian Christian king.[17]

Similarly, the monks of St.-Bénigne of Dijon, which is not known to have had monks until the final decades of the sixth century, used a reference by Gregory of Tours to the discovery and translation of the relics of Saint Benignus around the year 500 as the basis for their assumption that their monastery was founded around 500.[18] For them, their basilica was inconceivable without a monastic community. Even though Flavigny had a dated foundation charter from 717, its chronicle from around 1100 still sought to give the house greater antiquity. Hugh of Flavigny, when discussing his house's foundation, suggested that it had been founded in 601 and added details about supposedly contemporary early seventh-century events; he also attributed a charter of

Pippin the Short to his grandfather, Pippin of Herstal, to push the monastery's origins back in time.[19]

It was easy to assume that any ancient church rebuilt in the eleventh century with an organized religious community must also have had a religious community in the sixth. The monks thus tended, not surprisingly, to give their predecessors of five centuries earlier their own assumptions. When King Robert II gave the church of Notre-Dame of Losne to the bishop of Chalon in 1027, he asserted that it had been an *abbatia* founded by King Theoderic II at the beginning of the seventh century.[20] Now in fact Losne does seem to have had a basilica at the period. One Palladius, referred to as *episcopus* of Losne, attended the 614 Council of Paris, and Childeric II held a council at the basilica of Notre-Dame of Losne in 673/5.[21] But there is no actual evidence of a body of monks in the basilica until a generation *after* Robert II's gift of the church to the bishop: in the middle of the eleventh century the church was submitted to the monastery of Bèze, resulting in the establishment of a monastic community there, which soon became a Cluniac priory.[22] In all these cases the monks took it for granted that their houses had their origins in late antiquity. The sources on which they drew for details were interpreted on the basis of this belief.

The high medieval chroniclers in Burgundy were in fact correct that many monastic houses had plausible roots in the Merovingian era, even if in the seventh century rather than the sixth, and even if those roots cannot be equated with monastic communities of a later type. As detailed in Appendix I, there were relatively few completely new foundations in the Burgundy-Champagne region between 717, when Flavigny was founded, and the late eleventh century. The few monastic houses founded in the region in these four centuries had mostly had their origins in the two generations between the middle years of the ninth century and the first decade of the tenth, from the foundations of Vézelay and Pouthières in 858/9 to that of Cluny in 909/10. This brief period of monastic expansion was not significantly slowed by the Viking invasions, which hit the region in the 880s. Houses were devastated, but efforts to regroup and rebuild usually followed quickly. After Cluny's foundation, however, there were essentially no new foundations in the region for the next century and a half.[23]

When first bishops and then powerful laymen began again to establish monastic communities in the final decades of the tenth century, they refounded and rebuilt long-deserted houses in preference to completely new foundations. Even when nothing remained of a long-abandoned church but a few stones, bishops, dukes, and counts wanted a monastic community that was *not* new but rather an ancient one reborn. A place that had once been sanctified maintained an aura of holiness. And the memory of the distant, holy past could, in spite of everything, be supported by the written word. At Bèze, although there was no monastic life to speak of from the first half of the eighth century to the latter decades of the tenth, at least some of their documents survived 250 years of turmoil. The monastery's chronicler said that the "ancient parchments" of his house told him its history of desolation, and he copied a great many of those old sources into his chronicle.[24]

A refounded house was as hard to establish as any brand-new foundation. Initially such houses might be put under the direction of another monastery for a generation—most famously but not exclusively Cluny—and then elect its own abbot.[25] The number of Merovingian-era monasteries and basilicas was so great that it was not necessary to look far for a church to refound. When entirely new monasteries finally began to be founded in any numbers in the late eleventh and twelfth centuries—especially Cistercian houses—they were almost exclusively out in the country, away from the cities and their Merovingian-era churches.

Monks of the eleventh and twelfth centuries, looking backward at this complicated history, tended to simplify. Chroniclers in houses with origins before the ninth century created a straightforward account of ancient foundation, several cycles of difficulty and renewal, and recent triumph. The twelfth-century chronicler of St.-Bénigne of Dijon summarized his monastery's history in a few short phrases: "This monastery was founded by Bishop Gregory of Langres; endowed and given a stable life by King Guntram; restored by Emperor Charles the Bald and Bishop Isaac; and renewed by the most honorable men Bishop Bruno and Abbot William, especially by building a new church."[26]

The Past Remembered at Sens

The chronicler of St.-Pierre-le-Vif of Sens provides a case study of how a monk of the high Middle Ages conceptualized his abbey's history. As already noted, he dated the house's foundation to about 500, but Sens did not again play a major role in his account until he reached the second half of the seventh century, where he had sources to work with. He gave special emphasis to the bishops of Sens, whom he always called archbishops even though they did not actually have that title until the eighth century. For example, his account dwelled at length on the 675 death of "Archbishop" Emmo, who, the chronicler said, had granted Abbot Agilenus a "privilege of liberty" at a synod attended by over thirty bishops, when Clothar III was king and his mother, Balthildis, queen.[27]

The chronicler here relied on a charter issued around 660, in which Bishop Emmo granted such a privilege to Abbot Agilenus and the monks, who were then following, he said, the Benedictine Rule according to the *modo* of Luxeuil. The chronicler's version left out any mention of Luxeuil, as meaningless in the twelfth century, and added Queen Balthildis to the charter's mention of King Clothar.[28] Balthildis is known from her nearly contemporary *vita* (late seventh century) to have sought to establish monks under a regular life in the monasteries of the realm and to grant them immunities, and her biographer said that she considered St.-Pierre-le-Vif one of the "senior basilicas" of that realm.[29] The chronicler clearly knew this *vita* and its laudatory mention of his house, and her presence was thus indispensable in his chronicle.

His history of Sens continued with a *vita* of Archbishop Ebbo. The chronicler was quite well informed about a seventh-century bishop he considered a saint; it is possible that he had a *vita* or even a *Gesta* of the bishops of Sens before him, which no longer exists. Archbishop Ebbo, he said, was outstanding (*clarus*) "both for his miracles and his nobility." The heir to the county of Tonnerre, according to the chronicler, Ebbo decided to become a monk instead of a count and entered St.-Pierre-le-Vif, where he quickly became abbot. From there he was promoted to the see of Sens, where his uncle had preceded him, but in spite of playing an active role in driving back the "Vandals," he much preferred the *heremetica vita*. Thus he retreated from the world, and from his cell he healed all those who came to him with their problems. Both his sisters were nuns, who made generous gifts to St.-Pierre-le-Vif, and all three were buried together at the monastery.[30]

Here the chronicler took the material in his monastery's archives and made it seem perfectly normal in a twelfth-century context: the young lord who decides to join a monastery, the abbot who is promoted to a bishopric, the uncle-nephew dynasty within the see of Sens, gifts from close relatives who sought to be buried at the monastery, even the county of Tonnerre itself, located a short distance south of Sens.[31] It is thus not difficult to see why he should have told his story of Ebbo in this way. The question is what were the sources of his information that he so interpreted.

In addition to a possible earlier *vita* of Ebbo, this account was inspired in part by two donation charters from the early eighth century, which had already been copied into the monastery's eleventh-century cartulary and which were copied again into the chronicle of St.-Pierre-le-Vif.[32] Two wealthy women did indeed make generous gifts to St.-Pierre-le-Vif, even though their charters, issued a decade or two apart, do not say that they were sisters or that Ebbo was their brother. In the charters, only one of the women asks for burial at the monastery, and only one (the other one) is identified as a nun (*Deo sacrata*). Nothing in either of the charters suggests a family connection to a count of Tonnerre, even though the nun did give property located in that *pagus*. But from a series of names in the charters the chronicler was able to create a whole family group, including an unnamed count and his wife, their three children, and an archbishop, brother of either the count or his wife (the chronicler calls him Ebbo's *avunculus*, which technically meant maternal uncle but was often used for paternal uncle). Such a family group made excellent sense in the twelfth century; there was no reason for him that it not make sense for the seventh.

He also created a holy man who fit right into early twelfth-century patterns. The man from a wealthy family who gives up his status and position for the monastic life, as well as the abbot promoted to bishop who still prefers retreating to a small church to get away from worldly hubbub, were commonplaces in the first decades of the century; real-life models were found in the diocese of Auxerre, a short distance from Sens.[33] Thus the chronicler's account of his city's history was an attempt to combine the material he could elicit from the sources with his own, twelfth-century assumptions about how a bishop who was also a saint would have behaved.

From the perspective of the twelfth century, the principal danger to a Christian life came from "pagans." The chronicler used the same term, *pagani*, to describe ancient Romans, ninth-century Vikings, and tenth-century Magyars. The juxtaposition may be seen in his account of the churches destroyed during the Viking raids of the late ninth century.[34] One of those destroyed by the "pagans" was located on a hill a short distance from Sens and was dedicated to Saints Sancho and Beata, a brother and sister supposedly martyred there at the time of the Emperor Aurelian in the third century—an obvious effort to give Sens saints with the same antiquity as the earliest Burgundian martyrs (see Chapter 12).[35] The hill, the chronicler of Sens informed his readers, was called "Ad Martires," because "there the pagans were accustomed to behead martyrs."

The two sets of pagans, Romans and Vikings, though six centuries apart in time, were thus conflated into an Other: enormously destructive to the religious life but also in some ways positive because their attacks, whether beheading the faithful or burning down churches, provided an opportunity for true Christians to show their worth.[36] In the same way, the chronicler recounted how the Magyars ravaged the Senonais region in the 930s and burned down the monastery of St.-Pierre-le-Vif, but in the telling this destruction became an opportunity for reform and the translations of the relics of the monastery's saints, accompanied by appropriate miracles.[37]

The monastery's other chief potential enemies, besides pagans, were the archbishops of Sens. Some, of course, like Emmo and Ebbo, were saintly men who paid what the chronicler considered proper and reverent attention to his monastery. They were almost all buried at St.-Pierre; the chronicler was as careful to include the deaths and accessions of bishops as of abbots. For the most part, he tried to show that the cathedral and the monastery were on good terms, as indeed they may have been.

But there were always at least potential sources of tension between the bishops and the monastery. These burst out especially in the late tenth century, just when the attacks from pagans had ended, when Archembald was archbishop of Sens. According to the chronicler, Archembald sold all the monastery's possessions or gave them to his friends. When the few remaining monks all died, he moved from the episcopal palace to the monks' refectory, where he cavorted with "harlots" (*meretricibus*). Even having all the hounds and falcons he had brought with him unexpectedly expire was not warning enough for him, and this "bishop in name only" as the chronicler called him was finally found appropriately dead and stark naked. During this time, the monastery's few remaining treasures and its archives were preserved, but only because an archdeacon, the son of a local knight, thought to take them for safekeeping.[38]

Here the chronicler combined an account of his monastery's cycle of troubles and renewal with an account that showed clearly the relative merits of bishopric and monastery: the bishop was hopelessly sinful and corrupt, responsible for the difficulties at St.-Pierre even once the pagans were gone. Yet in spite of everything, the monastery was still able to persevere and even flourish because, according to the chronicler, the monks retained what was most important: the archival documents in which was recorded their memory of the past.

In the same way, when Paul of St.-Père of Chartres put together his house's cartulary in the 1080s, its real history began with the Viking invasions and the greed and malevolence of Bishop Elias of Chartres, who took whatever the Vikings did not. Paul had no knowledge whatsoever of the history of the house before the ninth century, but this did not keep him from assuring his readers that it had been one of the most outstanding monasteries of Neustria, noted both for its magnificent buildings and for the piety and education of its monks. The Vikings served as an excellent explanation for why there were no records of such a community. For Paul the destruction by the Vikings was an opportunity for the Virgin to enact vengeance on the pagans, demonstrating her power in case anyone in his own time doubted it, and for his monastery to be restored by Bishop Agano in the middle of the tenth century. Only under his rule did documents begin to be issued and preserved in sufficient numbers that Paul was able to start copying them. Devastation thus made an excellent foil for the magnificence of St.-Père in late antiquity and again for the reform of the house's religious life and the multiplication of its charters.[39]

In this context, the tendency of Crusade chroniclers from the early twelfth century to call the Muslims "pagans" makes excellent sense. More than just the product of a gross misunderstanding of the nature of Islam, it was due to an effort to integrate these "enemies of Christendom" into a story that had already accommodated Roman paganism and the beliefs of Norsemen and Magyars. In this story, the exact nature of the beliefs of non-Christians was unknown and irrelevant. Pagans were those who were not Christians themselves and who killed Christians or harmed their sanctuaries. Calling the Muslims pagans certainly indicates ignorance, but it also indicates an effort to make them understandable to people who assumed there were only two possible religions, Christian and pagan (with perhaps the slightest room in the equation for Jews).

The Past Remembered by Hugh of Flavigny

At about the same time as a chronicler at St.-Pierre made Sens a central part of world history, Hugh, monk of St.-Vanne of Verdun and abbot of Flavigny, set out to do something very similar.[40] His chronicle was in its first sections heavily borrowed from earlier chronicles, especially Gregory of Tours and Fredegar for the Merovingian period and the chronicle of St.-Bénigne for the Carolingian period.[41] He began with the birth of Christ, which he rather grandly dated to year 5198 of the earth and year 752 of the city of Rome.[42] From there he proceeded through popes and emperors and the Christianization of Gaul, working in references to the early bishops of Verdun, information he said he learned from the (no longer extant) *Gesta* of the bishops of that see.[43] With the foundation of Flavigny, however, his story began to narrow. In the following folios, though continuing to relate the histories of kings and popes, he focused especially on Burgundy and Lotharingia.

The memory of the monasteries with which Hugh was associated was improved in part by the context in which he told their history. For example, the story of the establishment of the Carolingians on the Frankish throne was interspersed with accounts of the successions of abbots and bishops at Flavigny and Verdun.[44] He clearly had the cartulary of Flavigny before him (in its original version from the first decades of the eleventh century) because he worked the majority of the documents into his narrative, but he did not simply paraphrase them; rather, he put each in a context where it would reflect best on the house. From Hugh's point of view, one of Charlemagne's most significant acts was to free Flavigny from royal tolls throughout his realm. Charlemagne's charter was the fourth in the cartulary, following only Wideradus's two foundation charters and a donation charter from Pippin the Short.[45]

This was only one of the charters Hugh incorporated. He had already utilized the first charter in the cartulary for information on Flavigny's foundation, namely that King Theoderic had confirmed Wideradus's testament in the first year of his reign and sealed the charter (although he was mistaken about which Theoderic was meant).[46] Probably because much of the testament concerned gifts to houses other than Flavigny, Hugh skipped the details, however. He also noted that the monks had received a gift of property at Glanon, again using information from the cartulary, though he dated the event a century too early, and recorded the gifts from the couple Baio and Cylinia in the seventh year of King Childeric.[47] The cartulary was also doubtless the source of his statement that a Frankish king had authorized the monks of Flavigny to establish a daughter-house at Corbigny, though he named the king as Carloman, while the cartulary gives Charles (Charlemagne).[48]

These eighth-century documents were artfully interspersed with broader political events to indicate that Flavigny's history had an importance beyond the cloister itself. For Hugh, the memory of his two monasteries was as important as the memory of kings and battles. He continued the same pattern for the ninth century, where the succession of Carolingian kings, the succession of bishops of Langres, the translation of the relics of Ste.-Reine from Alise to Flavigny, and the establishment of a priory at Corbigny were all recorded together.[49]

Not until he reached the eleventh century did Hugh go beyond his sources and give his own version of events. Here he concentrated especially on bishops and abbots in Verdun and on the quarrels between Pope Gregory VII and Emperor Henry IV in the 1070s and 1080s. Then, in the 1090s, his narrative became personal, for he was elected abbot of Flavigny in 1096. His election, coming shortly after his account of broad reform in the church, was treated as another aspect of reform, for the house was "desolate" when he arrived and had lacked an abbot for seven years.[50]

The memory he wanted his readers to retain of his election was composed both of his personal reaction—mostly surprise and an anxious feeling of unworthiness—and of the material improvement he made to the monastery's patrimony. Immediately after giving the details of his consecration, Hugh launched into what was essentially a pancarte, brief summaries of dozens of pious gifts or of quarrels settled with the local laity. He interrupted this account at several points to provide such information as the deaths or elections of local bishops and abbots, then returned to the gifts and quarrel settlements.[51] None of these were in the cartulary; he clearly considered that one of the purposes of his chronicle was to create a permanent memory where none had existed of gifts received.

His chronicle also became a justification of his own actions, for Hugh had a difficult relationship with the bishop of Autun. Not long after he became abbot he incurred the new bishop's ire because he did not attend his consecration, although Hugh argued that he had had a good excuse and indeed had sent a representative. The situation quickly deteriorated, and his house was put under interdict before Hugh was eventually able to reestablish cordial relations.[52] He wanted to make sure that anyone who heard about the quarrel would remember the events his way: an obedient, reverent abbot maltreated by a bishop who was both irrational and wrathful.

But the fullest section of the entire chronicle concerns Hugh's quarrel with his own monks, who drove him out. He began this section with a prayer to Christ, begging for his compassion. The conflict, which Hugh apparently recorded as it happened, stretched out with many an accusation, effort at settlement, and postponed resolution: it involved councils, the bishop of Autun (again) as well as other bishops, the papal curia, a monk at Flavigny whom Hugh accused of selling himself to the devil, and the monks of St.-Bénigne of Dijon.[53] Ultimately Hugh's efforts to retain his monastery failed, and the bishop of Autun ordained the prior of Flavigny as abbot. Although Hugh wrote "Amen" at the end of this section and proceeded to describe the adulterous affair of King Philip I, thus managing to return to broader history, his personal difficulties were for him a central part of his world history. Memory was individual: remembering kings and battles needed, at least for Hugh, to be supplemented by remembering how unfairly he had been treated.

Bishops and Abbots

In the twelfth century the effort to control the past—and hence the present—could, as well as taking the form of charters and chronicles, also be played out through access to the saints. The constant, low-level tension in many bishoprics between the bishops and the abbots of major monasteries, already seen at Sens and Autun, could find expression in competing claims to the see's holy past.

Most French cathedral cities in the high Middle Ages were dominated by two churches, the cathedral, home of the bishop, and the major monastery, chief rival of the bishop within the ecclesiastical structure. The cathedral was physically in the center of the city, generally built on the highest point in town since the fourth or fifth century, indeed often on the site of the Gallo-Roman governor's palace. The monastery was typically built outside the Roman *civitas*, perhaps only a short distance away, perhaps a kilometer or more. The cathedral had been the original church of a city in Gaul, and the only other churches within the Gallo-Roman walls were part of the cathedral complex, leaving the monasteries outside. The chief monastery would be a newer foundation than the cathedral, often established in what had been a basilica dedicated to a local saint.[54]

Both cathedral and monastery were considered holy, of course. But there certainly could be a vigorous debate on whether the bishops, considered the institutional heirs of the first apostles, had precedence or whether the monks did, living, they maintained, in the same style as the first apostles. The bishops represented the height of the ecclesiastical hierarchy, whereas the monastery, more withdrawn, represented on at least some level the desert of contemplation.

The debate took on an added sharpness in that both bishops and abbots often looked to the same individual for legitimation: an early holy bishop, buried at the monastery. A basilica might have originally been dedicated to a saint whose relics had been set there, but with the arrival of the body of the holy bishop, the church took on a new designation. For example, in Auxerre Bishop Germanus was buried in the mid-fifth century at the basilica he had dedicated to Saint Maurice, but it almost immediately became known in his honor as St.-Germain. The monks later established there always remembered that they had the greatest saint the see had ever produced in their crypt.[55] In Tours, the cathedral with its bishop and canons looked to Saint Martin, who had after all been bishop there in the fourth century, but the monks of Marmoutier, which Martin had founded, could argue plausibly that they better represented the legacy of the saint. The situation in Tours was further complicated by the presence of a third locus of holiness, the basilica of St.-Martin, which had the saint's relics, even though the canons who served that church in the twelfth century could not claim to be following as holy a lifestyle as did the monks of Marmoutier.[56]

Auxerre and Tours were not alone in the debate over who could claim and shape a holy bishop from late antiquity. At Reims, Remigius, the bishop who had baptized Clovis around the year 500, was claimed by both the cathedral and the monastery of St.-Remi. The archbishops of Sens, as already noted, were routinely buried outside of town at St.-Pierre-le-Vif, where their saintliness augmented that of the monks. At Verdun, the monks of St.-Vanne went so far as to create fictive graves for Merovingian-era bishops of Verdun within their monastery to claim their legacy for themselves.[57] At Limoges, it was the monastery of St.-Martial, not the cathedral, that was able to make the most of the deliberately created "tradition" that Martial, putative first bishop of the see, had been an apostle of Christ.[58]

At Rouen, both the bishops and the monastery of St.-Ouen had initially claimed the authority of the seventh-century bishop Audoin (Ouen), but in the eleventh century, as the competition became more marked, the bishops began vigorously promoting the cult of Romanus, an earlier bishop, rather than that of Audoin.[59] The bishopric of Langres had no significant early bishop over whom to contend; their chief spiritual competition came from the monastery of St.-Bénigne of Dijon, in their diocese but not their city. The original Saint Benignus was not a bishop but a martyr, perhaps imported from Byzantium. The bishops of Langres were still frequently buried at St.-Bénigne, and indeed in the early Middle Ages they often resided in Dijon rather than their own city.[60] Langres was thus unusual in not having, a short walk from the cathedral, a monastery that could claim that not only was its way of life superior but that it was preferred by the see's principal saints. The memory of saints of the past, even the very distant past, thus could be used to validate a church's position in the present, especially its position in relation to other churches, which might, however, refer their own status to the same saints.

The monastic chroniclers of the high Middle Ages had a clear purpose for their narratives: to organize the past, make sure its most important events were not forgotten, and give the details of their own houses' place within the history of human salvation. In doing so they used the documents in their archives to support and supplement the accounts they obtained from other sources. Cartularies and chronicles, very different for modern historians, were for high medieval chroniclers both ways of organizing and presenting the past. They simplified what may now seem complicated series of events, assumed that the accepted definition of spirituality had always been the same, and readily applied current expectations for the religious life, or for Christian versus infidel, to the past. Yet even though they knew how the story ought to run, chroniclers were not creating a fictive past, for they did their best to base it on the written word.

Some words were easier to understand than others. The documents of the Merovingian era, with their challenging handwriting, abbreviations, and protocols, always seemed strange. But at least in those documents high medieval monks could recognize pious gifts and royal immunities. Carolingian-era polyptyques, though not as distant in time, presented a bigger challenge, as discussed in the following chapter.

Chapter 4

Polyptyques: Twelfth-Century Monks Face the Ninth Century

Polyptyques, the great ninth-century inventories of monastic holdings, stand at a turning point in the medieval exercise of memory.[1] On the one hand, they were originally created in order to have a clear record of property holdings and expected revenues. Their creation was thus part of a ninth-century effort to organize memory and make it unchanging, as well as to rationalize records—like the first cartularies, created at exactly the same time. On the other hand, polyptyques in the high Middle Ages were also part of the memory of the past that later scribes had to deal with, had to try to rework into something that would make sense in their own time.

Modern debates over the precise meaning of terms in the ninth-century polyptyques, how they can be related to the agricultural practices of late antiquity, and the creation of "classic" manorialism have absorbed most recent scholarship on these sources. I intend to approach them somewhat differently, as sources that were originally created to preserve memory and then, three centuries later, had lost their meaning when their context was forgotten.

Polyptyques in the Ninth Century

Polyptyques, listings of the property holdings of and dues owed to major churches, were a ninth-century innovation. There were a few earlier efforts to make records of estate holdings, in particular at St.-Martin of Tours,[2] scraps of which still survive, but no efforts were made to enumerate property on the scale of the great polyptyques until the Carolingian era. Charlemagne's "Capitulare de villis," which ordered that such surveys be done on his own estates, is generally taken as the impetus for the creation of all polyptyques.[3] If his orders were carried out on royal manors, however, no records survive, and indeed most polyptyques date from at least two generations later.

The word "polyptyque" itself was used in late Roman administration to mean a record or account book, a census of people and property for taxation purposes. A significant difference, however, is that Roman census rolls, unlike ninth-century polyptyques, did not specify how much each property was expected to pay, as that had to be worked out annually.[4] Even though the ninth-century form of a polyptyque, a recording of property and dues regularly owed on great manors, was therefore something new, it was built on an older sense that sources of income ought to be written down and organized.

A number of monastic houses, primarily in the time of Charles the Bald, sent agents around to their villas to make systematic surveys of land, of dues and obligations, and of those who owed these obligations. Fewer than a dozen ninth-century surveys still survive more or less intact from west Francia: those from St.-Germain-des-Prés, St.-Remi of Reims, St.-Maur-des-Fossés, St.-Victor of Marseille, St.-Bertin, Prüm, Wissembourg, Lobbes, and Montier-en-Der. St.-Germain's is the only one to survive as an original; the others are all later copies.[5] The polyptyque of St.-Bertin is preserved because when the monks wrote the *Gesta* of their abbots in the 960s they copied into it the text of a polyptyque already over a century old.[6] There are also scraps and mentions of others, such as the polyptyques of St.-Père of Chartres and Marmoutier, enough that it seems highly likely that many more monasteries produced such inventories than those that have survived.[7] Like the Domesday Book in England two centuries later, the polyptyques were composed with the hope and belief that once everything was in writing it would be easier to tell what was owned and what was owed.[8]

Again like Domesday, the polyptyques were never uniform or complete. Some property was simply never recorded in a polyptyque. Because different villas would be surveyed by different men, what was recorded and even how it was counted would have varied.[9] Even if we know the names of those who surveyed the monastery's holdings for the polyptyque, we do not know whether they were monks, monastic agents, or perhaps (and indeed most likely) men of local importance. Sometimes the original polyptyque scribe, writing from the notes of several different surveyors, duplicated or accidentally omitted entries.[10]

And of course a monastery's properties were not static. Although scholars have sometimes tried to date polyptyques based on certain material within them,[11] at best one can determine a date after which certain materials could have been added. Over the generations after a polyptyque's initial composition, new entries were often made or old entries emended.[12] The mid-ninth-century polyptyque of Montier-en-Der, for example, includes a great deal of property that was confirmed to the monks by Charles the Bald but also includes property they acquired only in the late ninth, tenth, or eleventh centuries.[13] In the polyptyque of Wissembourg the ninth-century material is overshadowed by later additions.[14] By the twelfth century, polyptyques would have been heavily worked over, with marginal comments, interlinear notations, and whole folia of additions. Although scholars have tended to concentrate on the polyptyques as ninth-century productions, they should be seen instead as tools that continued to be used and added to over the following centuries.[15]

A copy of a polyptyque done in the high Middle Ages may now look clean and tidy—and for most polyptyques that is all we have[16]—but the parchment from which the scribe worked would have been anything but tidy. This very messiness must have been an incentive for a cartulary scribe to skip over certain sections. The surviving twelfth-century version—when we have it— would have been the product of a determined effort to clean up what would have been hardly comprehensible. Faced with unusual terms, scribes seem to have abbreviated heavily and hoped for the best.[17]

Even now, although scholars have better access to late Roman law than twelfth-century monks would have had, there are debates about a number of the terms that appear in polyptyques,[18] suggesting that when they were originally composed the agents doing the surveys and the scribes recording the information may not have had an entirely clear set of categories with which to work. For example, the word *colonus* was a perfectly valid word for a free tenant in late antiquity, used in some polyptyques, such as that of St.-Germain-des-Prés, but absent in others; it is never found, for example, in the polyptyque of Montier-en-Der. Scholars are still debating whether an early medieval *colonus* would have owed labor dues, and how much, just as they are also still debating whether *ingenui* were (as seems most probable) freemen or just another version of *servi*; the information in the sources is far from unambiguous or uniform. *Mancipia* and *hospicia* were servile dependents who were still not as subject to arbitrary demands as were slaves;[19] the differences between the two terms were never spelled out in the ninth-century sources and may indeed be an artifact of different monasteries using different words.[20] A polyptyque, then, should be seen not so much as an application of general rules about categories of status and ownership to the particular manors of a monastery but rather as an attempt to try to create those categories.

There has been a concerted if controversial scholarly effort to describe the polyptyques as fiscal documents and the payments described in them as connected with royal government and public tax revenues.[21] But the polyptyques themselves show no sign of the monasteries having fixed obligations to the state. In the case of Montier-en-Der, Charles the Bald confirmed the monks' possession of many of the same villas as are enumerated in their polyptyque, in a manner that made clear that he, at any rate, considered the land, the tenants, and the revenues as the monks' own, not his.[22] The range of formats adopted in the different polyptyques and the fact that all surviving ones are from ecclesiastical institutions that were not part of royal lands also argue against any public fiscal purpose. Those who created the polyptyques were doing more than following some governmental mandate; they were creating what they hoped would be an orderly record for their own monastic successors.

Ideal and Messiness in Polyptyques

Although it has been argued that a polyptyque was an "ideal form" rather than, strictly speaking, an accounting,[23] one should not overdo the distinction. Of course the monks had in mind an ideal, in which all of their lands and revenues would be systematically described, but the differences in the vocabulary used by various monasteries and the differences in the ways they organized their entries indicate that they were not following a formula.[24] Nonetheless, the ideal of a "classic" ninth-century manor has a strong hold on scholars. If a polyptyque does not seem to reflect the classic system, for example, in not showing a clear division between seigneurial domain and *mansi* granted to dependent tenants, then it is asked what might be different or strange about the polyptyque one is studying.[25] But the very idea of a classic manor and of a polyptyque that reflects that manor assumes clarity and stability. A polyptyque was rather a messy effort to construct memory out of a fluid set of people and obligations, and in the form that it has survived it reflects three centuries of changes.

It should also be noted that it would be very unwise to attempt to use the apparent exactitude of the figures to try to give precise totals for the rural population or the extent of a monastery's holdings.[26] The monks' tenants were surely not the only inhabitants of a region or even a particular villa. The eleventh-century scribe Paul of St.-Père of Chartres said that one would be "deluded by vain hope" in thinking to get exact figures for his house's income from its polyptyque.[27] Even aside from the fact that there was never a perfect correspondence between a monastery's holdings and what was recorded in a polyptyque, the figures within it cannot be assumed to add up. The example of the entry for St.-Dizier in the polyptyque of Montier-en-Der, an entry for which two independent witnesses survive, indicates the figures' unreliability.

The first appearance in the twelfth-century cartulary of an inventory of the monks' possessions at St.-Dizier is attached to the end of an 876 donation charter of Count Boso. A very similar inventory appears in the polyptyque (further along in the cartulary), but a comparison of the two indicates significant differences.[28] In the polyptyque, the entry for St.-Dizier is attached to an inventory of the property held *in precaria* at Effincourt, where it clearly does not belong, suggesting that it was written in the margin or on a separate piece of parchment and the cartulary scribe just copied it where he found it.

Both of the accounts of the holdings at St.-Dizier start with a church and the *iornales* of arable land associated with it. However, the polyptyque says these *iornales* numbered 33 (*xxxiii*), while Boso's document put the number at 123 (*cxxiii*). Next, both say that there were three *iornales* of meadowland and continue with identical enumerations of the manse attached to the church, with its arable land and meadowland, of the *mansus dominicatus* with its lands and five serfs (*hospicia*), and of the woodland. But then the polyptyque says that there were four (*iiii*) additional mansi at St.-Dizier, whereas the document puts the number at eight (*viii*). The number of men on these mansi is the same in both (eight), but it clearly would make a difference to our understanding of the ninth-century rural economy if there were two male tenants per manse or only one.

Next the amount of arable land and of newly cleared land (*de exartis*) is the same, except that the polyptyque adds an extra half *iornalis* to the latter. Both accounts proceed with identical enumerations of *mancipia,* of a flour mill and measures of grain, but then the polyptyque says that the monks received eight (*viii*) measures of salt a year there, although the document gives only six (*sex*). Then comes a phrase different in the two versions: "De denariis libra i" in the polyptyque and "De pice solidum i" in the document. Interestingly, the polyptyque, which (unlike Boso's document) strikes a total at the end, gives "de argento solidus i," which suggests that the document, not the polyptyque, gave the correct reading earlier (and that the odd word *pice* meant "specie"). The two accounts finish with the same figures for land at two adjacent hamlets.

The differences in the details in these two accounts throw into question the accuracy of all of the figures in the polyptyque.[29] Even though the majority of figures are the same in the two versions, the differences suggest that the twelfth-century scribe consistently had trouble reading his Carolingian original. There is no way to tell which version more correctly represents the original. Because the polyptyque of Montier-en-Der, like most surviving polyptyques, is known only in copies, one is always left unsure as to which figures in such a polyptyque actually reflect what the ninth-century survey really said.[30]

Polyptyques in the High Middle Ages

As this example suggests, cartulary scribes of the high Middle Ages must have looked at polyptyques and scratched their heads. Clearly these were important compilations, spelling out at least some of a church's possessions. And yet they would have seemed extremely foreign to monks of the high Middle Ages. In the ninth century a number of terms and categories were employed that then dropped out of usage in the following generations. The ninth-century rural landscape was undergoing rapid changes, and five or six generations later, when west Frankish cartularies were first being composed, polyptyques would have seemed inherently strange.

The changes taking place were more than changes in vocabulary. The monk Paul, compiling the cartulary of St.-Père of Chartres in the 1080s, commented that the *rolli conscripti* in the monastery's archives showed that in days of old the *rustici* were not subject to the same obligations and did not pay the same dues as in his day, and that in addition those who wrote these rolls did not have the same names for things (*vocabula rerum*).[31] These "rolls" were almost certainly an old polyptyque of the monastery. He copied at least a portion of these rolls because, as he said, he wanted a record on "new leaves" of what the house of St.-Père had once owned, but even some of the place-names of the polyptyque were strange to him, and he said that the places had "vanished or were unknown."[32] Between the seizure of property by lay abbots and bishops, which had deprived St.-Père of most of its Carolingian-era holdings, and the changes in the ways that estates were administered, an eleventh-century monk like Paul found the ninth and tenth centuries disturbingly foreign.[33]

The polyptyque of Prüm, copied a century and a half after Paul worked, also indicates the difficulties the monks of the high Middle Ages found with a ninth-century text. The monk Caesarius said in his preface that he had transcribed the polyptyque, which he said was written in 893, "to the best of his ability and knowledge."[34] But this *librum antiquum* had given him many problems, especially the names of the villas: the old names, he said, seemed "almost barbarous," and he felt obliged to change them to their modern form, even though he tried to leave the other *vocabula* as he found them. Still, through all his difficulties with the text, he felt obliged to copy it conscientiously; it contained the "rights and revenues" of Prüm, he said (*iura et redditus*), and he wanted to be sure not to weaken the "authority" of the old book. He closed his preface with a prayer, indicating that although he described his copying as a work of "temporal administration," it also had a strong religious component.

Caesarius also realized that many of his thirteenth-century contemporaries would have difficulty with the terminology used in the polyptyque. On the folio facing the first entry in his codex, he added some notes to aid understanding.[35] For example, he said that the book mentioned four different kinds of *mansi*, which he set out to define—doubtless deriving his definitions from context. *Mansi serviles*, he said, were those on which the tenants were obliged to work for the monks three days a week all year long, as well as render various other dues. Modern scholars, who also have had to derive their definitions more or less from context, although with the advantage of multiple polyptyques to look at, would agree with Caesarius here, although perhaps not with the specificity of three days a week.[36] *Mansi lediles*, Caesarius continued, were those that also owed many dues but not year-round. Here he seems to be guessing. *Mansi ingenuales*, he went on, was the term for *mansi* in the Ardennes. Here he missed completely the distinction between "servile" and "free" *mansi*, which scholars now associate with the legal status of the men who lived on them in the ninth century, although he did comment that these Ardennes *mansi* were also called *kunihkgeshuve*, a term meaning "royal households."[37] Finally, *mansi absi* were to him, as to modern scholars, ones empty of cultivators. The necessity he perceived to explain these terms—as well as some others like *camba*, a "bakehouse and brewhouse" he said correctly (*bahchus et bruhus*)—indicates that they were no longer in use at the beginning of the thirteenth century.

The lack of connection between the experience of a copyist and the polyptyque he was copying is further illustrated by the frequency of people's names in polyptyques. Those copying the "old books" must have realized that the Reimbald or Nantcher whose dues they were carefully writing out (to give examples from Prüm) had been dead for three centuries. And yet many polyptyques list by name those living on the *mansi* along with their dues. Much of the polyptyque of St.-Remi of Reims is a list of names, of people generally identified as *servus* or *ingenuus* (for men; the female versions were *ancilla* and *ingenua*), sometimes with the rents they owed, sometimes with the number of their children. Caesarius of Prüm carefully copied the names of the tenants at *Wetellendorpht* and what each owed, even though he then gave a brief history in a marginal note of the very different use to which this property had been put in the succeeding three and a half centuries.[38]

That names should be found in polyptyques originally is not surprising. The Merovingian-era administrative documents from St.-Martin of Tours are little more than lists of names, with annotations to show how much each person owed. What is surprising is that these names were copied in the high Middle Ages. Many other copyists must have been less patient than Caesarius. The twelfth-century scribe at St.-Bertin deliberately omitted from his polyptyque the lists of precarial grants that had been included—and which he characterized as benefices granted to knights, *milites* and *cavillarii*.[39] Yet at Montier-en-Der, a number of names are found in the list of grants made *in precaria*, which was incorporated into the polyptyque. These names were the same as those whom Charles the Bald had confirmed as holding *in precaria* from the monks, and thus the precarists were dead over two centuries when Der's polyptyque was copied,[40] but the scribe recorded them anyway, unlike the scribe at St.-Bertin. Clearly he thought it important to reproduce what was before him as well as he could.

Caesarius wrote a personal note at the end of the polyptyque of Prüm, which sums up very well the changes from the ninth century to the high Middle Ages.

> One should realize that 329 years have passed since the old book was written or compiled. . . . And in that time there have been almost daily changes, woods have been cut down, villas built, tithes established, many mills constructed and vineyards planted, and the land broadly cultivated. The possessions of the church of Prüm are found in many provinces, both far and wide. And therefore no one should wonder why all the possessions and fiefs are not mentioned here.[41]

Paul of Chartres's and Caesarius of Prüm's puzzlement in examining their houses' polyptyques must have been widespread. The unfamiliarity of peasant obligations and the uses to which land was put would have worried many a cartulary scribe. The differences between what was in the polyptyque and what they took for granted in the high Middle Ages was, again, much more than changes in vocabulary.[42] Although the places in which the monks owned property generally remained the same, the way that the rural economy was organized and the kinds of dues the peasants on the land owed had completely changed. Even the large estate, worked by dependent tenants, generally assumed to have characterized Carolingian as well as Merovingian agriculture,[43] had been transformed by the twelfth century.

Much more scholarship has gone into characterizing the great estates of the Carolingian era, along with their relationship with the *latifundia* and estates of late antiquity, than has gone into discussing what happened to these estates after the ninth century.[44] Scholars have tended to assume that the "seigneurial system" of the high Middle Ages was built, without too much difficulty, on the bases established by the ninth century.[45] The interesting questions have been considered to be whether ninth-century serfs were the descendants of Roman slaves—or were perhaps slaves themselves—and the extent to which seigneurialism owed more to Roman or Germanic practice. But the evidence of the polyptyques suggests that additional questions deserve attention, for the manorialism of the ninth century was *not* that of the twelfth.

Here looking at polyptyques through the lens of memory can help address issues about their purpose and their survival. The great slave-worked plantations of late antiquity, as well as the Carolingian-era broad seigneurial estates, were long gone by the high Middle Ages. By then small holdings that might pay rent, infrequent in the Carolingian era, had come to dominate. That is, although the monks of the high Middle Ages owned land in the same places as had their ninth-century predecessors, and had tenants on that land, the kinds and amounts of obligations of those tenants were changed.

The small attention given to the change from ninth-century manors to twelfth-century seigneurialism may in part be due to the paucity of evidence on tenth-century agricultural practice, what has been called a "hidden turning point." Although rather general efforts have been made to characterize this "turning point," specifically as a regrouping of the peasantry and a disintegration of the great estates,[46] the exact details remain unexamined. Scholars have instead preferred to discuss the much better documented eleventh century and its supposed mutations.

Debates have raged over the supposed "transformations" of the year 1000, whether the eleventh century was categorically different from the late tenth. Recently something of a consensus has developed, that the institutions of the tenth century were not revolutionarily turned into feudal society by the mid-eleventh century.[47] But the real question, and the one that scholars have not been asking, is how the ninth-century economy turned into that of the tenth. Instead, all of the debate has focused on knighthood, law, and the exercise of power, not the rural economy. Most scholars have assumed that the agricultural and commercial developments of the ninth century led fairly seamlessly into the economic expansion of the eleventh and twelfth centuries.[48]

Perhaps it is time to reconsider this assumption. Polyptyques describe a world that clearly made sense in the ninth century but did not make sense by the end of the eleventh. Rather than looking for feudal mutations of the year 1000, it may be better to look for agricultural mutations of the year 900. Whatever the nature and causes of the changes between the ninth century and the eleventh, one point is clear: the polyptyques described an agricultural world that no longer existed by the time that late eleventh- and twelfth-century monks began to compose their cartularies.

The failure of more polyptyques to survive, therefore, cannot be simply accidental. Nor can it be blamed on the fragility of papyrus, as can the disappearance of most Merovingian-era documents, for by the ninth century Frankish monks were using parchment exclusively. The disappearance of polyptyques has to be considered the result of a deliberate choice: a choice not to bother to copy out a long, confusing, and, it seemed, often meaningless series of entries. Ninth-century donation charters and royal confirmations *were* copied as worth remembering because the land was still the monks'. Ninth-century polyptyques, detailing obligations that had not been fulfilled for two or three centuries, must often have been deliberately forgotten.

Such forgetting, it should be stressed, was not a rejection of a monastery's past in general or of the ninth century in particular; otherwise, there would not be so many surviving records of Charlemagne, Louis the Pious, and Charles the Bald. Nor was there some universal rejection of polyptyques, because a few monks *did* make the effort to preserve them in their cartularies. These brave copyists knew that a polyptyque had once been an important guarantee of their house's possessions and was thus worth copying for that reason alone. But for the most part, the scribes of the high Middle Ages who created cartularies were organizing their houses' archives in ways that would be useful in their own present and anticipated future. Polyptyques that had once been put together out of a similar mission to organize had lost their usefulness and were thus allowed to slip quietly into oblivion.

Chapter 5

An Age of Forgery

Creative memory was at its most creative in the ninth century, when church-men forged unprecedented and monumental runs of entirely false charters. The modern study of medieval documents long focused on "what really happened" and thus either ignored forged documents completely or at best relegated them to the *spuria* section of an edition. But if one examines memory as an active process, in which it was but a small step from thinking about the past, to reconceptualizing the lessons of the past, to reworking the past to how it should have been, then forgeries become an important element.[1]

For example, it is not enough to say that forged Merovingian documents do not tell us anything useful about the sixth and seventh centuries. A high proportion of Merovingian-era documents have been characterized as *unecht* by scholars at one time or another—indeed, the majority of those that do not still exist as originals, and even some of them[2]—although the more recent tendency is to recognize a core of authenticity and speak rather of "interpolation."[3] Yet even obvious forgeries tell us a great deal about how the writers of the Carolingian and Capetian eras thought about their own pasts.

In this chapter I shall discuss several of the more egregious sets of forgeries from the ninth century, which became a true age of forgery.[4] Falsification reached a height not equaled earlier or later. The forgers were all churchmen creating an imaginary past: monks trying to assert or reestablish the value of their monasteries; monks and bishops seeking either to dominate or to free themselves from each other; bishops attempting to free themselves from judgment.

The forgers of the ninth century primarily created documents with purported dates in late antiquity rather than documents they could attribute to Charlemagne. It has been estimated that less than 10 percent of all spurious

"Charlemagne" documents were created during the century after his death; most instead were fabricated during the twelfth and thirteenth centuries. The majority of false Charles the Bald documents, too, appear to date from after the Capetians took the French throne.[5] Given Charlemagne's reign of over forty-five years and his subsequent central place in medieval epics, one would have expected him to have made a bigger impact on the minds of ninth-century creators of false documents. Even the rather indiscriminate forgers of Le Mans preferred Louis the Pious. As I shall argue further in Chapter 8, during Charlemagne's years as king of the Franks the ecclesiastics of his realm had come to know him all too well. If they wanted an ideal king who was supportive of the church, they knew better than to label that king Charlemagne. Only in later centuries, when his publicists' image of him as exactly such a monarch had taken hold, could he become a suitable figure to be presented as the originator of forged privileges.

The Written Word and Forgeries

It is usually assumed that the growing frequency of charters in the eleventh and twelfth centuries led to a new interest in forging records. The rapid changes in political, religious, and economic structures, it is suggested, led to an attempt to resist change by writing records of a dimly remembered if doubtless golden-hued past.[6] I would argue instead for the ninth century that it was not the frequency of the written word but rather its infrequency that inspired forgers and that they were not reactionary but innovators, trying to create new structures and institutions that would benefit them.[7] Between the relatively document-rich Merovingian era and the high Middle Ages, documents in the Carolingian period, because infrequent, took on greater normative value, and thus the forgers could hope that their careful creations would carry greater weight.

The ninth century and the sixth were so different—including chancery practice and diplomatic protocols—that it was not sufficient, or in many cases even really possible, for ninth-century scribes to make clean, complete transcriptions of the papyrus documents they copied onto parchment. And yet they knew they had to try, for otherwise some of their most important early records would soon be gone.[8] Under this relentless pressure, the line between making the past make sense and making it more useful was extremely thin and often crossed. To some extent then forgeries (or at least "interpolations") might be seen as almost accidental, the result of misunderstanding, misreading, and filling in the gaps. But ninth-century forgeries went well beyond accidents.

New or refounded monasteries, increasingly frequent in the mid-ninth century, needed to assert both that they had a glorious past and that they were as worthy as their contemporaries. Thus the abbot of Glanfeuil created in the 860s a *vita* of Saint Maurus, disciple of Saint Benedict, in which Maurus was the first to bring Benedictine monasticism to Gaul in the sixth century by founding Glanfeuil. The monastery of Fleury, located not far away on the Loire, claimed to have the body of Benedict himself, so the choice of Maurus gave Glanfeuil an almost comparable prestige.[9] The abbot's assertion that he took the *vita* from an "ancient" booklet of Roman provenance gave it an air of specious authenticity.

At many other houses, the overall efforts at regularization that emerged from the Carolingian court, the growing scarcity and thus value of written charters, and a need to regain control of a past that was in danger of crumbling into dust all gave a new meaning to the written act as a mediator between past and present. Such a record became more than just the normal product of any sort of formal interaction. It was a guarantee of rights. Although the written charter was no longer the everyday event it had been in the Merovingian era (see Chapter 9), literacy was still presumed among those in authority, and important decisions were recorded and promulgated in writing.[10] What was different in the ninth century was the special, almost iconic nature of the charter. When written records were fewer, individual charters could take on much more significance. Memory became associated with the charter that preserved that memory.

The value of such documents is spelled out in the *Gesta* of a bishop of Le Mans from the middle of the ninth century. Several times the narrative paused for a few—or sometimes quite a few—charters, sometimes given as summaries, sometimes as integral copies. "It has seemed right to insert a few of our privileges into this little book," the author said, "so that if in the future some question should arise, and someone tries to conceal a privilege because of his machinations and evil plans, the *exemplar* will still be found here."[11] In a suit in the imperial court, the author has everyone declare to Louis the Pious that the bishop should prevail because he had "the charters and royal pronouncements of your father and your other predecessors, that is, the kings of the Franks."[12] Indeed, according to the Le Mans account, the bishop had brought twenty-five separate charters with him to show the emperor.[13]

This was a novel concept of property law, that kings themselves could be bound by earlier royal decisions, as long as those decisions were in writing. The author asserted that antiquity of written record of ownership was more important than mere present possession. He preferred purported royal charters confirming other royal charters of greater antiquity to charters in which recent kings made new pronouncements.[14] Thus those claiming authority in the present bolstered their position by creating documents they could claim were from the past. The document that emerged from a royal ruling was almost more significant than the ruling itself. Thus it became tempting to forge as many authoritative texts as possible, preferably ones of considerable antiquity.

Certainly the mid-ninth century was not the first time someone had written a document and attempted to pass it off as older than it actually was or as written by someone else. Most famously, the Donation of Constantine had been composed in the eighth century, as members of the papal curia sought to assert rights with a four-hundred-year pedigree. The Donation indeed may have served as an actual precedent for ninth-century forgers. It was incorporated into the Pseudo-Isidorian decretals, whose author seems to have found there the inspiration to confect a much larger series of early decisions to support the power and authority of bishops. If "Pseudo-Isidore" recognized the Donation's falsity, however, he was virtually the only one. The Carolingians— and indeed everyone until the Italian Renaissance—assumed its authenticity.[15]

The Le Mans forgeries and the Pseudo-Isidorian decretals are the two most famous forgeries of the ninth century, both the products of concerted campaigns to create a useful past that was completely false. These two sets of forgeries were composed nearly contemporaneously; it is even possible that both were created in Le Mans, although current scholarship tends to put the Pseudo-Isidorian author(s) instead into the archdiocese of Reims.[16] They were both written in response to perceived attacks on episcopal authority and possessions in the middle of the ninth century. Both sets of authors reacted similarly, by going into ancient times to find supportive (if false) statements by ancient, eminent authorities. The Le Mans authors relied on the earliest kings of the Franks, Pseudo-Isidore on the earliest popes.

The Le Mans Forgeries

The Le Mans forgeries were put together at the episcopal curia in several stages, over a generation or more, starting in the 830s.[17] The compilers artfully combined forged and authentic charters. They quite consciously rewrote a past that had come to them in pieces but could be reorganized into a unified whole. In forging they created a coherent story where there had been no coherent story. The past with which they had to deal was composed of a number of authentic documents of greater or lesser antiquity, *vitae* of local saints, testaments of earlier bishops, and various other narrative sources. The past they re-created was a "History of the Bishops," a narrative studded with *pièces justificatives*. The ninth-century bishopric pressed its claim to authority within the diocese primarily by creating a narrative where bishops were the principal players.[18]

The two major components of what are now known as the Le Mans forgeries are the *Actus pontificum Cenomannis*, a brief history of each of the bishops of Le Mans, going back to the origins of the see; and the *Gesta domni Aldrici*, a much more detailed account of the life and activities of one ninth-century bishop, probably he who held office when the forgeries were composed. In addition, the Le Mans authors rewrote some of their earlier saints' lives. They were wide-ranging in their activities, so that virtually no charter from ninth-century Le Mans can be taken at face value without careful consideration. Even the testament of Bishop Aldric seems to have been heavily reworked after his death.[19]

Because the Le Mans authors so skillfully combined real charters with those they confected, it is clear that they did not set out to fabricate a completely specious past but rather an improved and more useful one. Major parts of the Le Mans corpus are no more forged than was any effort to retell the story of the past.[20] But unlike most chroniclers, the authors of the forgeries created completely new documents to which they attempted to give a spurious antiquity. Both forged and real documents were intended to enhance the bishopric's authority and holdings.

The bishops of Le Mans tried for a decade, without notable success, to assert their authority over the little monastery of St.-Calais. The quarrel began in the final years of Bishop Aldric's reign. In 855, the abbot of St.-Calais complained to a council at Bonneuil that his house was being "oppressed" and brought out for inspection royal immunities issued by three generations of

Frankish kings. Impressed, the assembled bishops at the council agreed that his house was not subject to the bishop, a decision confirmed by Charles the Bald. This council's findings were repeated at a council at Pîtres seven years later, which decision was signed by all of the assembled bishops who had not already signed the first decision.[21] But Bishop Aldric of Le Mans ignored the decision of the first council (he was at any rate dying), and his successor, Bishop Robert, was no more willing to accept the 862 decision. Instead, when he appeared before Charles the Bald in 863, he made sure to arrive with plenty of supporting documents of his own.

The bishop's supporters had every reason to expect that their own volume of forged royal charters would carry the day. But in spite of their daring initiative and imagination, the Le Mans authors were unsuccessful; their efforts ended in devastating failure. Bishop Robert claimed in 863 at the council of Verberie that St.-Calais was dependent on the bishopric, but Charles the Bald ruled that the monastery was not an episcopal but instead a *royal* monastery. He noted that the bishops had subjected the monastery to themselves for only a few years, not for centuries as they claimed. He also ordered destroyed the charters from Le Mans that the council pronounced false, "so that they could not be used again in fruitless lawsuits and needlessly take up judges' time."[22]

The claims of the bishopric of Le Mans rested primarily on the value of the written word. At Verberie, even when the case was going badly, the bishop's spokesman continued to insist that their many *legitima instrumenta* proved their point. However few or many years the bishops had exercised dominion at St.-Calais was irrelevant. Possession was not at issue: antiquity of charters was. But Charles the Bald was working from an entirely different set of principles. It proved impossible to convince the king that the written decisions of earlier kings altered what Charles himself believed: that the monastery was in fact his.

Significantly, there is no indication that the charters he ordered destroyed were even examined. Witnesses attested that earlier bishops had held St.-Calais for only a few years, and then only as a royal *beneficium*, that is, a temporary grant, which did not change its fundamental status as a royal possession. The bishop's charters must be false because they contradicted this, no matter what verisimilitude the forgers may have given them. A belief in the power of the written word was strong enough at Le Mans to inspire extensive forgeries, but others were not ready to accept this.

The dossier that the bishop of Le Mans unsuccessfully presented at Verberie had been carefully put together, and thus both these documents and their sources are worth further examination, to see how the forgers picked and chose elements from a real past to rewrite the narrative that linked past and present. The records of the council do not specify what was in the charters ordered destroyed, but the bishop had not brought his only copies with him. Some still exist in the *Gesta* of Bishop Aldric, as well as summaries of many more; still others had been copied into the *Actus* of the bishops. In addition, Aldric's biographer added a "memorial" or memorandum that summarized the long and difficult relations between the bishopric and the monastery of St.-Calais.[23]

The starting point for the Le Mans authors was the *vita* of Saint Carilef (Calais), a sixth-century hermit. Carilef was considered St.-Calais's founder, establishing the house, according to his *vita*, under the name of Anisola. This *vita* dates from the eighth century or possibly the seventh, at any rate well before the forgers set to work.[24] Conspicuously absent is any mention of the bishop of Le Mans. Rather, it is the story of a saintly man from the Auvergne who came to the region seeking solitude and found it in the ruins of a spot once called Casa Gaianus, located on the Anisola stream, now overgrown with brambles. Here the hermit Carilef settled. The transition from hermitage to monastery, the *vita* continued, was made at the suggestion of King Childebert, who stumbled upon Carilef while hunting, and of Queen Vultrogoda, who had learned of the reclusive saint's "holiness, abstinence, and humility." Both made generous gifts to the saint, even though he initially insisted that a monk could not own land.[25]

The ninth-century Le Mans authors kept playing with this *vita*, using it in different ways. Their purpose was to make it clear that St.-Calais had always been dependent on the bishops of Le Mans, without denying or going against any part of the *vita*. Rather, their strategy was creative addition, both in the biographies of the bishops in the *Actus* and in the rewritten *vita* of Turibius, one of the earliest bishops of the see. For the *Actus* authors, Bishop Turibius was the second bishop of Le Mans, who founded a little monastery, St.-Pierre, in the late second century. This supposed episcopal monastery (a good two centuries earlier than Saint Martin's Marmoutier, the first real monastic foundation in Gaul) was intended as an early version of St.-Calais. The house was explicitly said to be founded at Anisola, which the authors said "the pagans" had called Casa Gaianus.[26] The dedication of his little monastery to Peter was meant to recall the supposed apostolicity of the see's bishops. The account of this bishop in the *Actus* was fleshed out in a rewritten *vita* of Turibius, in which a converted pagan, named Gaianus, gave his former house to the bishop, who established a monastery there with the avowed purpose of converting the infidel.[27]

All this was preparation for the *Actus* account of Bishop Innocent, a contemporary of King Childebert I.[28] Into his story the authors inserted the story of the hermit Carilef, suitably reworked. Carilef still arrives in the region and establishes a monastery on the Anisola, but now the old ruins have been reconceptualized as the second-century monastery of St.-Pierre, established by Bishop Turibius. Bishop Innocent is rightly concerned about a new monastery established in his diocese without his permission, but Carilef immediately rushes to subject himself and his monastery "humbly" to the bishop, along with all its possessions. He does so with written charters, *per strumenta cartarum*.

The *Actus* authors would not have wanted to leave this assertion of charters unverifiable, so they created a testament for Carilef, which they inserted at the end of their account of Bishop Innocent. In it, Carilef recalls that, for the remission of his sins, he had built a little monastery on the Anisola, where Bishop Turibius had earlier built a church in honor of St.-Pierre. He recalls that King Childebert had given him fiscal property but also adds that Bishop Innocent had been rightly concerned about a monastery in his diocese that was not subject to him, and thus that he, Carilef, had given everything into the bishop's hands.

Following this "testament," the *Actus* authors added two more confected documents, one in which Bishop Innocent granted the monastery to Carilef *in precaria*, to explain why the monastery had functioned independently in subsequent centuries, and another one from King Childebert, confirming that Carilef had built Anisola and given it to the bishop.[29] Other forged charters, supposedly issued between the mid-sixth and mid-seventh centuries by Bishops Domnolus, Hadoin, and Berarius, confirmed the whole episcopal version of the foundation of St.-Calais. Each had the bishop grant the monastery *in precaria* to the current abbot, thus simultaneously stressing its dependence on the bishop and creating an explanation for the abbots' apparent independence.[30]

Finally, the author of the *Gesta* of Bishop Aldric created a charter of Louis the Pious, in which Louis supposedly recalled the origins of St.-Calais, including King Childebert's confirmation of its dependency on Bishop Innocent.[31] Thus with a few suitable additions, the story of a hermit founding a house with the input of the king, but not the bishop, had been transformed into a story in which St.-Calais had been from its foundation—indeed, from even before its foundation—a dependency of the bishopric.

It is ironic that in confecting a story of episcopal control over St.-Calais, the authors of Le Mans used a false St.-Calais document as their model in forgery. The monks claimed to have what would be (were it authentic) one of the earliest charters from a Merovingian king for any monastery in Gaul, dating from the first decades of the sixth century. Scholars once accepted as authentic Childebert I's charter in which he granted Carilef some fiscal land on which to build a monastery.[32] Although this charter, borrowed heavily from the *vita* of Carilef, is not now seen as genuine,[33] it does seem to have impressed the episcopal curia of Le Mans in the ninth century.

In fact, the monastery of Anisola (St.-Calais) was probably founded in the second half of the sixth century, not the first half, as everyone in the ninth century assumed. It may be the monastery at Le Mans that Venantius Fortunatus said, very unspecifically, was founded by the bishop of Poitiers in the middle of the sixth century; it first appears unambiguously in Gregory of Tours's account of the events of 576, when the royal claimant Merovech was forcibly tonsured and intended to be a prisoner there.[34]

But the ninth-century authors at the episcopal see did not try to counter the monastery's "Childebert" document by critiquing its dating but rather by producing a "Childebert" document of their own. Surely it is no accident that the purported earliest royal charter granted to the bishopric is *also* from Childebert I, in which the king recalls that Carilef has built the monastery of Anisola and then subjected it to Bishop Innocent of Le Mans.[35] The best way to counter a Merovingian charter that failed to suggest any dependence of the monastery on the bishop was to create another charter, from the very same Merovingian king, that asserted that dependence.

Efforts to improve the records of the past required a diplomatic knowledge of the form in which the Merovingians issued their documents. The ninth-century authors knew some of the aspects of sixth-century scribal practice, recognizing, for example, that the kings then usually called themselves *vir inluster*, rather than "king by the grace of God," as did the Carolingians. They even recognized that no bishop was called an archbishop before the eighth century and that Merovingian-era bishops who signed charters did not give the names of their sees. The ninth-century authors were successful enough that some of their creations were still accepted as authentic in the nineteenth century, even while their tendency to forge has cast into doubt the authenticity of some documents that otherwise appear perfectly authentic. They possessed a genuine charter from Theodebert II from the end of the sixth century, in which the king confirmed that a couple had built an oratory outside Le

Mans, dedicated to Saint Martin.[36] Although this document said nothing about St.-Calais, their major topic of interest, and was in fact rather vague on the subjection of the new oratory of St.-Martin to the bishop, it did give an excellent example of the scribal practice of three centuries earlier from which to work.

When the bishop of Le Mans and his spokesmen took their collection of improved sources before the Council of Verberie, they could thus expect that they would be successful. When instead they completely failed in asserting authority over St.-Calais, they had to explain what had gone wrong. This explanation is found in the "memorial" attached to the *Gesta* of Bishop Aldric. The author of this little work tried to re-remember the events at Verberie as demonstrating the weakness of the monastery's position.

According to this "memorial," the question should have turned quite simply on documentation. The sole document, it said, that the abbot of St.-Calais was able to produce, showing that his house depended on the king rather than the bishop, was one of Pippin the Short, in which Pippin said that the monastery was under his *mundeburdo vel tuitione vel dominatione*. This is indeed the language that Pippin would have used in the eighth century, and in fact the text of not one but two charters still exist, in which Pippin extended his protection to two successive abbots of St.-Calais.[37]

In spite of a somewhat sneering tone adopted by the author of the "memorial" toward the pathetic efforts of St.-Calais, Pippin's charter(s) must have been a shock. Since the forgers at Le Mans were such believers in the value of the written word, they could not dismiss it easily. Even the bishopric's four charters attributed to Louis the Pious (some of which may in fact be authentic), one referring to the Council of Chalcedon's ruling that monasteries be subject to bishops and all concluding that St.-Calais depended on the bishop of Le Mans,[38] were not enough if antiquity of charters was the final arbiter. (Here it is worth noting that the author of the "memorial" mentions neither of the "Childebert" documents, the bishopric's nor St.-Calais's; he doubtless knew both to be false.)

So the author of the "memorial" had to discredit Pippin's charter for St.-Calais. He claimed that the abbot eventually admitted that the only reason Pippin issued the charter of immunity was because of an undeserved "hatred" of Gauzlin, then bishop of Le Mans. (Interestingly, the cathedral canons who had written the *Actus* of the bishops of Le Mans also hated Gauzlin, whom they called rapacious, unlearned, indeed illiterate, and said was put into office by tyrants. Their own account indicates that Pippin the Short reappointed

Gauzlin to the see after another man had briefly held it, which gives little support to the theory that Pippin hated him.)[39] A discredited charter could be overruled, but it shows how much the Le Mans authors valued antiquity that they could not simply supersede it with documents from Pippin's grandson Louis.

Even in subsequent generations, the canons of Le Mans did not give up their efforts to rewrite the past. The *vita* of Bishop Robert, who unsuccessfully tried to claim authority over St.-Calais, reinterpreted the events at Verberie to the point of outright falsity. This somewhat later *vita* insists that in spite of the monks' best efforts to stir up Charles the Bald against Bishop Robert, he was able to obtain a confirmation of his authority over them from Pope Nicholas I (858–867).[40] In fact the monks, not the bishop, prevailed with Pope Nicholas, and Charles never recognized anyone's authority over the monastery but his own. When the creation of elaborate false charters failed to win the bishop's party what they sought, the solution was simply to assert to posterity that it had.

The monks of St.-Calais, who wanted independence from the bishop, fought back as the cathedral had fought, with the written word. The monks, like the bishops, had argued for a decade before Verberie that ancient documents, or at least their own ancient documents, must be the final arbiter. The monks had the advantage of more relevant charters in their archives. They had authentic privileges of immunity freeing them from episcopal oversight, granted by Charlemagne, Louis the Pious, and Charles the Bald, as well as from Pippin the Short.[41] Just as the bishopric of Le Mans produced a "memorial" after Verberie to explain how the council should be remembered, so the monks of St.-Calais felt it necessary after 863 to put together a coherent story of their own.

Once the king ruled in their favor, they created a little book, a "cartulary" as it is now called, including all their charters. The cartulary was intended for Pope Nicholas I, to earn the monks a papal privilege. They were in fact successful in this effort—although initially the pope had been more inclined to support the bishop's authority.[42] This cartulary sought to demonstrate that their church was part of the royal fisc and had always been, going back to the sixth century. Most of the charters in it were genuine, but others were forgeries, many created for this very purpose. The first is the supposed foundation charter of Childebert I, in which the land he gives to Saint Carilef is called fisc land, to account for later kings saying that the monastery was of the royal fisc.[43] Childebert was the logical choice as founder because the ninth-century monks of St.-Calais had already seen him play a prominent role in their saint's *vita*—although they now eliminated any role for the queen and also discreetly left out the saint's insistence that he did not want land.

The next three charters in the little cartulary of St.-Calais were also forgeries, attributed to Childebert I again, Chilperic I, and a King Theoderic (probably Theoderic I), all created on the model of the charter of protection granted the monks by Pippin the Short and given dates before the monastery even in fact existed. But St.-Calais also had genuine Merovingian charters of immunity, starting with ones issued by Clovis III and Childebert IV just before the year 700.[44] Pope Nicholas, to whom the monks showed their privilege collection, assumed that these were much earlier kings, Clovis I and his son Childebert, and the monks did not disabuse him.[45]

These royal charters used the Merovingian version of an immunity (see Chapter 11), in which a king freed a monastery from paying certain fees or even allowing his agents entry into the monastery. In these charters the brothers Clovis III and Childebert IV referred to earlier immunities granted by their father, Theoderic III; grandfather Clovis II; great-grandfather Dagobert I; great-great-grandfather Clothar II; and to their uncle Clothar III; first cousin (the latter's son) Clovis; and relative (*consobrinus*) Guntram (uncle of Clothar II).

The charters of none of these earlier kings were preserved in the ninth century; otherwise, the monks would certainly have copied them into their dossier. The charters of Clovis III and Childebert IV may well, from their dates, have been the first for the monastery to be written on parchment rather than papyrus, so in the next hundred and fifty years the earlier charters that these two kings had seen and confirmed had all disintegrated. The oldest charters to which the royal brothers referred were those of Guntram and Clothar II, both of which would have been from the second half of the sixth century, the time that the monastery was most likely founded.

At the end of their little book, the monks copied the final decision of the Council of Verberie, as a triumphant charter-based indication that they had defeated the bishop's charters.[46] Even though Charles and his council had not privileged the written word in his ruling that St.-Calais was a royal house, both parties, the winners and the losers, continued to believe that charters recording decisions made in the past were their best guarantee for the future.

An interesting comparison may be drawn between the failure of the bishop of Le Mans to make his case at Verberie and the success of the bishop of Rouen, who obtained a royal privilege from Charles the Bald some two weeks later, while the king was still at his palace at Verberie. In this case the bishop of Rouen had no charters whatsoever. That was his problem. The Vikings had burned them when they sacked the city. Charles, however, generously offered to confirm whatever the charters might have contained and was willing to take the bishop at his word. Significantly, however, his confirmation document, which still exists as an original, did not detail the property that had supposedly been listed in the now-lost charters.[47]

This incident provides an illustration of the differences between how the churchmen of Le Mans and the king used and viewed charters. Charles used the document he gave the bishop of Rouen—which he called a *testamentum* or a *pancarta*—the way that kings had long used documents: as an indication that a royal decision had been made but *not* determinant in its own right. The royal charter thus simultaneously reaffirmed the worth of the past—what the bishop had once held must be confirmed—and the ability of the king to change the present by his own decision, based on his own memories or on witnesses, without having to rewrite the past.

Immunities at Le Mans

The Le Mans authors certainly knew that what they were doing was wrong. They gave citations to Roman law against producing false documents and using them in court—said citations being used to argue that the bishop's opponents, but of course not the bishop himself, ought to have their evidence dismissed.[48] They doubtless tried to justify what they were doing as serving some higher good, but their own citations showed that their creations were criminal. Thus their cause must have seemed highly compelling.

The Le Mans authors wanted control over ecclesiastical property, and they wrote, as discussed in Chapter 8, in a time when ecclesiastical property and even the episcopal office were held at royal whim. Charles Martel had summarily deposed a bishop of Le Mans he considered hostile to his interests, and he and his descendants continued to appoint favorably disposed laymen or at best corrupt clerics to the see, while further reducing episcopal holdings through precarial grants and simple seizures. It was not until Aldric became bishop in 832 that the bishops were able to begin regaining control of property in their diocese.[49] In response the cathedral of Le Mans fought back with both Merovingian-era documents (of greater or lesser authenticity) and forged documents of Louis the Pious, in which the emperor happily agreed that property belonged not to the royal fisc but to the bishops.

In addition, the Le Mans authors worked at a time when episcopal authority was being challenged by a new form of immunity: a pronouncement, by king or other powerful secular leader, that a monastery was not subject to the direction of its diocesan bishop. Such direction, spelled out at Chalcedon, had been the norm for four hundred years. Before the ninth century, secular leaders had rarely tried to break the dependence of monasteries on bishops.[50] Merovingian royal immunities, though freeing monasteries from intervention by the king and his agents, had not affected monastic obedience to the bishop.

Episcopal immunities of the Merovingian period, although they might include the provision that an abbot could have an altar consecrated by any bishop he wished, were primarily declarations that the bishop would not take a monastery's holdings and income. These immunities were thus a voluntary renunciation of the power the bishop would otherwise have enjoyed over the monasteries of his diocese. The kings, much less other lay lords, never issued what would have been, in effect, episcopal immunities in the Merovingian period. Although one of the marks of a "regular" monastery in the Carolingian period continued to be free election of the abbot by the monks, such houses were still under episcopal authority.

But in the middle decades of the ninth century, great lords began freeing favored monasteries from their bishops. Although the example of Cluny is the best known, with this freedom written into its foundation charter of 909/10 from the duke of Aquitaine,[51] such immunities had begun to appear with some regularity half a century earlier. One of the earliest examples is from Flavigny, where in 849 Charles the Bald freed the house from a variety of tolls, as Louis the Pious had done a generation earlier, but then added a novel detail. He ordered that the diocesan bishop should not exercise *dominium* over the monks.[52]

An additional development was to declare that a house, free from episcopal oversight, was instead dependent on the pope. Although a few Italian houses became papal dependencies in the eighth century, the practice did not reach Francia until the mid-ninth century. Perhaps the earliest examples of laymen granting monasteries immunity from the local bishop, in favor of papal rule, are Vézelay and Pouthières, freed from episcopal oversight when they were founded in 858/9 by Bertha, sister of a Carolingian queen, and her husband, Girard of Roussillon. Neither house is listed in subsequent royal confirmations of the rights of their diocesan bishops, those of Autun and Langres, so they were clearly considered free from episcopal authority from their foundations onward.[53]

The mid-ninth-century changes in the meaning of immunity are illustrated by the quarrel of the bishopric of Le Mans with St.-Calais. Both episcopal representatives and the monks read into the term *immunitas* a freeing of a monastery from the direction and correction of its bishop. The monks brought forward immunities from Merovingian kings that promised no royal agents would enter the monastery precincts, and immunities from an Arnulfing that promised protection, and read them as giving the monastery independence from its bishop. Even though the bishop's agents disagreed with the conclusion, they agreed that that was what immunity could mean and therefore had to create royal charters that denied the existence of such an immunity. Charles the Bald, however, was not interested in the meaning of immunities. He cut through all the contradictory documents to announce that St.-Calais depended solely on the crown. In trying to counter St.-Calais's charters with other charters, the bishopric of Le Mans gave its attention to the wrong opponent.

The Le Mans authors were thus trying, ultimately unsuccessfully, to assert the supremacy of their bishopric when episcopal authority seemed threatened. But their efforts were not unique. A far broader program, intended not just to advance the interests of a single see but rather of all bishops, was carried out nearly simultaneously by another set of forgers, the creators of the Pseudo-Isidorian decretals.

The Pseudo-Isidorian Decretals

The Pseudo-Isidorian decretals are a collection of mostly forged papal letters and mostly authentic decisions of councils, put together in the middle of the ninth century.[54] The heart of the corpus is a collection of letters supposedly written by the popes of the first four centuries of Christendom, but it includes other letters, many authentic, to and from popes down to the first years of the seventh century (Gregory I). The Pseudo-Isidorian decretals have long needed a new edition.[55] They take their name from the attribution in many of the manuscripts to one Isidore *Mercator*, apparently intended to suggest Isidore of Seville, who collected the decisions of early church councils during the seventh century. The decretals themselves, the supposed statements by early popes, were part of a broader, very ambitious program of compiling and forging.

Back in the fifth century, some jurists had begun collecting statements of popes, as well as those of councils as had been done for some time. These were used to address important issues of church law. Western bishops had been writing at least occasionally to the bishop of Rome since the fourth century to get his decision on troublesome matters of governance, and collections of these decisions, or decretals, soon became, along with conciliar rulings, the basis of canon law.[56] By creating papal letters for the first through fourth centuries, the Pseudo-Isidorian forgers not only filled in a gap but also created the oldest and thus most authoritative body of papal decisions. The texts were valued in the ninth century for their combination of antiquity and clarity on the points the forgers wanted to make; a major proportion of all extant Pseudo-Isidorian manuscripts were copied within two generations of the work's composition.[57]

These decretals should be seen as part of the intellectual ferment of the Carolingian Renaissance. The forgers, who appear to have had an excellent library (or at least an excellent collection of *florilegia*), combined biblical exegesis with an appreciation of Roman judicial structures to create a new vision of hierarchy and legal responsibility.[58] They made explicit for the first time the position of bishops as at once legal and sacred, representatives of God, the "apples" of God's eye—to use the language of Zacharias 2:8, their most commonly quoted Bible verse. Bishops' grievances were not merely their own but also God's, for they were his agents. As such, they could not have their offices taken from them or even be subject to the rigors of correction without suitable process, in particular appeal to the pope.

The Pseudo-Isidorian decretals have received surprisingly little scholarly attention within the context of the mid-ninth century, the period in which they were written. They have chiefly been studied for their impact in the eleventh and twelfth centuries, when they were used to justify ecclesiastical reform and the popes' position at the head of the church hierarchy.[59] Every indication is that the eleventh-century papacy used the false decretals in good faith, though they did not accept them entirely uncritically, and other early decretals and pronouncements (some also false) were added to the mix.[60] But my concern here is not how the decretals were received two centuries later but how and why they were put together originally.

Central to the decretals was the judging of bishops. Five different popes (Victor, Zepherinus, Sixtus, Julius, and Felix II) issue virtually identical statements in these decretals: if a bishop is accused by his fellow bishops, he may appeal to the Roman pontiff. Not until the pope has judged the bishop guilty may other bishops remove him or ordain a replacement. In fact, although the bishops may "examine" the case, they are forbidden to render judgment without consulting the pope, even apparently in the absence of a formal appeal.[61]

In the ninth century the primary interest of the decretals was not the authority of the papacy per se but rather the position and status of the bishop within his own see, so that even his fellow bishops could not judge him too readily. When the decretals had Urban I cite the biblical verse "Whatever you bind and loose on earth shall be bound and loosed in heaven" (Matt. 16:19), the statement explicitly applied not just to Peter or to Peter's vicar in Rome but to all bishops.[62] Here the most significant aspect of the decretals was their effort to rewrite the history of popes and church councils. It was not enough to assert that bishops had a special status within the church's legal structure. Rather, it was considered necessary to create a useful if fictive past, in which one of the major papal concerns was to support and protect bishops' positions.

In addition, the decretals contained within them a stout defense of ecclesiastical property. Learned men of the Carolingian Renaissance knew as well as the monks and friars of the twelfth and thirteenth centuries that the New Testament had stressed radical poverty and that in the Book of Acts there had been no sign of the manors, fields, waterways, vineyards, rents, and serfs that not only were owned by every bishopric or monastery but also enumerated in every royal privilege. The forgers used a double approach to the property question: not only did they justify ecclesiastical property, but they also took the opportunity to threaten with "anathema maranata" anyone who dared turn church property to other uses.

The fullest justification was attributed to Pope Urban I (222–230).[63] In his supposed *decreta*, the pope notes that it had been the custom, since the first days of the church, for people to sell all that they had and lay the purchase price at the feet of the apostles (Acts 4:34–35). But now, the pope continues, it has become clear that much greater "utility" would be served if the property itself were given, rather than the money for selling it. Then churchmen could live on the revenues of the *hereditates et agros* that had been given them, a continuing source of income, whereas the purchase price would be exhausted relatively quickly. Such gifts of property, the forgers have the pope declare, shall be called *oblationes*, offerings, the normal term of course in the ninth century.[64] The forgers even make a dark suggestion of what may happen if property itself (rather than the purchase price for such property) is *not* given. They recall Ananias and Sapphira, who sold their property but offered only some of the money to the apostles, "defrauding" them of the rest. Quite appropriately they both fell down dead (Acts 5:1–10). But such risks of divine wrath can be avoided if land and other hereditary property are given directly.

The challenge for a church was holding onto what was given. The same *decreta* of Pope Urban stress that the offerings of the faithful are to be used *only* for bishops, clerics, and religious brothers, except as these men choose to employ them for the support of the indigent. Anyone who tries to take such property is to be cursed. Other forged papal letters explained why seizing church property was so heinous. A decretal letter attributed to Anaclete announces that someone who seizes anything belonging to his father or mother is guilty of more than just an ordinary sin; he has committed the moral equivalent of homicide. Since God is our father and the church our mother, Anaclete continues, anyone who takes church property (*pecunias*) is guilty of homicide. Pope Lucius (253–254) repeats the equation of taking church property with committing homicide, then adds that not only are the perpetrators themselves to be damned but so are all their associates.[65] The creators of the Pseudo-Isidorian corpus were thus erecting a coherent theological justification for church property, along with divinely sanctioned punishments for those who violated it.

The Pseudo-Isidorian Decretals and Episcopal Autonomy

The problem with reading the Pseudo-Isidorian decretals backward from the Investiture Controversy, as has too often been done, is that they are viewed through the lens of Gregory VII's efforts to assert the plenitude of papal power in his quarrels with the emperor. Ninth-century bishops, too, struggled with the emperor, but they faced different struggles and a different emperor.

The autonomy that bishops had taken for granted during the Merovingian period was seriously threatened by Charlemagne and his successors. Church property was frequently appropriated by royal favorites. The kings routinely appointed, removed, or reassigned bishops. The chronicler Notker's characterization of the Frankish bishops as weak creatures who needed to be closely directed by a Christ-like emperor nicely reflected the imperial attitude, which Pseudo-Isidore felt compelled to counter.[66] The efforts of the forgers, therefore, need to be seen not as a program to create the papal supremacy asserted in the eleventh and later centuries. Rather, this was an opportunity for the bishops to use the authority of a distant pope, unlikely to interfere in their own daily exercise of power, to fight back against their own kings.

Although the requirement that episcopal synods receive papal approval before removing a bishop is the most coherently developed in the false decretals, the starting point was to reject any removal of a bishop from office or any seizure of church property, whether done by cleric or layman. In the preface the author discusses bishops deprived of their goods and driven from their sees because of their "depravity and cupidity." The first letter in the collection, attributed to Pope Clement, states that bishops are to be "judged or removed" by God alone.[67] Although the decretals range widely, they keep returning to the central issue of the evil of judging bishops as a pretext for exiling them or seizing property.

The forgers of the decretals worked within the same tradition that generated episcopal *gesta* in the ninth century.[68] They had clearly read the *Liber Pontificalis* (*LP*) closely, for the forged letters attributed to early popes were arranged in the same order as the "lives" of those popes in the *LP*. Every pope from Clement at the end of the first century to Miltiades in the early fourth century has at least one decretal letter composed for him. Given the complex manuscript tradition it is hard to draw definitive conclusions about how the forgers organized their material (which they themselves added to and reworked), but the early part of the decretals, from Clement to just before the time of Sylvester I, forms a coherent unit, letters from early popes followed by the Donation of Constantine.[69]

It is surely significant that this section concludes just short of Sylvester, Constantine's pope. The Donation, forged a century earlier than the decretals, exactly served Pseudo-Isidore's purposes by having Constantine declare the church's leadership superior to any emperor.[70] The forgers thus created a tidy if false story, in which all of the important questions on church leadership and governance were worked out before there even were Christian emperors, by popes who were commonly martyred and thus sainted. When Constantine becomes emperor, the glorious story of early Christianity comes to a triumphant close. Constantine gives his western empire to the pope and leaves, not just the city of Rome but also the story.

The Pseudo-Isidorian decretals, therefore, should be seen as a commentary on Constantine in contrast to the "new Constantine." The Carolingian court of course was quick to draw parallels between Charlemagne and the fourth-century emperor who first embraced Christianity, who acted in essence as the head of the church in calling the great ecumenical council of Nicaea. The forgers accepted those parallels. But for them the intrusion of their own emperor into ecclesiastical affairs did not redound to his glory, as in Constantine's case, but rather to the detriment of the church.

Just as lay founders sought to ensure the continued success of Frankish monasteries in the later ninth century by making them dependent on a distant pope, so the Pseudo-Isidorian decretals attempted at the same time to strengthen bishops' positions by making them dependent on the pope alone. Episcopal power and papal power had to be asserted by reference to the first centuries of Christendom in order to counteract the very real imperial power operating upon the Frankish church in the ninth century.

Strikingly absent from Pseudo-Isidore are any of the biblical verses used in contemporary political theology to draw an equation between a king and Christ.[71] Although the publicists of the Carolingian court described the Carolingians as the new Hebrew kings, the Pseudo-Isidorian forgers created a story with the opposite message: kings were not heads of God's kingdom on earth, were not in any sense closer to God than priests and bishops. Rather, the pope (conveniently far from Francia) was the chief representative of God's authority. Part of the continued success, even after twelve hundred years, of the publicists of the Carolingian court has been the ready assumption that churches flourished under Charlemagne. The Pseudo-Isidorian decretals are often seen as seeking to re-create a lost Golden Age, once the deaths of Charlemagne and Louis the Pious had opened the way for *potentes* to depose bishops, to alienate ecclesiastical property, or to drag churchmen into secular courts.[72] But the problem as the forgers saw it was not one of regional lords unrestrained by strong kings. The problems originated with the kings themselves.

The works of Pseudo-Isidore thus need to be seen as a response to the authority of the Carolingian kings over the Frankish bishops. For Notker, this authority meant that kings, already halfway to God, should correct erring bishops at every turn. Pseudo-Isidore, in contrast, sought to establish a principle asserted as totally "traditional," that no regional authority, even a king, should judge and discipline bishops. For both, royal authority over bishops was a given; the only question was whether it was valid.

It is therefore ironic that within a decade of the composition of the false decretals they were quoted in a synod held by Charles the Bald at Quierzy in 857. In an *Admonitio* most likely composed by Archbishop Hincmar of Reims, the Pseudo-Isidorian decretals of Anaclete, Urban, and Lucius are quoted verbatim. There is no discussion here of whether church property needs to be justified, no reference to the poverty of the original apostles. Rather, the council equates taking church property with homicide, states that those who do so will share the fate of Ananias and Sapphira, and damns not only the perpetrators themselves but all their associates.[73]

This was the first use of the Pseudo-Isidorian decretals in west Francia to argue for the inviolability of church property, but the decretals were not used to argue for episcopal independence until over a decade later. Then, around 870, Bishop Hincmar of Laon asserted his independence from his uncle and metropolitan, Hincmar of Reims.[74] The elder Hincmar knew the Pseudo-Isidorian collection well. But he was not impressed with the central tenet that bishops could not be judged by other bishops, even their own metropolitans. The younger Hincmar had to yield, in spite of all his citations from the false decretals. Indeed, bishops were not able to escape judgment by appeal to Rome for another two centuries.

The popes, the ultimate authorities according to the forgers, became aware of the collection of the supposed decretals of their earliest predecessors almost immediately, but the weakness of their position at the time long prevented them from being able to develop Pseudo-Isidorian ideas into a program.[75] Ironically, then, the elaborate efforts of the forgers had very little practical effect in their own period, in spite of their significant later success.

They thus need to be seen, like the forgers of Le Mans, as privileging the written word, although not everyone else was ready to agree. But they must have assumed that at least some would accept their conclusions. The failure of the bishop of Le Mans to prevail against Charles the Bald or of Hincmar of Laon to prevail against his uncle should not obscure their belief that even the most powerful *might* be swayed by written texts of supposed antiquity.

Benedictus Levita

A third major set of forgeries were also composed in the ninth century, probably in the Rhineland in the 840s, by someone calling himself Benedictus *levita*, Benedict the deacon.[76] Benedictus compiled an astounding collection of decretals, hundreds of brief pronouncements on church discipline and proper Christian behavior, some real but most false (or at best improved), and attributed them to Pippin the Short, Charlemagne, and Louis the Pious.

At first glance this collection might seem to undercut the argument that forgeries represented an effort by ninth-century churchmen to challenge the authority of the Carolingians, since these decretals were attributed to them. But nothing in the collection promoted royal authority, much less the right of kings to do with churches as they wished. Rather, Benedictus took as his starting point Pope Zacharias's letter to Boniface in the 740s on holding a synod, in accord with the mayor of the palace Carloman, and he sought to make his whole collection a continuation of that synod. Thus the kings were for him not those who made rules for the church but rather helpful agents of popes and missionaries in assuring ecclesiastical prosperity.

Significantly, one of his first decretals (1.13) dealt with those who held church property *verbo domni regis*. Charlemagne himself had issued capitularies concerning church property granted to laymen "at the king's command" (see Chapter 8), but here Benedictus turned the meaning of that phrase on its head. Instead of giving church property to his followers as a reward, the king of his decretals gave it to them specifically so that they might improve it (*emendare debeant*). In addition, they were to distribute any tithes or other church income they received with a generous hand—and not keep the income for themselves. If they did not do so, they would lose the property.

In addition, Benedictus sought to make it harder to judge priests and bishops. While he did not go as far as the Pseudo-Isidorian decretals did only a few years later, he determinedly rejected the possibility that churchmen should be judged by laymen. In a group of several decretals (1.390–93), he began by having the king announce that no one could bring an accusation against a bishop or priest before *publicos iudices*. Even in an ecclesiastical court, no judgment could be made unless both the accuser and the accused were present. Benedictus's king also states that his synodal decree only repeats the "Roman and apostolic" statute that anyone who accused an ecclesiastic would first have his own faith and way of life closely examined. These decretals were artfully created in order to make it very difficult to judge ecclesiastics, especially for laymen to do so.

For the most part, however, Benedictus was not concerned with the relations of kings and churches. Most of his decretals concern issues such as proper baptism, avoiding incest, honoring one's parents, and the like. These were concerns of ninth-century bishops and priests, and according to Benedictus they were the proper concerns of kings as well. He used his forgeries to define the role that the Carolingian kings *should* adopt: to be the attentive supporters of churchmen. While Pseudo-Isidore and the Le Mans forgers made early, pre-Carolingian kings and emperors their focus, Benedictus was ready to put Charlemagne and his family at the center of his story. But his Carolingians did not threaten ecclesiastical property and independence. He idealized them by taming them. He created a series of forged decretals that showed the way they ought to interact with churches by suggesting that they had always done so.

The Failure of Forgery

The great mid-ninth-century forgeries were an effort at reworking memory at a time when the written word carried its own force, at least in the minds of some. In spite of the power of antiquity and of writing, the creators of the Le Mans forgeries and the Pseudo-Isidorian decretals were not as successful in their own time as they would have hoped, because their audience was not nearly as credulous as they would have liked.[77] Benedictus *levita*, whose forgeries were not as radical, received only a small amount of attention.

The forgers wanted a charter to be the final arbiter: something in writing could not be ignored. But truth and falsehood were not so simple to others, and the central premise of the Le Mans forgers, that not even a king could overthrow the decisions of earlier kings, failed to gain acceptance. After all, Charles the Bald rejected the carefully created Le Mans documents not because they failed to follow correct protocols but because he disagreed with their conclusions.

A case from a generation later, this time involving the pope, suggests the uneasiness the authorities felt when confronted with something that might have been a forgery and also indicates one way of dealing with it. Pope John VIII was presented in 878 with a charter purporting to be from the recently deceased Charles the Bald, saying that the monastery of St.-Denis was subject only to the pope.[78] Hincmar of Reims, from whom our information comes, believed—and suggested most believed—that it had been created by Bishops Frotgar of Bourges and Adalgar of Autun, in an effort to get the monastery away from Abbot Gauzlin. It would have been easy enough for them to confect such a charter in Charles the Bald's name; Adalgar had previously been royal chancellor.[79]

Even though the pope would have benefited from this grant of authority, he seems to have had doubts. He resolved these doubts by telling Louis II, Charles's son, that he should confirm the charter, thus making the original document's authenticity irrelevant by having St.-Denis's immunity granted by the current king. However, Louis had his own doubts—or did not want to take St.-Denis away from Gauzlin—because he never confirmed the charter and, according to Hincmar, nothing ever came of the affair. This was a distinctly different view of the power of the written word than the forgers': an assertion that a document obtained its value only when reconfirmed by a living authority. It was an effective way of dealing with possible forgery because it avoided having to accept as true a dubious charter without actually proving its falsity. But it meant that the iconic value of the written word did not persuade all.

Some of the early Middle Ages' most ambitious efforts at creating a useful past by outright forgery took place in western Francia in the middle of the ninth century. Both the Le Mans authors and the creators of the Pseudo-Isidorian decretals used the authority of past popes and kings, as embodied in the written word, to counter the very real and present power of the Carolingian kings. Benedictus *levita* countered Carolingian power instead by making the kings themselves announce their support for episcopal programs and renounce their ability to judge churchmen. All artfully combined authentic (or only slightly reworked) documents with outright fabrications, so that the past they sought to create had at least some resemblance to the real past.

The popes had little effective authority in Francia in the ninth century, and the Merovingians were long gone, which of course made them more malleable for the forgers. The (partially created) memory of the Merovingians as more supportive of Frankish churches than the Carolingians doubtless encouraged the forgers of Le Mans to hope that their creations would seem plausible. All three sets of forgeries, however, had at best a mixed success in their own period.

In the eleventh century, however, the Pseudo-Isidorian decretals experienced a rapid and widespread acceptance. As the papacy rose, rather abruptly, to prominence, it found that a useful past had already been created, a useful past in which bishops were already assigned their place in a hierarchy that had the popes at the top. There was no need for additional forgeries or delicate reworkings; an apparent thousand-year-old tradition already existed, offering just what the eleventh-century popes needed. The forgers' greatest triumph thus took place in a context they could not have imagined.

Chapter 6

Remembering the Carolingians

Everyone knows that the Carolingian age was a glorious turning point.[1] The reason we all know this is because certain writers of the late eighth and ninth centuries went out of their way to tell us so. In recent years, however, scholars have begun to see Einhard and his contemporaries not just as simple reporters but as publicists for the Carolingian dynasty.[2] It is not surprising that members of court wanted to remember a divinely constituted emperor, who was always successful, both morally and politically. But their accounts need to be seen as more than transparent recitations of events, instead as deliberate efforts to control how the Carolingians would be remembered.

In this chapter, I shall discuss the models used at the time to construct the memory of Charlemagne and his family, the image promulgated of them as religious and just rulers, as representing both Roman and Germanic traditions, culminating in the creation of an appropriate dynastic history. The publicists' program to make the Carolingians into glorious kings, far better than their decadent predecessors, was extremely successful, not only in the ninth century but ever since, as witnessed by the chansons de geste of the twelfth century.[3] My purpose here is not to denigrate the lineage's quite real achievements, but rather to discuss the ways those achievements were meant to be remembered, while the shades of their predecessors still lingered in Frankish lands.

Charlemagne as Christian Leader

One of the most laudatory descriptions of Charlemagne was the poem "Karolus magnus et Leo papa," probably written by a member of the palace school on the eve of Charlemagne's imperial coronation.[4] This poem manages to combine every possible image of holiness and strong government. Charlemagne is victorious in battle, more just and powerful than any other king, strong and wise and yet modest. He is associated with the pope, though in a way to suggest his superiority even to the heir of Peter—for the pope needed his help against evil enemies. He is a new David. He is associated with both classical Rome and the heroes of Troy by frequent phrases borrowed from the *Aeneid*. He is explicitly called the Father of Europe. He is made Christ-like by raising up the humble and ensuring that the last be first. His name, Carolus, is given the etymological root of "dear light," *carus lux* (lines 55–56).

The theme of Charlemagne as Christian leader, as proclaimed by the poem's author, was picked up by other writers—and indeed seems to have been taken seriously by the Carolingians themselves.[5] A specific liturgy was developed of masses for the kings and prayers for their success. Both Charlemagne and his successors patronized artists, scribes, and scholars as part of an effort to promote the correct Christian faith.[6] The kings had a special, sacred role because they were assumed (at least by their publicists) to have been chosen by God.[7] In the preface to Charlemagne's "Admonitio generalis" of 789, he spelled out the key issue for a ruler: his people needed to be brought closer to God for his rule to be successful. Charlemagne thus found it appropriate to assemble a church council in which he issued directives both to his people as a whole and to the "shepherds" who were supposed to lead their flocks, "lest the wolf devour them."[8] It is surely significant that although the Merovingians had never labeled themselves kings "by the grace of God," Pippin the Short assumed this title, beginning in the 760s, and of course it was continually used by Charlemagne.[9] The king believed he needed to remind the leaders of the church of their duties, and he assured their morality.

There had long existed a special relationship between the Arnulfings and the popes. The so-called *Codex Carolinus*, composed in 791 at Charlemagne's orders, was a collection of letters from popes to Charles Martel, Pippin the Short, and Charlemagne himself over the course of three-quarters of a century.[10] The papyrus originals were carefully copied, with rubrics indicating their contents, a decade before the imperial coronation of 800. This *Codex* indicates that Charlemagne found in his connection to the papacy a support and justification for the inherent religiosity of his reign.

And yet on occasion Charlemagne sought to be "more Catholic than the pope." An intriguing example is the *Libri Carolini*, treatises on proper Christian doctrine, drawn up at the Frankish court at royal initiative. They were written in response to the (misunderstood) Byzantine position on images in the 787 Council of Nicaea.[11] The Greek church had sent their synodal decrees to the West, and Charlemagne distrusted the papacy's efforts to answer correctly. Rather, he had the theologians of his own court, notably Theodulf and Alcuin, assemble in response a full statement of true Christian faith. The *Libri Carolini* did not receive nearly the wide circulation Charlemagne intended—the pope himself ignored the report, if he saw it at all.[12] But what is significant is that Charlemagne believed that, as anointed king, he had a personal responsibility to promulgate the Christian faith, and that by exercising this responsibility he was also able to demonstrate how entirely appropriate it was that he be king of the Franks.[13]

Once Charlemagne was crowned emperor by the pope, of course, he received full Christian legitimation by the successor to Peter, the Rock on whom the Church was based. But the "Admonitio generalis," the *Codex Carolinus*, and the *Libri Carolini* all predated his coronation, as did the extremely laudatory "Karolus magnus et Leo papa." His semisacral status, all these works suggest, proceeded naturally from his own position and family. He was very sensitive to the possibility that he enjoyed divine favor only at the pleasure of the Roman pontiff, a danger even before 800, as his father's accession to the throne was at least partly due to papal intervention. Therefore, even being good Christians was not sufficient, and the Carolingians were described in addition as the new Romans, the new Franks, or the new Hebrews.

Romans, Franks, Hebrews, and the Law

When the Carolingians and their publicists identified them as Rome reborn, the model was the Rome of antiquity, not the Rome of their own day.[14] They took it for granted that this Rome was Christian rather than assuming, as had earlier writers, that Rome was to be equated with persecution of Christians.[15] "Rome" could be a problematic concept in the ninth century, in that it could either mean Christian emperors triumphing over all foes or else popes granting authority to their subordinates, the emperors. The Carolingians avoided much of the problem by creating connections to the great Christian leaders of late imperial Rome, especially Constantine and Theodosius I. The earliest, pagan emperors were irrelevant compared to Constantine and his successors, who took seriously their Christian duty to lead their people to God.

The identification with Rome at its height can be found, it has been argued, in Charlemagne's efforts to rule all of the old western Empire,[16] but it was expressed especially through art and architecture. Indeed, Roman-inspired art was so ubiquitous that it dominates modern discussions of the "Carolingian Renaissance."[17] The church at Aachen was inspired by imperial churches in Benevento and Ravenna, and Aachen's great hall, around which all business and politics revolved, was modeled on Constantine's palace at Trier. In spite of some uneasiness about the Byzantines, whose long-held title of "Roman emperor" Charlemagne took in 800, Carolingian art is also full of borrowings from Byzantium, the "new Rome."[18] Within a decade or so of his imperial coronation, Charlemagne began issuing coins modeled on imperial coins of antiquity, a style that persisted through the reign of Louis the Pious and became a symbolic assertion of their position. Louis himself adopted an H-shaped monogram similar to that used by earlier Byzantine emperors.[19] Both Charlemagne and Louis the Pious chose for their tombs pieces of old, reused Roman marble.[20] They thus were able to assert even from beyond the grave that their imperial authority was the same imperial authority of half a millennium earlier.

One of the most striking examples of art equating the Carolingians with the ancient Roman emperors must have been the wall paintings at the palace at Ingelheim. The paintings themselves have long since disappeared, but a description survives in poems written for Louis the Pious by Ermoldus Nigellus. In his description, the wall paintings connect the Carolingian line and the Caesars of antiquity, without intervening popes or Merovingians. There is no gap between depictions of the accomplishments of Julius Caesar, Constantine, and Theodosius, and those of Charles Martel, Pippin the Short, and Charlemagne. "The acts of the Caesars are joined (*iunguntur*) to the deeds of the Franks," Ermoldus said.[21] But the Ingelheim paintings did not merely show imperial deeds, for according to Ermoldus they began in the chapel with the story of Adam and Eve and proceeded through the events of the Old and New Testaments, before continuing in the royal chambers with depictions of the great rulers of antiquity. Thus the iconography of one of the greatest Carolingian palaces made the family's rise part of both the Christian story of sin and redemption and the history of ancient emperors.[22]

Of course the Merovingian kings had also sought to become Romans. In many ways Clovis's *gens* had a more plausible claim to being Roman, since there was no temporal gap requiring finessing. But the Carolingian court quite deliberately forgot this. In part, the Carolingian effort to tie themselves to Rome was an effort to efface the memory of the previous dynasty. Even the

Gallican liturgy used in the churches of Francia was to be replaced by the Roman liturgy.[23] If a straight line led from the Caesars to Charlemagne, then the first race of Frankish kings became nothing more than an unproductive detour.

More difficult to overlook was the possibility that being Roman meant being subject to the Roman pontiff. Thus the Carolingians sought alternate models. One would expect that their Frankish ancestry would be stressed; after all, Charlemagne's family *were* Franks. But there were problems with so defining themselves. For both Gregory of Tours and Fredegar, the Franks had been those who were led by the Merovingians. Perhaps as a result, during Charlemagne's lifetime there were few efforts to connect his line with the Franks. Even his mustache, though based on Germanic rather than Roman models, was most likely meant to evoke Theoderic, the Visigothic conqueror of Rome.[24]

The Carolingians' Frankish heritage only began to be asserted after Charlemagne's death, when Einhard became one of the most fervent spokesmen for the idea of Charlemagne as embodying Frankishness, even if for him the Carolingians were Franks redeemed, Franks who had shaken off any taint of the *fainéant*. The emperor's conquest of the Saxons and of the many other people against whom he waged war was not merely a military victory for Einhard; it was a Frankish victory. He said that the *regnum Francorum* was doubled in size by the emperor's victories. The Saxons, he added, finally "gave up the worship of demons and the other ceremonies of their fathers, and adopted the sacraments of the Christian faith and religion, and were joined to the Franks, so that they became one people."[25] The conquered people were thus not merely conquered; they *became* Franks. Indeed, for Einhard being a Frank and being a Christian were essentially synonymous.

But in order to glorify the Carolingians as Franks Einhard had to redefine the Merovingians as non-Frankish. The *gens Meroingorum* with which Einhard's "Life" of Charlemagne begins is both a term for a coherent patriarchal family, of the sort that the Carolingian court had to use as an uncomfortable model in order to create their own *gens*, and also a term for a nation or people. If the kings before Pippin the Short were not truly Frankish but of some different race, then the Carolingians could be Franks with impunity. Here it is surely significant that Einhard never called Childeric III (the only Merovingian king who merited a name) a Frank. Rather, Einhard said that "the Franks were accustomed to make men from the Merovingian race their kings."[26] This kind of delicate distancing made the Merovingians not the essence of Frankishness, as they had been for Gregory of Tours, but rather some foreign outsiders, whom the Franks needed to depose before sensibly beginning to choose their kings from among their own numbers.

Charlemagne of course had to be elected by the Franks, as Einhard made clear he was, but he also had to *be* a Frank.[27] Thus Einhard spoke of the Frankish people (*Franci*) twice choosing him as their king, once after the death of Pippin the Short, again after the death of his brother Carloman. Einhard also added that, like all Franks, Charlemagne loved riding and hunting, and he preferred to dress in "the costume of his Frankish forebears."[28] The suggestion was strong that not only had the Carolingians replaced the Merovingians as kings of the Franks, but for the first time the Franks were ruled by someone truly their own.

In the decades after Einhard, the royal family continued to be characterized as Frankish. The so-called Astronomer, writing a "Life" of Louis the Pious some time after 840, simply assumed the natural superiority of Franks. Charlemagne, he said, appointed Franks as his *vassi* in Aquitaine because their "wisdom and strength" could not be overcome with "cunning or force."[29] Once the fundamental Frankishness of the Carolingians had been asserted, moreover, there was a deliberate effort to re-create Carolingian imagery as a *combination* of Roman and Frankish elements.

This synthesis is evident in the portrait of Charles the Bald in the lavish so-called Vivien Bible, created for Charles at Tours.[30] Charles sits enthroned, wearing Roman garb, every bit the Roman emperor. A divine hand emerges at the top, showing that this emperor was favored by God. Poems accompany this portrait, equating Charles with King David and calling him a source of justice and a patron of the church, in case anyone missed the point.[31] On one side stands a man dressed as a Roman soldier, holding a sheathed sword, ready to hand to the emperor. On the other side stands a shield-bearer similarly attired, holding a long lance and a shield, also ready for the emperor to take up arms.[32]

Although this image has often been analyzed, one crucial point has been overlooked: although the emperor's garments and posture are Roman, as are those of his weapons-bearers, the arms themselves are Frankish. The sword is a Frankish long-sword, not a short Roman *gladius*; if hung at the belt it would reach to the heel of the man holding it—a bearded man, not a boy. The shield is of the round medieval type, not the rectangular shield of the legions. The long lance depicted had become an important weapon in the previous several centuries, but it had not been carried by the Romans. In such a carefully constructed image, this cannot have been a simple slip by the artist, who would have known perfectly well that he was depicting Frankish weaponry.[33] Rather, he deliberately depicted weapons considered symbolic of Frankish royal rule.

Gregory of Tours had had King Guntram place a lance (*hasta*) like that in the Vivien Bible in the hand of his nephew Childeric, specifically to indicate that he intended to make Childeric his heir.[34] The same equation between weaponry and rule was made by the Carolingians. When Charlemagne made his young son Louis the Pious ruler of Aquitaine, he indicated the boy's status by giving him weapons "suitable for his age" and setting him on a horse, even though he was less than five years old.[35] The iconography of the Vivien Bible therefore can best be seen as a deliberate effort to make Charlemagne's grandson both Roman and Frankish.

But even this was not enough. In addition, efforts were made to identify the Carolingians as the "New Israel," beginning when Charlemagne first became king and intensifying after his imperial coronation.[36] The ancient Hebrew kings provided a religious precedent *not* based on any connection to the papacy. The kings of Israel had stood halfway between their people and God, without needing the mediation of priests. It is surely no accident that another Bible done for Charles the Bald uses a portrait of Charles to represent Solomon.[37] As the new David and Solomon, Charlemagne and his heirs could assert a similar position: one that required great responsibility, certainly, but one in which no one stood between them and God. Pippin the Short had not only assumed authority, he had been *anointed* as king, as the Hebrew kings had been anointed—and the Merovingians had not.[38]

Central both to the Carolingians' sense of themselves as Christian leaders and to their attempts to emulate the ancient Israelite kings was a focus on law and justice: the establishment of written laws, the insistence that judges rule on the basis of those laws and not on the basis of gifts they had received, and the regular use of *missi* to check that justice was being carried out properly everywhere. As the preface to Charlemagne's "Admonitio generalis" spelled out, he was like King Joshua of the Old Testament, with a "kingdom given to him by God," and therefore had a charge to exercise justice within that kingdom.[39]

In spite of the long scholarly tendency to see Louis the Pious as a far less effective ruler than his father, scholars have recently argued that he, too, through his councils and his interactions with both lay and ecclesiastical leaders, advanced a strong and practical form of administration.[40] Here it should

be stressed that judicial authority legitimizes: he who dispenses justice is connected with a sense of right and what ought to be that goes far beyond personal rule. Both the Carolingians' self-proclaimed status as the new kings of
Israel and their very practical interest in promulgating laws and enacting good
judicial procedures served to justify their position.

All of the models adopted by the Carolingian court for the kings underscored that they and they alone deserved to rule. Because Charlemagne's ancestors had been Frankish aristocrats rather than kings, both Pippin the Short
and Charlemagne were in a potentially perilous position: if one family could
mount the throne, defining the previous dynasty as unworthy, then any might.
To counter this idea an effort was consciously made to create a consensus, an
agreement among the most powerful, the *proceres* and *viri inlustri*, that while
it was natural that the Carolingians be kings, the same reasoning could not be
applied to others.[41] This "consensus," of course, was created in part by simple
force. Pippin and especially Charlemagne ruthlessly pursued anyone who tried
to contest their rule. It is surely significant that the territory they sought forcibly to conquer was identical with the old Merovingian *regnum*.[42] But force
alone is a very difficult way to establish or maintain authority.

The consensus that the Carolingians were and ought to be kings of the
Franks was built on many elements, as scholars have long recognized, including *missi* who reported directly to the king, a network of sworn fidelity, the
careful distribution and redistribution of counties, and even the support of
newly established lineages (*Reichsaristokratie*) who would be faithful from the
beginning. Theoretical discussions at the time of the nature of good kingship,
especially its sacral nature, always suggested that the aristocracy would naturally follow such kings.[43]

The complex imagery of the Vivien Bible is symptomatic of the multiple
models the Carolingian dynasty used to define themselves. They were excellent Christian rulers, emperors dispensing regular justice like Roman emperors of old, Hebrew kings mediating between their people and God, and
Franks, with all that people's sturdy virtues. The very diversity of models with
which they simultaneously associated themselves suggests that the Carolingians had some doubts about their position and sought to identify themselves
with multiple sources of authority.[44]

But one should not stop at seeing this search for justification as a sign of
unease. The synthesis of these multiple models was also a source of strength for
Charlemagne and his descendants. If there were doubts about his dynasty's
legitimacy, then the best way to prove decisively that his line deserved to be

kings and emperors was to demonstrate their excellence: as war leaders, as givers of justice, as supporters of Christian doctrine. It is not enough to say that the king corresponds to one or another admirable model—the king must then live up to it. The indubitable achievements of the Carolingians may in fact have been driven in part by their efforts to prove they were not usurpers. In seeking to demonstrate that they deserved to rule the Franks, they pursued both religion and justice to create an account of themselves that ceased to require such proof.

The Deposition of the Merovingians

One of the ways that Carolingian publicists could underline their kings' Christian and legal authority was by pointing to the papal approval and sacred anointing of both Pippin the Short and Charlemagne, ceremonies that had no Merovingian precedent.[45] But it was the audacity of replacing King Childeric III in 751, after three centuries of Merovingian kings of the Franks, that made Pippin the Short turn to the pope for legitimation. This is a topic that has been worked over so thoroughly that it has become an obvious truism, invisible by nature of its very obviousness.[46] Indeed, scholars may have overlooked the radical nature of the transfer of royal authority because the eighth- and ninth-century authors themselves strove to downplay its significance.

The earliest source to mention Pippin's accession is the continuation of the *Chronica* of Fredegar, sponsored by Pippin's uncle Hildebrand and perhaps written within a year or two of the events.[47] Strikingly, the rather laconic account does not note that a Merovingian king first had to be deposed before Pippin became king. The text says simply that Pippin, with the *praecepta* of the apostolic see and the *electio* of all the Franks, became king and was consecrated by the bishops. The author commented that all was done according to "ancient tradition," *ut antiquitus ordo deposcit*, but Pippin was not following any time-honored ritual. He was not the first Frankish king to be elected, but he was the first to be consecrated and the first to receive *praecepta* from the pope on his accession to the throne. He was breaking entirely new ground.[48]

The next source to discuss Pippin's accession in any detail is the "Clausula de Pippino," a short text once thought to be a ninth-century creation but now accepted as composed at St.-Denis in 767, at the end of Pippin's life.[49] The "Clausula," like Fredegar's continuation, describes Pippin's accession in 751 as having three separate sources of legitimacy: it took place at the orders (*per auctoritatem et imperium*) of Pope Zacharias, with the consecration (*unctio sancti chrismatis*) of the bishops of Gaul, and by the election (*electio*) of the Franks. The "Clausula," like Fredegar's continuators, is silent on the last Merovingian.

The only eighth-century source even to note that a king first had to be removed before Pippin's coronation could take place was written some forty years after the event. The *Annales regni Francorum* have Pippin's representatives ask Pope Zacharias obliquely whether it was good that the Frankish king not have royal power and receive the answer that he who exercises power ought to be called king. Childeric III is then tonsured and put in a monastery.[50] It is worth noting here that any letter Pope Zacharias might have sent Pippin was not copied into the Carolingians' collection of papal letters, even though both earlier and later letters are found there—none, however, mentioning any deposition.[51]

Although the account in the *Annales regni Francorum* of Pippin's question to Zacharias is usually read through the lens of Einhard's account of *rois fainéants*, it does not actually say that Childeric was incapable of exercising *potestas*, only that he did not have it. In this account the pope is given all the responsibility for Childeric's deposition. Paul the Deacon, who wrote a few years before the *Annales regni Francorum* were composed, and the annalist of Metz, writing a generation later, both skip over Childeric's deposition entirely.

Einhard's account is thus only the second even to note that another king had to be deposed before Pippin himself could become king. First Einhard declares that the Merovingian line of kings was ended "by the order" (*jussu*) of the pope. Next he comments that Childeric III, the last Merovingian king, was "deposed" (*deponebatur*), using the passive tense to avoid discussing who did the deposing—in essence structuring the entire series of events as a product of papal initiative. Then he finishes by saying that Pippin became king "by the authority of the Roman pontiff."[52] Given Einhard's loquaciousness on other topics, especially the ridiculousness of the last Merovingians, it is surprising that he does not have more to say on this all-important accession of the first Carolingian king in 751, and especially nothing on Pippin's own initiative. It is of course possible that Childeric was not in fact deposed but simply died, and that the story of his deposition was a later concoction, to explain why Pippin did not search for another Merovingian to replace him.[53]

The popes of course needed the Carolingians. They recognized that they could not expect assistance from the emperors in distant Constantinople; at this time they even abandoned the long practice of dating their documents by the Byzantine emperor.[54] But the papacy discerned a potential ally in the vigorous new Frankish lineage. Already, some dozen years before Pippin became king, Pope Gregory III had sent costly gifts to Charles Martel and told him, according to the continuators to Fredegar's *Chronica*, that he was ready to leave the party of the emperor and join with "Prince" Charles.[55] Nothing came of this overture, but the papacy clearly realized its best potential defense lay in the Arnulfing line.

The importance of the papacy is indicated by an event three years after the coronation of 751—even if the popes may have actually played no role in ending the Merovingian line. Pippin found it desirable in 754 to be anointed again, this time by Pope Stephen II rather than by his bishops, on the same day as the pope consecrated the church of St.-Denis, where Pippin's advisor Fulrad was lay abbot. The events are known from the contemporary *Liber Pontificalis* and the "Clausula de Pippino" as well as from the *Annales regni Francorum* of a generation later.[56] Pippin's sons, Charles and Carloman, were consecrated with him, as was his wife, Bertrada.[57] The significance of this papal consecration is underlined by Einhard's identification of the pope who ordered the deposition of the last Merovingian as Stephen, the name of the pope who blessed Pippin with his wife and sons in 754, rather than Zacharias, the pope who reigned in 751.[58]

The accession of Pippin to the throne was thus accompanied by an entirely novel and complex series of acts and rituals. It required not just the usual election but also consecration with a chrism,[59] reflecting Old Testament models and probably also the baptism of Clovis with holy oil. It also required the pope's approval to put someone on the throne who was not of the Merovingian line. Maintaining him there was shaky enough that it required, three years after Pippin's initial coronation, the personal appearance of the pope in Francia to anoint not just Pippin but also his wife and sons at a ceremony that also included the consecration of the church dedicated to the first apostle to Gaul. Everything that ritual could do was done to equate Pippin's family with the leadership and continued well-being of the Franks. That such ritual was considered necessary indicates how fragile that equation must have been.

When Pippin the Short succeeded the last Merovingian, he did not merely replace one king with another. He replaced an entire lineage with another, which therefore had to be defined and confirmed as appropriate kings. The "Clausula" adds a rather startling detail: Pope Stephen II ordered, under pain of excommunication, that "no one in the future should ever elect as king someone issued from any other loins" (*numquam de alterius lumbis regem in aevo presumant eligere*). No one, whether some offshoot of the Merovingians or perhaps of another family that had seized power as the Arnulfings had, could replace Pippin and his descendants.[60] The pope thus made it explicit that not only the new king partook in consecrated kingship but also the wife who had borne the fruit of his "loins" and the sons who had issued from those loins.

The participation of the entire family in the papal blessing is also suggested in a 757 letter from the pope, preserved in the *Codex Carolinus*. The pope acknowledged the novelty of the Arnulfings as kings but did not even allude to the Merovingians. In this letter Stephen II said to Pippin, "May you be blessed, my esteemed son . . . and your beloved offspring, my spiritual sons, Lords Charles and Carloman, established by God as kings of the Franks and patricians of the Romans, with their most Christian mother, the most excellent queen, your dearest wife . . . and may God expand your seed (*semen*) and bless it."[61] The biblical parallels with the seed of Abraham were unmistakable.

Twenty years later, another papal letter, also preserved in the *Codex Carolinus*, spoke of Charlemagne bringing his newborn son (Carloman, soon renamed Pippin) to Rome so that the pope could personally baptize him.[62] According to the so-called Astronomer's "Life" of Louis the Pious, Louis was also taken to Rome around the same time—already baptized but still young enough to be wearing his baby clothes—so that Pope Hadrian I could bless him, "with the benediction appropriate to one destined to reign," and crown him with a diadem.[63] Even for the popes, much less the Carolingians themselves, Pippin's sons had been established as kings along with their father; the mother who bore them took part in the divine blessing; and the papal blessing was to be extended to the next generation. Kingship was a family affair.

It is indicative of the importance of establishing the Carolingians as the only rightful family to rule Francia that, some seventy years after the events of 751, court publicists still found it necessary to disparage the previous royal lineage. Doubts about Carolingian legitimacy could be assuaged only by raising even more serious questions about their predecessors. The strident insistence by Einhard and his contemporaries that the Merovingians needed to be put aside (one might almost say "put down") as a kindness, both to themselves and to the Frankish kingdom, suggests that not everyone agreed with them. Even while Louis the Pious represented the third generation of Carolingian kings on the throne, there were deliberate efforts to reshape the memory of the Merovingians—to make them a lineage best forgotten. Writing the Merovingians out of history gave contemporaries a reason to be glad that a new lineage had replaced them. The glory of the Carolingians, as constructed in the decades surrounding the year 800, was built at least in part on the rejection of their predecessors.

Forgetting the Merovingians

The Merovingian kings were remembered in their own time as active, exciting, dangerous, and solid Christians who supported the rise of monasticism. In the ninth century, however, they came to be remembered as incompetents who desperately needed to be replaced, for the good of both church and state. This memory proved so compelling that it became the standard image of the kings for the next twelve hundred years.[64] Here I shall reexamine the picture created around the year 800 of Merovingian degeneracy, which then became a post facto argument for the accession of Pippin the Short.

Einhard's "Life of Charlemagne" tells a compelling story of how entirely appropriate it was that Charlemagne's father become king, rather than someone from the decrepit Merovingian line. These were weakling kings, Einhard tells us, incapable of riding a horse and therefore having to be driven around in an ox-cart like peasants,[65] parroting whatever the powers behind the throne told them to say because they were too feeble-minded to be trusted to come up with anything themselves. They only remained on the throne as long as they did due to the good-hearted attentions of their Arnulfing mayors of the palace: "The kings, happy just to have the title of king, had nothing else left to them by the mayors of the palace than being allowed to sit on the throne and give the impression of authority with their long hair and dangling beards."[66]

These are strong words. Other contemporary sources are also generally read as reinforcing the picture of Merovingian kings drinking themselves into early graves, when they were not promiscuously procreating or trying to kill each other in pointless vendettas. The *vitae* of Merovingian-era saints that were written in the Carolingian era all stress that these saints were surrounded by hordes of pagans—in marked contrast to those *vitae* written in the seventh and eighth centuries, which assumed a Christian milieu. Ninth-century *vitae* thus created a picture of an irreligious Merovingian-era society.[67] The Annals of Metz, composed shortly after Charlemagne became emperor, give a clear date to the triumph of the Arnulfings over their weakling predecessors: the battle of Tertry in 687. According to the Annals, with this victory Pippin of Herstal (Charlemagne's great-grandfather) was able to correct the "depravity" that had grown up at court as a result of the "cupidity" and "iniquity" of the kings.[68]

Thus in the early ninth century a conscious effort was made to create a new justification for removing a king from office: not cruelty or gross injustice but incompetence. Rulers had always been overthrown with the justification that they were fearsome tyrants; in contrast, the Merovingians, according to Einhard and his contemporaries, had to be removed because they had become ridiculous.[69] Einhard was doing more than noting that the mayors of the palace in the early eighth century kept a firm hand on the kings they put on the throne; he was saying that given the kings' debility, the mayors had no choice.[70]

Until recently scholars tended to accept this conclusion uncritically,[71] indeed often assuming in addition that the kings were illiterate and half pagan. But the image of the Merovingians promulgated since the year 800 should rather be seen as the product of a deliberate effort to make it seem evident and logical that the Carolingians should replace them.[72] To scholars twelve hundred years later the Carolingians may scarcely appear to need legitimation. They are now remembered as saving western Christendom from Islam, becoming the true successors to the Roman emperors of antiquity, and uniting continental Europe in a manner that might be considered, by not *too* big a stretch, as the model for the European Union.[73] But their very real achievements were seen at the time as requiring additional validation, and thus they constructed memories of the preceding dynasty.[74]

The Merovingians, of course, have always had a bad press. Much of what we know of the dynasty's first hundred years comes to us through the eyes of the sixth-century historian Gregory of Tours, who was not much more of a flack for the descendants of the sea serpent than was Einhard over two hundred years later. Clovis was undoubtedly the hero of his story, but a deeply flawed hero, and Gregory could not resist being ironic in describing him as, for example, loudly and bitterly bemoaning his shortage of relatives, in the hopes of luring some residual relatives out into the open where he could kill them.[75] With such a progenitor, it is not surprising that Clovis's sons and grandsons are described as cruel, cunning, and absolutely ruthless throughout the rest of the *Historia*.

It is, however, striking that Gregory's Merovingians and Einhard's Merovingians do not match. The active and bloodthirsty kings of the sixth century do not accord with the dim-witted weaklings of the eighth. Curiously, for a long time scholars did not worry about the gap between the bloodthirsty Merovingians and the *fainéant* Merovingians, instead assuming that all that violence debilitated the line, so that the transition from cunning to retarded took place almost naturally.

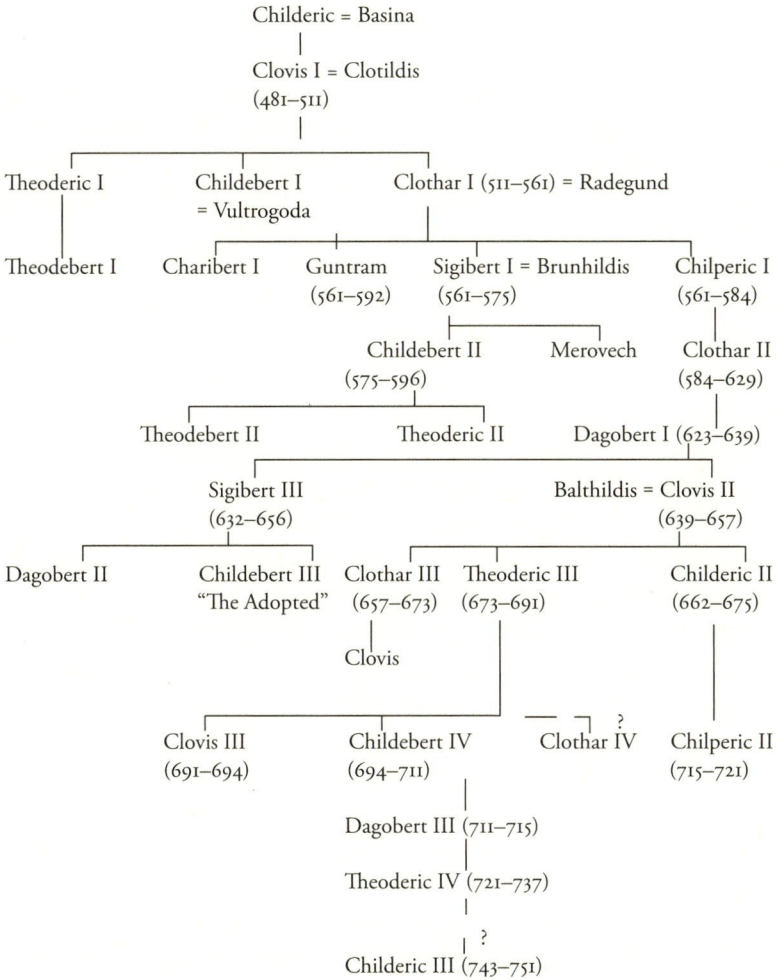

Figure 1. The Merovingian dynasty (simplified).

Now, it might be argued that some sort of change gradually overcame this line of kings, but the seventh-century kings in the sources do not look especially "transitional." Fredegar, the principal narrative source for this period, describes kings who were overall closer to Gregory's violent schemers than to men slipping into irrelevancy, and two of his kings, Clothar II and his son Dagobert, are considered among the most successful of the lineage.[76] But he did insert a suggestion into his reworking of Gregory that the line of kings had fallen from their early glory: Basina (Clovis's mother), he said, had a vision that the first generation of her descendants would be as lions (i.e., Clovis), the second as leopards and unicorns, the third as bears and wolves, and the fourth as dogs. While this certainly suggests a decline, it does not suggest a progressive *weakening* of the line, for Basina's fourth generation of descendants are still described as having *fortitudo*. The chief danger expressed in this vision was of a "people without fear of princes" who ended up tearing each other apart.[77] Fredegar thus characterized the kings of his own time as below the level of the heroes Gregory described but still marked neither by brutish violence—that was rather the feature of a people without strong leadership—nor by imbecility.

The closest one comes in pre-Carolingian sources to a description of Merovingian royal violence leading to decadence is the description of Clovis II (d. 657) in the *Liber Historiae Francorum*: "He was dedicated to every kind of filth, a fornicator, a defiler of women, and full of gluttony and drunkenness. History recalls nothing worthwhile about his death and final end." But even this account, written some seventy years later, does not accord with the *vita* of his wife, written much closer to events; it calls him a "pious king" and says that the royal couple proved generous to the poor.[78]

Recently scholars have begun efforts to rehabilitate the Merovingians.[79] The kings have benefited from a recharacterization of their era, the fifth through eighth centuries, as "late antiquity" rather than some deplorable Dark Age gap between the "fall of Rome" and the (unfortunately named) "feudal" period.[80] The old "official" date for the end of the western Roman Empire, 476, is no longer taken seriously as a turning point.[81]

As late antiquity has gained new attention, so scholars have stressed the many examples in the Merovingian lineage of literacy, piety, and a determined pursuit of *Romanitas*.[82] The kings sought to make themselves into Roman imperial officers—if not indeed virtual emperors. Clovis received the office of *consul* from Emperor Anastasius, according to Gregory of Tours, and was hailed with imperial titles, and his grandsons received Roman-style panegyrics. Frankish kings routinely minted coins modeled on imperial coins.[83] In addition, as discussed further in Chapters 9 and 11, the Merovingian era was a literate age, and the kings supported monasticism with gifts and privileges of immunity.

A memory of the Merovingians as crude barbarians, originally perpetuated by publicists at the Carolingian court and accepted until very recently, was thus constructed by deliberately forgetting many aspects of their culture. But even in the ninth century not everyone agreed that the Merovingians had been irrelevant weaklings. Indeed, they were often remembered positively.

The Merovingians Remembered

The "Mirrors for Princes" that described ideal kings, beginning around the time of Charlemagne's death, were based directly on earlier admonitions written for Merovingian kings.[84] The ninth-century *vita* of Faro, a seventh-century bishop of Meaux, includes a reference to the great military victories of Clothar II over the Saxons, still celebrated in special songs at the time the *vita* was written.[85] A Merovingian king recalled as a victorious battle leader two centuries later was not the king that Carolingian publicists would have wanted to remember.

Some monasteries indeed tried to reconstruct their history so that the Merovingians rather than the Arnulfings/Carolingians held pride of place. For example, Adela of Pfalzel made testamentary gifts to the nuns of Oeren in the 730s, but when her testament, along with many other monastic documents from the Trier region, was copied during the Carolingian period, she was said to be daughter of the Merovingian king Dagobert.[86] Here the scribe undertook a deliberate suppression of the Carolingian kings: Adela, who was most likely Charlemagne's great-aunt,[87] was reconceptualized as a Merovingian princess.

The Le Mans forgeries, the program of falsification based primarily on forged Merovingian documents as discussed in Chapter 5, are another example of the continuing prestige of the descendants of Clovis. Writing in the middle of the ninth century, when Carolingian hegemony was unquestioned, the forgers did not try to pass their "right" to coin money off as a privilege from Pippin or Charlemagne. Instead they attributed it to a grant from Theoderic III. They did present Charles the Bald with a forged charter of Louis the Pious, purportedly confirming this grant of the seventh century, but it is striking that they had the Carolingian emperor merely confirm what a Merovingian king had granted.[88]

The monks of Micy, contemporaries to the forgers at Le Mans, created a parallel series of false charters also intended to give their house rights far older than the Carolingian dynasty. Their monastery, St.-Mesmin of Micy, on the Loire, claimed in the ninth century to have been founded by Clovis himself.

Hagiographic accounts of the house's founding saints, written during the time of Louis the Pious, stress that the first Frankish king to have been baptized chose *their* house as his special foundation. Charters purporting to be written by Clovis were put together on the basis of these *vitae*.[89] Here, during the height of Carolingian power, the monks of Micy chose to associate their house not with that dynasty but with the Merovingians.

More than just antiquity was sought because foundation by an Arnulfing mayor of the palace would also have been ancient. Rather, the choice of Clovis as founder was in many ways a rejection of the current Carolingians. Even more specifically, it was a rejection of Theodulf, bishop of Orléans and a member of the Carolingian court circle, who refounded the monastery at Micy during the time of Charlemagne. With no extant charters from before the time of Theodulf, the monks had no way to argue that they should not be subject to the bishops of Orléans (as indeed they were throughout the ninth century), except by creating for themselves a past of independence and royal favor in which a Merovingian rather than any Carolingian ancestor played the central role.[90]

It was, however, possible, as writers sometimes attempted during the late eighth and ninth centuries, to speak well of both the Merovingian and Carolingian lines, thus recognizing the virtues of the current line of kings without denigrating their predecessors. For example, the *vita* of Saint Liutfred of Croix-St.-Leufroy in Normandy, written at the end of the eighth century, referred to Charles Martel as the "most noble prince" and said that he served Dagobert III, son of the "most glorious" King Childebert IV.[91] For this author, the Merovingians were admirable kings, but he also made clear that he found nothing to criticize in the early Carolingians.

The image of the Merovingian dynasty as weak incompetents, an image created several generations after the dynasty had left the throne, needs to be seen not as a description of what the kings of the seventh and early eighth centuries were really like but rather as the product of a deliberate campaign of denigration. Such a campaign indicates that doubts lingered long after 751 whether Childeric III's deposition had been the right thing to do, doubts underlined by the infrequency with which the deposition was even mentioned. Portraying Childeric and his predecessors as an embarrassment to the Franks was a refutation of those doubts.

The elaborate rituals by which Pippin was made king are themselves an indication of what an unusual, indeed problematic event it was. Even the later efforts to downplay these rituals or to give, as Einhard did, all the responsibility to the pope who had recently crowned Charlemagne emperor are a suggestion that the transition to the new lineage still remained a sensitive issue—one underscored by the number of monastic chroniclers and forgers who continued to remember Clovis and his descendants with affection.

But it was not enough to reject the Merovingians. Those at the Carolingian court in the late eighth and early ninth centuries also sought to create a positive image of the new dynasty as strong and just leaders, one the kings themselves tried to adopt. Being a dynasty was itself crucial; in the next chapter I shall discuss the ways that the Carolingian family was conceptualized, arguing that what is now considered their lineage was in fact a deliberate creation of the years around 800. Writers then also constructed the myth that the Carolingians had always been kings, or at least had been the effective kings of the Franks for a good century before Pippin the Short deposed the last Merovingian. The vision of a lineage that competently governed for generations, while weak-headed long-haired kings occupied the throne, was more than an exercise in self-aggrandizement: it was intended to help create the consensus that the Carolingians, and they alone, should be king.

Chapter 7

Creation of a Carolingian Dynasty

As discussed in the previous chapter, the scorn heaped on the Merovingians from the court of Charlemagne should be seen as a retrospective account, intended to make their replacement by the Carolingians seem sensible and natural. In this chapter I shall focus on how the ancestry of Charlemagne was described—and that description modified—in order to make it seem a royal dynasty, of the sort that could or should have been ruling all along.

Specifically, the Carolingians had to be reconceptualized as a male-line dynasty, where power had always passed smoothly from father to son, without any long detours or dead ends. Paul the Deacon said at the end of the eighth century that a new "lineage" (*prosapia*), the one now called the Carolingians, had taken up Frankish rule—even while implying, by making this comment in the context of the deeds of Charlemagne's great-grandfather, that this lineage had done so a century and a half earlier. This new lineage needed a new history that explained that it was not new at all.[1]

Creation of a Dynasty

The Carolingians were uncomfortably aware that their predecessors on the Frankish throne had all been related in the male line, indeed the only group of relatives at the time with their own collective name, "Merovingian." The term "Carolingian" arose only much later. Indeed, at the end of the twelfth century the compiler of the cartulary of Echternach, a house founded with the assistance of Charlemagne's ancestors, was able to give an accurate *genealogia* of the line from Pippin of Herstal to Charles the Fat but had no name with which to label them collectively; he simply called them "our Pippins and Charleses" (*Pippinos et Karolos nostros*).[2]

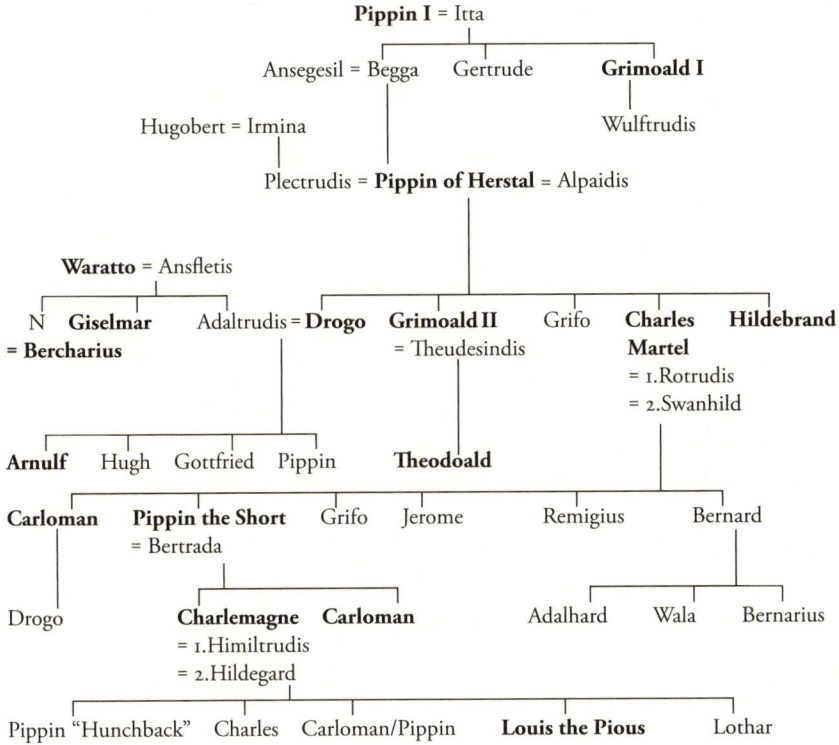

Figure 2. The Carolingian dynasty (simplified). Names of kings, dukes, and mayors of the palace in bold.

The Merovingians had taken their name, according to the seventh-century chronicler Fredegar, as the descendants of Meroveus, the son of a sea serpent, a source of power unmatched by anything in the Arnulfing family tree. Einhard appears acutely conscious of the cohesiveness of the Merovingian line, for the words *gens Meroingorum* are the very first words in the first chapter of his "Life" of Charlemagne. But he had no comparable term for the *gens* of Charlemagne, making it much harder to describe the Carolingians as a dynasty.[3] The logical conclusion, that of course no one at court wanted to draw, was that Pippin the Short and his successors were usurpers. The very slowness of the Arnulfings to get rid of the previous kings suggests that they, too, had long believed that all Frankish kings should come from the Merovingian line.

It is here worth stressing that until 751, *only* male-line members of that dynasty could be kings of the Franks.[4] In spite of wars with each other, with unfaithful followers, with neighboring kings, and with pagans, the Merovingians kept on producing kings. They might be illegitimate, or they might have to be recalled from the monastery; it did not matter, as long as their fathers were of the royal lineage. The emphasis on the male line was indeed such that royally born women of the sixth and seventh centuries are nearly undocumented.

Two illuminating passages in Fredegar illustrate the importance of Merovingian paternal descent. The infamous Brunhildis tried to stir up Theoderic II against his brother by telling him that the brother was not their father's son but rather son of "some gardener"; and in contrast she tried unsuccessfully to get the holy man Columbanus to bless Theoderic's sons who had been born "of adulterous unions," telling Columbanus that they were "sons of the king."[5] Theoderic refused to attack his brother, and Columbanus refused to bless the boys, but Brunhildis was clearly using as justification contemporary assumptions about royalty. Even someone brought up to rule could not do so unless he could be convincingly demonstrated to be a king's son, and in contrast any king's son held a privileged place, whatever the status of his mother. For three centuries, the father's lineage alone defined kingship, and only direct descendants of Childeric (Clovis I's father) were crowned Frankish kings.

The so-called "coup" in 656 by Grimoald, one of the Pippinid mayors of the palace, is instructive here.[6] Grimoald, son of Pippin I, had already had a respected career as mayor of the palace for a decade or so.[7] His king, Sigibert III of Austrasia, had just died, leaving only a young boy born to his queen. According to the *Liber Historiae Francorum*, Grimoald promptly had the boy tonsured and shipped off to Ireland on "pilgrimage."[8] At this point the modern reader might expect a preview of what happened a century later, when Pippin the Short tonsured the last Merovingian king and had himself crowned in his place. But Grimoald did nothing of the sort. He did not try to have himself crowned king; the idea was apparently inconceivable. Instead, declaring Sigibert's other (probably illegitimate) young son Childebert his own adopted son, he set about trying to rule Austrasia in the boy's name.[9]

Grimoald was here following the same strategy that King Guntram of Burgundy had followed some seventy-five years earlier: seize control of a kingdom by making oneself the "protector" of a son of the late king. Guntram took control of his late brother Chilperic's kingdom in 584 by taking Chilperic's infant son into his own custody, acting as godfather to him, and establishing the child on his late father's throne, rather than any of Guntram's other nephews.[10] In this case Guntram was successful, and the child (Clothar II) ruled for over forty years, eventually becoming sole king of all the Frankish kingdoms.

In contrast, Grimoald's success at ruling through his adopted son was relatively short-lived. After seven years at the most, Childebert died and Grimoald was promptly put to death.[11] At first Merovingian cousins from Neustria took the Austrasian throne, but eventually the "pilgrim" to Ireland was recalled to become King Dagobert II.[12] This incident made no more than a ripple in seventh-century history, but its significance for Frankish kingship is clear: even a powerful mayor of the palace who wanted to act as king had to do so through a boy with Merovingian blood.[13]

It is also worth noting that two generations later, Charles Martel ruled as mayor of the palace without actually having a king to serve. It was not that he preferred not having a king: he had already set on the throne one Merovingian (Clothar IV) so obscure that scholars cannot agree on who his father was and had brought another (Theoderic IV) out of the cloister and had him grow out his hair. And yet Charles Martel made no effort to have himself crowned, even when his final Merovingian king died, leaving him to rule Francia as mayor without a king for the last years of his life.[14]

For Charles Martel as for his predecessor Grimoald, the Merovingians were the only kings of the Franks. Pippin the Short and his brother Carloman also found a Merovingian king to serve for close to a decade. When Pippin finally decided to break with that tradition, he did so only after his brother had become a monk, only after his son Charlemagne was about three and thus past the dangers of infancy, and thus only when a new dynasty could plausibly be asserted. He still required the full support of the earthly representative of Saint Peter behind him. The shock that the end of Merovingian kingship must have caused clearly still resonated two generations later and was surely felt by Charlemagne himself. The concerted efforts by his publicists to assert how entirely appropriate it was that the Merovingians be deposed indicate that it was considered anything but appropriate at the time.[15]

The Carolingians after 751, like the preceding dynasty, had wars with each other, with unfaithful followers, with other kings, and with Muslims and pagans, but for them it was not much over a century before the first non-Carolingian king—Boso of Burgundy—took the throne in the heart of Frankish territory. Boso was only the first of a number of kings, most notably the Welfs, the Robertians, and the Ottonians, who soon set themselves up as alternatives to the Carolingians, even while Charlemagne's male-line descendants still lived.[16] But these descendants were either illegitimate or underage[17]—conditions that had not prevented descendants of Clovis from becoming king but presented almost insurmountable challenges to the Carolingians. Pippin the Short deposed the final male-line Merovingian; Boso in contrast established his short-lived kingdom a good century before male-line Carolingians stopped contending for, and often successfully holding, their thrones.

Einhard

Thus the Carolingian line never acquired the same unique claim to Frankish kingship as the Merovingians had had before them. When Einhard wrote in the early ninth century, a male-line dynasty was clearly crucial. And yet the "family" of the new line of kings included women in a way that the Merovingian dynasty had not. If Pippin's consecration was novel, then the papal blessing of his wife was even more original. Merovingian queens had of course appeared in the sources from time to time, often in the context of founding churches, but they had never been major players in politics. Carolingian queens, in contrast, had a significant public role. They acted as partners to their husbands much more than had their predecessors—indeed, the Merovingian kings often took lowborn brides rather than the aristocratic women always chosen by the Carolingians.[18] Thus the attempts to define the Carolingians, like the Merovingians before them, as a strictly male-line concern were undercut by the increased inclusion by Carolingian men themselves of women within the group of significant relatives.

Faced with these challenges, Einhard went out of his way to suggest that the Carolingian dynasty had existed as a hereditary line even before they became kings. His insistence on this point, and the differences in the way that he portrays the Arnulfings and the way earlier sources do, suggests that both for Einhard and for his contemporaries, there was a connection between being royal and being part of a dynasty.

According to Einhard, during Childeric III's reign Pippin the Short was mayor of the palace, "as it were by heredity" (*velut hereditario*). His father, Charles Martel, had himself obtained the office of mayor of the palace directly from his own father, Pippin of Herstal, also according to Einhard. This characterization is of course a gross oversimplification.[19] Although Pippin the Short, the future king, succeeded Charles Martel fairly smoothly as mayor of the palace, Charles had experienced much more difficulty succeeding his own father and was for a while imprisoned by his stepmother, who preferred her own grandson, son of her husband's older son, to Charles. Not heredity but success in scheming and war eventually gave him office and authority in Austrasia.[20]

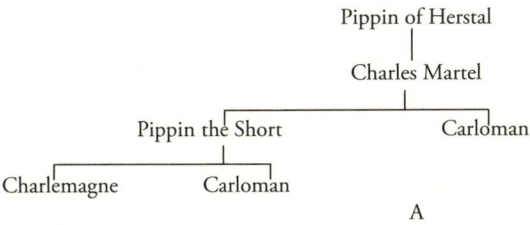

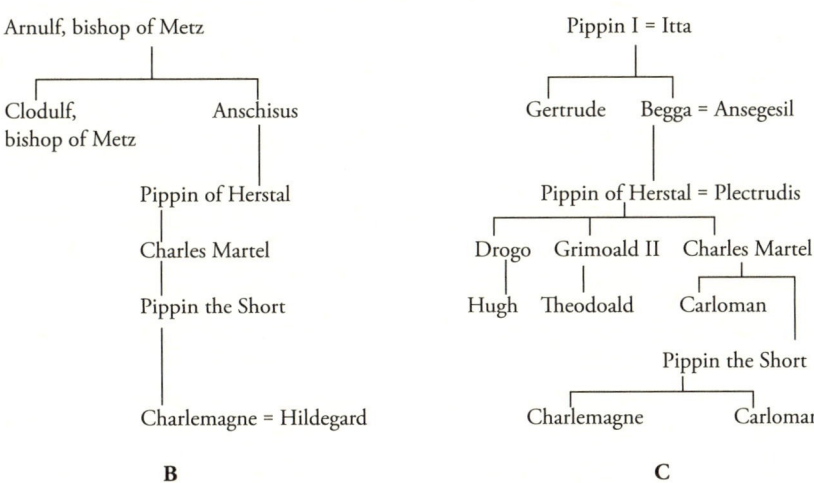

Figure 3. The Carolingian dynasty according to Einhard (A, top), Paul the Deacon (B, lower left), and the Annals of Metz (C, lower right).

Because Einhard wanted to emphasize the father-son line that led to Charlemagne, he did not even mention Charles Martel's older half brother Grimoald II, who had in fact been mayor of the palace long before Charles took that office and whose son Theodoald succeeded Grimoald as mayor of the palace, or Charles's other half brothers, Drogo, duke of Champagne, and Grifo.[21] Nor did he mention any of Duke Drogo's relatives: his wife, Adaltrudis, her parents, Ansfletis and Waratto (also a mayor of the palace, and thus someone who would have muddied the picture of Arnulfings as sole mayors of the palace); Drogo's son Arnulf, who succeeded his father as duke of Champagne; or Drogo's second son, Hugh, archbishop of Rouen and bishop of Paris and Bayeux, as well as abbot of St.-Wandrille (Fontenelle) and of Jumièges in Normandy.[22] He did not even mention Charles Martel's probable full brother, Hildebrand.[23]

Einhard, by not mentioning Grimoald II or Drogo or their sons and in-laws at all, was also able to suggest that, starting with Pippin of Herstal, no one but direct ancestors of Charlemagne held the office of mayor of the palace. He thus left out not only the mayor Waratto and Waratto's son, Giselmar, briefly mayor himself,[24] but also Waratto's other son-in-law (besides Drogo), Berchar-ius, who also acted as mayor of the palace.[25] In addition, he passed in silence over Raginfred, another nonrelative who competed with Charles Martel for the office of mayor of the palace.[26] Einhard was thus able to portray Charlem-agne's ancestry as a successful male-line dynasty, but only by means of radical pruning.

And the history of the family before Charles Martel's father, Pippin of Herstal, shows even less evidence of male-line heredity. Einhard made no at-tempt to carry his story back before the time of this Pippin; for him it was enough to establish a male-line dynasty back to Charlemagne's great-grandfather. But two other major attempts to draw the Carolingian family tree, that of Paul the Deacon and that of the Annals of Metz, respectively forty and twenty years or so before Einhard's work, both took the story back an additional two generations. Here it is striking to note that these two accounts do not match. One speaks only of Pippin of Herstal's maternal ancestry, the "Pippinids" as they are now known, and one only of his paternal ancestry, the "Arnulfings." There still seems to have been considerable doubt at the end of the eighth century as to how a canonical history of Charlemagne's ancestors was to be constructed.

Modern scholars, like historians in the high Middle Ages, have had no trouble combining the two accounts. Pippin of Herstal, it is widely agreed, was son of the couple Ansegesil and Begga. Ansegesil was the son of Arnulf, bishop of Metz, who had married long before becoming bishop; Charle-magne's ancestors are generally now called Arnulfings in recognition of his status as first male ancestor of the line. Begga in turn was the daughter of Pippin I (or Pippin the Ancient) and his wife, Itta. With Carolingian ancestry thus carried back to the first decades of the seventh century, to two men—Arnulf and Pippin I—who are known from the seventh-century chronicler Fredegar to have been political allies,[27] neither modern scholars nor the histo-rians at Charlemagne's court felt any compelling need to extend the family tree any further.

But this clear identification of the two parents and three of the four grand-parents of Pippin of Herstal, it should be stressed, was not put together during Charlemagne's lifetime. Rather, two competing versions both attempted to create a male-line dynasty but to do so in different ways. Only by combining the two can scholars create the version that has been taken for granted for the last twelve hundred years. That Paul the Deacon and the author of the Annals of Metz, originators of the two accounts, each resisted the other's version suggests that they, at any rate, would not have accepted a simple combination. (It is even possible that Einhard, who wrote after both, stopped his own account of Carolingian ancestry with Pippin of Herstal to avoid taking part in the debate.)

Paul the Deacon

The first attempt chronologically to create a Carolingian family tree was that of Paul the Deacon, who wrote toward the end of the eighth century.[28] For him Charlemagne's lineage, his *prosapia*, mattered as much as individuals. Paul's description of his own family tree (*genealogia*) suggests how he thought families should be conceptualized: male-line, with repetition of names used to indicate family membership and women unnamed if mentioned at all. Paul's own *abavus*, he tells us, was Leupchis, who was captured by the Avars with his five sons. One son escaped, also named Leupchis, Paul's *proavus*—the other four went nameless. This man's son, Arichis, was Paul's grandfather, who had Warnefrit, Paul's own father, who had Paul and his brother Arichis, "who recalls our grandfather by his name."[29] This was what a family tree ought to be like: a straight line, with repeated names showing family unity, stripped of extraneous branches or names of wives, and leading to people of interest in the present.

Paul set out to create a similar family tree for Charlemagne, based, he said, on what the king himself had told him of his ancestry.[30] Paul's account, like that of Einhard after him, mentioned women only in passing, if at all.[31] All of Paul's emphasis was on the men. Charlemagne, according to Paul, had said that he was the great-great-great-grandson (*trinepos*) of the blessed Arnulf of Metz. Paul embedded the family's genealogy within his "Gesta" of the bishops of Metz, which became less an account of that see's bishops and more an account of the descendants of Bishop Arnulf, who was of the "race (*stemma*) of the most noble and most powerful Franks." Arnulf, he continued, was father of Anschisus, father of Pippin of Herstal. He gave the name neither of Arnulf's wife nor of Anschisus's wife. Indeed, he gave the names of neither wives nor brothers as he carried the line of descent from Pippin of Herstal to

Charles Martel to Pippin the Short to Charlemagne. Charlemagne is the first in this family tree whose wife is named. Paul explained that Charlemagne's son Pippin was named for his own grandfather, and his son Charles was named both for his father and great-grandfather, reinforcing the image of a male-line dynasty.[32]

Paul the Deacon was certainly correct that Anschisus—or at least a man with a name only slightly different than that—was the father of Pippin of Herstal because Pippin named his father Ansegesil (*Ansgisilius*) in his own charters.[33] But Paul's father-son connection between Bishop Arnulf of Metz and Anschisus/Ansegesil is not attested by any contemporary source, indeed by any source less than a century and a half after the fact, when he was the first to put it forward.[34] Paul probably had read Fredegar's chronicle, which shows Bishop Arnulf of Metz and Pippin I acting together—without, however, suggesting that there was any tie of blood or marriage between them. The "continuations" of Fredegar's account call Ansegesil a "noble Frank" but again do not make any suggestion of a family connection with Bishop Arnulf.[35]

Even though no contemporary source says that Charlemagne was Arnulf's descendant, there is no way to disprove definitively what could well be the lineage's oral memory. There is, however, enough evidence suggesting otherwise to justify the recent doubt that has been cast on accepting Arnulf as Charlemagne's ancestor.[36] The *vita* of Arnulf, probably dating from the mid- or late seventh century, is remarkably unhelpful here, not giving the names of his parents, his wife, or his two sons, though stressing that they were of the highest nobility—but that did not stop Paul the Deacon, a century later, from confidently naming the sons. Charles Martel's son Jerome recopied this *vita* as a youth in the early eighth century, perhaps in the monastery at Metz, and identified himself proudly as son of Charles and grandson of Pippin of Herstal but showed no sign that he thought of Saint Arnulf as his own ancestor, which would be very unusual if there was indeed a family memory of descent from him.[37]

The most persuasive evidence that any family members before Charlemagne considered Arnulf of Metz to be in their family tree is that Drogo, son of Pippin of Herstal, named one of his own sons Arnulf. But it is possible that Drogo was not commemorating a great-grandfather but only naming a son for a famous bishop of a century earlier, at whose church Drogo's father was buried. After all, Drogo's half brother Charles Martel named a son Remigius, who became bishop of Rouen, almost certainly for the bishop of Reims rather than for a relative, as well as giving another son the distinctly non-family name of

Jerome. It is possible, however, that Charlemagne himself believed that the name Arnulf, held by one of his father's cousins, indicated a descent from Bishop Arnulf of Metz.

In addition, even if one accepts Bishop Arnulf into the Carolingian family tree, the line of descent from Arnulf was not nearly as tidy as Paul the Deacon implied; even his own account suggests a few genealogical twists and turns. First of all, Arnulf appears in Paul's "Gesta" without any relatives, other than his descendants. And yet the seventh-century *vita* of Bertulf, abbot of Bobbio, says that Arnulf was Bertulf's cousin (*consanguineus*);[38] if Paul knew this he ignored it, as needlessly complicating the story. Then, according to Paul the Deacon's own account, Arnulf of Metz had two sons, and Anschisus, the Carolingian ancestor, was not the older but the younger; Clodulf, the older, became bishop of Metz like his father.[39] Paul commented, "No further information on him comes to us, except for his family origins"; Clodulf clearly lacked interest because he was not part of Charlemagne's direct ancestry.[40]

Paul also failed to note that Pippin of Herstal was a cousin (*propinquus*) of Wandregesil, founder and first abbot of St.-Wandrille, a connection recorded in a *vita* written during Pippin of Herstal's lifetime and thus with a fairly good chance of being accurate. The similarity of name elements between Ansegesil and Wandregesil does suggest that he was a relative of Pippin of Herstal.[41] Interestingly, almost no modern scholar puts Wandregesil into the Arnulfing family tree,[42] even though he appears to have a better claim to be there than does Arnulf himself. Then, Paul the Deacon leaves out any mention of Pippin I, because he was only father-in-law of Anschisus/Ansegesil, and his own account is focused on the men, not the women.

Moreover, Bertulf and Wandregesil are not the only persons known from contemporary sources to be connected to Pippin of Herstal and yet ignored by Paul the Deacon. A certain Adalgisel lived slightly earlier than Ansegesil, a man of great wealth, known from the testament he issued in 634. In this testament, he referred to himself as Adalgisel-Grimo, a *diaconus* from Verdun, and noted his nephew, Duke Bobo. He was almost certainly the same person as the Duke Adalgisel who served the Merovingian kings in Austrasia in the 630s, accompanied by a Duke Bobo.[43] This person too received no place in the Arnulfing family tree, at least in the account of Paul the Deacon.

One could not, of course, identify this Adalgisel with Ansegesil, in spite of the name similarities. Either he, in his testament, or Fredegar in his chronicle would have been likely to mention a son if he had one, much less one as important a figure in Merovingian politics as Pippin of Herstal. But, like

Wandregesil, Adalgisel's name, his wealth and status, and his activities in the Metz region would all seem to indicate someone who should be attached to the family tree of Carolingian ancestors. Even his *cognomen* Grimo recalls the names Grimoald and Grifo in this family's lineage. One cannot help but feel that the complete lack of modern interest in this seventh-century figure— although his importance in his own period is well attested in seventh-century sources—is due to his absence in the accounts of a hundred and fifty years later.[44]

Interestingly, Paul the Deacon asserts that Anschisus is a Trojan name. Indeed, Paul seems to have chosen to call him Anschisus rather than Ansegesil in order that he might have the same name as the father of Aeneas. In designating him a Trojan, Paul was trying to claim ancient origins for the Carolingian dynasty, in essence displacing the Merovingians from the position, which they had claimed since at least the sixth century, of being the New Troy.[45]

But Paul was remarkably leery about commenting directly on the end of the Merovingian line. Although he had made a vague reference to Clovis earlier in his "Gesta" of the bishops of Metz, he gave no explanation to how the transition from Merovingian to Carolingian kings took place. He had, in his *Historia Langobardorum*, spoken of the kings of the Franks as having "degenerated from their accustomed strength and skill" in the early seventh century, at the time of Bishop Arnulf—far earlier than any other source would put Merovingian decadence. Paul added that the mayors of the palace had taken over "whatever the kings used to do" and that it was due to "heavenly disposition" that "the Frankish realm was translated to this lineage."[46] Here he is very reticent about exactly how this transfer took place, or even when—though the implication is that it was in the seventh century.

In Paul's "Gesta" of the bishops of Metz, he is even more reticent, and the topic of Merovingian decline never even arises. Here Pippin the Short is "wise" and "brave," but his only achievement that Paul found worth mentioning was that he put down a Gascon rebellion, not that he was crowned king of the Franks and consecrated by the pope. Pippin is not even designated as *rex*, although Charlemagne is *magnus rex*. This very silence is telling. Because Charlemagne is described as a king, Paul seems to be hoping that his ancestors will enjoy a royal aura as well—without needing to discuss directly the perhaps dubious transition to Carolingian kingship. Paul comments that it was "not unworthily that the kingdom of the Franks should be transferred to his lineage" (*non inmerito ad eius prosapiam Francorum translatum sit regnum*), with the clear implication that his king's many accomplishments fully justified it.[47]

This comment is placed in the context of the achievements of Anschisus/Ansegesil, which made it possible for Paul to suggest that the Carolingians had already enjoyed over a century and a half of rule by the time that he wrote. His silence on Pippin the Short's deposition of the last Merovingian in both his *Historia* of the Lombards and his "Gesta" of the bishops of Metz may well indicate that the 751 transfer of the crown from one lineage to another was still a highly sensitive issue in the late eighth century, one that he did not care to touch.[48]

The Annals of Metz

A quite different version of the Carolingian family tree is given by the Annals of Metz, which were composed twenty years or so after Paul the Deacon's account, most likely in response to a political crisis in the first years of the ninth century.[49] Much had happened in the intervening years, most notably Charlemagne's coronation by the pope as emperor, but the annalist's concern was the same as Paul's: to construct an image of a male-line dynasty of considerable antiquity that led inevitably to Charlemagne, suggesting that his family had always been the appropriate leaders of the Franks.[50]

It was more challenging for the annalist of Metz[51] to create a plausible male-line dynasty reaching from Charlemagne back to the early seventh century because the Annals covered the maternal, rather than paternal, ancestry of Pippin of Herstal.[52] The Annals open with the succession of this Pippin to the "principality" (that is, the office of mayor of the palace) of his father, Ansegesil. But then almost immediately the annalist turns to Begga, Ansegesil's wife, a "glorious" mother for Pippin and "worthy of all praise." Begga, the annalist tells us, was daughter of Pippin I, and although this account (like Paul the Deacon's) was written a century and a half after the fact, it is essentially confirmed by sources much closer to the events (unlike Paul's). Interestingly, while the annalist had no choice but to discuss Begga, given the intention to link Pippin of Herstal with Pippin I, the Annals also included Saint Gertrude, Begga's sister, and Pippin I's wife, Itta, also known from seventh-century sources.[53]

In trying to create an image of a male-line descent, the annalist attempted to present Pippin of Herstal's maternal grandfather as the moral equivalent of a paternal grandfather. Pippin I, we are told, had "no offspring of the masculine sex, and thus left both his name and his principality to his grandson

Pippin [of Herstal]."[54] But Pippin I *did* have a son of the "masculine sex," Grimoald I, who was mayor of the palace in the 650s, as discussed earlier.[55] The problem for the annalist was that this Grimoald was not of the line that led to Charlemagne. Moreover, although Grimoald had been mayor of the palace, the eventual accession of his sister's son to that office had nothing to do with his ultimately failed efforts to rule through an infant Merovingian. Pippin of Herstal commemorated this maternal uncle through the name of his second son, Grimoald II, but he himself only became mayor of the palace a good generation after the first Grimoald's death.

The annalist of Metz, unlike Paul the Deacon or Einhard, *did* mention many people in Charlemagne's family tree besides his direct ancestors. Interestingly, however, Bishop Arnulf of Metz in this account is not Ansegesil's father but only a "paternal relative" of Pippin of Herstal, *agnatione propinquus*.[56] The fact that Arnulf is mentioned but *not* placed in the family tree must indicate a deliberate rejection of Paul the Deacon's version of Carolingian ancestry, in preference to the line leading back to Pippin I.

The Annals, following the continuations of Fredegar, included the older sons of Pippin of Herstal, Drogo and Grimoald II, although not Grifo or Hildebrand. Interestingly, Drogo's ecclesiastical son Hugh appears but not Drogo's other son and heir, Arnulf, the duke—indeed, the annalist said that Grimoald succeeded to Drogo's offices after Drogo's death, thus simplifying the story.[57] The appearance of Drogo and Grimoald II in these Annals indicates that Einhard surely knew about them, even though he does not mention them.[58]

The annalist was able to assert that Charles Martel was the "legitimate" heir to Pippin of Herstal by skittering around the fact that Charles was born to a different woman than were Drogo and Grimoald, indeed perhaps to a concubine. Interestingly, the annalist dismisses Theodoald, son of Grimoald, as a possible competitor to Charles Martel by saying that he was "just a boy" and in addition born *ex concubina*, and thus "scarcely worthy" to succeed, morally incapable of challenging Charles Martel for leadership of the Franks. It was only the "womanish" notions of Plectrudis, Charles Martel's stepmother, that made her oppose him, the annalist states. In this account, she attempted unsuccessfully to rule with her "infant" grandson, whom the annalist suggests quickly and conveniently died, thus leaving no further sons or grandsons of Plectrudis.[59]

The legitimacy—or not—of Charles Martel is an issue that has concerned modern scholars as well as Carolingian publicists. Pippin of Herstal, it is clear, married Plectrudis as his first wife and had sons by her.[60] But Charles Martel was not born to Plectrudis but rather to one Alpaidis, who in some later accounts was a lowborn concubine—although Fredegar's continuator calls both Plectrudis and Alpaidis an *uxor nobilis*.[61] Even if Alpaidis was a well-born wife, she was a bigamous later wife, for Plectrudis survived Pippin of Herstal and attempted to regulate his inheritance as his widow. A possible issue here is that bigamy, while relatively common among the powerful in the Merovingian era (especially if only one of the wives was highborn),[62] had become morally stigmatized by the ninth century. While Pippin of Herstal might have had two wives,[63] for his descendants four generations later such an arrangement was impossible, at least if the son of the second wife would succeed.

Bertrada, wife of Pippin the Short, had after all been consecrated by the pope along with her husband, and in spite of their efforts to create a male-line dynasty, all the Carolingians treated their queens as guarantors of the legitimacy of that dynasty. By the time the annalist of Metz was writing, Pippin the Hunchback, Charlemagne's oldest son, had been thoroughly removed from the line of possible succession on grounds of supposed illegitimacy.[64] That assertions of illegitimacy could be used against Theodoald and Pippin the Hunchback indicates that those writing at court were highly concerned that the same label not be attached to Charles Martel by making him the son of a bigamous union. Therefore Plectrudis and her children, Pippin's older sons, had to be eased out of the family, even if it meant suggesting, as did the annalist of Metz, that Plectrudis was nothing more than a classic bad stepmother.

In fact, other sources suggest that Plectrudis's support for her grandson Theodoald as mayor of the palace was not nearly as ridiculous as the annalist of Metz asserted. Theodoald may not really have been born to a concubine at all: the *Liber Historiae Francorum*, which, like the Annals of Metz, says that he was, also says that his father, Grimoald II, married Theudesindis, daughter of the Frisian leader, and it is tempting to assume that Theodoald was given a name composed of elements of both his parents' names. Pippin of Herstal himself promoted his grandson Theodoald in preference to his son Charles Martel. Theodoald also does not seem to have been as young or to have died quite as quickly as the Annals of Metz suggest, for he served as mayor of the palace for Dagobert III and appears in a later charter along with his uncle Charles Martel.[65] The court of the ninth century portrayed Charles Martel as succeeding legitimately to Pippin of Herstal; Plectrudis herself saw his succession as anything but right and fought to resist it.

In addition, the annalist of Metz, unlike Paul the Deacon, made the

Merovingian kings a part of the story, even though the annalist was no more impressed by those kings than Einhard some two decades later. The annalist's Merovingians, however, unlike Einhard's, are active figures, cruel and untrustworthy perhaps, but never figures of fun. When they stopped being active and cruel, they stopped being mentioned at all. The last Merovingians simply do not appear, and the account of the consecration and coronation of Pippin the Short does not even note that a final Merovingian king first had to be removed. The annalist of Metz, like the earlier authors of the *Liber Historiae Francorum*, the *vita* of Bishop Eucherius of Orléans, and the "continuations" of Fredegar, had been calling the mayors of the palace "princes," and a prince could be crowned king without much fuss.[66] This version of Carolingian family history, therefore, got around the problem of justifying the transfer of the crown from one lineage to another by not even mentioning it.

Competition Among Carolingians

All early ninth-century efforts to create a correct Carolingian genealogy also downplay the fact that both Pippin the Short and Charlemagne had brothers named Carloman who were initially their co-rulers—and in fact Carloman, son of Charles Martel, was the *older* brother of Pippin the Short. Indeed, the early ninth-century chronicle of Moissac, which did not mention the final Merovingian at all, much less his deposition, called this Carloman *rex Francorum* with the implication that Arnulfing kingship began with the death of Charles Martel.[67]

The two Carlomans died rather conveniently, the first after resigning to enter the church, close enough in time to when the annalist of Metz and Einhard were writing that some explanation might be expected. Both passed in silence over the fact that Pippin the Short's brother Carloman had a son named Drogo, who, as oldest son of the oldest son, should probably have taken precedence.[68] In naming his son, Carloman had most likely been mindful that his grandfather, Pippin of Herstal, had named his own oldest son Drogo. Fredegar's continuator said that Carloman commended Drogo to Pippin the Short upon converting to the monastic life. Drogo indeed was not only his father Carloman's heir but also Pippin's heir when Carloman left for Italy to became a monk, for Charlemagne was not even born yet.[69] But Drogo, son of Carloman, after briefly succeeding as mayor of the palace, was tonsured and disappears from the records.[70]

The annalist of Metz did not say why Pippin's brother Carloman became a monk, only relating that he did so;[71] the annalist also gave no cause for Charlemagne's brother Carloman's sudden death. Interestingly, the annalist quickly turned from the account of the first Carloman's resignation to an account of the perfidy of Grifo, Carloman's and Pippin's half brother, apparently with the hope of implying that *all* of Pippin's brothers were troublesome and unworthy to rule. According to Einhard's own rather airy explanation, Pippin's brother Carloman decided to go to Rome and become a monk for "some unknown reason, most likely out of love for the contemplative life." Charlemagne's brother Carloman died of "some disease," and Einhard, having insisted that the two brothers truly loved each other, professed himself unable to understand why Carloman's widow fled with her sons and sought refuge in Lombardy. (His insistence on brotherly love is of course undercut by his own comment that Charlemagne bore Carloman's hatred and jealousy with equanimity.) Such concerted efforts to divert suspicion immediately make the attentive reader suspicious.[72]

Besides the two Carlomans, full brothers of Pippin the Short and Charlemagne, who had been respectively mayor of the palace and king, there were also other family members who could be pruned away more easily. Pippin the Short also had at least four half brothers, although Einhard mentions none of them.[73] One, Grifo, born to the Bavarian woman Swanhild, is mentioned by both the Annals of Metz and Fredegar's continuators,[74] but the annalist of Metz calls Swanhild a concubine, and both of these chroniclers make Grifo into a troublemaker who inappropriately tried to seize authority that was rightfully his brothers'. As a troublemaker, he could easily be set aside from a story that stressed legitimate continuity, especially as he was killed shortly after Pippin the Short became king of the Franks. And note again that the assertion "born to a concubine" is used—deliberately but probably incorrectly—to dismiss someone from the family.[75]

Another half brother of Pippin's, named Remigius, was overlooked by all the royal annalists, even though he appears in papal letters to Pippin from the 760s and became bishop of Rouen. Still another half brother, named Jerome, also seems to have entered the church as noted earlier; he copied the *vita* of Saint Arnulf as a youth and accompanied the pope back to Rome in the 750s after the pope had consecrated his brother Pippin as king.[76] Once Remigius and Jerome were in the church, they could safely be ignored by those writing their family's political history.[77]

A fourth half brother of Pippin the Short, in this case most likely really born to a concubine, was named Bernard. He is mentioned in a tenth-century genealogy of the counts of Flanders, along with his brothers, Pippin, Carloman, Grifo, Remigius, and Jerome. Bernard was the father of Adalhard and Wala, cousins to the Carolingian royal line and important figures at court, according to their ninth-century *vitae*. Both became abbots of Corbie, and a third son of Bernard, Bernarius, probably was also a monk there.[78] But because these three cousins of Charlemagne were in the church, they, too, could be ignored in discussions of the Carolingian family tree, as could their sisters Gundrada and Theodrada, even though all five were alive and active when the royal *genealogia* was being conceptualized.[79]

Interestingly, when the so-called Astronomer wrote his biography of Louis the Pious, he suggested that Wala was a potential rival to Louis upon the death of Charlemagne in 814.[80] The fear that he might plot against Louis was immediately assuaged, the biographer continued, when Wala hurried to submit himself to Louis, but the incident still raises an interesting issue. Wala was Charlemagne's first cousin, and in spite of probable concubines in his immediate ancestry, the Astronomer expected his readers to recognize him as a plausible focus of a sinister plot. By the middle of the ninth century, therefore, there was at least some sense that everyone connected in the male line to Pippin the Short and Charlemagne might be a potential king, the same attitude Brunhildis had demonstrated in regard to Merovingian boys over two centuries earlier: this even though Wala's father, Bernard, as Pippin's half brother, had never taken part in any of the papal blessings and was in no way a product of Pippin's "loins." The deliberate effort to create a Carolingian *gens*, therefore, as one that began in the seventh century and included all the descendants of Pippin of Herstal, was beginning to be accepted by the time of Charlemagne's grandsons, ironically to such an extent that it could sometimes create dangerous confusion.

The Carolingians and the Merovingians

All of the efforts discussed so far, to construct some kind of coherent Carolingian genealogy in the late eighth and early ninth centuries, had one point in common: the Carolingians were different from the Merovingians. But some Carolingians themselves seem to have been conflicted as to whether to reject the Merovingians as a dynasty best forgotten or to present themselves as the new (and undoubtedly improved) Merovingians. By the time Einhard wrote, the consensus among Carolingian publicists seems to have been to ridicule the descendants of Clovis—if an author saw fit to mention them at all. But during the three generations between the coronation of Pippin and the time of Einhard, there were several efforts by the kings themselves to identify themselves with the previous dynasty.

Most obvious, of course, is Charlemagne's choice of the names Clovis and Clothar (Louis and Lothar) for the twin sons born to him not long after he became sole king of the Franks. These names clearly identified his lineage with that of the first Christian Merovingian king and that king's oldest son. His daughter Chrotildis appears similarly to have been named for Clotildis, Clovis's queen.[81] Interestingly, Paul the Deacon, who tried to keep the Merovingians as far out of his account of the Arnulfings as possible, did mention Charlemagne's twin sons, but he spelled the name now known as Louis as *Lodobich*, whereas he had called Clovis *Chlodoveus*, perhaps in an effort to separate what Charlemagne himself tried to bring together.[82]

Another indication of the Carolingians identifying themselves with the previous dynasty is the choice of St.-Remi of Reims as the burial place for King Carloman, Charlemagne's brother. No one in his family had been buried there before, and Carloman did not even die there, but his request to be buried there, accompanied by a generous gift to the church of Reims, seems a conscious effort to forge a connection with the saint who had baptized Clovis three centuries earlier.[83] Carloman died only a short time before the birth of his twin nephews with their Merovingian names, so clearly Clovis was on the minds of both Charlemagne and Carloman. A further connection between the Carolingians and Reims was established when Louis the Pious had the pope come there to give him the imperial crown rather than going to Rome; this was the first of what later became regular coronations of French kings at Reims.[84] The Carolingian dynasty might have deposed the Merovingians, but they could not reject everything associated with the first Frankish royal line.

These efforts to create connections between Merovingians and Carolingians might have been symbolic only of the transfer of rule from one line to another, but they could also have been meant as an assertion that the Carolingians actually had Merovingian ancestry—a possibility indeed made explicit in a *genealogia* composed in the early ninth century. This version of the emperor's ancestry relied on Paul the Deacon as far back as Bishop Arnulf, but then gave Arnulf a father and a paternal grandfather, the grandfather being identified as of senatorial *genus* and as having married a Merovingian princess.[85] In an even more elaborate version produced slightly later, the senatorial grandfather is given several brothers, including Agiulf, bishop of Metz (fl. c. 600).[86] The very differences among all these accounts suggest that even in the ninth century there was still a scramble to create a canonical version of how the Carolingian line ascended to authority—as a hereditary line of fathers and sons.

This inclination of the Carolingians to make themselves more like the Merovingians than their publicists suggested they were is perhaps most clearly evident in the constant divisions of the realm. These divisions, which caused all sorts of political trouble when some brothers were excluded or others felt they had not been given their fair share, have also proved irritating to modern scholars, who have always assumed that a single, centralized monarchy would have been the preferred model.[87] But division of rule had been a constant among the Merovingians,[88] and from the beginning of the Carolingian dynasty's royal rule, all sons—or at least all capable, legitimate sons—shared in kingship. Charles Martel made his sons Carloman and Pippin the Short co-heirs as mayors of the palace in 741. Pippin the Short made both his sons Charlemagne and Carloman kings. Charlemagne and Louis the Pious ended up as sole kings, but that was essentially an accident. The sons of Louis the Pious fought each other ruthlessly—but one cannot help but conclude that they would have done the same if Lothar I had been named sole heir. At the death of Louis the Pious, the Carolingian dynasty had ruled the Franks for close to a century, and family members had internalized the same conviction as members of the Merovingian dynasty had held: all men born to the family were entitled to be kings.

Interestingly, when the Arnulfings had been mayors of the palace, there had been little sense that siblings were co-equals. If one brother took the office, then other brothers were excluded—or at best found a different king to serve. The only example in the Arnulfing line of brothers serving peacefully together as mayors of the palace was the sons of Charles Martel. But this is atypical, for there was no king: Charles Martel, though not king himself, acted like a king in dividing the Frankish *regna*, according to Fredegar's continuator.[89] Being a king was thus different from being a mayor of the palace: now brothers could be co-equals. The idea that only one son would inherit changed once family members became kings. Being a king meant that every relative was royal as well—even ones like Bernard and Wala.

It should thus be clear that the Carolingian dynasty, the way that it was presented by Einhard and accepted for the next twelve hundred years, is a product of creative memory. Many of the details that modern scholars have taken for granted as firmly grounded parts of the story, such as descent from Bishop Arnulf of Metz or even the deposition by Pippin the Short of the last member of the Merovingian dynasty, are curiously absent from some contemporary accounts. Chroniclers' pruning of the family tree, sometimes silently, sometimes with sunny but dubious suggestions of how Carolingian relatives departed the picture, indicate that their purpose was never to give a complete list of Charlemagne's ancestors. Paul the Deacon told the story of the paternal ancestors of Pippin of Herstal and the annalist of Metz the story of this Pippin's maternal ancestors, but Einhard passed in silence over anyone ancestral to Pippin. Einhard vehemently insisted how little the Merovingians had deserved to be kings, even while Charlemagne and others at his court attempted to create imagined ties with the Merovingian lineage, the lineage that the descendants of Pippin of Herstal themselves seem to have taken for the model of how they ought to organize and conceptualize their own family. Saints had always been malleable, changing to meet the changing needs of the present. The example of the Carolingian dynasty shows that ancestors could be equally malleable.

Chapter 8

Western Monasteries and the Carolingians

The publicists of the Carolingian court, as discussed in Chapter 6, sought to portray these anointed kings as great Christian leaders. As part of their program, they sought to distinguish the Carolingians from their predecessors by suggesting that the Christian world of late Merovingian Gaul was decaying and corrupt, requiring the strong reforming hand of a new dynasty. For example, Alcuin, one of Charlemagne's chief advisors, wrote around 800 a *vita* of Willibrord, missionary to Frisia a century earlier. Here Pippin of Herstal urges Willibrord to exterminate the "thorns of idolatry" and plant the "most pure seed of the word of God," and sends him to Rome for a blessing. Charles Martel in turn has Willibrord baptize his son Pippin, whom the saint prophesies would "devoutly spread the Christian religion in his realm."[1] The Arnulfing line was thus identified with the extirpation of paganism and the establishment of the true faith, in the context of Roman orthodoxy. The Merovingian kings who held the throne during Willibrord's life were not even mentioned.

This retrospective effort to portray the Merovingian church as in disarray was a great success. Scholars have long accepted the Carolingians' increased control over the church as a positive development, for Frankish monasticism and for good government itself. The Carolingians are seen as reforming both decayed monasteries and a church structure that had been inappropriately taken over by lax bishops, due to the weakness of the final Merovingian kings.[2] Some monks, at least two or three hundred years later, looked back on the Carolingian era as a golden age, when Charlemagne himself founded and endowed communities of monks.[3] Implicit in both the modern and this high medieval view is the assumption that late Merovingian churches lacked the internal discipline or the religious commitment to survive without royal patronage. Here, however, I shall suggest that by the end of the eighth century, if many churches were in need of reform, much of the responsibility for their difficulties must be attributed to Charlemagne's family members, not their Merovingian predecessors.

The Modern Image of Merovingian and Carolingian Monasticism

The memory of the Merovingians as essentially pagan had its greatest success in the nineteenth and twentieth centuries. There was long a topos that if not for the intervention of the Irish abbot Columbanus at the end of the sixth century, Christianity itself might not have survived long enough to be revived by the Carolingians.[4] The Anglo-Saxon missionary Boniface wrote to the pope in 742 that "ecclesiastical religion" had been on the decline for some "sixty or seventy years."[5] His description of the decline in the Frankish church has often been taken as emblematic of a whole sad history of the monasteries before the rise of the Carolingians.[6] More recently, however, the religiosity of Merovingian Gaul has begun to be rehabilitated, and "pagan practices" discussed by writers of the period are now seen primarily as literary devices. Scholars now recognize that the image of a flourishing Christian culture in late antiquity, essentially destroyed by fierce Frankish invaders who reduced the churches to misery, is false, a product of romanticizing by Renaissance humanists.[7]

Yet many have continued to assume that Carolingian accomplishments necessarily included a thorough overhaul of the monastic life. The image of a ninth-century age of ecclesiastical growth and reform is so strong that it has been considered very unusual, for example, that the monastery of St.-Wandrille appears more vigorous and successful in the eighth century than the ninth.[8] Any difficulties that churches may have experienced before the middle of the eighth century are routinely attributed to the last Merovingians. Any difficulties from the 840s onward are attributed to the Vikings or to the decline of imperial authority under Charlemagne's grandsons. The age in between is assumed, almost without discussion, to have been a high point for monasticism.

But the difficulties of the Frankish churches under Charles Martel and Pippin the Short demonstrate that eighth-century problems cannot merely be blamed on the Merovingian kings. Similarly, a wholesale destruction of the organized Christian life by Viking raiders is an exaggeration, even though it is indisputable that many houses, from St.-Wandrille on the lower Seine to

Montier-en-Der on the borders of Lorraine, suffered devastating attacks. But Frankish monasteries had been facing serious challenges well before the Vikings came rowing up the rivers, and it trivializes the difficulties they experienced in the ninth and tenth centuries to treat these as the almost inevitable results of the weakening of Carolingian central government.[9]

Between the time of the Merovingian kings and that of the grandsons of Charlemagne, scholars have almost uniformly described the relationship between the kings and the Frankish church as a necessary program of reform. For example, when scholars note that during the eighth century most monasteries in central Gaul fell into Arnulfing hands or that Charlemagne and his successors routinely chose bishops and abbots who would be reliable administrators of royal interests, this practice has been described as a constitutive element of Carolingian good government.[10] Some even attempt to give a positive twist to the well-documented Carolingian stinginess with gifts to monasteries or conclude that the kings must have been more generous to religious houses than the sources suggest.[11]

I shall demonstrate instead that Arnulfing rulers, from Charles Martel and Pippin the Short to Charlemagne and Louis the Pious, treated monasteries as royal possessions, from which the kings could obtain land and revenue, rather than primarily as holy places that kings should support. The freedom these monasteries sought was not the independence from secular meddling in elections and liturgical issues embraced by the Gregorian Reform; rather, it was an end to having their property taken away and lands devastated. Although the royal practice of making the churches support the kings, rather than the other way around, has been taken as a marker of Carolingian success,[12] I shall argue that in many ways the rise of the Carolingians did not contribute to the regularity and well-being of Frankish churches but was instead a disaster for them.

Charles Martel and Church Property

The era of Charles Martel (d. 741) is a generally recognized turning point, in which monasteries suffered losses of both property and prestige. The common scholarly assumption is that because Charles held power during the reigns of the last Merovingian kings, the latter need to bear much of the blame. But the evidence does not support this conclusion.

The eighth century was of course a violent period, especially marked by the Saracen incursions into the Frankish realm, which not surprisingly took a toll on the churches. Bishop Betto of Langres asked Louis the Pious in 814 to confirm him in his possessions and authority in his diocese, saying that all his records had been destroyed during the Saracen attacks. According to the twelfth-century chronicler of Bèze, the whole Burgundian region was devastated by the Saracens in 731.[13] Charles Martel essentially campaigned every year, between his long struggle against the Muslims, whom he stopped at Poitiers in 732[14]—although, less famously, he also had to fight them in Gothia five years later—and his wars against the Frisians, Bavarians, and Saxons, as well as against his Frankish rivals. The "Annales Petaviani" found the most remarkable feature of the year 740 was that it was a year without a military campaign.[15] In the next generation, Pippin the Short went to war against Waiofar, duke of Aquitaine, and during his campaign laid waste to the countryside, including houses of monks. "Many monasteries were depopulated," commented the continuator of the *Chronica* of Fredegar, without emphasis.[16] Such devastation had become too commonplace to treat as an aberration.

But the ongoing wars cannot bear the entire blame for the disruptions churches suffered. The question is whether the mayor of the palace played an active role in this overall decline. Scholars always used to think so. The image of Charles Martel in much of the twentieth century was shaped by what might almost be termed an urban legend: Charles won at Poitiers because he seized church property, "secularized" it, and distributed it to his warrior vassals— thereby creating feudalism—allowing them to use their new lands to raise horses, develop the stirrup, and defeat the Muslims through heavy cavalry charges. Like all good urban legends, this one has possessed remarkable staying power,[17] even though scholars have long pointed out that stirrups first appeared in the West only a great deal later, that heavy cavalry had nothing to do with the victory at Poitiers, that vassals in the eighth century were generally lowborn dependents, not knights, and that even if Charles redistributed land, it was as gifts, not fiefs.[18]

More recently, there has been a concerted effort to rehabilitate Charles, now freed of the label of feudalism's founder. Scholars have argued that in his own time he was well regarded for his military triumphs and that the vision of Charles as seizing church property to give to laymen only really began in the later ninth century.[19] It has even been asserted that what was later considered confiscation of church property was a perfectly legal appropriation by kings and their agents because church property was all really royal property.[20] Such touching stories as the one in the late eighth-century "Vita Leutfredi," in which Charles Martel appears as "nobly governing the republic," a pious prince concerned for his soul who prayed fervently for the healing of his son, would seem to support a new image of a conscientious and religious leader.[21]

I would argue, however, that recent efforts at rehabilitation may have gone too far and that Charles really did seize church property in a manner that created a sharp contrast with his Merovingian predecessors, and churchmen were not happy about it. Without attempting to resurrect eighth-century feudalism and the stirrup as subjects of inquiry, there is still plenty of contemporary evidence for Charles Martel and his successors taking the church's possessions—which cannot easily be explained away as a legal exercise of power—and then either giving it to laymen or keeping it.

Charles seized secular property as well as church property, of course. Shortly after his victory at Poitiers, he turned to Burgundy and the Lyonnais, where, according to Fredegar's continuator, many men had become "rebellious and disloyal" (*rebelles et infideles*). He then granted the Lyonnais to his followers (*fidelibus*) and had these grants judicially confirmed.[22] Of course, the kings of a century earlier had also seized property from those who turned against them. What was different about Charles is that he did not draw a distinction between seizing church property and seizing the property of rebellious secular lords, whereas the Merovingians had been careful to do so (Chapter 11).

Difficulties for the churches under Charles Martel are evident in the letters of Boniface, who worked beyond the Rhine with both the papacy's mandate and Charles's intermittent support.[23] Boniface himself saw Charles as a leader who routinely and improperly seized church property. In a letter to King Aethelbald of Mercia, Boniface announced the death of Charles Martel, a "destroyer of many monasteries," who "transferred ecclesiastical goods to his own use."[24]

Boniface's negative comments are echoed in another letter that he wrote to England. Although he mentions no one by name, he certainly suggests that he is alluding to Charles Martel (dead for six years by the time he wrote) or to his son.

> Any layman, whether emperor or king or someone exercising secular power as an official (*prefectus*) or count, any of these who violently seizes a monastery from a bishop, abbot, or abbess, and who begins to rule over the monks in place of the abbot, and takes the house's property (*pecunia*), which was bought with the blood of Christ: such a layman is one of those whom the Fathers of old named a thief and a sacrilege and a

murderer of the poor, the devil's own wolf entering the sheepfold of Christ; and may he be damned with the most powerful bonds of anathema before the judgment throne of Christ.[25]

This is a powerful statement. The triple mention of Christ, as sacrifice and good shepherd and final judge, leaves no doubt of Boniface's position against someone who would take church property.

Boniface must have had specific individuals in mind; even a cranky old man would not fulminate like this against merely hypothetical cases. The Byzantine emperor played no role in Francia in the 740s, and the last Merovingian kings were firmly under Arnulfing control. Boniface's anger was turned on someone who exercised "secular power" as a royal official, which could mean only Pippin the Short or his late father, Charles Martel. For him the Arnulfings stole church property as "the devil's own wolves."

A contemporary and equally vivid portrait of Charles Martel appeared in a mid-eighth-century *vita* of Bishop Eucharius of Orléans. In a vision, the bishop saw Prince Charles "tortured in hell." To check the vision's veracity, the tomb of Charles Martel was opened (significantly by Boniface according to the story), and a horrible dragon emerged. Now Eucherius died a few years before Charles, so he could not actually have seen the tomb, but the *vita* explained the defiled grave as judgment for Charles's taking church property. "He had done cruel violence to a bishop" (Eucherius), and had also "usurped the property of other churches" and had then given what he "usurped" to "laymen and counts."[26]

Charles thus emerges from eighth-century sources as a man who may have had admirers but who also seized property that the churches considered theirs. If one separates this out from the old debates over the "origins of feudalism," it may seem almost trivial. After all, many contemporary dukes also appropriated ecclesiastical property for their own use. Even if Charles despoiled some churches, one might assert, he had no *systematic* policy of doing so.[27] But this was not trivial, for it marked a striking shift in those who ruled Francia. The Merovingian kings had rarely taken church property for themselves. The Arnulfings frequently did so. In the sixth and seventh centuries, the aristocratic enemies of monastic property had been the local or regional lords, not the kings.[28] The Arnulfings became kings in fact if not in name with Charles Martel, but Charles Martel did not behave like a king in the Merovingian sense, at least not when it came to church property. He behaved like a magnate.

Back in the 580s, King Guntram had had to resolve a messy political situation after the murder of his brother Chilperic I, including the problem that Chilperic's *potentes* had taken the opportunity to appropriate ecclesiastical goods. King Guntram ordered it all restored. According to Gregory of Tours, although Chilperic's followers had seized church property, he had not done so himself.[29] Considering that Gregory was no supporter of Chilperic, his distinction between the king's actions and those of his magnates carries special weight.

Magnate behavior toward monasteries is further illustrated by the seventh-century Duke Chatichus/Adalric of Alsace (of the lineage now known as the Etichonids; see Chapter 10). According to the *vita* of Abbot Germanus of Grandval, this duke began to "oppress" the monastery's men as soon as he took office. The abbot tried to resist this "enemy of God and Truth" and ended up martyred by the duke's men.[30] A similar example, a generation later, is provided by Duke Drogo of Champagne, Charles Martel's older half brother.[31] He took a villa belonging to the monastery of Tussonval, a dependency of St.-Denis. The abbot of Tussonval claimed Drogo had "stolen" or "devastated" all his house's property, including "serfs, flocks, and everything else." Significantly, Drogo was forced to yield his claim by the Merovingian king.[32]

This king acted in 697, a decade after the Arnulfings had supposedly taken firm control both of the Frankish realm and of the Merovingian kings. Now Childebert IV issued a royal edict rejecting Drogo's claim to Tussonval's property. He recalled that his own father, Theoderic III, had confirmed the villa to Tussonval in the first place, thus reinforcing the connection between Merovingian kings and well-endowed monasteries. Drogo made a half-hearted defense, saying that his brother-in-law had obtained the property from Tussonval, and it had then passed to Drogo, but he had no written records to support this claim and was not believed. Instead the king ordered him to repair all the damages he had caused and stated that no one in the future should try to take this property.

This edict indicates clearly the differences between Merovingian and Arnulfing attitudes toward church property: something to be protected versus something to be appropriated. The new race of kings felt none of the concern that Gregory of Tours had attributed to Guntram, of a relationship between the welfare of churches and of the kingdom. As further discussed in Chapter 11, the Merovingian kings, at least most of the time, had considered it best to remain in the good graces of the monasteries and their saints. These kings were frequently high-handed toward bishops, choosing their own (often unsuitable) candidates, as Gregory of Tours said Clothar II chose Badegisel, his mayor of the palace, for the see of Le Mans. But they were much less likely to show the same preemptory attitude toward monasteries and their property.[33] Monasteries in the sixth and seventh centuries were both uncommon and holy in a way that bishoprics were not. The rise of the Carolingians put Frankish monasteries in the same category as everyone else, the category of those who had to fear the wrath of the king.

The Call for Reform and the Problem of *Precaria*

In spite of Boniface's distrust of Charles Martel, there was one Arnulfing whom he believed to have potential for good: Carloman, Charles Martel's oldest son. Boniface and Carloman jointly organized councils that both they and modern historians have called "reforming" councils;[34] the conclusion is generally drawn that there was a great deal in Merovingian monasticism needing reform. But this is the wrong conclusion. If one examines what was criticized in these councils, one finds not corrupt or semipagan monasteries (much less lax Merovingian royal leadership) but rather bishops who were ineffective Christian rulers, allowing their flocks to go astray. The heresy and paganism that Boniface feared was a danger for the lay population, not for monks.[35]

Boniface argued that a council was necessary because negligent bishops allowed people to wear amulets, consult auguries, or celebrate January 1. Quoting Caesarius of Arles from two centuries earlier, he said that it availed nothing to act like a Christian, praying, giving alms, and attending church, if one followed such sacrilegious practices.[36] In particular, Boniface maintained that the Frankish bishops were no longer taking a leadership role. Writing in 742, he described the final decades of the seventh century and the first half of the eighth as a time of serious institutional weakness. The last Frankish synod, he said, had been held some eighty years earlier, that is, in the 660s.[37] In the years since, when the bishops did not hold synods, they also "did not have archbishops, and did not found or renovate churches." Worst of all, many episcopal sees were taken by "greedy laymen" or, at best, by corrupt clerics who turned them to "secular" uses. The answer for Boniface was a synod, to be held by Carloman, "duke of the Franks." The bishops could not be trusted to hold a synod on their own.[38]

His letters would date the start of ecclesiastical decline to about the same time as Pippin of Herstal was consolidating his power. Boniface's comments may have been somewhat rhetorical, but he was right that under the Arnulfing mayors of the palace the Frankish bishops rarely if ever held synods.[39] Other evidence suggests a break in many episcopal lists in the last quarter of the seventh century, especially in regions of Arnulfing conquest, and that a higher proportion of the episcopate was composed of laymen or of pluralists than had been the case in the sixth century. It should thus not be surprising that one of the last Merovingian-era councils was devoted to the problem of bishops who lived and behaved like secular lords.[40] The situation of the monasteries, however, was not addressed at these councils—except when the Arnulfings wanted monastic property. Then Charles Martel and his successors were described not as the solution but rather as a key part of the problem.

Boniface's synods have to be considered in the context of *precaria*. These were grants that would now be considered extended leases, by which a church made a temporary donation, generally recorded in writing, to a layman, most commonly for his lifetime, in return for an annual payment. Although there are some similarities between *precaria* and conditional grants in late Roman law, the medieval form appears to have developed only in the eighth century.[41] *Precaria* and their relationship to the seizure of ecclesiastical goods were first addressed in the synod over which Carloman presided in 742 (a year after the death of Charles Martel), a synod attended by Boniface and the bishops of Austrasia.

This council was concerned with both religious belief and church discipline. It rejected various practices labeled as pagan and forbade priests from being fornicators or adulterers, carrying arms, or hunting with dogs. But among these items of church discipline the council began by ordaining that a synod be held every year from then on and that at these synods "property of which the churches had been defrauded should be restored and returned to them."[42]

The question of restoring property to the church would not have been such a central one—this statement was indeed in the first canon of the synod's decisions—had not churches at the time been losing what they considered rightfully theirs. And the problem was centered on the Arnulfings themselves. In a second synod, held at Estinnes the following year, Carloman admitted as much. The canons began with fulminations against adulterous or fornicating clerics and ordered that monasteries follow Benedict's Rule, but they also addressed *precaria* that monasteries and other churches had been making. Specifically, they had made them to Carloman.[43]

Precaria in themselves, of course, should not be considered automatically as a sign of secularized church property (any more than they should be treated as proto-fiefs). Bishops and abbots throughout the early Middle Ages made temporary grants, sometimes to a layman whose friendship they sought to cultivate, often in order to generate income from a piece of property located an uncomfortable distance from the church.[44] There are also instances of a precarial grant functioning as a *post obitum* gift: a layman granted a piece of property to a church and then received it back, *in precaria*, for his lifetime.

But precarial grants were readily subject to abuse because they involved the granting of ecclesiastical property for extended periods to a layman, with little way to enforce its return.[45] In discussing precarial grants at his synod of Estinnes, Carloman doubtless addressed practices that had grown up under his father, as well as in his own Austrasian territories. That precarial grants were one of the first issues churchmen wanted to present to the prince, at a synod called specifically to address ecclesiastical abuses, certainly indicates that this was a real problem in the eighth century.

At the council, Carloman argued that the *precaria* he received from Frankish churches were completely justifiable: they were intended to support the army in a time of war and invasions.[46] Further, he promised to pay a *solidus*—twelve pennies—a year for each of the households on the land he had received and to return the property if the precarial grant was a source of poverty (*paupertas*) for the churches. The provision for restitution in case of poverty certainly suggests that such precarial grants could be a real hardship—and also contains a hint that these grants were not always made voluntarily.[47] Finally, the synod made it clear that a precarial grant should not be made in perpetuity but would at most last for a generation: when one of the householders died, for whom Carloman had been paying an annual *solidus*, that property would revert to the church. The precarial grant could still be renewed if the *princeps*—Carloman—judged it necessary, but it would have to be written up as a new agreement.

An example of a problematic precarial grant is provided by the bishopric of Le Mans. In the 720s the count Rothgar and his son had taken over the bishopric, apparently with the cooperation of Charles Martel. Both were laymen, but according to the *Actus* of the bishops of Le Mans, written a century later, "the people" clamored for a real bishop, so Rothgar made his unlearned second son bishop—he was at least a cleric. Under this bishop, Gauziolenus, property belonging to the bishopric began to be granted to laymen *in precaria*. One of Gauziolenus's surviving charters in fact specifies that he made such a grant "at the orders" (*per jussionem*) of King Pippin.[48] This is just the sort of precarial grant that became such a source of concern at Carloman's councils.

And sometimes ecclesiastical property was simply taken without even the pretext of a precarial grant. In 746 Carloman restored to the twin abbeys of Stavelot and Malmedy some property that the abbot said Pippin of Herstal (his grandfather) had originally given to the houses by testament but that had improperly and unjustly ended up in Carloman's own hands, *malo ordine* and *iniuste*. Carloman said in his charter for Stavelot-Malmedy that the abbot had produced Pippin's testament and that he himself had read it and found it *verum*.[49] Because Stavelot-Malmedy had been one of the Pippinids' earliest monastic foundations, established by the mayor of the palace Grimoald I in the seventh century with the assistance of King Sigibert III, it is striking that within a generation of its foundation family members were appropriating its property.

Carloman's recognition of the problem of church property in lay hands, along with his synods, have made him look to modern scholars like at least a potential restorer of church property.[50] But he was not typical of the Arnulfings, and his sudden decision to head off to Rome and enter a monastery put an end to any project of church reform. Significantly the son of Charles Martel himself saw deep-seated difficulties in the Frankish church, even though he was unable to deal with them beyond restoring some property under his own control that appears to have been taken by Charles Martel on the death of his own father.

The Frankish churches continued to remember the Arnulfings as those who appropriated ecclesiastical goods. Around 780 the bishop of Marseille was able to recover some of his church's property by successfully asserting in Charlemagne's court that it had been secularized by Charles Martel, who had given it to a powerful layman whose family still held it.[51] In fact this church may have lost the property under Pippin the Short, rather than Charles Martel, but it is suggestive that the bishop blamed Charles—and if the problem actually arose under Pippin, then that indicates that succeeding Arnulfings continued to confiscate church property. Pippin was perfectly capable of generosity to monasteries—he made gifts to "churches, monasteries, and the poor" when he felt himself dying.[52] But he, like his father Charles Martel and brother Carloman, also seized monastic property, even after becoming king.

None of Charlemagne's own capitularies on ecclesiastical issues addressed a need to restore church property, indicating that for him such restoration was not a priority.[53] Yet the problem of property appropriated by kings or royal agents eventually became such a concern that there developed a specific procedure to report it. A formula drawn up in the second half of the eighth century records the proper way to complain to the king that one of his agents had improperly seized a church's possessions.[54] The formula appears based on a real complaint from the abbot of Murbach, issued shortly after Charlemagne became king in 768. In it, the abbot complains to the king that the royal agents had despoiled the monastery of goods acquired through pious gifts. The problem was clearly both common and serious enough that it was worth creating a formula to use when it occurred.[55] Another eighth-century formula insisted wistfully that precarial grants should be for one lifetime only.[56]

Charlemagne himself, in a council at Herstal in 779, made a distinction between *precaria* granted "voluntarily" (*spontaneo voluntate*) and *precaria* granted at the king's command (*de verbo regis*).[57] The clear sense was that the king could order churches to grant *precaria* to his followers even if they would not have done so voluntarily, and the monasteries had to obey. Soon someone making a gift of property to a church would anticipate receiving it back again, and indeed would hope for even more. As Charlemagne commented at the 813 Council of Tours, in the context of a church's "rectors" granting gifts back to the donors *in nomine precarie*, "Hardly anyone gives his goods to a church, without receiving back as much as he gave, or indeed two or three times as much."[58]

Precarial grants continued to be an issue for the Frankish churches in the following generations, as can be seen in two charters copied into the *Gesta* of Bishop Aldric of Le Mans. Their authenticity might be questioned, as they form part of the Le Mans forgeries, but that does not reduce their usefulness here: either they were two authentic statements on *precaria* from the 830s or else they were statements that were carefully prepared a decade or two later, and thus included only details that the forger's readers would readily accept.[59]

In the first of these, one Bavo asked for some property of the cathedral of Le Mans to be given to him *in precaria*, which indeed it was, by direct "order" of Emperor Louis the Pious. Although Bavo agreed to pay the bishop twenty-five solidi a year, this was not the property's real value, for half a dozen years later, according to the second charter, he began to think of the salvation of the soul and worry that it had been alienated from the church "through his greed." The property was further identified as being held *in beneficio* from the emperor. Authentic or specially confected, the charters give a lucid picture of ecclesiastical attitudes toward precarial grants: they were greedy appropriations of ecclesiastical possessions, and the Carolingian royal family was deeply involved.

Charlemagne, Louis the Pious, and Church Order

Just as the councils of the 740s have been taken as indicating a need for monastic reform, so Charlemagne's "Admonitio generalis," with its statement that it was crucial to "correct what is erroneous," has been assumed to show that much in Frankish monasticism needed correcting.[60] But the "Admonitio" was addressed to secular clerics and to laymen as much as to monks and had more to say about faulty Latin and proper Sabbath observance than about corrupt monastic practices. Many of its canons are derived from a list of canons sent to Charlemagne by Pope Hadrian I[61] and thus are more illustrative of what the Roman pontiff thought important than actual conditions in Francia.

The major advance in Carolingian-era monasticism to which scholars normally point is that monasteries were all ordered to follow the Benedictine Rule. Benedict of Aniane had promoted the Rule in the eighth century; it was certainly observed at some Frankish houses in his time but generally in a "mixed" form. This "second Benedict" interested the Carolingians in promulgating Benedict of Nursia's rule as the sole Rule of their realm, as Charlemagne indeed ordered at the 813 Council of Chalon-sur-Saône.[62] Louis the Pious again ordered adherence to the Benedictine Rule for monasteries and gave canons a semimonastic Rule of their own at his council at Aachen in 816.[63] This effort to establish uniformity of monastic rule has often been taken as another sign of monastic debility before the age of Charlemagne.[64]

But a diversity of Rules need not imply monasticism in disarray. Similarly, Charlemagne's orders, reflected in his "Capitulare de villis,"[65] that monasteries carry out systematic surveys of their property should not suggest monastic decadence and in fact can be given a more sinister interpretation. The "Capitulare de villis" was not the first effort to make churches spell out what they owned. Pippin the Short had ordered the churches of his realm to create a *descriptio* of their holdings, an injunction that Charlemagne repeated. At St.-Wandrille, the *Gesta* of the abbots reports that in 787 a complete enumeration of the abbey's dependent *mansi* was made at Charlemagne's orders.[66] Someone who considered that a monastery's property was really his own would have been very interested in having that property fully inventoried.

For there is plenty of evidence that Charlemagne and his heirs controlled ecclesiastical property. When Count Hugh of Tours made an exchange of property with the monastery of Wissembourg in 820, the agreement had to be approved by the emperor, Louis the Pious, for the monastery's property was said to be "in his hands."[67] Wissembourg has a large number of seventh- and eighth-century documents, and yet in none of them had royal permission been required as it now was. In the next generation, Louis the Pious and Queen Judith granted the monastery of Ferrières a cell, St.-Josse, which the monks had Charles the Bald confirm in 841. But just a few years later Charles gave the same cell to one of his counts, explaining himself to the monks by saying that he did so out of "some necessity." Abbot Lupus, understandably distraught and referring to the count as a man of "dangerous greed," tried to remind the king that it had been his own mother's wish that Ferrières have the cell and that the king himself had confirmed it, but the best Lupus could obtain from Charles was a promise that whenever the count died or decided to give up the cell—because the king gave him something else instead—he would ensure that it returned to the monks.[68]

Whereas under the Merovingians a monastery might be considered a royal monastery if it enjoyed special privileges from the kings and queens, in the Carolingian era the giving of gifts went the other way: monasteries were expected to make gifts *to* the kings. This expectation was spelled out at Aachen in 819, when Louis the Pious ordered twenty-five Frankish monasteries to give him *dona*—an order also extended to dozens more monasteries in the Midi and east of the Rhine.[69] For each Louis indicated whether each owed him *dona*, *dona* plus military service, or merely prayers for the royal family. Even here it was clear: those prayers were *owed*, not just something the monks were glad to offer.

The military service was indeed expected not just of monasteries but of bishoprics. A generation later Hincmar of Reims tried to justify churches' property holdings—which he recognized was contrary to the New Testament account of early Christians getting rid of all their possessions—in part by noting that Frankish churches were obligated to provide military service to the state. This obligation cost a church, he estimated, a fifth of its income to pay for its soldiers, because they were not given a stipend "from public resources."[70] Such military service seemed perfectly normal to Hincmar; it was what the Carolingians required.

The monasteries Louis listed as owing *dona* were not all of the monasteries in the Empire, because there are certainly others known to have had monks at the time. In the Burgundy–southern Champagne region (further detailed in Appendix I), the list included only Ferrières, Nesle, Moûtier-St.-Jean, Flavigny, St.-Seine, and Melun. It may well be significant that the list included none of the monasteries that Queen Balthildis had called the "senior basilicas" of Gaul, St.-Denis of Paris, St.-Germain of Auxerre, St.-Médard of Soissons, St.-Pierre-le-Vif of Sens, St.-Aignan of Orléans, and St.-Martin of Tours (Marmoutier). For her, houses were to be listed as receiving immunities from royal interference; for Louis the Pious, the houses on *his* list were there to serve the king.

Curiously, the imperial demand for gifts has sometimes been interpreted as part of the monastic reform movement, as related to the establishment of the Rule of Benedict of Nursia at Frankish monasteries. But the houses on the list already housed regular monks. Many had received privileges from bishops and sometimes from the Carolingian kings. Regularity and royal privilege did not, however, result in freedom from oversight in the ninth century; instead they meant royal control.

Exemptions and Protection

The uneasy relationship between the Carolingians and the Frankish church is illustrated by their use of privileges of exemption. The Merovingians had used such exemptions as well (as discussed in Chapter 11), but the institution changed fundamentally during the eighth century. Scholars used to take the granting of royal exemptions as a sign of weakness, as one more indication that the Merovingian line was debilitated. But more recent analyses have revealed that exemptions were a sign of strength, not weakness.[71] Kings and queens prohibited anyone from invading monasteries as a sign both of their piety and of their power, and because the prayers of grateful monks, as the *vita* of Queen Balthildis stated, would help assure the kingdom's peace and stability.[72]

Here a significant development is the appearance of Carolingian "protection" of monasteries (*tuitio*), the word "protection" carrying somewhat ominous overtones. Grants of exemption changed from prohibitions against entry—by either the king himself or his agents—to a rather more paternalistic type of protection, where it was clear that a monastery was safe only as long as it was firmly under the royal eye.[73] Indeed, this "protection" might better be termed control.[74] It was in many ways the opposite of a Merovingian-era exemption. Earlier kings had promised that neither they nor their agents would intervene; now the Carolingians promised intervention, even if supposedly for a monastery's own good.[75]

This new form of protection began innocuously enough with a seventh-century incident. A Merovingian king was concerned about the "illegal attacks by evil men" on a monastery and placed it under the protection of his mayor of the palace, *sub mundeburde vel defensione*. The royal charter does not survive, but Marculf used it as a model in his formulary.[76] The charter that Marculf used may be the earliest example of this new kind of protection, suggesting—as does its specific mention of the *maiores domi nostri*—that it was an innovation of the Arnulfings themselves.[77]

The concept that mayors of the palace would exercise such "protection" was immediately taken up, even without an illegal attack by evil men. For example, Pippin of Herstal and his wife confirmed Willibrord's foundation of Echternach in 706 by saying that they took the house "under our defense and that of our heirs."[78] The couple went on to say that after Willibrord died the monks might elect a new abbot—as long as he was faithful (*fidelis*) to Pippin and his heirs, and as long as the house continued under their "protection and defense" (*mundiburdio vel defensione*). The Arnulfings clearly wanted to involve themselves in the house's affairs.[79] This kind of protection quickly replaced the granting of liberties to monasteries that had been the Merovingian norm.

Carolingian privileges conveyed not freedom but control. The *Gesta* of Bishop Aldric of Le Mans speaks explicitly of Pippin the Short taking the monastery of St.-Calais under his *mundeburdo vel tuitione* as a gesture of authority: Pippin did so to keep their house out of the hands of the local bishop.[80] Whether or not Pippin actually used such terms in relation to St.-Calais, a mid-ninth-century author could incorporate these terms into his text and expect his readers to assume that Pippin intended authority and control. In case anyone might somehow miss the point, the author added to the phrase *mundeburdo vel tuitione* the words *vel dominatione*.

This domination of the Frankish churches by the Carolingians was quite real. The same section of the *Gesta* of Bishop Aldric relates how the abbot of St.-Calais was three times summoned before Emperor Louis at Aachen, and three times failed to appear, thus demonstrating according to the author that he was "disobedient and contumacious." This disobedience was enough that Louis ruled against the abbot. The emperor went through the motions of asking those assembled at Aachen, both laymen and clergy, for their opinions, but the decision against someone who had disobeyed an imperial summons was clearly the emperor's. His decision was made with his own "full authority," not "with the consent" of the clergy and laymen present but rather "before" them (*coram illis*).[81]

The author of the *Gesta* found it entirely appropriate that Louis so rule, not simply because his own hero, Aldric, had won, but because he expected his ninth-century audience to take such imperial decisions for granted. The author followed up with a few papal decretals taken from the collections of Isidore of Seville, stating that those who do not answer a repeated summons to court should be ruled against.[82] But the precedent he tried to establish did not in fact work, for the pope's decisions he cited all concerned ecclesiastical courts. His use of examples of ecclesiastical courts to justify the actions of the imperial court is telling. For him there could be no doubt that the emperor could make valid rulings in ecclesiastical cases.

Laymen in Monasteries and Bishoprics

It has long been noted that "lay abbots," that is, laymen who received the revenues from a monastery and directed its affairs, were much more common in the Carolingian than the Merovingian era.[83] The monk Notker, writing a "Life" of Charlemagne three generations after the emperor's death, took it for granted that kings would control monasteries and use these political plums as gifts both to bishops and to laymen. Notker has Charlemagne explain the benefit of such gifts: "With a piece of fiscal property or a manor, with a little abbey or a church, I can make me as good or better a faithful vassal than any count or bishop!"[84] Notker here, as well as equating counts and bishops as royal vassals, has the emperor equate land and churches as suitable gifts for laymen. Both, Notker assumes, were royal property.[85]

Rewarding political allies with the office of abbot was a new practice in the period. If political leaders entered monasteries in the Merovingian period, it was as exiles, tonsured to keep them out of the way; royal councillors and allies did not take monasteries as rewards. The roots of this practice, however, go back to when the Arnulfings were mayors of the palace. When studying the monasteries and bishoprics where they named the abbots or made sure the bishops took the correct political line, scholars have focused on the question of where the Arnulfings and Pippinids had their original seats of power.[86] Yet the authority the family wielded over religious houses reveals much more. It reveals a pattern of controlling ecclesiastical office even before the Arnulfings became kings.

Scholars have often attributed the lower number of lay abbots before the eighth century to a less astute political use of monasteries by the Merovingian dynasty. It has been surprisingly easy to represent the Carolingians' imposition of secular lords onto religious houses as a positive good.[87] Alternately, if the prevalence of lay abbots is seen as due to ninth-century aristocrats seizing power, then they are considered to be in rebellion against state control. In either case, lay abbots are assumed to serve a political function.[88] Thus scholars studying the distribution of abbatial offices to the Carolingians' followers have generally treated this as an exercise in state-building.[89] But if one looks at the appointment of lay abbots from the point of view of the churches, one sees a different picture.

Eigenkirchen, churches closely controlled by laymen, are sometimes considered one of the abuses that the Carolingians had to work against—but in fact this practice became common for the first time only under Charlemagne.[90] In Alsace, for example, in the seventh century great lords had at most put monasteries under the direction of a clerical relative, but in the ninth century the counts acted as abbots themselves.[91] Indeed, the Carolingian kings also held *Eigenkirchen*. For example, Charlemagne became abbot of the Alsatian monastery of Murbach during the 790s.[92] Hugh "the Abbot," of the powerful Welf family, took over many Burgundian monasteries in the middle of the ninth century, usually having been given them by his cousin, Charles the Bald. In Auxerre, he was abbot both of St.-Germain and of St.-Julien—the latter even though it was a house of nuns.[93] Conversely, Lothar II's daughter Gisela became lay abbot of the monastery of Fosses at the end of the ninth century, hers by gift of her cousin Louis the Child—even though she was a woman and it was a male monastery.[94]

The bishopric of Metz, the see of the man whom the Carolingians claimed as their ancestor, remained vacant for twenty-five years, from when Bishop Angilram died in 791 until two years after Charlemagne's death. The best explanation for this long vacancy is that the see was held vacant for Pippin the Hunchback, Charlemagne's oldest but disinherited son. Pippin had rebelled against his father not long after Angilram's death but was allowed to live, though cloistered, finally dying just a few years before the emperor.[95] Even the reestablishment of bishops in the see of Metz had a family aspect: in the 820s, Drogo, half brother of Louis the Pious, was made bishop there, and although the so-called Astronomer said that the "clergy and people" clamored for Drogo and assured his readers that Drogo was following a canonical rule at the time, it is hard to see this "election" as other than royal control of the see.[96]

Charlemagne rewarded some of his most loyal counselors as well as family members by making them abbots or bishops. For example, he appointed a member of his royal court as bishop of Le Mans at the end of the eighth century and, as a great favor, restored to his candidate some of that bishopric's property that he himself had taken.[97] One Hucbertus, called a *magnificus vir*, became under Charlemagne abbot of St.-Marcel of Chalon, a house originally founded and endowed by the Merovingian kings.[98] Alcuin, Charlemagne's trusted advisor and the head of the palace school, was made abbot of Ferrières and of St.-Loup of Troyes by the king around 782; he also served as abbot of St.-Martin of Tours and became abbot of Flavigny a short time later. The author of Alcuin's *vita* tried to excuse this pluralism by saying that God had found him worthy of heading all these houses.[99] After Alcuin died, Flavigny was given to one Apollinaris "as a gift from the emperor" according to the monastery's later chronicle. Apollinaris also headed multiple houses, for he was in addition abbot of Moûtier-St.-Jean and of St.-Bénigne of Dijon.[100]

The so-called Astronomer, writing during the reign of Charles the Bald, took it for granted that Charlemagne and his successors should control the church's most important offices. Referring to Aquitaine, he said that Charlemagne had settled both counts and abbots there, all of them his *vassi*, with a primary duty to serve the king. Similarly, Charlemagne was said to have "tightly bound" all the bishops of the region to young Louis the Pious "in whatever way was available." Bishops' first obedience, the Astronomer assumed, was to their king.[101]

These loyal bishops were given increased authority over Frankish monasteries. Synods from Carloman's forward had treated the bishops as suitable protectors of the monastic life, rather than seeing them as potential threats to the sanctity of that life, as had been the case in the Merovingian period.[102] But if, as often happened, the local bishop was more interested in a monastery's property than in the regularity of its life, then the house could not appeal to the king, as Merovingian monasteries had once done.

To a large extent of course the Carolingians really were concerned about the welfare of the churches of their realm. But while the Merovingians had seen staying well away from the churches and their property as a chief way to guarantee their sanctity, the Carolingians believed that they could best promote Christianity from within the ecclesiastical structure. Louis the Pious's works, according to his biographer, showed that "not only was he a king, but even more so a priest." As a priest, a *sacerdos*, it was entirely appropriate that he ensure that the secular clergy in his *regnum* were thoroughly educated, rather than spending their time in warlike activities, and that monasticism in Aquitaine, which had "fallen into ruin," be restored.[103] There is an ironic contrast here between the young king who becomes a virtual priest, and the real priests who have to be warned against the weapons and the horseback exercises that the biographer had earlier indicated were signs of royal rule.

Passages like these have earned Louis the nickname "the Pious," appearing to distinguish the warrior Charlemagne from his rather weak and priest-ridden son.[104] But such an invidious comparison was not the biographer's intention. He had, after all, depicted Louis with weapons in his hand from the time he got out of diapers and leading his men into glorious battle in his teens. For him royal priesthood was not a sign of weakness but a sign of control. As high priest of the realm, it was natural that all churchmen defer to him and that all churches be treated as his property.

The Carolingians at St.-Wandrille

The authority the Carolingians wielded over the Frankish churches can be demonstrated by the example of St.-Wandrille (Fontenelle). Pippin of Herstal's grandson Hugh (d. 730/2) became simultaneously bishop of Rouen, Paris, and Bayeux, as well as abbot of St.-Wandrille and of Jumièges, at the instigation of his uncle Charles Martel.[105] Hugh appears to have been close to Charles, perhaps because he, unlike the rest of Charles's half brothers and nephews, was in the church and thus did not represent a challenge for authority in Francia. The early ninth-century *Gesta* author at St.-Wandrille had trouble with this arrangement, knowing it was "against the canons," and said that these churches had been a "royal prize." However, he was reluctant to say anything directly against Hugh or members of his family because Hugh, though a pluralist, ended up being very generous to St.-Wandrille; the chronicler said that he was "noble by blood, but not less so in religion." Therefore, to explain how Hugh acquired all his offices, he asserted (somewhat unconvincingly) that it was not due to any "perverse greed" or "secular arrogance" but rather in order that the church's heritage be preserved and that Hugh have the opportunity to make gifts.[106]

The author showed a real ambivalence whether to connect his monastery to the Merovingians or the Carolingians. He ended up attempting a balancing act, trying to connect his house with both. But while he found plenty to praise in both lineages, criticisms were leveled solely at the Carolingians.[107] He attempted to connect his monastery to both lines of kings in the opening of the *Gesta*, while discussing Saint Wandregesil, founder and first abbot of the house in the seventh century. Wandregesil, he said, was a first cousin of Pippin of

Herstal, a piece of information he probably obtained from the *vita* of Bishop Ansbert of Rouen, written a century and a half earlier.[108] The ninth-century *Gesta* author fleshed out this connection between the founding abbot and Pippin, saying that their fathers, Waltechisus and Ansegesil (also known as Anschisus), were brothers.[109]

But in the very next sentence after establishing a connection with the Arnulfings, the chronicler of St.-Wandrille said that Saint Wandregesil was educated in the court of the "most glorious king Dagobert" in the "most noble" manner. He added that his house was founded on land given by Erchinoald, mayor of the palace for Dagobert's son Clovis II.[110] Erchinoald was not an Arnulfing, but a ninth-century author, knowing that the Carolingians had begun as the mayors of the palace, would probably have assumed so—indeed, he wrote at the same time as Einhard was attempting to suggest that no non-Arnulfing had ever been mayor. Then, having established connections between Saint Wandregesil and both the Merovingians and the Arnulfings, the author made clear that the Merovingian connection was more valuable.

A generous donation made to St.-Wandrille and its subsequent fate illustrates the change the author saw accompanying the transition from Merovingian to Arnulfing rule.[111] In the 670s Childeric II, along with his queen and the chief men of his court, made a large gift of property. In the 730s, however, Abbot Teutsind started granting his monastery's possessions away, both to his own relatives and to the "ruler's men," until according to the ninth-century chronicler a third was gone, including King Childeric's pious donation from half a century earlier. A certain count took what Childeric had given, originally as a *precaria* for which he agreed to pay sixty solidi a year. But the property had still not been returned by the 780s, and by then the sixty solidi were no longer being paid.[112] The contrast here was clear between the period of the Merovingian kings, whose generosity helped establish the fortunes of St.-Wandrille, and of the Arnulfings, especially if, as appears most likely, Abbot Teutsind was an Arnulfing appointee.

This was not an isolated example. When the *Gesta* author described a gift that Clovis II confirmed, he copied portions of the royal charter into his narrative. He did so again when describing how Pippin of Herstal, with his wife and sons, gave St.-Wandrille the little monastery of Fleury that Pippin had founded in the Vexin. But there was a significant difference. Clovis's confirmation was described as the generous response to a request. Pippin's gift was said to be in reaction to the "guilt" he felt after he had driven Bishop Ansbert of Rouen from his see—a bishop who was also abbot of St.-Wandrille—so that the bishop died in exile.[113] The author was interested not only in what was given but why. St.-Wandrille's transition from a monastery that regularly received gifts from Merovingian kings to one controlled by the Arnulfings has sometimes been taken as emblematic of a transfer of power to a new royal lineage.[114] But more than a political change was involved, in the eyes of the ninth-century *Gesta* author. The Merovingians had come to the monastery to make gifts. The Arnulfings, who came to appoint the abbots, were generous only under duress.

Indeed, the author of the *Gesta* seems if anything to have toned down his sources' suspicion of the Arnulfings. The *vita* of Bishop Ansbert of Rouen, written shortly after Ansbert's death around 700, is far more critical. In this account, a Merovingian prince, the future Theoderic III, is out hunting, comes across the saint working in the vineyards, and predicts that Ansbert will be a great and revered Christian leader. Significant is *who* makes this (correct) prediction. Theoderic, an adolescent, is still able to recognize exceptional spiritual qualities. He goes on to be very generous to the monastery and gives the monks a privilege of exemption. In sharp contrast, Pippin of Herstal, mayor of the palace, is influenced by the "enemy of all humankind" to accuse Ansbert of things he had not done and to drive him into exile, where he dies. The dead saint's body almost immediately begins to work miracles while carried home to Rouen. Pippin, whom the *vita* author compares to Nero to make sure the point is not missed, felt so rebuked by these miracles that he ended up making St.-Wandrille a large gift.[115] This *vita* was among the sources for the author of the *Gesta* a century later, an author who carefully did *not* accuse an Arnulfing of diabolical inspiration. But it is still clear that even in the heyday of Carolingian authority, they were not perceived at this monastery as friends of the monks.

Thus, in spite of intermittent efforts to avoid accusing the Carolingians too strongly of being enemies of the church, the early ninth-century St.-Wandrille author preferred to remember the Merovingian era as a time of monastic prosperity. The perception of the Carolingians as glorious supporters of monasticism only began to take hold in the later ninth century. The author of the Jumièges version of the *vita* of Hugh, abbot of both Jumièges and St.-Wandrille in the early eighth century, lacked any of the ambivalence toward the Carolingians of the earlier St.-Wandrille author—who was, however, his principal source. Writing in the second half of the ninth century, the Jumièges author proudly made Hugh a son of Charlemagne (instead of a nephew of Charles Martel) and said he was made bishop by the emperor and then retired to Jumièges. His account seems quite confused, both genealogically and chronologically, but it is clear that he had rewritten his source, the *Gesta* of the abbots of St.-Wandrille, to give Charlemagne a much more central and positive role.[116]

Saint Dagobert at St.-Denis

A preference for the Merovingians rather than the Carolingians, even at the time of their greatest hegemony, may also be seen in the "Gesta Dagoberti," composed at St.-Denis in the first half of the ninth century to commemorate the Merovingian king buried at the monastery.[117] It is striking that St.-Denis, where Pippin the Short was anointed as king by the pope, along with his wife and sons, and where both he and Charles Martel were buried, should have chosen to describe as a saint a king from the lineage that Pippin the Short deposed.[118]

The "Gesta Dagoberti" has never received much scholarly attention, both because it is very derivative, with large sections lifted straight out of the *Chronica* of Fredegar, and because it was written two centuries after its subject lived and is thus not a trustworthy witness to Dagobert's actual deeds.[119] But this very remoteness means that the text is highly revelatory of the way that a monk at one of Francia's most important monasteries conceptualized a saintly exemplar of kingship. In his opening line, the anonymous author insists on the fundamental Christianity of Dagobert's family: Dagobert's father, Clothar II, was "fourth in line from Clovis, the first king of the Franks to convert to the worship of God."[120]

And yet at the same time the author glorified the Merovingians, he also made some efforts to tie Dagobert to the Carolingians. He calls Dagobert's mother Bertrada, the same name as Charlemagne's mother, even though neither Fredegar nor the *Liber historiae Francorum* gives Dagobert's mother's name. He has young Dagobert undertake his studies with Bishop Arnulf of Metz, considered in the ninth century to be the ancestor of Charlemagne.[121] But both of these cases carried a subtle suggestion that the Merovingian king was superior to the later Carolingians: a woman and a bishop were no match for an activist king.

The most Christian king Dagobert, according to his hagiographer, showed his sanctity primarily through generosity to the church of St.-Denis: "He enriched churches and priests and the poor and pilgrims." He made gifts to embellish the church, from the martyrs' tombs to the crucifix on the high altar, as well as donating revenues from an annual market and from tolls that he collected.[122] In addition, Dagobert made St.-Denis his "heir" for a good deal of land and other property, including the one hundred cows he had been receiving from Le Mans. Indeed, the list of what he gave the church is specific enough that it seems most likely that the ninth-century author had authentic charters of Dagobert in front of him. He is even able to present the gifts that the king's brother-in-law made as redounding to the king's advantage, because he agreed to them. King Dagobert's death, according to the ninth-century author, filled everyone with unbearable sorrow. He made further gifts by testament, charging his sons with ensuring that the testament was properly carried out and preserving the memory of his generosity by having four identical copies of this testament drawn up, one to be kept at Laon, one at Paris, one at Metz, and one in the royal treasury. The Paris copy, the author said proudly, was still at St.-Denis.

A king like Dagobert, who had numerous wives and concubines and who frequently was engaged in wars, might seem like an unlikely candidate for a saint. The ninth-century author of his *vita* could not even come up with any decent miracles. Indeed, there is no sign of his cult beyond St.-Denis itself. But the author was doing more than laying a mantle of sanctity over someone who had been very generous to the church in which he was buried. He was also creating an image of what a king ought to be. That he chose to glorify a Merovingian king during the heyday of Carolingian rule can only be an indication that the monks of St.-Denis had doubts about the Carolingians' fulfilling their role as Christian kings.

Such doubts also animated Hincmar of Rheims, who a generation later began what would have to be considered a systematic campaign to discredit Charles Martel. Hincmar was intimately involved in the affairs of the royal court, organized the western bishops to oppose Louis the German, and led the opposition to the divorce of Lothar II, so he was entirely capable of criticizing the Carolingian royal family. But his complaint against Charlemagne's grandfather was quite specific. Hincmar sternly criticized Charles Martel for giving bishoprics to laymen. He also broadcast the story that had started a century earlier: that when the tomb of Charles Martel was opened, a horrible dragon emerged.[123] With such an ancestor, Hincmar suggested, it was not surprising that the Carolingians of his own day needed correction by the bishops.

Even in the high Middle Ages some writers still recalled the ninth century as a dark period. For example, the eleventh-century monk Paul spoke with full conviction of the glories of his monastery, St.-Père of Chartres, before the ninth century: it had many monks who mortified the flesh for the love of Christ, he said, and the monastery's extensive walls, beautiful buildings, and thorough study of the liberal arts made it outstanding in Neustria. This highly successful and Christian community was, however, devastated during the Viking raids.[124] Interestingly, Paul credited the eventual successful opposition to the Vikings to the "Franks," a group that in his formulation included the Robertians/Capetians but not the Carolingians.

Moreover, memories of grievances at the hands of Carolingians lingered long. A twelfth-century chronicler at Bèze, describing the desolation of his monastery in the eighth century, which he said he had read about in "ancient parchments," related that Remigius, specifically identified as brother of Pippin the Short and uncle of Charlemagne, had taken the house of Bèze and given it to a woman named Angela. Understandably, the monks all fled, "to Luxeuil or to other monasteries where they knew the monastic order still persisted." Bèze, according to the chronicler, did not recover from this disaster for a century, and he compared it to sackings by Vandals, Saracens, and Vikings.[125] That this chronicler knew that Charlemagne had an uncle named Remigius, which was certainly not general knowledge, suggests he may really have had "ancient parchments" with accurate information about the eighth century. For him, the Carolingian age was a disastrous one for his monastery.

The supposed fatal monastic decline under the last Merovingians does not seem nearly as dire when reexamined, and the seizure of church property by the Arnulfing rulers and their granting of *precaria* were considered more serious at the time than they are now often characterized. An unnuanced image of the Carolingian era as a heyday for Frankish monasticism is overdue for qualification. The ideal that the Carolingian publicists sought to establish of the kings as excellent Christians, an ideal the kings themselves sought to live up to, did not translate into royal support for western monasticism.

The decline and abandonment of many monasteries in the West, and the notable gap in recorded donations to many others, as discussed in the next chapter, paint a different picture, as does the change from kings restricting their own power through grants of immunity to kings offering not immunity but control in the guise of protection. Moreover, some ninth-century monastic chroniclers made invidious comparisons between the Merovingian monarchs and those of their own time. For them the Carolingians had not rescued decadent monasteries; rather, this line of kings respected monks only under duress and suffered in comparison with such Merovingians as the holy King Dagobert. In part of course they were exercising creative memory, constructing an image of a golden time when secular rulers supported monasteries the way they would have liked to be supported. But eighth- and ninth-century evidence suggests they may have had a point.

Chapter 9

Eighth-Century Transitions: The Evidence from Burgundy

Memory always has gaps. In this chapter I shall examine a curious lacuna in the documents from west Frankish monasteries, occurring during the transition from Merovingian to Carolingian rule. Monasteries in the early eighth century functioned in a world very different from that of the early ninth, and yet that transition is nearly silent, for it was not recorded in memory. In addition, this gap in the documents corresponds to a period in which no new monasteries were founded.

In part this chapter will be an argument for seeing the rise of the Carolingians as a true historical turning point. Ever since adoption of the broad term "late antiquity" muted the question of exactly when the Roman Empire ended, turning points of the early Middle Ages have been defined more by social and economic developments than by politics. Some scholars have revived the Pirenne thesis, focusing on changes in the agricultural economy and the impact of Islam in the sixth and seventh centuries, while others have spoken of a "feudal transformation" that took place only in the year 1000.[1] The rise of the Carolingians, in contrast, has generally not been viewed as a transition point in any area other than political leadership.[2] Adherents of sixth- and seventh-century transitions, those who see as most significant the breakdown of Mediterranean trade and the establishment of an agricultural system that Marxists call "feudalism," put the Carolingians into a later, or "feudal," age. Yet adherents of eleventh-century transitions, those who argue for the continuity of Roman institutions until the year 1000, put the Carolingians instead into a prior, "pre-feudal" age.[3]

Only recently has the eighth century begun to receive attention in its own right.[4] For example, Chris Wickham has argued that in the eighth century in

Francia "aristocratic economic dominance" replaced the "peasant mode" of agriculture, which had allowed relative peasant autonomy in the Merovingian period.[5] Economic historians of this poorly documented period have naturally used all sources available to them, and monastic records, along with archaeology, have been a major source of information.

But monasteries were more than landlords or economic entities. They did not simply partake in broad economic developments, nor can such developments be extrapolated from secular and ecclesiastical sources interchangeably. In this chapter I shall move the monasteries of west Francia back into the foreground, concentrating on the significant, if strangely silent, changes that took place during the eighth and early ninth centuries, changes that correspond to the transition from the Merovingian to the Carolingian dynasty. My focus is Burgundy, a region never particularly favored by the Carolingian kings, though located in the center of their realm. Many of this region's significant transitions occurred in documentary darkness; the records of Burgundian monasteries are marked by distinct lacunae, corresponding to the reign of Charlemagne.

Especially noteworthy are a change in literacy among the laity and a change in human geography. Before the ninth century, monastic transactions were recorded in writing, generally drawn up by a lay notary for a reasonably literate population. Settlement patterns as revealed by monasteries' records continued to follow those of the Gallo-Romans, with the *pagus* and the *ager*, the old Roman administrative subdivisions, still significant. From the ninth century onward, however, settlement patterns were substantially different, with the old villas long gone and new villages established, many of which still exist today. Moreover, as the general lay population became less literate, the written word became almost exclusively the province of the church. And this period of decreasing literacy and changing settlements was also a period without monastic foundations.

Literacy in the Merovingian Era

The Merovingian age was a literate age. Like imperial Rome, it assumed a well-educated upper class.[6] Although reading was surely reserved for the well-to-do, rather than for the great mass of the population (many still unfree), it was taken for granted that all important events in life should be recorded in writing, and literacy at some level was required for public life.[7] Venantius

Fortunatus, writing at the end of the sixth century, described Queen Radegund—whom he had known personally—as studying Christian literature in the royal court when she arrived there as a girl, even though she arrived as a captive.[8]

When Gregory of Tours wanted to show how cruel Chilperic I was to the bishops of Gaul, he said that the king routinely tore up the wills by which people bequeathed property to them, thus taking such written wills for granted. In addition, Gregory mocked Chilperic *not* for being illiterate, which he clearly was not, for he wrote two books himself and attempted to improve written Latin by incorporating four new letters into the alphabet, but rather for not appreciating the difference between long and short syllables in his awkward efforts at versification. Although the king composed some hymns and sequences for the Mass, Gregory continued dismissively, they could certainly not be used.[9] Interestingly, Venantius Fortunatus found the best way to defend his friend Gregory against Chilperic's unjust accusations was through writing a panegyric.[10] Even one of Gregory's worst kings was highly literate.

In the seventh century as in the sixth, the wealthy routinely drew up written testaments.[11] The monastery of St.-Wandrille still had in the Carolingian era a great many Merovingian-era documents recording transactions between laymen. The author of the ninth-century *Gesta* of the abbots included phrases and whole portions of seventh-century documents in his narrative. He proudly announced that his monastery had in the archives a privilege of King Dagobert, by which he gave one Rotmar the property Rotmar later gave to the monks.[12] When Irmina, mother-in-law of Pippin of Herstal, drew up her own testament at the end of the seventh century, she referred to serfs that she had earlier freed by giving them written charters.[13] If even serfs could expect the written word to confirm their new status, then free men and churches too must have taken charters for granted.

The persistence of literacy is also demonstrated by the formulary book of Marculf, put together in the seventh century. A formulary was a collection of sample letters and charters a scribe could use to compose letters for people quickly and easily. Marculf included a whole series of model documents for use in family affairs: gifts between a husband and wife or between a parent and child, the establishment of heirs in the absence of children, the payment of a dowry or issuance of a testament, the selling of a house or the freeing of a slave.[14] When it was composed it was assumed that such important yet private matters between laypeople would be memorialized in writing. A century later, the formulary put together at St.-Martin of Tours similarly suggested that laypeople were routinely using documents.[15]

Books of "popular" literature were regularly copied, bought, and sold during this period. Although scholars are still debating whether the transition from late Latin to proto-French ("Romance") took place in the eighth century or the ninth, it is clear that in the sixth and seventh centuries Latin was still a spoken language, and anyone with the rudiments of an education should have been able to read literature, saints' lives, and charters.[16] It has even been argued that in eastern Francia, where Roman influence had never been significant in the heyday of the Empire, written records became prevalent for the first time in the seventh century, suggesting an *increase* in overall literacy under the later Merovingians.[17]

Written records were also important for legal proof in this period. In 697, Drogo, duke of Champagne and son of Pippin of Herstal, claimed property belonging to the monastery of Tussonval. He asserted in the Merovingian king's court that his brother-in-law had obtained the property in question in exchange for some other property and that it had then come to Drogo via his wife, after the brother-in-law's death. But no one believed him. The court asked Drogo "if letters of exchange had been drawn up and if he could present them." Without anything in writing, Drogo did not have a chance. The court ruled summarily against him, giving as reason that "he never presented documents and could offer no other evidence."[18] Here everyone, ecclesiastical and lay, assumed that all important transactions would be put in writing, to the extent that written evidence had a legal authority it would in fact lose in subsequent centuries.

But one must still explain the shortage of surviving documents from the Merovingian era, the original reason the period was once labeled the "Dark Ages." To a major extent this sparsity should be seen as due to the fragility of papyrus in a damp climate. In a Gaul that still thought of itself as Roman, papyrus continued to be considered much more appropriate than parchment, and people were willing to pay well as long as it was possible to import it.[19]

Monks of the Carolingian era preserved some of their houses' earlier charters by copying them, but they did not copy all. Because the cursive script in which most Merovingian-era documents were written would have become nearly unintelligible to monks of the tenth and later centuries, accustomed instead to Caroline minuscule, many of these early charters must have fallen unread into dust.[20] The abbey of St.-Denis accounts for a major proportion of the surviving original papyrus documents from Gaul, but there is no reason that this particular abbey should have received charters when other abbeys did not, although its monks were better able to preserve some of theirs.[21] And of course the more normal and ordinary the written record is, the less likely that individual written records would be treasured and preserved, once their initial purpose had passed.

Furthermore, it is possible that monks in the Merovingian era were not as conscientious about maintaining their own archives as their successors would be, not because they were unconcerned with the written record but for the exact opposite reason: they assumed that public notaries and municipal archives, keeping records of transactions as they took place, would always be available.[22] Indeed, the ease with which donors even to houses such as Flavigny, located outside any major urban agglomeration, could find a public notary in the first decades of the eighth century indicates their prevalence.[23] Ironically, one of the signs of a literate society (as again much later during the Italian Renaissance) is the presence of notaries who keep records of all important transactions, and yet this very institution made it easier for records to be lost.

With the disappearance of notaries in west Francia in the middle decades of the eighth century, the monks' records also disappeared. Those houses with good archival runs back into the seventh century are all houses founded on the margins of Merovingian Gaul, where municipal archives had never penetrated. Monasteries in the Rhineland such as Lorsch and Fulda, not founded until the eighth century, have far more records of transactions from before the year 800 than do many older monasteries in the heart of Frankish Gaul.[24] Part of the reason must be that the western monks assumed that the local authorities would keep their records for them, as they always had, whereas east of the Rhine such a service had never been available, and even when records were drawn up by secular notaries they went straight into monastic storerooms.[25] Thus we now have access to only a tiny percentage of sixth- through eighth-century documents, and the small number of extant charters cannot be taken as a reflection of how many were produced.

Charters and Formularies at Flavigny

Late eighth-century changes in the use of the written word are illustrated by the monastery of Flavigny. The cartulary of this house contains documents from both sides of the key transitional period, with twelve documents from the eighth century and eleven for the ninth, a large number for the period in western Francia. The monastery also produced a formulary around the year 800. It is thus possible, using this house's materials, to look at scribal practice in three different periods: the early eighth century, when its great testaments were drawn up; the years around 800, when these testaments and other materials were shaped into a formulary; and the late ninth and subsequent centuries, when the monks discovered it was impossible to use their formulary as intended, even though it dated from only a few generations earlier.

Flavigny was a Benedictine house founded in 717, when a wealthy man named Wideradus made his testament, specifying that he had built the basilica of Flavigny and established monks there. He indicated rather vaguely that they should follow the practices of "Luxeuil, Lérins, and St.-Maurice of Agaune," all influential versions of the monastic life in early monasticism in Gaul. Two years later he drew up a second testament, confirming everything he had given to Flavigny and ordering observance of the Benedictine Rule.[26] Though virtually the last of the great Merovingian foundations—indeed the last new house in the region for 150 years—Flavigny came into existence in a world which, from its charters, still looks very "Roman." Wideradus's two testaments were drawn up in the tradition of late Roman notarial practice.[27] Both were written not by a monk but by a notary named Aldofredus. The first refers explicitly to the *gesta municipalia*, official municipal registers that kept track of legal transactions. Such registers were rapidly disappearing, having been gone from the Mediterranean region since the seventh century and never having been established in the east, but they persisted in central Francia into the eighth century.[28] The first testament was witnessed at a public gathering by King Theoderic IV and the royal chancellor, but only Wideradus himself and the notary signed when he reissued the testament at Flavigny.

As well as distributing much of his property to four basilicas in his great testament, Wideradus specified what portion was to be preserved *in falcidia* or *in faucidia*; Roman testamentary law specified the "falcidia," the minimum amount of property a man was obliged to leave to his relatives.[29] The donated property was listed by *ager* and *pagus*, the Roman administrative units into which Gaul was divided. There was little attempt to assign people specific social or political status. Wideradus himself, though a modern scholar would consider him a powerful noble, based on the enormous extent of his hereditary property, was given no noble title. He was simply called *abba*—which confused the eleventh-century historians of the abbey, who ended up naming *both* Wideradus and Magoaldus, Flavigny's actual first abbot, as the first abbot of the monastery.

For the next fifty years Flavigny flourished, receiving gifts from local laymen and even from Pippin the Short. Here Flavigny is unusual among west Frankish monasteries in that any of its pre-Carolingian charters survive, even if in later copies, but not unusual in that they once existed. Its charters record gifts from both men and women, usually without giving any indication of their position (except for the few from kings), at most calling a layman *vir inluster*. Notaries drew up the donation charters. Since those who made these gifts were apparently all literate and certainly knew their own status, they saw no need to spell it out. Property was defined by *pagus*, *villa*, and *finis*. Most charters included no witnesses, for the charter itself had important legal and symbolic value. The insertion of a penalty clause, directed against anyone who might disturb the monks' enjoyment of their property, meant that there was no need for the long list of witnesses found in monastic charters from the ninth century on.[30] Thus the eighth-century charters assumed a legally established system of public power, which could be trusted to enforce a charter's provisions.

For example, in 748 the couple Baio and Cylinia, Baio calling himself a *vir inluster*, gave Flavigny land at three villas, including fields, a vineyard, buildings, serfs, freedmen, the right to collect tolls, and a church. Three years later, the couple donated land at three more villas to the monks, land Cylinia had inherited from her father. A man named Maurengus, who may have been their son, made a gift of his own a generation later, in 768, including land at three villas.[31] Additional gifts from around the same time came from both priests and laymen, including one Hildebrand, probably the same Hildebrand who sponsored the continuation of Fredegar's *Chronica*.[32] The culmination of this initial period of prosperity for the monastery came in 775, when Charlemagne freed the monks from a variety of tolls and gave them a silver reliquary.[33]

Several features stand out in these eighth-century records. First is the explicit assumption that there were many more contemporary charters in existence, including private charters in which parents detailed what their children would inherit. Baio and Cylinia referred to his parents as having granted them the church that they later gave Flavigny, a transfer made with *strumentis cartarum*. An additional indication that the eighth-century monks of Flavigny assumed they lived in a period of lay literacy is provided by a manuscript that the monks completed shortly after the year 800.[34] It includes a list of popes up to Hadrian I (d. 795); a brief chronology of world history, finishing with Charlemagne's rule as emperor; doctrinal discussions of substance and essence; some church law and councils; and a list of ecclesiastical provinces. But its best-known section is a formulary of letters and documents, partially based on Flavigny's archives.

The scribes used a number of examples from the seventh-century formulary of Marculf, as well as formulae from eighth-century Tours. The monks of Flavigny were not alone in continuing the formulary tradition, for at the same time scribes at the monastery of St.-Denis created one of their own, based on their own archival documents.[35] At both of these houses, therefore, the monks wanted to create a template for the future and found it logical that such a template should be based on their own past.

At the beginning of the ninth century, both secular courts and religious houses were concerned with improving the written word, with correcting Latinity and regularizing records. The role of Alcuin at Charlemagne's court in establishing and disseminating a corrected copy of the Bible is well-known (interestingly, Alcuin was briefly abbot of both Flavigny and Tours). Continuing this process of regularization, Louis the Pious, almost immediately after succeeding Charlemagne, set out to rework the formulary of the imperial court, the *Formulae imperiales*. In this climate, it is not surprising that the monks of Flavigny, drawing up a volume of collected knowledge and law in a handsome Caroline miniscule, should have included their own formulary in the volume.

It might at first appear that this formulary and the manuscript in which it appears are no more than an example of the energetic scribal activity at Flavigny in its first century, already made clear by other manuscripts.[36] For example, Flavigny's scriptorium produced a handsome manuscript of the four gospels, written in uncial letters. It is known to be from Flavigny because of an inscription (also in uncial), written in two columns, LE SIPTI AFIICNI and IBR CER LUNAESS, an anagram for LIBER S. PREI[E]CTI FLAUINIACENSIS.[37] This manuscript was almost certainly copied from a slightly earlier—and much rougher-looking—gospel that the monastery had acquired.[38] The monks' scribal activities are also suggested by the gift to them from Pippin the Short of a set of ivory tablets, of the sort commonly used as Bible covers.[39] In the early ninth century, at about the same time as the monks were creating their formulary, they also produced a glossed copy of the Pauline letters.[40] Given this context, the importance of the monks' formulary might too easily be overlooked.

But Flavigny's formulary is significant in several respects. It was composed for use by monks, not by the lay notaries who had drawn up a great number of Merovingian documents—and used such formularies as Marculf's. It includes testamentary formulae based directly on the two long testaments that Wideradus had issued in 717 and 719.[41] And yet, strikingly, these testamentary formulae were never used for Flavigny's subsequent donations, even those donations explicitly called testaments. The changes in the way that later monks recorded gifts cannot be due simply to a forgetfulness of the past. After all, Wideradus's testament, the monks' most precious document, still existed as late as the seventeenth century. Rather, the format for charters was rapidly changing even as the monks used their eighth-century testaments to create their formulary.

The formulae from Flavigny, though often treated as a late, static example of Merovingian scribal practice, should instead be seen as an unsuccessful attempt to provide a blueprint for the future. When the monks of Flavigny compiled their formulary around 800, they did not expect to ignore the formulae in it;[42] they thought they were organizing and regularizing the way they would draw up their charters, just as they organized everything from doctrinal issues to a list of popes in the same volume. But the very fact that monks, not lay notaries, compiled this formulary meant that its forms, being based ultimately on notarial practice, almost immediately became outdated. It is ironic that the monks of Flavigny looked backward in planning for future charters and yet quickly discovered that their scribal needs were very different from the models their formulae provided. Thus Flavigny's formulary provides a window into the eighth- and ninth-century transition in how transactions were recorded.

For if the period around 800 was a time of regularizing and organizing the written record, the first half of the ninth century was a time when written records rapidly became a much less significant aspect of lay-clerical relationships, even while the written word took on increased importance within the confines of the cloister. Lay literacy, while it did not disappear, became much less prevalent as clerics gradually attained a monopoly on the written word. No longer did literate laymen, accompanied by notaries, arrive at the abbey to record their donations by preparing documents reflecting Roman law, which would then be presented to the monks. No longer was the charter itself considered a legally binding instrument. Instead the monks themselves drew up charters intended to serve as memoirs of transactions that had taken place orally, as records of ceremonial actions by donors and witnesses.[43] Here the social context was more important than the legal context, and witnesses were vital.

An illuminating comparison may be made with the monastery of St.-Gall. Although this house preserved far more eighth-century records than Flavigny, it also experienced a significant change in the format of its charters in the ninth century. Before 800, donation charters were drawn up by laymen themselves, speaking in their own voices. Starting in the second quarter of the ninth century, the abbot routinely drew up the charter and attested in the third person to what a layman had done. Although not universal, this new practice is still a significant change from the eighth century, when the abbot never drew up the charter.[44]

Witnesses are listed in virtually all ninth-century charters for Flavigny, except royal ones. Charters from the mid-ninth century onward also described the social and political status of all people mentioned. The monks, outsiders to worldly society, felt compelled, as the lay donors of the previous century had not, to define exactly where these donors stood in the social hierarchy. Bishops and counts were not merely *episcopus* and *comes* but bishop or count *of* somewhere. The county also began to replace the *pagus* as the territorial unit in which property was localized. When the Merovingian kings and the first Carolingians had issued confirmations to monasteries, they often stated that they confirmed what was in charters now lost or burnt. But in the ninth century, such confirmations frequently suggested that the donations had *not* originally been recorded in writing. The list of witnesses, whose social position was carefully recorded, gave credence to the assertion that all had been properly done.

In light of these changes in practice, it is not surprising that Flavigny's formulary became a dead letter within a few decades of its compilation. The volume containing the testamentary formulary continued to be known and used at Flavigny—the list of popes, which had originally stopped at 795, was continued in the eleventh century to the 1030s. Therefore the change in diplomatic practice at Flavigny can be considered deliberate. The monks of Flavigny no longer received gifts from literate laymen, recorded in charters drawn up by lay notaries, and the charters the monks drew up to record their gifts could thus not be modeled on the charters of the previous century.

In 878, for example, a layman named Ardradus gave the monks of Flavigny several *mansi* with their serfs, in exchange for fifty measures of grain, fifty of wine, and ten pigs a year.[45] At first glance, the charter looks very similar to one of the formulae, described as the format for a gift *a die presente*. But upon closer examination the similarity goes no further than the fact that both the document of 878 and the eighth-century formula begin with the phrase, "Domine sacrosancte," and include a penalty clause, "Si quis vero." The property was defined and delineated not simply by its administrative location (*pagus, ager, finis*) but by its specific and highly local social context: the charter, drawn up by a cleric and witnessed by twelve men, listed the names of the individual serfs and gave the names of those who held the adjoining property.

The difference is even more striking if one compares Flavigny's formulae with the testament that Count Aymo of Auxois had drawn up in 1004, when he gave Flavigny an oratory and a large amount of land, saying that he wished to "meet God face to face in Zion."[46] Interestingly, this charter was completed by Aymo's monogram, even though a monogram would have been reserved for a king two centuries earlier; the only monogram mentioned in Wideradus's original testament is that of King Theoderic IV. Count Aymo's charter, though called a *testamentum*, does not begin with a statement that someone, son of someone, made his testament to a certain monastery where a certain man was abbot, as drawn up by a certain notary, even though this is the way Flavigny's testamentary formula begins. Rather, the testament of 1004 opens with a long series of biblical quotes: "We do not have here a 'lasting city,' and thus we should, while in this 'vale of tears,' as much as we can, 'put off the corruptible and mortal and put on the incorruptible and immortal,' to be changed to 'the liberty of the sons of God,' giving 'a cup of water for Christ's sake,' since 'as water extinguishes fire, so alms extinguish sin.'"[47]

Here a monastic scribe drew up an important testament without the slightest diplomatic reference to the formulary of the early ninth century, even though he wrote not long before a monk of Flavigny updated the list of popes in the same volume as the formulary. It is also worth noting that Count Aymo's testament was drawn up only a few years before a monastic archivist began assembling Flavigny's cartulary, in which the original testaments of the eighth century would be the first documents copied. Thus at the beginning of the eleventh century, Flavigny's founding testament and testamentary formulae were considered highly important relics of the monastic past, but relics that had no contemporary relevance to the eleventh-century scribe who drew up the generous testament of one of the abbey's most powerful neighbors.

Changes in Settlement Patterns

In addition to indicating a change in lay literacy and diplomatic practices from the eighth to the ninth century, Flavigny's charters also reveal an important change in human settlement patterns in the same period. Such a change is especially noteworthy because no such transformation took place in late antiquity when, in spite of the disruptions of the fifth century, new villages—or even new villas—were often built on the same sites as ruined Roman villas.[48]

Archaeologists have long noted a major gap between the city of late antiquity, with its grid-work streets, public monuments, and central forum, and the city of the eleventh century onward, with its tightly packed streets laid out according to no overall pattern, dominated by a central cathedral. These differences are especially striking in regions where the ancient and the medieval city were built on the same spot. Often archaeological remains of a growing eleventh-century French city are found on top of the remains of a late classical city, separated by a stratum of "dark earth," which was once considered agricultural soil and has more recently been argued to be traces of light housing.[49] This evidence suggests a disjunction in settlement patterns between late antiquity and the high Middle Ages; documentary evidence such as Flavigny's can help pin down when the most significant shift took place.

While charters from the middle years of the ninth century onward list villages that persisted throughout the Middle Ages—and indeed still exist today—the documents from the eighth century indicate a very different human geography. Wideradus's original foundation charter of 717 describes Flavigny as located in the *ager* of Bornet (Burnacinsis),[50] an *ager* being the chief subdivision of a *pagus* in Roman provincial administration. And yet a century later Bornet had completely dropped out of all references to Flavigny and its region, and the name is preserved today only in the names of two farms. A fair proportion of the rest of the property enumerated in Wideradus's testament, between a quarter and a third, is located at places that either cannot be identified at all today or whose names at best have long since been reduced to the names of woods or farms or bridges, not villages. That the places that cannot be identified today are also not found in any later medieval inventories of Flavigny's possessions also indicates that many areas, like Bornet, which had been at least small agricultural and population centers in the eighth century, lost their population as well as their importance in subsequent years.[51]

Even the twelfth-century cartulary scribe did not recognize all the places mentioned in Wideradus's testament from four centuries earlier. Where the villa mentioned still existed and still belonged to Flavigny, the scribe knew it at once and modified the Merovingian spelling to the twelfth-century standard: thus the eighth-century *Bagatiacus* became the twelfth-century *Pagatiacus* (today Pazy).[52] But the scribe simply reproduced exactly the names of those places he did not know, names that were important to him because they were in his monastery's foundation charter but that possessed for him no other content because they no longer designated for him property his monastery owned.

Archaeology provides another tantalizing indication of the changes in settlement patterns in this region.[53] A few kilometers north of Flavigny is the steep hill of Alesia (today Mont Auxois), probably best known as the site where Vercingetorix long withstood Caesar. Today the crown of the hill is empty of human activity, except for an archaeological site. It has in fact been empty since the seventh century. But excavations reveal that from the time of early imperial Rome through the period of Merovingian Christianization, the hilltop supported a small but bustling town. After the region's conquest by the Romans, the hill where Vercingetorix made his final stand became a commercial settlement and a regional center for metallurgy.[54] When Christianity reached Gaul, a small basilica was built within a few yards of the old Roman temple. Here we know that a noble priest named Senator served in the 430s and that he had a wife named Nectarolia.[55] But at some point, doubtless when the aqueduct ceased to function, this settlement lost its population.

A new village (today Alise-Ste.-Reine) was then established halfway down Alesia's hill, with its own Merovingian-era basilica—even though the cemetery stayed next to the old basilica on top of the hill. It was to this new basilica that Wideradus made gifts in his testament at the beginning of the eighth century. Settlement patterns were thus already in flux.[56] When the Auxois region was burned over in the ninth century by the Vikings, the lower but not the upper church was rebuilt—the upper church had doubtless become nothing more than the oratory for the cemetery. The Roman settlement at the top of the hill was permanently abandoned. By the twelfth century, shepherds' huts were being built from the bits of stonework that still protruded above the soil. Alesia thus provides a striking example of the discontinuity in settlement patterns in Burgundy between the eighth and late ninth centuries.

A Lacuna in Monastic History

If Flavigny in the first three-quarters of the eighth century was still very much part of the late Roman world, then the monastery in the mid-ninth century had passed into a different era. Understanding how this transition took place is rendered much more difficult by the marked lacuna in the documents in the cartulary from the crucial period of the late eighth and early ninth centuries. Although a cartulary was always more than an unproblematic collection of whatever charters existed in the archives, it is hard to conceive any explanation for why the cartulary compilers would have selectively omitted late eighth-century and early ninth-century charters while including both earlier and later ones. The manuscript that contains the formulary is thus almost a solitary voice at Flavigny. A sixty-five-year silence in its documents, from 775 to 840, is broken only by one charter, Louis the Pious's confirmation in 816 of the privilege his father had given the monks forty years earlier.[57]

When one emerges in 840 from this gap in the evidence, many things have changed. No longer do well-to-do laymen, speaking of charters by which their parents had confirmed them in their possessions, engage notaries to draw up records of gifts to Flavigny. Members of the new authority structures had to be recruited to guarantee the monastery's continued possession of its property. Both disposable wealth and literacy had passed into the hands of a governing elite, composed of church leaders and of those attached to the royal court, including the counts whom the kings still appointed.

Interestingly, the cartulary records more ninth-century grants of immunity and privileges enumerating the monks' existing possessions than new donations. Despite this flurry of reconfirmation, much of the property spelled out as the monks' in Wideradus's foundation charter of 717 is nowhere mentioned in the royal and episcopal privileges of a century or more later. It is clear that most of the monks' original patrimony, the land spread over many kilometers with which they were first endowed, was no longer producing enough to be worth owning. Although there are a few names of places in the ninth-century documents that cannot now be identified and do not appear in later charters, these are different than the unidentified places of the eighth century and far fewer in number.

Yet there is not the same gap in the evidence between the ninth century and the tenth as between the eighth century and the ninth. Even though Flavigny lost its regularity of life in the late ninth century when taken over by the bishops of Autun and was not again an independent Benedictine monastery until the end of the tenth century when Bishop Walter of Autun appointed a monk from Cluny to head the house,[58] the world of the year 1000 in which the newly reformed monastery emerged was not so different from the world of a century earlier. The property that Bishop Walter confirmed to the monks in the 990s is very similar to the property Lothar I and Charles the Bald had confirmed to the monks a century and a half earlier.[59] Land from which the bishops of Autun had gathered dues and rents for a hundred years was still populated by agricultural workers and still worth owning when it returned to the monks' hands, unlike much of the land Wideradus had originally given Flavigny. Thus, although Flavigny's evidence indicates an important transformation in human geography between the eighth century and the ninth, the new patterns then persisted through the ninth century and the tenth.

The example of Flavigny, therefore, suggests that the real transition period, during which both settlement patterns and access to the written word changed, was the late eighth and early ninth centuries, the period of the establishment of Carolingian rule, the period for which this monastery produced no surviving documents. Moreover, even though it is always dangerous to argue from silence, Flavigny is not alone in this gap in its documentation.

For example, the monastery of St.-Marcel of Chalon-sur-Saône, also a Merovingian foundation in Burgundy, has only one charter in its cartulary from the century between 779 and 873, again, as with Flavigny, this single exception a charter of Louis the Pious.[60] The monastery of St.-Bénigne of Dijon, another Merovingian-era foundation located between Flavigny and Chalon, does not have quite so big a chronological gap in its cartulary, but the thirty-year period from which no charters survive, from 783 to 815, corresponds to the first portion of the silent period in the charters of Flavigny and St.-Marcel.[61] The twelfth-century chronicler of nearby Bèze, a Burgundian monastery founded in the seventh century, commented himself that the monastic *ordo* disappeared at his house from the time of Pippin and Charlemagne to that of Louis the Pious, when it was restored around 830. Bèze preserved at least a few Merovingian-era documents, but when its cartulary was compiled in the twelfth century, the scribe could find nothing between 679 and 816.[62] At the monastery of Montier-en-Der, located north of Flavigny on the border of Champagne, the monks' cartulary has a similar gap in its records. Although the monks' cartulary contains six charters from the seventh century, the century of its foundation, and sixteen from the ninth century, it contains only two authentic eighth-century charters, both from before 760, and a seventy-year gap after 760 is broken only by two charters from Louis the Pious from 815/6, one of which is a possible forgery.[63]

A similar gap in the records also occurs elsewhere. For example, the monastery of Fosses, in northern Gaul, was a seventh-century foundation, attested to both by documents and by contemporary saints' *vitae*, but it experienced a documentary silence from the accession of Pippin the Short to the year 830. This gap is especially significant because the Pippinids had exercised almost exclusive power in the region since the late seventh century.[64] At St.-Martin of Tours, the property found in Merovingian-era documents and that confirmed to the house by Charlemagne is mostly the same, but a good two-thirds of the places mentioned then are not found in documents from the middle of the ninth century onward.[65]

What was happening during this silent transitional period, from the late eighth century to the mid-ninth? There have been various hypotheses put forward over the years by scholars who have also noticed the changes. The wars of the first half of the eighth century, wars that involved the Saracens, local Frankish leaders, and the Pippinids/Carolingians,[66] are often credited with creating upheavals in social as well as political organization. However, the lacuna in the documents and the transformations that took place then fell half a century later and thus cannot be simply explained by them.

Instead, the most common explanation for the social transformations of the beginning of the ninth century is that the rise of the Carolingian kings was accompanied by a new kind of lordship, in which people were rousted from their old settlements and rearranged in a way that made better economic sense for the newly powerful lords, who were also at this time beginning to draw up polyptyques. It has even been suggested that provisioning of the Carolingian armies created a demand for grain to which energetic landlords responded. The archaeological evidence suggests the abandonment at the end of the eighth century of sixth- and seventh-century centers of habitation and the building of new, nucleated settlements, which scholars have associated with increased authority in the hands of the regional aristocracy.[67] But it is difficult to see the changes that Burgundian documents indicate as merely a new exercise of lordship. After all, the development of castellanies and banal lordship in the eleventh century, much better documented, is accompanied by no comparable changes in settlement patterns.

The changes in where people lived and how their settlements were organized, it has also been suggested, may instead owe much to the rapid population decline of the sixth and seventh centuries. This was in part the result of what scholars have termed the mini-ice age of the late Merovingian period and the widespread effects of the plague, accompanied by the breakdown of Roman trade routes and the last of the urban civilization that had sustained the residue of Roman culture.[68] The overall decline of both the rural and urban economy of the Roman Empire intensified during the Merovingian period, and the economic nadir has been put around the year 700, with the turn-around only becoming evident a century or so later.[69] It is certainly easy to speculate that a drastic drop in population and a migration of those who survived to the most promising agricultural areas, where people huddled together in small groups against the terror of the wild wood, would have spelled the end both of widespread literate culture and of many rural villas where people had once worked and lived.

But the gap in monastic records, corresponding in time to the rise of the Carolingians, is indicative of more than changes in climate, the broader economy, or patterns of lordship. Indeed, the gap comes after, not before, the economy is considered to have begun to improve. The lacuna seems tied especially to the situation of the monasteries, not just broader society, for, as will be discussed below, there were also essentially no new monastic foundations in the region during this period. Indeed, the records of the monastery of St.-Pierre-le-Vif of Sens suggest that the documentary darkness in the eighth century was the result of a uniquely terrible time for the monasteries.

This house later claimed to have been founded in the early sixth century by a daughter of Clovis, which seems unlikely, but it was certainly established by the first half of the seventh century, when it was considered one of the six chief monasteries of the west Frankish realm.[70] It received privileges from the bishops of Sens and donations from the laity in the late seventh and early eighth centuries. Its unusually large collection of relics from this time, one of the largest in the West, is indicative of the monastery's importance. Over seventy authenticating bits of parchment, attached to relics, survive from before the age of Charlemagne.[71]

In the first decades of the eighth century two women (perhaps sisters), Ingoara and Leotharia, made generous gifts to the monks of Sens, including land, serfs, and a church. Leotharia asked in return to be buried at the house. Everything about these donations indicates a flourishing monastery, the kind of place a wealthy matron would choose for her burial.[72] The monastery must have continued to thrive for at least a few more years because the monks drew up a formulary using these charters as their model, apparently expecting to receive more gifts of this type.[73] But this formulary was the last appearance of St.-Pierre-le-Vif in the records for a century.

The next known record from St.-Pierre is an 822 charter of Louis the Pious directed to the archbishop of Sens, submitting the house to his direction. This gap of a hundred years in the records is not the product of a recent loss of documents, for even in the twelfth century the house's chronicler had nothing to say about eighth-century Sens after the gifts of Ingoara and Leotharia. But clearly much had changed by 822. Now St.-Pierre is not called a monastery but a *cella coenobialis*. According to the charter of 822, "Here monks ought to follow a religious life under the discipline of a holy rule," but they no longer did so, "due to various causes and diverse setbacks, including human frailty." Instead, for a long time the church had been in episcopal hands, and the house's property "was diminished by being divided" until the monks "did not have enough left to sustain them." The emperor ordered that regular monks be reestablished there and their property returned to them.[74]

And yet, even as he faulted the archbishop's predecessors for having taken monastic goods and issued a privilege saying that no one in the future should do so, Louis still confirmed episcopal authority, saying that when the house should have monks again the archbishop would choose the abbot and, if necessary, correct him. In this case, St.-Pierre did not have any documents surviving for the space of a century for the excellent reason that the house was in complete disarray, indeed without monks for much of the time. Such disarray may well be at the base of the documentary silence for other houses in the same period.

If the second half of the eighth century and the early ninth were difficult times for Burgundian monasteries, a possible explanation may be found in the counterexample of monasteries without a comparable gap in their records. Such monasteries were either located in eastern Francia, away from the heartland of Charlemagne's rule, or else were closely associated with his family—or both. The nunnery of Chelles, for example, supported in the later seventh century by the Merovingians, continued to flourish throughout the eighth century. At least one Carolingian princess held a prominent position in the house. The nuns, skilled scribes, have been credited with much of the manuscript copying that formed the basis of the Carolingian Renaissance. The identifying tags attached to their many relics indicate that they were acquired in the decades immediately before and after the year 800, the exact period when many other Frankish monasteries experienced a lacuna in their records.[75] Here a western house with an intimate connection to the royal family avoided a major gap in its records.

But monasteries without an eighth-century lacuna in their histories were preferentially in eastern Francia, in territories that had recently been converted to Christianity. The map of Frankish houses founded after the end of the seventh century is heavily weighted toward those established in the Rhineland and east, rather than in the territories once ruled by the Merovingians.[76] Here monasteries founded by a missionary, who took the title *episcopus et abbas* in his new house because a system of diocesan bishops had not yet been established, received gifts fairly steadily during the eighth century from regional lords. The houses were not sacked by the Saracens as were many farther west and did not have their property appropriated by the Carolingians or other great lords. Some indeed were intimately connected with the Carolingians. Fulda, for example, was founded in 744 by the missionary Boniface, who had been working closely with Carloman, Pippin the Short's older brother. The house was supported by the Carolingians, who still made sure that the abbots were their own loyal men.[77]

Other older houses of eastern Francia with Carolingian connections continued to receive gifts from family members. Echternach had been founded by Pippin of Herstal's mother-in-law, and it was doubtless the family connection that inspired Pippin and his wife to make their own gifts to Echternach.[78] Similarly, the monastery of Prüm, originally founded by the grandmother of Pippin the Short's wife, received gifts from Pippin and his queen.[79] Such monasteries, favored by Charlemagne's family, were able to flourish at a time when houses not so favored not only failed to thrive but indeed suffered serious setbacks.

The monastery of Wissembourg, a seventh-century foundation, received privileges from the Carolingians after they took over Alsace, and its cartulary indicates a surge in donations in the final decades of the eighth century, the same period as the gap in Burgundian charters.[80] This Rhineland monastery also experienced, much earlier than houses like Flavigny, the change from charters being drawn up by laymen to being drawn up by monks or abbots. Throughout the eighth century donation charters were drawn up in the monastery itself, doubtless because notaries were unavailable in the countryside. The exceptions were few; a telling example is that of Duke Liutfrid of Alsace, who, rather than coming to the monastery to make gifts in 739, had his donation charters drawn up *publice* in Strasburg, by a notary—perhaps the only one in the duchy.[81]

Other eastern Frankish houses were able to prosper without much royal notice, indeed, perhaps precisely because of the lack of such attention. Documents were dated by Pippin the Short and his successors, but otherwise the Carolingians were rather distant figures. The monastery of St.-Gall, for example, has one of the richest collections of early medieval documents from any monastery north of the Alps, and a total of some one hundred and sixty from before the year 800, of which more than half still exist as originals.[82] Such monasteries, which did not fall into disarray in the eighth century and had always preserved their own documents, did not experience the same gap in both records and regular life as those houses that had counted on notaries to preserve their records and that suffered from the depredations of Saracens, Vikings, and Carolingians.

The Decline in Western Monasticism

A further indication of the difficulties western monasteries faced during the age of Carolingian rise and hegemony is the steep decline in the number of new monastic foundations in western Francia after about 720, with extremely few foundations for the next century and a half.[83] Charlemagne himself founded no monasteries, in spite of what, much later, monks in search of an august founder might assert.[84] The flourishing monastic world of the year 700 had included many houses, both venerable and newly established foundations. But two centuries of rapid expansion in the Merovingian era were followed by two centuries of far fewer new foundations. Such that did occur, moreover, were more than offset by the number of houses that failed. Indeed, enough monasteries were abandoned or at least fell into decline that it took most of the late tenth and eleventh centuries to reform or refound them all.

The author of the *Gesta* of Bishop Aldric of Le Mans, writing around 860, assumed that his readers would accept the idea of old, abandoned monasteries, long since empty of monks, of the sort that Louis the Pious presented to the bishop. After all, according to the roughly contemporary *Actus* of the bishops of Le Mans, there had been thirty-six monasteries in the diocese early in the eighth century, but there were hardly any left by the end of the century, as they had all been given to "laymen" and "secular men" *in beneficia*.[85] In the Burgundian region, after Flavigny was founded in 717 with the assistance of the Merovingian king Theoderic IV, there were no more new foundations until the foundations of Vézelay, Pouthières, Corbigny, and Charlieu in the second half of the ninth century (see Appendix I).

At the close of the ninth century, seven Burgundian monasteries grouped together in an association of prayer, most of those that still followed a communal life: St.-Martin of Autun, Flavigny, St.-Bénigne of Dijon, St.-Seine, Corbigny, St.-Pierre of Chalon, and St.-Symphorien of Autun.[86] There were a few other Burgundian houses observing a regular life at the time, most notably Vézelay and Pouthières, founded only a generation earlier—though even Vézelay had already experienced troubles, as its original nuns had had to flee from raiders and been replaced by monks.[87]

Cluny, founded at the beginning of the tenth century as a completely new house (rather than a refoundation of an old house), one that would have dozens of priories by the late twelfth century, may seem like an exception. But its later success should not obscure how typical it was at the time, a house founded in the region in the half century starting around 860. Cluny, it should also be noted, owed neither its foundation nor its subsequent prosperity to the Carolingians; William I of Aquitaine, its founder, was married to the daughter of Boso, who had been the first king successfully (if briefly) to challenge the Carolingian monopoly on the thrones of the West.[88] Thus in the classic region "between the Rhine and the Loire," monasticism flourished in the early eighth century, and by the late tenth century many new houses were flourishing again, but in between there was a serious gap in the regular monastic life.

The era of Charlemagne and Louis the Pious was not nearly as difficult for eastern Frankish monasteries, for those in old Austrasia or across the Rhine, as for those in the West—even though they, too, experienced new challenges. The map of gifts and privileges from Charlemagne to churches is heavily weighted toward the east.[89] The scholarly characterization of the Carolingians as supporters of monasticism is generally based on their role in the establishment of houses in east Frankish areas. It would be hard not to see this reorientation as the lineage's rejection of the Merovingians and their churches.

Eighth-century eastern foundations were far more numerous than western ones. For example, the missionary Willibrord founded the monastery of Echternach in 706. Not long thereafter the missionary Boniface, like Willibrord titled *episcopus*, founded the monastery of Fulda. Prüm was founded in the middle decades of the eighth century by Pippin the Short. Similarly, the monastery of Gorze, located a dozen kilometers outside of Metz, was founded at about the same time by Chrodegang, bishop of Metz.[90]

Chrodegang was a significant figure in eighth-century Austrasia: a man who owed his position to secular patronage—according to Paul the Deacon he grew up in the court of Charles Martel and acted as his *referendarius*—but who was genuinely concerned with religious issues.[91] Pippin the Short had made Chrodegang bishop of Metz, his capital, not long after becoming mayor of the palace. Chrodegang himself was a *consanguineus* of those who founded the monastery of Lorsch, according to the *Traditionsbüch* of the house.[92] When Cancor and his mother, Williswinda, Chrodegang's cousins, founded Lorsch in 764, with monks drawn from Gorze, first Chrodegang himself and then his own brother Gundland became abbot there.[93]

Chrodegang is also significant because of the privilege for Gorze he issued at the Council of Compiègne in 757, a privilege that became the new model and greatly increased the authority of a bishop over a monastery. Royal privileges had, during the late seventh and eighth centuries, evolved from grants of immunity to offers of (perhaps unwanted) protection, as already noted. Now episcopal privileges made the same transition.[94] Even while faintly echoing some language of "privileges of liberty," Chrodegang's privilege stated that a monastery should be "subject to the protection and defense" of its bishop, using the same terms that Pippin of Herstal had used in a charter for Echternach two generations earlier (*subiectum sub mundeburde et defensione*). Elections of new abbots, according to Chrodegang, were to take place with the "consent and desire" of the bishop. Earlier privileges had spoken of bishops "invited" to a monastery; Chrodegang in contrast spoke of a bishop arriving "when it pleased him" (*quando ei placuerit*). For him a monastery's well-being was best preserved by being firmly under episcopal—and, by extension, royal—control.

It is surely significant that this privilege was issued only half a dozen years after Pippin removed the last Merovingian king. A decade earlier, when the Merovingians were, at least nominally, still kings, Chrodegang himself subscribed a privilege that the bishop of Strasbourg issued for the monastery of Arnulfsau-Schwarzach, containing all the exemptions and liberties of the sort that had been issued by bishops for a century.[95] But Chrodegang issued his privilege for Gorze with, he said twice, the "consent and desire" of Pippin the Short. Indeed, this privilege has parallels with the privilege that Charlemagne later issued for Lorsch, in which he said that Chrodegang himself had put it under the king's personal control, *in mundeburdem vel defensionem nostram*.[96]

Even houses that escaped domination by the Carolingians in the eighth and early ninth centuries, moreover, could not do so indefinitely. At Echternach, the late twelfth-century history of the house recalled that, after having been ruled by abbots from its foundation until 848, it was then headed by counts for over a century, until 974. At St.-Gall, the abbot was removed by King Arnulf of Germany around 890 and replaced by the king's chaplain.[97] Although Arnulf was careful to express regret and promised that the monks could freely elect their own abbot again after the chaplain's death (a right St.-Gall had had confirmed by all Carolingian kings back to Louis the Pious), there was no disguising his assumption that monastic offices were his to dispose.

One of the reasons for the relative decline of Frankish monasteries under the Carolingians, I would therefore suggest, was a new, close relationship between the kings and the bishops—a relationship the Merovingian kings have been faulted by modern scholars for not pursuing. A number of Carolingian administrators, men like Chrodegang, also served as bishops.[98] For a period of seventy years, all the bishops of the Burgundian see of Langres were from Bavaria and other regions east of the Rhine, men chosen by the Carolingians for political purposes—and indeed the abbots of houses in Dijon were also chosen from this region. The ninth-century bishops of Langres took personal control of most of the monasteries in their diocese, and they were confirmed in this control by the kings.[99]

Throughout the Merovingian era, monasteries—and the saints whose relics they conserved—had both challenged and counseled kings. Now that role was taken over by bishops.[100] A few favored monasteries, like Lorsch, continued to receive attention and gifts from the king, but for the majority of both eastern and western Frankish monasteries, including those with charters in their archives issued by Merovingian kings, the early Carolingian period was an empty one.

The Burgundian evidence thus suggests that the rise of the Carolingians was accompanied by crucial social and economic changes in west Francia, changes that, for the monasteries most affected, took place in a period of documentary silence. Not only were very few documents produced during this period in the west, but essentially no new monasteries were founded. A time of societal breakdown and reorganization was a time uniquely suited for a new dynasty to consolidate its power and become rulers of the Franks. But the coincidence of the rise of the Carolingians, the lacuna in west Francia both in monastic records and in monastic foundations, and the transition from late Roman to medieval patterns of literacy and human settlement was more than just coincidence. I would argue that west Frankish monasteries experienced a major gap because they went into a period of significant decline in the late eighth century, a decline caused to a considerable extent by the rise of Charlemagne's family and their new attitude toward monasteries, their governance, and their property.

Chapter 10

Great Noble Families in the Early Middle Ages

Some aristocrats of the Merovingian era were enormously wealthy. But did these families become the very wealthy and powerful families of the Carolingian era? Curiously, they do not appear to have done so—or, if they did, that was not how they remembered their origins. It is striking that no one living within the borders of the old Roman Empire in the year 800 has demonstrable ancestors from the year 400,[1] even though a number of those living in 1200 can be demonstrated to be the direct descendants of Charlemagne. A gap in aristocratic family history marks the transition from late antiquity to the early Middle Ages, a gap that cannot explained simply by a shortage of evidence. The nature of the aristocracy in the early Middle Ages has been hotly debated, but in this chapter I shall address the question from another direction: that of memory.

Wealthy Merovingian-Era Families

Certainly there was no shortage of wealthy families in the seventh and eighth centuries. Testaments, many issued by bishops, indicate men and women with vast holdings that they were able to give to the church.[2] Of course, almost by definition, such donors left few secular heirs to inherit this wealth. But that did not mean that they were the last in their families. Bishop Bertram of Le Mans, who died in the first decades of the seventh century, named in his unusually long testament three nephews, four grand-nephews, and four cousins (*parentes*, including three men and a woman), one of whom had two sons of his own, as well as naming his two late brothers. He had both inherited and obtained from the royal court property that spread over much of western Francia, from the mouth of the Seine south nearly to the Pyrenees.[3]

Bishop Aunarius of Auxerre (d. 605) also made the church his principal heir, but, like Bertram of Le Mans, he had family members who outlived him. According to his ninth-century *vita*, he was brother of Austrenus, bishop of Orléans, and his sister Agia was the mother of Lupus, bishop of Sens.[4] These connections, chronologically plausible, doubtless came from his testament; the ninth-century authors of his *vita* spelled out what he had inherited from his father and where he wished to donate it when he died. But this powerful ecclesiastical dynasty disappears from the records as abruptly as it appears.

Another example of a wealthy family is provided by Bercharius, who used his substantial fortune to establish a monastery in the woods of Der in 666, originally called Puteolus but soon renamed Montier-en-Der. He gave his foundation, for which he served as first abbot, hereditary property located in twenty-two different villas south of the Loire. Like Bertram and Aunarius, he is known to have had relatives who might have expected to be his heirs because his charter included a specific curse against them if they tried to claim what he gave the new house, though he did not name them.[5]

Fifty years later, in 717, one Wideradus distributed a large amount of property spread across a giant square some 120 kilometers on a side to four basilicas, St.-Andoche of Saulieu, Ste.-Reine of Alise, St.-Férreol of Grigny/Vienne,[6] and especially to St.-Prix (Praeiectus) of Flavigny.[7] He founded Flavigny himself, as he announced in his testament, and he established Benedictine monks there two years later.[8] Wideradus referred to his late father Corbo as a *vir illuster*, an indication that he was of high social status—if the extent of his generosity were not already sufficient evidence. The names of Wideradus's other relatives are not known, even though he left property to them as well as to Burgundian churches.[9]

Similarly, a generation later, Fulrad, counselor to Pippin the Short, who was rewarded by being made abbot of St.-Denis, drew up a testament in favor of that monastery, including property in villas scattered across all of Alsace and adjacent territories.[10] Fulrad's contemporary, the wealthy *patricius* Abbo, made his foundation of Novalesa the recipient of his testamentary bequests in 739, bequests that were spread across an area twice as broad even as the region where Wideradus had owned property. We know the names of Abbo's closest relatives, including his parents, Felix and Rustica—good Roman names—as well as those of three of his four grandparents, some uncles and an aunt, plus a cousin.[11] But this whole wealthy family group disappears from the records in the middle of the eighth century, and although they must have had descendants in the ninth century, we do not know who they were.

The testaments may give only brief glimpses of powerful families, just as they gave away their wealth, but there is also other evidence of great landlords in the seventh and eighth centuries. The author of the seventh-century *vita* of Saint Bris expected his readers to be able to recognize the type of Porcarius, a *vir nobilissimus*, lord of many *servi* and vast fields, who discovered an abandoned oratory and prepared to tear it down, until Saint Bris punished him with a fever and then revealed himself in a vision.[12] If ninth-century nobles did not trace their families to men like Porcarius, it is not because they had not existed.

Women, too, could control vast fortunes. An example is Irmina, mother-in-law of Pippin of Herstal, who founded the monastery of Echternach in 698 and endowed the house richly, including making it the heir for all her property, as she specified in her testament.[13] About the same time, the wealthy matron Erminethrudis made her testament in favor of St.-Denis. Fragments of her original testament still survive, so one can be sure that no later copyist has improved her position.[14]

We know a certain amount about Erminethrudis. She gave St.-Denis and other basilicas in Paris property located in many different villas, as well as a number of serfs with their families, so she was clearly an important landowner in the area. She was the mother of a living but unnamed son, and also of Deorovaldus, buried at St.-Symphorien of Paris by the time she drew up her testament. She also had grandchildren (or just possibly nephews and a niece) named Bertegisilus, Bertericus, and Deorovara, and a daughter-in-law (*nora*) named Bertovara. One can make an informed guess that Deorovara was daughter of Deorovaldus, because their names are so similar, and that Bertovara was the mother of Bertegisilus and Bertericus, with whom she shared a name element.[15]

But this is *all* we know about Erminethrudis. Her testament does not give the names of her parents or her (presumably dead) husband. Bertegisilus and Bertericus do not appear in other sources. The only possible connection between Erminethrudis and individuals found in other sources is found in another fragmentary testament for St.-Denis, this one probably issued slightly earlier by an anonymous man—anonymous because the part of the papyrus with his name is gone—who was son of Idda and husband of Chramnethrudis, just possibly Erminethrudis spelled differently.[16] It may be that Erminethrudis was a member of a well-established and long-lasting dynasty, but if so we will never know it. No one in the ninth century remembered her as their ancestor.

With all these very wealthy people in the sources for the seventh and early eighth centuries, one would expect to find their descendants continuing to be prominent in the late eighth and ninth centuries. But there are surprisingly few lineages that cross the gap from the seventh to the ninth centuries. Seventh-century families often appear in the records without context, floating to the surface as it were with a great deal of éclat, only to disappear again without a trace. In the hundred years after Erminethrudis's death, something changed.

Transformations of the Frankish Aristocracy

These wealthy landowners of the seventh and eighth centuries, both men and women, were very different from the Gallo-Roman aristocrats of the fourth and fifth centuries. Yet the discontinuities between the aristocracies of the year 400 and those of the year 800 were not spread out evenly over four centuries; the sixth century has been seen as an especially crucial transition. Scholars have long posited a shift at the time of the victorious establishment of Frankish rule throughout Gaul during the sixth century, some even arguing that there was essentially no aristocracy at all then separate from the kings and that noble ranks were reconstituted *de novo* by the Merovingians as royal appointees.[17]

This argument clearly goes too far, in spite of such markers of change as the decay of Roman-style villas and the increased importance of connections to court. The kings could not possibly have obliterated an entire population of well-born landowners, and the wealthy of the sixth century continued to have inherited property as well as what they received by royal gift. Those who claimed senatorial nobility, like Gregory of Tours himself, were proudly conscious at the end of the sixth century of their ancestors a hundred years earlier. But if aristocratic families persisted, as Chris Wickham has argued, in many cases what he calls their "distinguishing marks" had changed when the state changed from empire to local kingdom, and the differences in their social position meant that their ancestors were rapidly becoming incomprehensible.[18]

Here I would like to carry the discussion of the transformation of the Frankish aristocracy one step further and focus on another major discontinuity in their history, that of the eighth century. Just as few fifth-century families persisted as self-conscious units through the sixth century and into the seventh, other than the Merovingian royal line itself, so there is a gap between the powerful of the seventh and early eighth centuries and those of the year 800 and after. This gap falls at the very same point as that in western monastic records (Chapter 9). Very few families cross this gap, other than the Arnulfings/Carolingians themselves.

For too long discussions of the eighth-century aristocracy were bogged down in debates about the extent to which they were representatives of the ethnic identity of the peoples of their regions or else royal appointees from elsewhere. That is, for some these aristocrats were the forerunners—perhaps indeed the ancestors—of the regional princes of the tenth century.[19] For others, they were the last remnants of the Merovingian age, shortly to be replaced by an "imperial aristocracy" composed mostly of men of Austrasian stock, established in the rest of Francia by the Carolingians as they rose to power and broke up many of the long-established hierarchies.[20] Although this simplistic dichotomy has rightly been abandoned, allowing a more nuanced view of a Frankish nobility that does not have to be either a conscious creation of the Carolingians or else the palpable expression of self-definition by the folk, it is still necessary to address the novelty of dynastic consciousness among the aristocracy in the ninth century.

In part, of course, in the seventh and early eighth centuries dynasty was not as crucial for the many people who owed their position to the kings as it was for the kings themselves. Dukes and mayors of the palace were appointed and replaced with some frequency. The great lords who appear in the records do not appear to have claimed that just because they were related to someone they had a right to their office. Fredegar certainly noted family connections in many cases. But that he did not bother to mention family for most of those he discussed implies that it was not a central issue. This suggests that there was a shift in the late eighth century in family structure as all great lords, led by the Carolingians, began for the first time to conceptualize themselves as male-line dynasties, in direct imitation of the now-gone Merovingians.[21]

The Arnulfings' family tree may now be pieced together for five generations, but it was only with the historians of the age of Charlemagne that it was portrayed as a clear dynasty. The lack of any such dynastic portrayal by earlier chroniclers—including the chroniclers upon whom scholars now rely for genealogical detail—suggests that non-Merovingians were not considered in the same terms as were the kings. Certainly it was important to know if someone was from a noble *gens* or *stirps*, but the chroniclers might well tell their readers this without bothering to name any specific relatives. Here an understanding of the great nobles, and the way that they remembered and commemorated their own pasts, can shed light on crucial issues.

The Etichonids

The example of the so-called Etichonids indicates how difficult it is to speak confidently of "families" and their boundaries in the seventh century and suggests that the ninth century, while also not having a simple or transparent conception of family, remembered their ancestors very differently.[22] It is possible, by combining a number of sources (some from appreciably later), to construct six generations of a family tree for this group in the seventh and early eighth centuries. But in the ninth century the way this family was remembered had changed—even though there may well have been biological continuity.

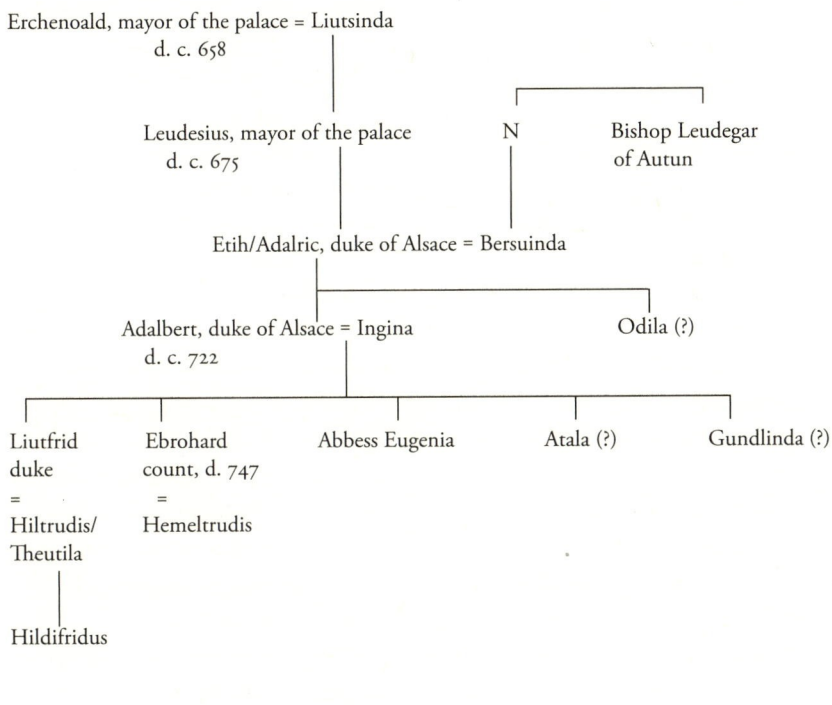

Figure 4. The Etichonids.

Evidence for these six generations is as follows. Erchenoald was the first known family member chronologically. He became mayor of the palace in the 640s,[23] and although there is no precise evidence for his family connections, Fredegar (a near contemporary) tells us that he was a *consanguineus* of the (unnamed) mother of King Dagobert I, implying that she was Clothar II's beloved wife Bertetrudis.[24] Erchenoald and the queen might have been aunt and nephew, or distant cousins. Fredegar was concerned with kin but did not define this kin as any straight-line lineage.

Although Erchenoald died around 658, his son, Leudesius, did not become mayor of the palace until the 670s; there was no presumption of heredity.[25] Leudesius was most likely born to Liutsinda, Erchenoald's second wife. Both the similarity of name elements and the fact that Leudesius did not become mayor until nearly two decades after his father's death suggest that he was born of this late second marriage. The *Liber Historiae Francorum* calls Leudesius noble, but its most interesting detail is a political alliance between Leudesius and Bishop Leudegar of Autun, at whose urging Leudesius was given the office of mayor.[26]

This alliance of course recalls that of the Arnulfings/Pippinids; Pippin I and Bishop Arnulf of Metz were allies in the 620s,[27] and from the marriage of Pippin's daughter and Arnulf's son came (it was later believed) the lineage that resulted in Charlemagne. Leudesius was not nearly as successful as was Pippin I, in spite of his own friendship with a bishop. Ebroin, mayor of the palace, who had been tonsured and made an unwilling monk at Luxeuil at the time that Leudesius came to power, soon left the monastery and had both Leudesius and Bishop Leudegar killed—even though Leudesius was his own godfather, according to the continuator of Fredegar's chronicle—along with Warin, the bishop's brother.[28]

At this point, after only two generations, the family of the Etichonids disappear from the seventh- and eighth-century narrative sources. But their subsequent history may be constructed from scattered charters, from occasional mentions in saints' lives, and from much later narrative sources, if one assumes that monks of the twelfth century had some now-lost earlier sources on which to draw. That such powerful individuals are not linked in a lineage by the narrative sources is itself an indication that such a dynasty was not of great concern.

If one can recognize Leudesius, briefly mayor of the palace, as Liuthericus, mayor of the palace for the "emperor" Childeric,[29] then the later "Vita Odilae" has further genealogical information. According to this source,

Liuthericus was the father of the very noble duke Adalric of Alsace, also called Etih. It is for him that the line is called the "Etichonids" by modern scholars.[30] An Edichus or Chadichus does appear as duke in Alsace in a 675 charter of Childeric II (though with no indication of his father) and, under the name of Adalricus, was accused of being unfaithful to King Theoderic III in a charter of 677. He also appears, under the name of Duke Chatalrichus or Chaticus, in the late seventh-century *vita* of Abbot Germanus of Grandval, though without any indication of his family. The twelfth-century chronicle of Bèze, however, which incorporates early charters of the house, calls Adalricus son not of Leudesius but of Amalgarius, founder of Bèze, and of his wife, Aquilina.[31]

Adalric/Etih, the duke of Alsace, and his wife, Bersuinda, also are referred to in a later document from Ebersheim, a document the monks attributed to Charlemagne. According to this retrospective document, the noble couple were the original founders of Ebersheim. The thirteenth-century chronicle of Ebersheim also identified Etih (here called Atticus) as the house's founder, with enough detail that it is possible that the chronicler had an authentic foundation charter before him. In addition, this chronicle specified that the duchess Bersuinda was related to Bishop Leudegar: according to the chronicle, she was the bishop's niece, daughter of a sister of Leudegar or of his brother Warin.[32] If the chronicle is to be believed, then the friendship between Leudesius and Bishop Leudegar was cemented by a marriage between Leudesius's son and Leudegar's niece. This connection between Adalric/Etih and Bishop Leudegar may, however, be undercut by the "Passio" of Leudegar, written within a few years of the bishop's murder, which identifies Duke Chadalricus from Austrasia (i.e., Etih) as one of the party of the bishop's bitterest enemies.[33]

A similar story is told by the "Vita Odilae." Here Duke Adalric was married to Persinda, related by "affinity" to Bishop Leudegar, and they were the parents of Duke Adalbert and of Saint Odila. Duke Adalbert does appear in the charters; he married a woman named Ingina, made a dying gift to Honau in 722, and is referred to again in a retrospective charter of Pippin the Short for Honau from c. 748, although with no specification of his parentage. The "Vita Odilae" says that Adalbert had three daughters, Eugenia, Atala, and Gundlinda, and charters from both Honau and Wissembourg give Adalbert sons named Liutfrid and Ebrohard. The charter for Honau also has the abbess Eugenia witness a gift from the brothers Liutfrid and Ebrohard, so it is indeed possible that she was their sister. (Atala seems less likely, however; this was the name of the abbess of Hohenburg, Odila's nunnery, in the 780s, some sixty years after Duke Adalbert's death.) A charter from Murbach from the late 720s calls Liutfrid a duke and Ebrohard a count, and in Theoderic IV's confirmation of this charter he called Count Ebrohard Murbach's founder and his own *fidelis*.[34] Duke Liutfrid, who referred in his own charters to his mother Ingina, married a woman named Hiltrudis or Theutila (although Theutila may be a second wife). He and Theutila appear for the last time in a 742 charter for Wissembourg, when he had a son named Hildifridus, about whom nothing more is known. Ebrohard married a woman named Hemeltrudis, with whom he appeared in charters for Murbach from the 730s, but is not known to have left any heirs. Ebrohard died in 747.[35]

One can thus, at least if one is willing to assume that later sources have some accurate genealogical information on the seventh and eighth centuries, give a family tree with six generations in the male line, from the original Erchenoald, mayor of the palace; through his son Leudesius, also a mayor of the palace and ally of a martyred bishop; to his (possible) son Etih/Adalric, a duke and husband of the bishop's niece; to his son Adalbert, also a duke; to *his* two sons, Duke Liutfrid and Count Ebrohard, and three daughters, all holy young women; and finally to Duke Liutfrid's son. But it is striking that the continuity of the line (even the rather shaky continuity thus established) is broken by the middle of the eighth century.[36]

Here the Etichonids were not *forgotten*, for Thegan, the biographer of Louis the Pious, still remembered them well into the ninth century. According to Louis's biography, Ermengard, the bride of the emperor's oldest son, was the daughter of Count Hugh, himself of the *stirps* of Duke Etih.[37] Count Hugh, who is identified as count of Tours by the Royal Frankish Annals, appeared in a document of Charlemagne's in 807, receiving property in the regions of Anjou and Rennes, and also received the nunnery of St.-Julien of Auxerre from him, a grant reconfirmed by Louis the Pious.[38] But Duke Etih/Adalric had been dead for close to 150 years when a girl from his *stirps* married the future emperor.[39] It is also worth noting that an Alsatian duke's descendant was established now in West Francia. Etih/Adalric had been important enough that his distant relative, Count Hugh, was honored by association with him, but the absence of other relatives worth mentioning during those missing generations certainly suggests a break in how families were considered and constructed in the eighth century.[40]

The example of the Etichonids, therefore, suggests that tidily constructed family trees were not the norm in the seventh and early eighth centuries. Once the Carolingians set out to define themselves as a patrilineage, as discussed in Chapter 7, and defined their kingship as hereditary in the male line, other groups of relatives had to follow suit.[41] But this new sense of patrilineage meant that the organization of even the most powerful nonroyal families before the late eighth century remained profoundly strange to their descendants.

The Robertians

The novelty of the ways that men of the ninth century thought about their ancestors can be further illustrated by the example of the Robertians, the ancestors of the Capetian kings of France. They are one of the very few groups of relatives, other than the Carolingians themselves, for which it is possible to construct a line of ancestors back from the ninth century into the early eighth or even seventh century.[42] And yet they themselves never evoked these ancestors—and neither do modern histories of the lineage. The narratives of around the year 800, focused on Charlemagne's ancestors, outshone any such effort the Robertians might have made, and by the mid-ninth century, when Robert the Strong (d. 866) became a major figure under Charlemagne's grandsons, ideas of family had shifted so much that neither he nor his contemporaries thought of him as a descendant of Merovingian-era royal officials.

Even today, historians cannot agree on the ancestry of Robert the Strong. The father of two kings and the male-line ancestor of all kings of France from 987 until the Revolution, he appears rather abruptly in the French sources of the mid-ninth century. Certainly he was no parvenu; he was wealthy and powerful, a count, a war leader against the Vikings, a lay abbot of multiple houses. The comments by Richer, who wrote a century and a half later, that Robert was a simple knight, son of one Witichin or Widukind, appear to have been made purposely to discredit his descendants and are given no credence by modern historians.[43] But that Richer could make such a comment at all shows how little information there was on Robert's ancestry.

One aspect of Robert's family is clear from his first appearance in the ninth century: relatives often held church property and acted as lay abbots, in the Carolingian tradition. In 845, Charles the Bald restored to the archbishop of Reims some property he said he had distributed in benefice to his *fideles*, including Robert. In 852, Robert was lay abbot of Marmoutier.[44] Indeed, Robertians continued to exercise authority over the relics of Saint Martin for the next century and a half; their possession of the legendary cape of the saint gave rise to the nickname Capet, eventually the name given to the whole dynasty. Odo, oldest son of Robert the Strong, was "count and abbot" of St.-Martin of Tours. Both King Robert I, younger son of Robert the Strong, and Robert I's son Hugh the Great are attested as having acted as abbots of St.-Martin in a 931 charter of King Raoul (Robert I's son-in-law).[45]

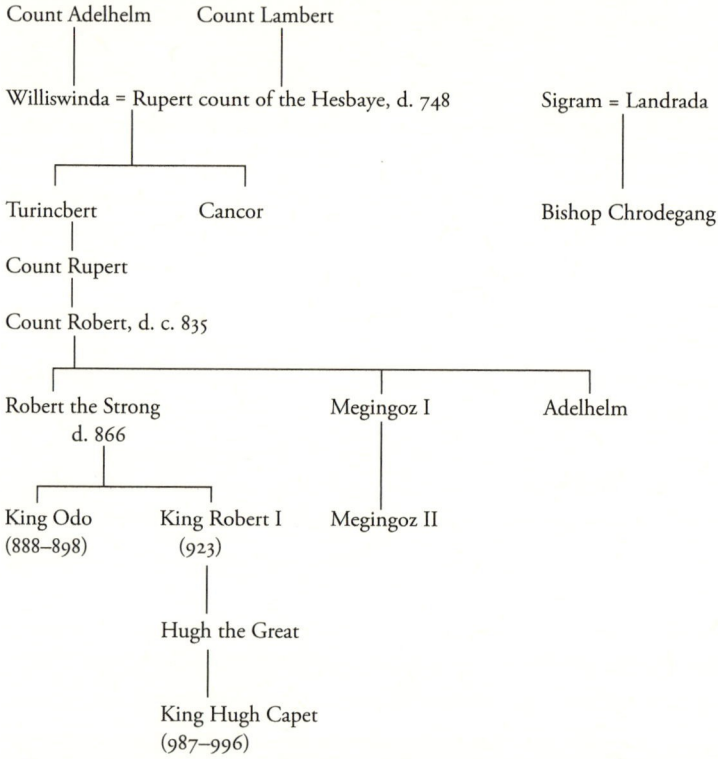

Figure 5. The Robertians, ancestors of the Capetians (simplified).

And yet this very powerful group of relatives appears to spring into existence with no background—or at least none that was obvious even at the time that they first took the throne. The difficulty of determining Robert the Strong's ancestry is more than the result of scant sources—or even of looking for sources in the wrong places. Rather, it is a reflection of how medieval writers themselves conceptualized their past, indeed an act of deliberate forgetting.

Beginning in the eleventh century, writers sought to reshape French history into three relatively tidy periods, the Merovingian, Carolingian, and Capetian.[46] This periodization was a great success and even now is taken for granted. But in putting ruling families into their "correct" compartments (481–751, 751–987, post-987), one risks overlooking if not indeed impatiently cutting away any branches of the family that hang out of their appropriate compartment, or even try to invade other compartments. To glorify the Capetian lineage their publicists concentrated only on those men who were kings, rather than nonroyal relatives, much less women. Indeed, by the thirteenth century Capetian family trees might leave out all pre-987 Robertians.[47]

Unlike the Carolingians, who quite consciously tried to push their own origins back into the seventh century, when the Arnulfings, they suggested, already "really" ruled the Frankish kingdoms, the Capetians were much less interested in their ancestry before Hugh Capet. The troublesome century (888–987) from Odo to Hugh, when alternately Carolingians and Robertians served as kings of the Franks, had to be smoothed out, often by being left out. As a result, even if Capetian histories strayed back before 987, they made no effort to go back before Robert the Strong.

And yet there is good evidence to construct a family tree of Robertian counts and dukes back to men who served at the Merovingian court at the time of Arnulf of Metz and Pippin I. Their documentary sources are indeed as good as the documentary sources for the early Arnulfings, even if the early Robertians tend not to feature as prominently in the narrative sources. This should not be surprising, given the pull the Arnulfings had on the historical imagination once Pippin of Herstal effectively eliminated opposition. But the biggest difference between the sources for early Arnulfing/Pippinid history and early Robertian history is that we have no ninth-century court of Robertians—as we have for the Carolingians—saying, "Yes, those are our ancestors."

Robert the Strong becomes much less a mysteriously appearing figure if one can avoid labeling him "French." The distinction between "French" and "German" is, of course, markedly unhelpful for the Carolingian era, but French scholars for generations resisted seeing the first ancestor of the Capetians as having any Germanic taint. This kept their attention away from the Rhineland and away from the sources that speak quite a bit about men named Robert or Rupert.[48] The challenge is in going beyond generalities like "the clan of the Rupertines" to knowing exactly how Robert's family was related to other people with whom they were allied—or against whom they competed for advantage.

The most likely family tree for Robert the Strong begins in the Rhineland with a Robert (or Rupert) who acted as royal *missus* in 825; Einhard wrote him a letter about this same time.[49] This Robert probably died around 835, for Robert the Strong—who is also doubtless the "Robert son of Count Robert" found in documents from the monastery of Lorsch in the 830s—received property in the Rhineland from Louis the Pious in early 836, when the emperor called him his *fidelis*.[50] Robert the Strong was probably brother—or possibly brother-in-law—of one Megingoz, who called Odo, oldest son of Robert the Strong, his nephew (*nepos*) when they made a gift together to Lorsch in 876; Megingoz's probable son, Megingoz II, was referred to some fifteen years later as Odo's cousin (*nepos* again—the word could mean either nephew or cousin).[51] Robert the Strong is also usually considered the brother (or possibly brother-in-law) of one Adelhelm, because Adelhelm was *avunculus* of Robert's son Odo.[52]

German scholars (followed in recent years by at least some French scholars) have created a family tree that gives Robert the Strong ancestry going back at least four generations. They make his father Count Robert (or Rupert) son of another Robert (or Rupert), son of Turincbert, son of Rupert I, count of the Oberrhein in the mid-eighth century.[53] Thus Robert the Strong's grandfather is identified as the Count Robert who appears in a charter for Lorsch in 795. As a youth this Robert appeared in a 770 charter with his father, Turincbert, who had a brother named Cancor.[54] Turincbert and Cancor were important figures in Alsatian history, sons of the widow Williswinda who founded Lorsch in 764. Williswinda, herself daughter of Count Adelhelm, was the widow of Count Rupert, according to the necrology of Lorsch.[55]

According to the *Traditionsbüch* of Lorsch, Cancor was the *consanguineus* of Chrodegang, the bishop of Metz who assisted in Lorsch's foundation and whose brother became the house's first abbot.[56] (It is rather ironic that Pippin the Short, who found Chrodegang's help invaluable when he became king of the Franks, was here relying on someone who can be worked into the family tree of the Capetian line that would eventually replace the Carolingians.)[57] Chrodegang, according to Paul the Deacon, was from the Hesbaye and was of the highest nobility, son of Sigram and Landrada.[58] It is unclear exactly how Cancor and Chrodegang were related, but the name element *Chrod-* suggests he was related to men named Robert.[59]

Williswinda's husband can probably be identified with the Count Robert who appears in the Hesbaye in several charters from the first half of the eighth century, the same region from which Chrodegang came. A 741 charter for St.-Trond refers to Count Robert as son of Lambert, and the eighth-century *vita* of Bishop Eucherius of Orléans says that when he was driven from his see by Charles Martel, he found refuge in the Hesbaye with *Chrodebertus dux*. Robert of the Hesbaye was probably the *Hotbertus* killed in 748, according to the "Annales Alamannici."[60] His father Lambert may be the same person as the Count Lambert who appears in a charter from Metz from 715, which would push the Robertians' ancestry back to a fifth generation.[61]

At this point all effort to find the ancestry of Robert the Strong becomes sheer speculation, yet Roberts, Ruperts, and Lamberts can readily be found even earlier, often serving the Merovingian kings. These often, however, appear in Neustria as well as the Rhineland. A Chrodoberthus signed a charter of Chilperic II in 716.[62] He may be the same as the Ruotbertus who signed a charter of Charles Martel in 723 and perhaps the same as the Rotbertus who acted as *advocatus* before Charles Martel on behalf of the monks of St.-Wandrille.[63] Another Hrodbertus, said to be of the highest nobility and to have a niece named Erintrudis, was bishop of Worms and Salzburg in the early eighth century.[64] A *referendarius* Chrodberchtus appears in a 692/3 charter of Clovis III.[65]

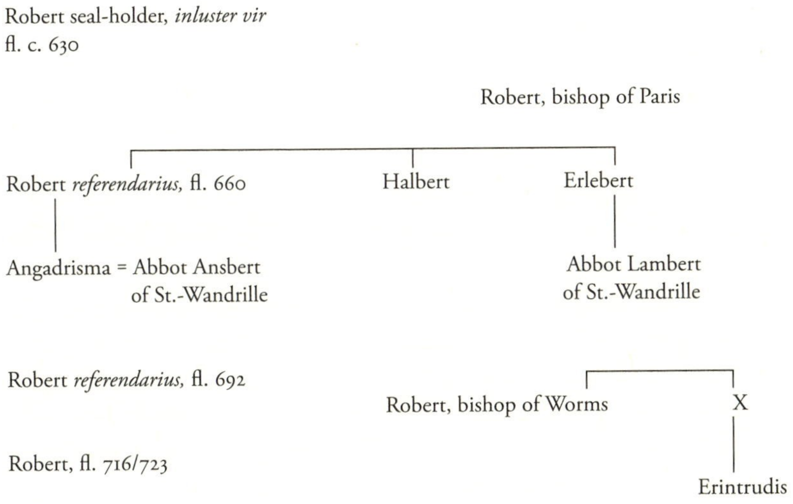

Robert seal-holder, *inluster vir*
fl. c. 630

                                                Robert, bishop of Paris

Robert *referendarius*, fl. 660   Halbert   Erlebert

Angadrisma = Abbot Ansbert   Abbot Lambert
            of St.-Wandrille   of St.-Wandrille

Robert *referendarius*, fl. 692
                              Robert, bishop of Worms   X

Robert, fl. 716/723
                                                                Erintrudis

Figure 6. Seventh- and early eighth-century men named Robert.

Another Hrotbertus *referendarius*, called "major domo of the sacred palace" in a charter from 660, appears a generation or so earlier. This one was apparently the brother of one Haltbertus; the two were said to be of the highest nobility and uncles (*avunculi*) of the seventh-century Abbot Lambert of St.-Wandrille, son of Erlebertus, according to a *vita* written not long after his death.[66] The slightly later *vita* of Abbot Lambert's successor Abbot Ansbert—who supposedly married Hrotbertus's daughter Angadrisma, although the couple maintained a chaste union—says that Hrotbertus kept the seal for King Clothar III (d. 673).[67]

This Hrotbertus was perhaps identical with the Rodebertus who was identified as count in the Alsace region in a royal charter from 675; the Alsatian count was doubtless the same as the Chrodobertus, "count of the palace," who acted as executioner on behalf of the mayor of the palace in the late 670s.[68] Another Chrodobertus, called "excellent prince," was bishop of Paris in the 650s.[69] An earlier Chrodobertus was seal-holder for King Dagobert, according to a 630 document, and was doubtless the same as the Duke Crodobertus whom Fredegar says fought at Dagobert's side against the Wends in the campaign of 631.[70] He may be the same person as the *inluster vir Rodbertus* who is referenced in a retrospective charter of Pippin the Short as having made gifts to St.-Denis at the time of Clothar II, and perhaps is the *inluster vir Daobercthus* in an original 625 document of Clothar II for St.-Denis.[71]

In studying the Merovingian-era curia, scholars have tended to give all their attention to the mayors of the palace, because some of them eventually gave rise to the Carolingians. The mayors of the palace were a power in their own right, attempting throughout the seventh century to make their office hereditary.[72] The counts of the palace, however, may have been nearly as important. They were after all responsible for overseeing the royal tribunal[73] and thus played an essential part in the king's function as lawgiver. A surprising number of counts of the palace were named Robert. One can semiplausibly take the history of the "Rupertine" counts of the palace back as far as that of the "Arnulfing" mayors of the palace (first decades of the seventh century). It is thus not too far-fetched to suggest that the ancestors of Capetians were consolidating their power as agents for the Merovingians at exactly the same time—if not initially as successfully—as the Arnulfings were doing so.

Constructing the family trees of the Etichonids and the early Robertians may now seem little more than an exercise in antiquarianism. But the details of this apparently arcane genealogical exercise become revelatory of how ancestors were remembered in the early Middle Ages if the process is compared to that by which modern scholars have worked out the ancestry of the Arnulfings/Carolingians.[74] For all three lineages, there is little indication of an effort to create a memory of the family before the ninth century; modern scholars have to piece earlier connections together from scattered references. Only when a lineage took the throne, or came close to doing so, did members create a memory of patrilineage. The Merovingians had always been a *stirps*; the other groups of relatives only began to define themselves as such at the end of the eighth or ninth century. If we know more about Charlemagne's ancestors in the seventh century than about Robert the Strong's, or about how (or even if) Louis the Pious's daughter-in-law was descended from a seventh-century duke of Alsace, it is because the Carolingians themselves were more assiduous in creating that memory.

The apparent gap in the eighth century, between the wealthiest Merovingian-era lords and the great nobles of the Carolingian and subsequent eras, may in part be due to the broad transformations taking place from antiquity to the Middle Ages. But in part it is due to more specific changes, a new way of thinking about lineage. Aristocratic Roman clans and lineages had disappeared from Gaul along with consciousness of senatorial status, not long after the time of Gregory of Tours, requiring a reconception of family among the powerful. Before the eighth century, although of course men believed that whatever their fathers had had was rightfully theirs, there was little sense of a long line of ancestors giving validity—except for the kings.

When the Carolingians ascended the throne, they, too, needed to remember a line of ancestors. Those who challenged them then had to create their own ancestral memory. The Robertians, however, who became kings for the first time only five generations after Pippin the Short, looked back no further than Robert the Strong. Thus modern scholars can attest to more ancestors in the distant past for the Capetians that they did for themselves—the opposite of the Carolingians. The Etichonids, in contrast to both, never seem to have constructed their family history as a lineage. The six generations of (probable) Etichonids of the seventh and early eighth centuries were never arranged into a lineage by men of the time but have to be created out of name similarities and later accounts, those dating from periods when the importance of lineage was self-evident for the powerful. Hugh of Tours, living when those at the royal court were acutely aware of patrilineal connections, was said to be of the *stirps* of Duke Etih because it seemed obvious in the ninth century that he must belong to some great dynasty, but no one at the time spelled out his line of descent, which modern scholars, too, have been unable to determine.

As all these examples suggest, with the rise of the Carolingians came a new way of thinking about one's ancestry, one that persisted into the high Middle Ages. If the many powerful lords of the Merovingian era cannot be demonstrated to have descendants in the ninth and later centuries, it was not because their lineages died out. Rather, it was because no one (except the Merovingian kings themselves) thought in terms of lineage before the end of the eighth century. When the lords of the ninth century began to do so, it was generally too late to create the appropriate memory.

Chapter 11

Early Frankish Monasticism

The sixth century was the period in which medieval Christianity was formed.[1] By the year 600, bishops were well-established political figures, asceticism was institutionalized in the monasteries, and saints worked through their relics. During the century after the conversion of Clovis, late antique Gaul developed the assumptions about church governance, monasticism, and the holy dead that dominated for the next thousand years. Once early medieval Christianity settled on its broad outlines, the tendency was to re-remember the past as having followed the same pattern.

Christians of the seventh century shaped their religious practices by contemplating their past, retelling the story of their predecessors until an account of fairly radical religious and structural innovation became the story of what had always been done. Earlier Christian communities in Gaul had had a much less orderly governance system and had witnessed far more independent hermits and wandering ascetics than monks living under a Rule, but that was not how they were recalled. Such an act of creative memory obscured for later medieval thinkers the differences between the Christianity of late antiquity and that of the following centuries in Europe. For it was not inevitable that the organized church take the form it had by around 600, something not presaged by the first centuries of Christianity, yet a form that then persisted for close to a millennium.

Early—that is, sixth- and seventh-century—Frankish monasticism did not think of itself as early monasticism. Some three centuries previously, Anthony had first attracted followers as he retreated into the Egyptian desert, away from both materiality and Roman society. Separation from the world, accompanied by fervent prayer, marked those who wanted a more intensely religious life than that followed by other Christians. In the late fourth and early fifth centuries, there was a virtual explosion of wandering monks all around the Mediterranean, men who claimed apostolic precedent for their wandering and begging but who were regarded with deep suspicion by the church hierarchy. Initially without legal status, being neither clergy nor laymen, they commanded no respect.[2] These *gyrovagi* (wanderers) could be perceived as holier than the established clergy, as they themselves asserted, or could be considered both lazy and crazy.

But in sixth-century Gaul most of these debates were either irrelevant or over. Hermits might still be found in ones and twos in any wild patch, but there were few crazed wanderers—indeed, it is estimated that a good two-thirds of sixth-century hermits were aristocratic men seeking spiritual purity.[3] Begging and solitary wandering became less viable with the collapse of Roman urban culture. Monks were now a recognized and respected legal category, subject to their bishops as specified in the 451 Council of Chalcedon.[4] They were supposed to be stable, live in groups, and follow some kind of a rule under a master or abbot.

Unlike their predecessors, sixth-century communities of monks had their own fields and orchards, as assumed in the Benedictine Rule written in this period, and generally their own serfs and peasant tenants to work these fields. The well-to-do could and did support the followers of holy poverty, but such support increasingly took the form of donations of property rather than a coin pressed into a beggar's hand. By the seventh century, such donations were explicitly tied to a search for salvation by the powerful, and new monasteries generally received a formal foundation charter, commemorating both their foundation and the donors' generosity.

When the monks of the sixth and seventh centuries constructed the memory of their own past, many of the transformations of the previous centuries were smoothed out, so that their predecessors were assumed to be almost like the monks of their own time, even while monastic authors also argued for the exceptional achievements of these predecessors. And yet the past remained foreign enough that monks felt compelled to create explanations for how their houses had reached what seemed their entirely self-evident Present.

The Origins of Monasticism in Gaul

Monasticism had reached Gaul when Martin, bishop of Tours, founded Marmoutier, the first Western monastery, shortly before 400.[5] Even more influential was Lérins, founded about a generation later. This house, on an island off what is now the Riviera, began as a hermitage of aristocratic men, many of whom went on to become bishops. Lérins also became an intellectual center for sermons, letters, saints' lives, and theological treatises. Its rule was one of several possible rules adopted subsequently by other monasteries.[6]

But Lérins was unusual. In the mid-fifth century, at the time of the Council of Chalcedon, there were few other monastic communities in Gaul. Brothers assembled at Arles and Marseille, also on the Mediterranean; at the monastic complex at Grigny, across the Rhône from Vienne; and at Agaune, the latter group replaced in the sixth century by a community established by King Sigismund of Burgundy.[7] In the half century or so after Chalcedon, groups of monks began for the first time to attain significant numbers in Gaul. But monasteries were still uncommon; in the 480s the scholar and preacher Caesarius, later bishop of Arles, had to travel over five hundred kilometers to Lérins from his native Chalon-sur-Saône in order to find a suitable monastery to join.[8] In fact, the evidence often suggests a very uneven and sporadic existence for monasteries. And fifth- and early sixth-century monasteries did not yet have a form that would be recognizable to their medieval successors.[9]

In the fifth century, when much of Frankish Gaul was Christian, if not yet its kings, houses were generally founded through the efforts of the monks themselves, as hermits attracted disciples or as wanderers settled down. Scarcely any laymen founded monasteries in Gaul before the middle of the sixth century, long after the conversion of Clovis. He himself played no role in the establishment of monastic communities, even though many monasteries claimed him as a founder centuries later. He did have the church of the Apostles built in Paris to shelter his own tomb, where Saint Genovefa was also buried, but this basilica had no community of monks.

In the sixth century, in contrast to the fifth, monasteries were typically founded by bishops or, in some cases, by kings. Such was the case with Sigismund's community at St.-Maurice of Agaune. Royal foundations then became increasingly common after the year 600. Highly influential here were the practices introduced at Luxeuil by the Irish missionary Columbanus (d. 615), who was celebrated in his *vita* for working with kings to found monasteries—when he was not cursing them for inappropriate behavior. Nonroyal though still wealthy laymen began founding monasteries in the mid-sixth century, but they were more unusual than royal founders until the seventh century.[10]

The Burgundy–southern Champagne region provides a typical example.

Only one monastery, St.-Marien of Auxerre, was founded there before the year 500, as a group of recluses supported by Bishop Germanus.[11] In the first half of the sixth century, Moûtier-St.-Jean became established, originally as a hermitage. In the second half of the century, St.-Seine was founded by a disciple of Saint John of Moûtier-St.-Jean, and monks also settled in the basilicas of St.-Marcel outside Chalon, St.-Symphorien of Autun, and St.-Bénigne of Dijon, all of which were dedicated to early martyr saints and were supported by their local bishops—and for St.-Marcel, by King Guntram. This is a remarkably skimpy list for a region later considered a great monastic center. St.-Remy and St.-Jean of Sens, as well as the houses of Ferrières and Nesle, may also have been basilicas in the sixth century, but there is no evidence of their existence as monastic communities before the seventh century. As detailed in Appendix I, although many more monasteries were founded in the region after the year 600, such houses were still unusual a century and a half after Chalcedon.[12]

A community of monks could, at least theoretically, be established anywhere. But sixth-century monasteries were most commonly established at sites that were already sacred—such as martyrs' tombs. Earlier burials helped make a site holy. Some churches were built over burial sites that appear to predate the region's conversion to Christianity.[13] Their dead, however, were considered holy dead. If they had not been Christian when buried, Christian services conducted above their bones brought them into the community of the faithful. In urban areas, where most sixth-century monasteries were located, the general sequence was church, then church with holy relics, then church served by a body of monks. In the countryside, the sequence was holy site, then holy site with an oratory, then holy site with a church and a body of monks. A basilica might have a body of monks for a period, lose them, and then reacquire them. The establishment of monastic communities took place at first slowly, almost silently. It created a new relationship between the dead saints and their bones on the one hand and the community of the faithful on the other. The idea that all major churches and basilicas should be served by monks or canons, although almost self-evident in later centuries, was novel in Merovingian Gaul.

The slow transition from church or oratory to house of religious brothers meant that one cannot now say with any certainty exactly when an early Frankish monastery was founded. Perhaps those at the time would have had equal difficulty giving a precise date. The presence or absence of monks was not even always indicated by whether a church was called a *basilica* or a *monasterium*, for some houses that certainly had monks were referred to as basilicas and other houses served by secular priests were called monasteries.[14] A church served by only two or three monks could not really be characterized as a monastery (contemporary sources might call it an *abbatiola*). Monasteries might appear abruptly in the sources and then disappear again. Even the presence of an *abbas* did not necessarily imply a community of monks. Monastic communities from St.-Martin of Tours to Bobbio were founded or refounded in structures that might have been an abandoned oratory or might once have sheltered an earlier monastic community.[15] Thus monasteries were not founded *de novo* but rather transformed an earlier site that had already acquired some of the holiness the new community wished to appropriate.

The presence of a sixth-century basilica often led seventh-century monks to push their foundation event back well before the actual establishment of a monastic community. The city of Auxerre had more known churches at the end of the sixth century than any neighboring see (see Appendix II), although in part this may be an artifact of better documentation.[16] But many of these were recent foundations. There is, significantly, only one urban monastery in the group, the fifth-century foundation of St.-Marien—and even it was not strictly "urban," as it lay across the river. All the other urban churches of the sixth century were basilicas, with a priest or two but no monks—even though they all acquired monks in the seventh or subsequent centuries.[17] The few rural monasteries were small houses that did not long survive and should better be considered as hermitages or communities of recluses than the well-established and well-regulated institutions of the seventh century.[18]

Foundations and Foundation Accounts

Foundation stories are always retrospective: one knows the end of the story, the full flourishing of the institution, and thus can look backward for the elements that led to its first establishment. The creation of such foundation stories for their houses by Merovingian-era monks required a decoding of the past—an examination of evidence that could disturbingly suggest a very different sort of institution—in order to find and highlight those elements that led to their present. Numbers of monks, the rule they followed, and even whether the inhabitants of such a house were male or female were constantly in flux. Such complicated series of events are rarely reflected in the foundation accounts written in the seventh century, which preferred a simpler story in which a church that lacked a body of monks then happily and permanently acquired one. The difficulty confronting monks of older houses was that monastic foundations before the end of the sixth century were not nearly as tidy, in spite of the best efforts of foundation stories to suggest otherwise.

For example, Moûtier-St.-Jean (Reomaus), dating from the early sixth century, began as a group of hermits, who adopted a version of the institutes of Lérins. But this was not enough for later monks of Reomaus, who went to the trouble of forging a charter they attributed to Clovis's son Clothar I, in which the king recalled that Clovis himself had taken the *monasterium* under his *emunitas*.[19] Although the charter shows some signs of genuine Merovingian chancery style, its mention of the king offering "immunity and defense" indicates an actual date in the Carolingian period. But a purported early royal charter gave Reomaus the appearance of always having been a monastery of the sort that later monks could recognize, thus removing the need to remember a more complicated—and strange—early history.

Even though to later monks the establishment of a monastic community was a step upward, it could have caused real difficulties in the sixth century. A simple basilica would generally have welcomed everyone to venerate its relics, whereas a monastery would exclude most laypeople, especially women. The monks became the mediators between the saint and the greater body of the faithful.[20] Earlier, the untutored could have direct access to relics—as suggested by Gregory of Tours's story of countryfolk gathering wax from the forgotten sarcophagus of Saint Benignus.[21] But seventh-century foundation accounts were not interested in such problems.

One of the earliest monastic foundations to be fully documented was the nunnery later called Ste.-Croix, founded at Poitiers in the sixth century by Radegund, queen and saint. Gregory of Tours reproduced two relevant letters in his *Historia*, one from Radegund to the bishops of Gaul, recounting the establishment of nuns at Poitiers, who would follow the Rule of Caesarius under Abbess Agnes, and the other from the bishops to Radegund, confirming this foundation.[22] Both letters were issued after the fact, once the nuns had already been assembled. Neither letter could be called a foundation charter. In hers, Radegund simply declared that she had deeded all her property to the house and that she expected new nuns to do likewise. The emphasis was on the spiritual relationship between the retired queen and the bishops. The difficulty that monks and nuns of later centuries had, therefore, in dating the origins of their houses was due in part to the fact that foundation charters were an innovation only sporadically employed in the sixth century, not a requirement even for such an important house as Radegund's.

The earliest aristocratic foundation charter from Frankish Gaul now considered authentic is that of St.-André of Vienne, from the mid-sixth century. According to this charter, Ansemundus, who also appears in the later chronicle of Ado of Vienne with the title of *dux*, founded the house as a nunnery; he and his wife made their daughter Eugenia the abbess. But Ansemundus established St.-André primarily as a burial place for himself and his wife rather than as a religious community such as became the norm a century later. The nuns attached to the basilica were described as an offshoot of another religious community for women, this one headed by his sister Eubona.[23] The real monastic "foundation" then was the earlier, undocumented one of Eubona's house—a house that seems to have soon disappeared, even though St.-André went on to have a long and distinguished history.

In the seventh century, in contrast to the sixth, all monasteries were expected to have formal foundations. The way a seventh-century writer thought about a sixth-century monastic foundation may be illustrated by St.-Marcel of Chalon-sur-Saône. According to the chronicler Fredegar, writing in the later seventh century, King Guntram of Burgundy founded the house in 584 by having a sumptuous church built where the saint's "precious" body rested and then brought in monks to establish a *monasterium*. Guntram convened a synod of forty bishops who confirmed both his foundation and the institution there of the liturgy of St.-Maurice of Agaune. Everything in Fredegar's account suggests great formality. He concluded by saying that when King Guntram died some nine years later, he was buried in the monastery of St.-Marcel.[24] Despite the detail and the notable people involved, no contemporary foundation charter for St.-Marcel exists. The monks later forged one, probably in the eleventh century.[25] King Guntram was not widely evoked in eleventh-century monasteries, which generally preferred Clovis, Dagobert, or Pippin the Short, if not indeed Charlemagne.[26] His presence here thus suggests that the creators of the forged foundation charter had read Fredegar.

The most notable aspect of this monastery's foundation is how long it had taken. Saint Marcellus was supposedly a third-century martyr, a missionary sent from Lyon who was killed shortly after he began preaching. His burial spot on the outskirts of Chalon was later discovered and acquired a basilica, probably in the early sixth century; Gregory of Tours, late in whose lifetime Guntram founded the monastery, refers to the basilica.[27] Significantly, Caesarius of Arles, who lived in Chalon as a youth in the fifth century, never mentions Saint Marcellus, who appears for the first time in the "Acta" of the Burgundian martyrs, written a generation after Caesarius had permanently left Chalon.[28]

It was at least two generations from the *inventio* of Saint Marcellus to the establishment of a community of monks at his basilica, but this was not how the church's history was later portrayed. In fact, the lapse of three centuries from supposed martyrdom to monastery, even though it put Marcellus into the heroic age of martyrs, was far too long and therefore needed to be shortened in memory. Thus for Fredegar the saint's martyrdom and the establishment of a monastery could be described essentially in the same breath. The establishment of this house was also presented as a royal act, carried out by the king with the assistance of a whole synod of bishops. Guntram, according to Fredegar, referred back to the synod that King Sigismund of Burgundy had held when establishing his monastery at Agaune a good seventy years earlier, both underscoring the ties between kings and monks and suggesting that Guntram did not have many closer models.[29] It is also possible that, if Guntram was a leader of the Frankish army that drove Lombard invaders out of Agaune in 574, he would have learned then of Agaune's liturgical practices.[30] The establishment of a monastery was evidently much more unusual at the end of the sixth century than it was for Fredegar, writing nearly a century later.

The multiplication of monasteries in the sixth and early seventh centuries did not mean that monks and nuns were numbered like grains of sand, whatever admiring hagiographers might have thought. In the middle of the seventh century Queen Balthildis, widow of Clovis II, became personally involved in the support and promulgation of monasticism.[31] But her nearly contemporary *vita*, speaking of the "senior basilicas" of the realm, was able to list only six: St.-Denis of Paris, St.-Germain of Auxerre, St.-Médard of Soissons, St.-Pierre-le-Vif of Sens, St.-Aignan of Orléans, and St.-Martin of Tours (Marmoutier).[32] Of these only one, St.-Pierre, was dedicated to a universal saint rather than a local bishop or martyr.

This list of senior basilicas was certainly not intended as a comprehensive list of religious houses at the time. The same *vita* had spoken only a few lines earlier of the queen's generosity to the nunnery of Jouarre and the male monasteries of Luxeuil, St.-Wandrille, and Faremoutier. She had also helped Saint Philibert establish the monastery at Jumièges later dedicated to him, and she herself founded the nunnery of Chelles and the male monastery of Corbie.[33] But these were recent foundations. The designation of *seniores basilicas* was reserved for houses that had had bodies of monks for at least a few generations.[34]

After the rather tentative beginnings of the sixth century, a great many more foundations for male religious—and increasingly for women as well—took place in the seventh century, including Queen Balthildis's foundations.[35] Indeed, the majority of French monasteries in existence in the eleventh century had originally been founded in this period, generally by the first decades of the eighth century.[36] That is, the period from about 550 to 700 or 750 was so rich in monastic foundations that these houses temporarily saturated the field. As discussed in Chapter 8, many were then ruined or abandoned in the eighth and ninth centuries, meaning that in the tenth and eleventh centuries many new communities could be established by refounding or reforming an old house. A long abandoned monastic site still had an aura of the holy and was considered suitable for such a new community, just as monks had settled half a millennium earlier in places where the saints already dwelled. Even in Normandy, the area most thoroughly disrupted by the Vikings, continuities between old and new were deliberately created, and the Norman dukes, the heirs of those Vikings, integrated themselves into their new territories by sponsoring restorations of religious houses their ancestors had destroyed.[37]

By the late seventh century, monasteries began to be founded in areas that had not previously had basilicas dedicated to revered saints. They were increasingly far from the old Gallo-Roman cities, either in rural areas or off to the east.[38] And these seventh-century foundations usually *did* have foundation charters. Those who settled monks at a new house now knew exactly what they were doing, even if the foundation accounts may have collapsed into a single day a process that took several years. Such foundations, like other important transactions in late antiquity, required a written record. Enough authentic seventh- and eighth-century foundation charters exist that one can assume that most houses established in this period once had them. For communities established in the sixth century, however, there was often a need felt later to go back and create the charter that, from the point of view of subsequent monks, inexplicably failed to exist.

This transition may be demonstrated by the monastery of Bèze, originally founded in the seventh century. In the 660s Abbot Waldalenus complained to King Clothar III that his house's property had been stolen, along with its foundation charter. The king promptly appointed a prosecutor to determine what the monastery actually owned and recover the lost property.[39] Here both Waldalenus and the king assumed that a monastery *ought* to have a foundation charter, which would not have been assumed nearly as readily a few generations earlier. Both parties also assumed that a monastery would keep such a charter at the house. This particular case is complicated by doubts about the seventh-century documents that give us the story. The early charters of Bèze are known only from the house's twelfth-century cartulary-chronicle, and the rather convenient stealing of the foundation charter, requiring the king to confirm a whole long list of possessions, may seem suspect. The three mayors of the palace who are said to have reported the abbot's complaint to the king, Reidbert, Chrodebert, and Emerulf, are not known as mayors of the palace from other sources (although men with those names do appear in authentic documents).[40]

On the other hand, King Clothar appointing an *inluster vir* as prosecutor to take charge of the monastery's possessions does not seem like a detail twelfth-century monks would have created, and the mention in the documents of the rule of Saint Columbanus and of the *pagus* of Attuyer also appear to be products of the seventh century, not the twelfth. Even if the twelfth-century creator of the house's cartulary-chronicle, who declared that he was copying original documents, did make certain improvements in what was before him, the most suspicious figure in the whole story is the seventh-century Abbot Waldalenus himself, who might well have used the convenient disappearance of his house's foundation charter to claim that it had contained much more than it did—a possibility to which King Clothar seems to have been highly sensitive.

Bèze is typical of seventh-century foundations in that now the bishops or great secular nobles, rather than the kings, often took the lead. Indeed, it has even been suggested that the monastic foundations of the seventh century helped integrate the Frankish aristocracy of Gaul with the predominantly Gallo-Roman church.[41] The "Vita" of Audoin, bishop of Rouen in the mid-seventh century, praises the bishop for having founded many monasteries for both men and women, as well as for gathering the relics of martyrs. The biographer admiringly compared the numbers of religious men and women established in Audoin's diocese to the number of monks in the Egyptian desert of earliest monasticism.[42]

By the late seventh and early eighth centuries, monasteries were routinely given foundation charters or the equivalent, providing specific and substantial detail on their establishment. An example is Echternach, founded at the very end of the seventh century by Irmina, usually considered the mother of Pippin of Herstal's wife Plectrudis.[43] In two charters dated 698, she said that she had founded a monastery in her villa of Echternach, given the house to Willibrord, and made her testament, making her foundation the heir to everything she had inherited from both her parents. The combination of foundation and testament may also be observed in the foundation of Flavigny by Wideradus

(Chapter 9). Yet houses also continued to be founded as they had been since the fifth century, as a community of disciples around a hermit that gradually became a house with a rule. Such was the case with the houses of Jumièges and St.-Wandrille, hermitages well before they became the recipients of the generosity of Queen Balthildis. In these cases, later generations of monks wanted to know exactly when their houses had been founded; the proliferation of foundation charters had created the expectation that all monasteries have precise points of origin.

Property and Poverty

The example of Balthildis also shows the determination by both lay and ecclesiastical leaders of the seventh century to ensure that monasteries were "regular," that is, that they followed a monastic rule. Although scholars have often assumed that the regularization of Frankish monasteries under Benedict's Rule took place only with the synods of Charlemagne and Louis the Pious—with the implication that the monasteries of the Merovingian era had become decadent (see Chapter 8)—the rapid spread of monastic houses in the sixth and seventh centuries was accompanied by a deliberate effort to make sure that those houses followed a *regularis ordo*. Balthildis was particularly interested in the rule of Saint Columbanus and sent firm letters to both bishops and abbots to this effect.

By her time, monasteries had settled on the ideal of community property and personal poverty, to be observed while monks lived in obedient groups under an abbot's direction. Because this ideal was set out in the Book of Acts, to which early medieval monks referred, it would be easy to take monastic thinkers at their word, that devout Christians had always lived like this. But in fact the monastic rules of this time were far more than the setting down of ancient practices; they were deliberate efforts to craft a compromise that would reflect the mandates of the Bible without leading to the extreme asceticism that had been the direction of early monasticism. These rules were intended to avoid situations such as that of Saint Paternus, whose *vita* was written by Venantius Fortunatus at the end of the sixth century. Paternus, made a monk as a young boy, decided when he grew up to take off "on pilgrimage" and was finally located three years later by his abbot, living unshaven in a cave, with no bed or change of clothing, seeing neither men nor women, subsisting on bread and water. The abbot urged him no longer to undertake such extremes of fasting and solitude, "beyond the Rule," and brought him back into the Christian community—within which Paternus eventually became a bishop.[44]

The creators of the major monastic rules of the sixth century—the rules that would dominate the West for the next half millennium—in essence substituted personal poverty and collective property for the pronounced and generally solitary asceticism of many of the original Desert Fathers, the asceticism Paternus had sought to emulate. They also gave personal poverty precedence over preaching in defining the religious life, and phrased their rules to make clear that they did not expect all new monks to be ready instantly to give up all that they owned, instead allowing for a transitional novitiate period.[45]

The Benedictine Rule, which by the ninth century was normal, was only one option among many in the sixth and seventh centuries. An interesting example is provided by the near-contemporary *vita* of Ansbert, abbot of St.-Wandrille and bishop of Rouen at the end of the seventh century. When he first decided to become a monk, he was set to reading appropriate texts and came across a statement of Jerome's: "A monk lives in a monastery, under the discipline of one father, in the company of many, learning humility from one, patience from another."[46] A century later, one would have expected such a novice to be learning the definition of the proper monastic life from Benedict; but if the Benedictine Rule was even known at his house in the seventh century, it was not made the first primer for new monks. The first mention of this Rule in the *vita* is of the election of the abbot *after* Ansbert, which indeed may be a later addition.

The growth both in monastic houses and in the property these houses owned (even if it was held in common, rather than individually) was linked to a new way of thinking about salvation. Both cloistered monks and the secular elites came to agree that one could hope to save one's soul by enlisting the prayers of holy men and women. Offerings to the gods had of course been made for millennia, and requests for health were often linked to specific sites: the sources of the Seine in Burgundy have yielded votive offerings from the Gallo-Roman period, made as requests for healing. Gifts to churches out of generalized respect were also well established in Christian Gaul. Sidonius Apollinaris, writing in the 470s, thanked a friend for a gift of property to the cathedral of which Sidonius was bishop (Clermont) but merely said that this friend would receive both heavenly and earthly rewards, with no mention of specific prayers in return.[47]

But in the sixth century, for the first time, texts began to speak specifically of monastic communities as sources of intercessory prayer. In the late sixth and early seventh centuries a new practice became established, with little precedent in either Roman or Germanic custom: giving property to a church in return for prayers to save one's soul. By the end of the seventh century, the missal of Bobbio included prayers for those whose alms had been accepted and names inscribed in a book on the altar.[48] Thus, from about the year 600 onward, the wealthy increasingly *wanted* to make gifts to religious communities if not indeed to found new ones, and monasteries flourished and expanded in response. By the end of the sixth century, the monk was no longer a marginal or even suspect figure but rather a well-established locus of holiness, the kind that seventh-century donors wished to establish and endow through foundation charters.

Monasteries and the Merovingian Kings

The Frankish monasteries developed, if not necessarily close ties, at least attitudes of mutual respect with their kings.[49] The proper relationship between Merovingian kings and churches was spelled out in the late sixth century by Gregory of Tours, in a statement he put into the mouth of King Guntram (d. 593). Guntram was furious with his men, who had been ravaging churches, and he made it clear that kings, at least, would never do such a thing.

> How can we obtain victory in these days, when we do not follow the practices of our forefathers? They used to build churches, for they put all their hope in God . . . with God's help, they won victories over their enemies. . . . But we do not fear God, and lay waste to his holy places. . . . We will never obtain victory as long as such deeds are being done.[50]

For Guntram, at least as Gregory presented him, the entire success of the royal lineage depended on not ravaging churches.

A series of events in which Gregory himself took part further suggests there was substance to this attitude of the Merovingian royal family. In 576, Merovech, who wanted to be king but was considered a dangerous threat by his father and uncle, was supposed to be tonsured and imprisoned but managed to escape. When he sought sanctuary at St.-Martin of Tours, his father threatened Gregory with burning the whole Tours region. Gregory's answer is revealing. He said rather complacently that it would not be possible for the king to do in "these Christian times" what had not been done "even in the days of the heretics." It was of course easy for him to write, after the fact, of the confidence he felt at the time, for indeed at his father's threat Merovech volunteered to leave Tours, saying, "Let not Saint Martin's basilica suffer violence because of me."[51]

Gregory could here assume that his readers would accept his characterization of his time as a Christian one, to be contrasted to heretical or pagan eras when churches and their possessions might indeed be attacked. He also wanted future kings to share his constructed memory of the Merovingian kings as men who respected the churches. Gregory lived in a violent time, but one of controlled violence. Even a royal father and son concocting deadly plots against each other—like Merovech and his father—would hesitate to attack a church. Sanctuary in a basilica was a valid option; Merovech came to Tours in the first place because another refugee, Guntram Boso, had long managed to stay safe there. And he left again because of his father's threat against the church that sheltered him. Respect for churches and churchmen could not always be counted on to triumph, of course. Gregory said that one of his own deacons was imprisoned when suspected of being a spy for Merovech, and Gregory himself agreed to offer Merovech the communion wafer, in spite of some qualms, because he feared otherwise Merovech might attack the congregation. But overall Gregory believed that the Merovingian royal family agreed, or should agree, that in "these Christian times," the churches, their edifices, and their possessions were sacrosanct, off-limits to royal violence.

Even Merovingian kings who were not in awe of the church could sometimes become friends to bishops and monasteries, as did Chilperic I. He was a horrible king according to Gregory, the "Nero and Herod" of his time, unjust, gluttonous, a cruel lover of torture.[52] He put Gregory himself on trial at one point, so the bishop of Tours was not a disinterested observer. When Chilperic was assassinated in 584, Gregory suggests, Gaul became a much better place; Gregory's complete lack of detail on the assassin could also indicate that he considered him something of a divine force. And yet Chilperic was not typical, even in the sixth century. Gregory can be seen as using Chilperic as a foil for his brother King Guntram—everything that was bad in one was good in the other.

Even more intriguingly, Gregory himself had had more positive things to say about Chilperic earlier in his *Historia*. Specifically, he could be fair and generous toward bishops.[53] Gregory's own rewritings and revisions of his work preclude any simplistic explanation such as that his earlier, more positive statements were made out of fear, especially since other contemporary sources, especially Venantius Fortunatus, also found much in Chilperic to praise.[54] The real point is that even for the author from which most of our negative information about Chilperic comes—Gregory—the king was not an unalloyed disaster. The same thing could be said for the Merovingians as a group. Rather, Gregory remembered or wanted to remember the Merovingian kings, violent as they may often have been, as major supporters of Christianity and the organized church.

A similar understanding of the proper king-monastery relationship was set out some two generations later by Jonas of Bobbio in his *vita* of Columbanus, an account picked up almost verbatim by Fredegar not long thereafter. Fredegar, as is clear from his preceding and succeeding chapters, considered Theoderic II (d. 613) a despicable adulterer and his grandmother Brunhildis a horrible old lady, but in both Jonas's *vita* and Fredegar's *Chronica* this king and queen are shown as recognizing (if reluctantly) the proper way to behave toward a holy man.

According to Jonas, Theoderic used to go to the monastery of Luxeuil and "humbly" beg the prayers of Columbanus, even though the saint kept rebuking him for keeping concubines. When Brunhildis showed her displeasure by ordering that no monk be allowed to leave the confines of the monastery (and not, notice, by seizing monastic property), Theoderic tried to placate Columbanus with gifts, saying, "It is better to honor a man of God with timely offerings than to provoke the Lord to wrath by offending one of His servants." When the saint cursed the gifts and forbade any layperson, even if royal, to enter the monastery's inner sanctum, both king and dowager queen were "terrified" and begged forgiveness.[55]

Theoderic did not give up his concubines, however, and Brunhildis continued to scheme against the saint, eventually banishing Columbanus from Gaul. Interestingly, Theoderic himself did not drive him out; he had one of his *proceres* do so, and was repeatedly struck by "terror" as he tried to rid himself of this troublesome Irish missionary. The king, according to both Jonas and Fredegar, told Columbanus that he was "not so insane as to commit such a crime" as martyring the saint, and he did not seize any of Luxeuil's possessions either. The final result, according to both accounts, was that Columbanus prophesied (accurately) that Theoderic's "kingdom should crumble and be destroyed with the whole royal family."[56] Monks and holy men wielded enormous spiritual power, which gave at least temporary pause to even the wickedest. Both Jonas and Fredegar thus suggest—or argue—that even the worst Merovingian kings and queens had to show deference toward monasteries.

The same image of Merovingian kings and queens showing proper respect toward the churches of Gaul appears again in the early eighth-century *Liber Historiae Francorum*. In retelling Gregory of Tours's account of Queen Fredegundis plotting to murder her brother-in-law Sigibert I, around 575, the eighth-century author puts a speech into her mouth as she urges on her assassins: "If you are killed, I promise to offer many alms for you to the holy sites."[57] Again, even the wicked recognized the spiritual power of the monasteries—and, the author suggests, the Frankish royal family believed this power was strong enough to cleanse someone even from the sin of murder.

Exemptions and Memory

The major Merovingian-era addition to monasticism was the development of exemptions. Although immunities from taxation and dues, granted routinely to imperial fiscal lands and as a special privilege to the favored few, had been a part of late Roman law and practice,[58] seventh-century exemptions were something new. Not only did they free certain places from certain payments, but they also contained entry prohibitions. The first such grant to a monastery was from a pope; in 628 Honorius I freed Bobbio from the jurisdiction of its diocesan bishop, putting the house under his authority alone.[59] From then on, both kings and bishops promised not even to enter the monasteries to which they gave privileges, thus putting limits on their own authority.[60]

These privileges were not a result of any monastic rebellion against the hierarchy, for they were granted by the very members of that hierarchy, deliberately restricting themselves, their successors, and their agents from interfering in the internal life of the cloister. Bishops and secular authorities, who had been seen since the fifth century as guarantors of monastic stability and regularity, might now instead be seen as impediments to that regularity. They sought to preserve the purity and regularity of the monastic life by guaranteeing the monks' possessions and by voluntarily absenting themselves from the monks' affairs.

The first known royal privilege of exemption, less than a decade after the pope's privilege for Bobbio, was that granted to the monastery of Rebais in 635. It and an episcopal privilege from 637, also for Rebais,[61] became a model in the following years, the basis for the entries in Marculf's formulary on how to issue a privilege.[62] Other privileges followed quickly, including a papal one for Luxeuil in 640/2;[63] an episcopal privilege for St.-Denis in the 650s, confirmed by the king; episcopal privileges for the two monasteries of Sens, St.-Pierre-le-Vif and Ste.-Colombe, in 660; and both episcopal and royal privileges for Corbie in the 660s.[64]

The circle of those who granted the first episcopal exemptions was small. Bishop Audoin of Rouen urged Bishop Burgundofaro of Meaux to grant the initial privilege to Rebais, and both Audoin and Burgundofaro were present when Emmo, bishop of Sens, granted privileges to the two monasteries just outside his city. Bishops Audoin, Burgundofaro, and Emmo were again all present when the bishop of Amiens granted a privilege for Corbie. Meanwhile Queen Balthildis (d. 680), according to her *vita*, granted monasteries "immunities," freedom from outside interference, most notably from the kings and their family members and agents.[65] But privileges did not remain limited to this small group of bishops or to those closest to the royal court. Examples from the second half of the seventh century include the bishop of Reims's privilege for Hautvillers in the 660s; royal privileges for St.-Denis and for St.-Denis's daughter-house of Tussonval in the 680s and 690s; and the privilege of the bishop of Châlons in the 690s for Montier-en-Der.[66]

Scholars have commonly focused on the monks' exemption from episcopal oversight, so that they could call on any bishop they wished to consecrate an altar or ordain a priest, but this was not the privileges' central concern— and some did not even include it.[67] Such a focus may be the result of reading backward from Cluny's tenth- and eleventh-century privileges. Rather, seventh-century exemptions stressed that no king, bishop, or cleric was to "usurp or diminish" the monks' property; that no one should dare to appropriate any monastic income, whether a pious gift or dues from their dependents; that the monks be able to elect their abbots freely; and that any necessary correction of monks be done by their abbots.

It was once thought that the missionary Columbanus imported exemptions into Gaul at the end of the sixth century as some sort of foreign Irish practice, but it has recently been convincingly argued that the establishment of what was called a "privilege of liberty" (*libertatis privilegium*) took place only in the generation after Columbanus, influenced by the concerns and needs of the churches of Gaul.[68] The precedent to which the monks referred was not Ireland. Rather, they invoked privileges that had supposedly been granted to Agaune, Lérins, St.-Marcel of Chalon, and Luxeuil, only the last of which was associated with Columbanus; all the others were earlier foundations. The list of houses may reflect those which the bishops and monks of the seventh century considered the major monastic centers of the sixth. But it certainly suggests that they saw their privileges as continuing ancient and accepted practices in Gaul.

Thus, even though privileges of liberty created a new relationship between monks and both bishops and kings, the earliest charters evoked memories of a distant past. A number of monastic exemptions refer vaguely to a council held at Carthage in 525 and to Augustine's "De moribus clericorum" as precedent.[69] But these memories were faulty. Those who composed them must have seen very fragmentary accounts of the Council of Carthage or misinterpreted what they read. This council had indeed referred to Augustine, but not in any way that could be construed as freeing monasteries from their bishops.

The council as a whole had discussed the *libertas* of the church in the context of whether the north African churches ought to have to report to Byzantium. It cited Augustine's sermon "De moribus clericorum" on Christian unity and service to God in the monastery, but the chosen quote said nothing about *libertas* or whether monasteries might be able to report to a closer bishop.[70] (In fact, the passages quoted seem irrelevant to the council's central concerns.) Because Augustine always argued for bishops' authority within the Church, he would have been highly unlikely to argue, as the 660 episcopal privilege for St.-Pierre-le-Vif said he did, that abbots and monks should have "a privilege of liberty, so that they not be bound by bishops' power."[71] There was thus an effort to take something new—the monastic exemption—and link it to antiquity: not just any antiquity, but that of one of the principal Church Fathers, even if it was necessary to mis-remember what he had actually said two and a half centuries earlier.

This "memory" of Augustine and a council at Carthage gained validity at least in part from a delicate suppression of the memory of the Council of Chalcedon. That council, held in 451, had first put monasteries firmly under the authority of their local diocesan. It had ordered that monks settle into monasteries and stay there, "subject to the bishop." A new house of monks had to be established with its bishop's approval, and he had to dedicate their church. This council had reacted against the potential disruption of episcopal authority by self-styled holy men, by putting them into stable monasteries and telling them to be quiet (*et quietem diligere*). Throughout the sixth century, councils in Gaul emphasized monasteries' obedience to their local bishops.[72] The privileges of the seventh century did not state that they were changing this bishop-monastery relationship as decreed at Chalcedon, even though this is exactly what they were doing. Rather, the topic of Chalcedon never even arose. There had to be some way, however, to fill in the gap between the fifth century and the seventh, which is why those issuing privileges added vague references to exemptions granted to Agaune, Lérins, St.-Marcel, and Luxeuil, reinterpreted so that they could be perceived as precedent. The formulary of Marculf included references to all of these but St.-Marcel in its model episcopal privilege, ensuring that they be mentioned in privileges from the middle of the seventh century onward.[73]

A review of these cases reveals how creatively memory could act on putative precedent. Luxeuil was probably mentioned in seventh-century privileges because of how infamous the quarrel between Abbot Columbanus of Luxeuil and King Theoderic II still was a generation later, in the 630s, when King Dagobert issued the first known royal privilege for Rebais. Dagobert represented the line of Merovingian kings who had succeeded after Columbanus cursed Theoderic and his progeny for daring to set foot within the monastery's "secret enclosure." The rule followed at Rebais at the time was that followed at Luxeuil, and the bishop who founded the house and issued its pioneering episcopal privilege—and urged Dagobert to issue his pioneering royal privilege—had been blessed as a youth by Columbanus himself.[74]

In the case of Lérins, a council held at the same time as Chalcedon had declared its abbot free of episcopal supervision when laymen converted to the monastic life. But this was scarcely an exemption from episcopal jurisdiction: the council was called to settle a quarrel between the abbot of Lérins and the bishop of Arles and had reached a compromise, reaffirming that the bishop should have authority in all other areas.[75] Somewhat closer to seventh-century exemptions was the decision rendered by the Council of Valence in the 580s for St.-Marcel of Chalon: no bishop or king in the future should dare to take whatever King Guntram and his wife and daughters now gave to St.-Marcel. While not granting monks exemption from episcopal authority, the council did prohibit both bishops and kings from treating monastic property as their own.[76]

St.-Maurice of Agaune might be more difficult to see as a precedent for seventh-century exemptions because King Sigismund's foundation of a monastic community there in 515, suppressing Agaune's earlier community and establishing a new form of liturgical practice (the famous perennial prayer), offered the monks nothing that could be construed as a "privilege of liberty."[77] The answer is surely the decision in the 580s at the Council of Valence, the council that declared that no one should take St.-Marcel's property, to treat Agaune as a precedent. By saying that the "institutions" of St.-Marcel were modeled on those of Agaune, Guntram and the council in essence pushed the idea of inviolability of property backward in time seventy years, which is why the formula of Marculf referred to Agaune rather than to St.-Marcel itself.[78] Whatever the precedent, monastic exemptions multiplied in the seventh century, as both kings and bishops began putting restrictions on their own ability to control monastic life and property.

Viewed from a later perspective, one can see a complicated history for monks in late antique Gaul. Marginal wanderers and hermits regarded with suspicion by the church hierarchy in the fourth and fifth centuries, they settled down under strict oversight in the later fifth and sixth centuries, only to be granted exemption from the hierarchy—by members of the hierarchy itself—in the seventh century. At the same time as monks began receiving such written grants of exemption, they began for the first time to receive formal foundation charters. But this rather messy progression was smoothed out in the seventh century. Rather, monastic houses were assumed to have *always* had recognizable beginning points, marked by the founding donation of property. Adherence to a monastic rule was assumed to have *always* been a sign of religiosity, and interference from bishops and royal agents had *always* been, at least potentially, a threat to such regular adherence. If not all monasteries were as dedicated to the holy life as they should be, then all that was needed was a return to the mandates and practices attributed to earlier centuries, to a time so ancient that monasticism had not even yet been established in Gaul.

Chapter 12

Remembering Martyrs and Relics in Sixth-Century Gaul

This study of the memory of saints and ancestors has now proceeded back to the sixth century, when thinkers at the dawn of the Middle Ages contemplated early Christianity and assumed that their predecessors had been just like them. But the fourth and fifth centuries, in contrast to the sixth, had functioned with few local saints and even fewer relics. Specifically, between about 400 and 600 Gaul multiplied its saints, and relics became for the first time the chief point of contact between the living and the holy dead. The past of every region became a Christian past, full of local saints who still had power in the present.

In the fourth and fifth centuries, the holy man had transcended time and place, unlike pagan cults tied to specific locations. Bishops of the fourth and fifth centuries had been commemorated for their missionary activity, for converting pagans in their regions. But in the sixth century, with few local pagans left, bishops reversed the trend toward universal sanctity and became noted instead for discovering and creating appropriate cults for the relics of their regions' saints, relics with specific ties to their localities.[1] The cathedrals may have been established where Roman provincial governors had once held court, but in the late sixth century the most exciting churches were those *outside* the city walls, dedicated to local saints. Pilgrimages to visit the site where a saint's relics lay became a major expression of religiosity.[2] These exciting developments, however, were not remembered as changes at the end of the sixth century. Earlier centuries were creatively re-remembered, so that martyrs and their relics had always been so venerated—or should have been.

The Multiplication of Saints

Sixth-century Christianity in Gaul was marked by the rapid multiplication of saints. In the previous two centuries, plenty of saints had been commemorated, but most were the original apostles or else universal saints like Stephen. The latter's cult became established in the West for the first time after his body's miraculous discovery in 415—and a number of cathedrals in Gaul, previously without patron saints, were dedicated to him.[3] The newly venerated saints of the sixth century, in contrast, were overwhelmingly from Gaul. Saints multiplied not because unusually large numbers of men and women of the sixth century performed saintly deeds but because saints from the Gallo-Roman past were remembered, discovered, invented, translated, and honored for the first time.

Even though the Roman narrative of the early establishment of Christianity had focused on persecuted communities of Christians and spectacular martyrdoms,[4] antique Gaul had only a small number of martyrs. Because few Christians were martyred there in the third and fourth centuries, few local saints were venerated there in the fourth and fifth centuries. Writers of the fourth century remembered the large group of martyrs supposedly killed in Lyon in the second century, but these were unusual—and, initially, nameless.

The first historically attested saint in Gaul was Martin of Tours, whose initial, enormously influential *vita* was written by Sulpicius Severus around the year 400.[5] He was, however, not a martyr but a confessor saint. Other confessors were slowly added to the saints of the region, including Germanus of Auxerre, who died some two generations after Martin, his contemporary, Lupus of Troyes, and Genovefa of Paris, who died another two generations after Germanus.[6] But by the sixth century these were *not* remembered as Gaul's first saints. Rather, during the course of the sixth century the region acquired a large and diverse collection of martyrs who, it was asserted, had been there all the time but had been unaccountably forgotten.

The shortage of martyr-saints in fourth- and fifth-century Gaul is attested by Sulpicius Severus, Saint Martin's first hagiographer. Sulpicius, writing his universal history in Gaul at the end of the fourth century, treated the first three centuries of Christianity essentially as characterized by waves of persecution. However, he commented rather regretfully, almost none of these persecutions took place in Gaul. Not until the time of Emperor Aurelian, he said, did the true faith cross the Alps so that people could be martyred there as well as in Rome.[7]

Sulpicius was somewhat vague on who these martyrs were, but his account of Emperor Aurelian as a major persecutor of Christians became nearly as influential as his *vita* of Martin. During the fifth century, two or three generations after he wrote, an anonymous author wrote the *vita* of Saint Symphorien of Autun, killed for his faith under Emperor Aurelian; Symphorien retrospectively became the first martyr in the area.[8] Indeed, the later attribution of virtually all Burgundian martyrs to the age of Aurelian is probably ultimately due to this hagiographer. His *vita* of Symphorien was short: a young man from a noble Christian family is brought before a judge for refusing to take part in pagan ceremonies, cannot be persuaded to sacrifice to the gods, and is beheaded.

After Symphorien's supposed martyrdom in the 270s, it was close to two hundred more years before a basilica was built over his bones, in the middle of the fifth century according to Gregory of Tours. A century or so after that, in the second half of the sixth century, the church of St.-Symphorien acquired a body of monks.[9] The saint thus made a slow transition, from almost forgotten martyr to relics venerated at a basilica to a monastery where he helped define the Christian community at Autun. If one accepts the date of his death given in his *vita*, then the process had taken three centuries. A ninth-century *vita* of a later abbot of St.-Germain-des-Prés was able to collapse this sequence, saying simply that in the sixth century Autun had a monastery dedicated to Saint Symphorien, where a church had been built after his blood had been shed under Aurelian.[10] But this was because by the Carolingian era it seemed self-evident that martyred saints should be the patrons of monastic houses where their bones were preserved. In the sixth century, the veneration of sainted martyrs and even the establishment of monastic communities at their churches were beginning to seem normal, but there was still a scramble even to identify all the local saints who needed commemoration, much less to explain why they had not been receiving it.

Sidonius Apollinaris, who became bishop of Clermont around 470 (that is, not long after the *vita* of Symphorien was first composed), wrote three generations after Sulpicius Severus of a Gaul that was still strangely empty of saints by medieval standards.[11] This urbane, witty writer virtually never speaks of healing miracles or hermits associated in ascetic exercises around the bones of a long-dead martyr. In part he was more interested in other issues, such as imperial politics, the reception of his poetry by the public, or, once he became bishop, the wars with the Visigoths that ravaged his region. But he became one of the stalwarts of fifth-century Christianity in Gaul, and it is thus noteworthy that his Christianity was not marked by pilgrimage basilicas, relics, or local saints.[12]

He assumed that, at least in the cities, the population would be Christian, but their faith was not supported by miraculous cures or divine vengeance. His sad description of the death of the thirty-year-old *matrona* Philomathia, leaving a father, a husband, and five children, certainly suggests that she was a good Christian. But there is no indication either that she would continue to be present from beyond the grave in her family's lives or that any holy miracle-workers were called in an effort to save her. Graves were nonetheless important. Sidonius was horror-struck when his grandfather's was heedlessly dug into, and he took the occasion to write an epitaph recalling his grandfather's conversion to Christianity at the beginning of the fifth century. But what lived for him was memory and honor, not the dead through their relics.[13]

Yet his rather breezy, sophisticated style cannot be taken simply as an indication that the well educated of the late fifth century were uninterested in saints and miracles. Sidonius referred to Constantius of Lyon as "most wise" in literary matters and accepted his advice to publish his own letters: this was the Constantius who wrote a *vita* of Germanus of Auxerre that includes many healings of the gravely ill (or even already dead), expulsion of demons, and hauntings by the unburied.[14] Sidonius thus marks a transition point between the skimpy saints of the fifth century and the many of the sixth.

Christians in Gaul at the beginning of the sixth century honored, in suburban basilicas built in old Roman cemeteries, a few early martyrs who had sought to bring Christianity to a pagan part of the Empire (where, according to their later hagiographers, the worship of Jove and Epona was carried on indiscriminately).[15] When the cult of the saints expanded, these early martyrs, now often reconceptualized as the founding bishops of the region's Christian community, were the saints around whom commemoration came to be focused.[16]

The first systematic composition of the *vitae* of multiple martyrs in Gaul dates from the early sixth century, when the "Acta" of the Burgundian saints put to death under the emperor Aurelian were composed.[17] Although the "lives" of individual saints were later separated out of this collection, the sixth-century author worked to create a coherent narrative of martyred saints in Burgundy, even if some (like the Holy Triplets) were heavily borrowed in outline from saints of Cappadocia. He seems to have picked up Aurelian from the *vita* of Saint Symphorien, whose author had in turn found this emperor in Sulpicius Severus.[18]

In an effort to tie Burgundy's martyrs to the martyrs of Lyon, the author unconcernedly reduced the century from the famous martyrdoms at Lyon in 177 to the emperor Aurelian in the 270s to a single generation. (He may have confused Emperor Aurelian, discussed by Sulpicius Severus, with Emperor Marcus Aurelius, discussed by Eusebius in connection with the martyrs of Lyon.) These "Acta," note, were composed two and a half centuries after Aurelian had supposedly persecuted Christians in Burgundy. The first historical saints of northern Gaul had been Martin of Tours, Germanus of Auxerre, Lupus of Troyes, and Genovefa of Paris. Two generations or more after their time, the "Acta" indicated that these had *not* been the first local saints after all but that Gallo-Roman martyrs had preceded them by over two hundred years.

The "Acta" told how the holy Polycarp, a follower of the apostle John, had designated Ireneus as a missionary to Lyon, and how Ireneus had come to Burgundy. Here his own disciple Benignus preached at Dijon and Langres and his disciple Andochius at Saulieu, while at Autun Benignus baptized the youthful Symphorien (who thus was given a somewhat lower status than the disciples, even though his *vita* predated the "Acta" of the Burgundian martyrs), as well as Symphorien's cousins, the Holy Triplets of Langres. Within a short time, all of these achieved glorious martyrdom.

These "Acta" were enormously influential. Benignus quickly became identified as the founding bishop of Langres (even though the "Acta" author may have gotten him from a Greek *passio* of a Saint Menignos). It is possible that Bishop Gregory of Langres, great-grandfather of Gregory of Tours, was responsible for the composition of the "Acta" at the beginning of the sixth century. Other supposed missionary-martyrs, including Peregrinus of Auxerre, Ferreolus of Vienne, Felix of Valence, and Marcellus of Chalon, were soon commemorated and associated with missionaries from Rome and/or Lyon and with persecutions under Aurelian.

This multiplication of local saints still did not mean that every city had its own powerful saint, and by later medieval standards local saints were still sparse. There were surprisingly few major churches dedicated to saints from Gaul even at the end of the sixth century, when Venantius Fortunatus wrote a poem enumerating renowned saints revered in Gaul.[19] His list was very short: Victor of Marseille, Caesarius of Arles, Denis of Paris, Symphorien of Autun, Privatus of Gévaudan (Mende),[20] Julien of Brioude, Ferreolus of Vienne, Hilary of Poitiers, and Martin of Tours—and of these nine, the second, eighth, and ninth had not been martyrs. (If the saints of Gaul made a skimpy list, at least they were more numerous than those of Spain and Britain, to which

Fortunatus gave one saint each, respectively, Vincent and Albanus.)[21] Though not intended to be exhaustive, his list is an indication that even when the first Gallic martyrologies were put together, the Christian landscape of Gaul was still not thickly populated with basilicas dedicated to early saints.

The rapid growth in the fourth through sixth centuries in the number of saints who formed an integral part of the Christian community may be clear to modern scholars. But sixth-century authors did not speak of an increase in the number of saints. Rather, the stories written to remember the martyrs of Gaul—as well as the more recent saints of the fifth and sixth centuries—seem designed to deny that any change in the saints' number and importance had taken place at all. The *vitae* were thus an act of creative memory, reaching back to the time of the martyrs. There may have been a time of temporary forgetting of the saints and their importance, the sixth-century hagiographers implied, but the saints, their relics, and their miracles had *always* been a central feature of Gaul.

The hagiography of the late fifth and early sixth centuries, including the *vitae* of Germanus, Lupus, and Genovefa, are all dense with healing miracles performed during the saints' lives. What the accounts of these saints' lives lack is relics: the close association between the living and the bones of those who had once lived in an area, bones that would ultimately become more effective in working miracles than the saints had been while alive.

Holy Relics

Christianity was so identified with funerary observance by the seventh century that it may be too easy to overlook the novelty of this development.[22] The joining of the church hierarchy with the cult of the dead slowly became a distinctive aspect of western Christendom, distinguishing it from the other religions that came out of Roman antiquity. Historians now see a fundamental transformation as having taken place in the late fourth and fifth centuries, when, in Peter Brown's elegant phrase, "tomb and altar were joined."[23] But the process was gradual, and in Gaul the discovery, translation, and veneration of saints' relics was not fully established before the second half of the sixth century.

Early Christianity had flourished without assigning holiness to very many particular objects or places. Although Sulpicius Severus, writing at the end of the fourth century, said that the "whole earth" had been spattered with the blood of persecuted martyrs, he was not interested in particular spatters. The only relic he mentions is the True Cross, discovered by Helena (Constantine's mother), which was successfully tested for authenticity, he relates, by its ability to resurrect someone recently dead.[24] Recounting the suffering of earlier Christians helped create a shared identity for Christian communities,[25] but these stories were rarely connected with concrete relics before the fourth century.

Even when the relics of the numerous (if often unnamed) martyrs killed at the orders of pagan emperors first began to be venerated publicly after Constantine's conversion, they were revered where they lay—in Rome, most commonly in the catacombs. The disturbance of bodies was forbidden by both pagan and Christian law, even if the repeated prohibitions indicate that such disturbance was common, and still highly controversial at the end of the fourth century. Until the final decades of that century, when Ambrose first translated martyrs' entire bodies (Saints Gervasius and Protasius), putting their relics into a church as part of its consecration ceremony, churches were not even dedicated to saints.[26]

Ambrose's effort to integrate relics into the definition of a church's holy space was not immediately adopted or broadly accepted. As Augustine said at the beginning of the fifth century, it was the congregation that was holy. He saw no benefit in being buried near the bones of saints and wanted the martyrs to be emulated, not to become powerful, sacred figures who might still be interested in one's problems.[27] Although Augustine became much more open to relics toward the end of his life, becoming one of the first bishops to acquire the relics of Saint Stephen and composing a book of these relics' miracles, his principal interest was the resurrection of the body, not the relationship of the holy dead to the living.[28]

Victricius, bishop of Rouen and a contemporary of Ambrose's, was one of the few immediately to adopt the saints and their relics as central to Christian practice. He wrote enthusiastically of translating relics into churches, and in fact he became the first bishop of Gaul to do so.[29] The relics he put into his church at Rouen—bits of dust and blood—were relics of the same martyrs Ambrose translated into *his* church. He also developed the theological explanation that because saints were with God they were not really dispersed when their remains were dispersed but remained whole within each fragment and that they could still hear and pass on petitions generated near where those fragments lay.[30]

As the fifth century progressed, other bishops obtained relics for their churches, but the practice was far from universal. When Bishop Germanus of Auxerre obtained relics—those of Albanus and Maurice—for his city's churches in the second quarter of the fifth century, he was the first bishop of Auxerre to do so. He apparently knew of no regional saints whose bones he might translate, for he found his martyrs in Britain and in the Jura.[31] At many sites, including Auxerre, no local saint had a cult before the late fifth century, and all churches before then either were dedicated to saints whose relics had been imported from some distance or were not dedicated to a saint at all. A chronicler writing a history of Gaul in 452 mentioned no ancient saints beyond Gervasius and Protasius and found only a few regional holy bishops worth noting.[32] The bishop of Vienne's discovery of the body of the martyr Ferreolus in the 470s and its translation into a basilica was considered strikingly unusual at the time, a particular mark of favor for the bishop, who could be compared to no other pontiff closer than Ambrose himself, three generations earlier.[33]

Before relics became a locus of veneration, far less attention was paid to tombs. At Auxerre, the first four or five bishops (depending on how one counts) were all buried at Mont Artre, in what was doubtless a Roman cemetery a safe half kilometer beyond the Gallo-Roman city walls.[34] The cemetery was not reserved for bishops; according to the *vita* of Bishop Amator (d. 418), he buried his wife, Martha, there when she predeceased him and was later buried beside her.[35] Although this *vita* postdates Amator's life by at least a century—a dating that itself suggests the novelty of the sixth-century interest in the burial places of the holy dead—the author had doubtless seen the tombs. A slightly later *vita* of Saint Mamertinus includes the story of someone passing the night in this cemetery of Mont Artre, described as overgrown and infested with snakes.[36] The author used here the same topos of the forgotten tomb as did Gregory of Tours at roughly the same time, as discussed shortly— but Gregory's forgotten tombs were far out in the country. Auxerre's were only a ten-minute walk from the city.

In the course of the fifth century this separation between tomb and Christian cult began to change. Bishop Germanus of Auxerre died in Ravenna, probably in 448, but the churchmen of Auxerre were not satisfied to let him rest there. His body was brought home by a long and difficult journey across the Alps. His relics—and thus presence—were wanted for Auxerre.[37] Even the men who had brought his body back became holy by association and later had churches of the Auxerrois dedicated to them. Germanus was buried at the basilica he himself had established just north of the city, dedicated to Saint

Maurice of Agaune. The basilica quickly started being referred to as that of Saint Germanus, not of Saint Maurice, and a monastery, St.-Germain, was established there in the sixth century.[38] It is striking that this new burial center for bishops—a great many bishops followed Germanus into the church's crypt in the following generations—was on the far side of town from the original burial site of Mont Artre. The older bishops were not forgotten, for a church, dedicated to St.-Amâtre (Amator), was later built in the cemetery. But bishops no longer chose this site for their tombs. Although it is unlikely that burial at St.-Germain represented a rejection of the diocese's early bishops—being rather an act of identification with the see's holiest bishop—it was a symbolic turning point in how members of the diocese thought about and celebrated their Christian past.

The transition in how relics were appreciated may be seen vividly at Lyon, the only city in Gaul recognized before the late fifth or sixth century as having had multiple local martyrs. Lyon's traditionally numbered forty-eight, who had supposedly all been put to death in 177, four generations or more before other martyrs in Gaul.[39] They were recalled with admiration from at least the fourth century, when the Greek historian Eusebius wrote about them as having already passed into dim and ancient history.[40] But they were originally treated as figures to be emulated—in courage and faith if not in fact in death—rather than as members of the community whose ongoing presence would be made concrete by their relics. In the later fifth century, as holy bodies began to take on importance, the lack of such relics was noted regretfully and explained by the burning of the martyrs' bodies and the dumping of their ashes into the Rhône.[41]

But a hundred years later, this problem had been overcome: Lyon *had* the ashes of its forty-eight martyrs. In fact, it had always had them! Gregory of Tours named them all (or at least forty-five); previous authors had been content to name just a few. (Some names, like First, Fourth, Saint, Mature, Maternal, Rhône, October, and Bibles, seem a bit unusual.)[42] Gregory knew and retold the story of how a wicked judge had ordered the bodies burned and the ashes scattered. But in his version, when the local Christians who had not suffered martyrdom were bemoaning the loss of their companions and especially the loss of their relics, the martyrs appeared to them in a vision. "Gather up our relics from this place," the martyrs said, pointing out their ashes. They also reassured their friends that they had not truly died but had been directly transported to heavenly rest. Their friends gathered up the presumably water-soaked ashes and put them into a church, built in their honor.[43] By the late sixth century, then, a lack of relics was no longer a problem in Lyon—and Gregory suggested that in fact it had *never* been a problem, that the ashes had begun receiving proper Christian attention within a very short time of the martyrs' deaths.

Gregory's assumption of the centrality of saints' relics finds an echo in the other Gregory, his contemporary Pope Gregory I, who was faced with so many requests from Europe's bishops for bits of Roman martyrs and so much enthusiasm among his congregation for the martyrs that he tried to restrict the outflow of relics from his city and make his congregation focus less on the deaths of the saints and more on their moral achievements.[44] This relic trade was new, but it was not remembered as new. Gregory of Tours assumed that the martyrs he commemorated had always been known—or at least should have been.

The Discovery of Forgotten Saints

The sixth century was the major period for the discovery, the *inventio*, of martyrs' relics in Gaul. That so many of the martyrs were said to have been put to death in the third century under Aurelian and had their bodies hidden by the faithful, only to be rediscovered in the sixth century, indicates a deliberate effort to create a narrative of early Christianization of Gaul to match the Roman narrative.[45] Sometimes the newly discovered saint would continue to be venerated where originally buried, in which case a basilica could be built over the tomb. But the new sense that churches needed relics meant that many early saints, once they had been discovered, were translated into a church in town.

Translation could involve the importation of relics from a considerable distance, as done by Bishops Germanus and Aunarius of Auxerre, the latter a contemporary of Gregory of Tours. Aunarius, like many other bishops, wrote the pope to ask that relics be sent for the churches he was building.[46] Or, increasingly, translation might require finding the holy dead in their forgotten tombs and bringing them into the heart of the community. Translation could also entail the transference of remains from one tomb to a new, adjacent one, more spectacular or better suited for veneration. Aunarius was not alone among sixth- and seventh-century bishops in believing that their dioceses needed more saints, more relics, and more connection to the past. The *vita* of Bishop Audoin (Ouen) of Rouen, written not long after the bishop's death in the second half of the seventh century, created a bridge between the early age of martyrs and his own age: "Just as, at the time of the persecutions, the martyrs of Christ . . . shed their precious blood," the author said, "so too this man, in a peaceful time when persecutions had stopped . . . earned the palm of martyrdom by emulation."[47]

The attempt to make Audoin a virtual martyr was not entirely successful; the biographer's own account shows that he died of a fever. But the biographer connected Audoin to the age of persecutions by describing how assiduous he was in accumulating the relics of various martyrs for his churches, going on collecting trips both to Rome and Cologne. Indeed, although the biographer states that the bishop's original purpose in going to Cologne was to try to bring about peace in the conflict between the Neustrians and the Austrasians, once there he availed himself of the opportunity to take a number of relics from the city. He may have taken them by permission, or he may have engaged in "holy theft"; the biographer is (perhaps deliberately) vague on this point.[48] But the bishop, at least in his biographer's eyes, saw the responsibility to gather relics and link his church to the glorious Christian past to be at least as important a part of his mission as bringing peace in a time of war.

This bishop would doubtless have been pleased that his own body was treated as a relic. He died near Paris, far from his diocese but not far from those who admired him. Everyone, according to his biographer, was stricken by sorrow, but they were also joyful to be associated with his body. The king and queen, the bishops and the mayor of the palace all disputed, according to the biographer, for the honor of carrying him to his glorious funeral, and then clerics and members of the general populace competed for the honor of transporting the saint on their shoulders as he headed homeward to Rouen.[49]

The heroic age of martyrs may have passed, as Christianity became secure and indeed privileged, but incorporation of the sainted martyrs into the present community meant that Christians continued to share in their glory. Auxerre, which had acquired its first local saint, Germanus, in the fifth century, added two of Germanus's predecessors to the list during the later sixth century, Bishops Peregrinus and Amator, the former remembered as a martyr under Aurelian. Here, note, the memory of the Christian past reached backward *before* Germanus to find local saints who were then commemorated for the first time *after* he was.[50] By this period in Gaul, it would have seemed self-evident that the holy dead of a region ought to be remembered and have altars erected over their bones.[51] But it had not seemed self-evident in the years when they had originally been buried, which meant that the sixth and seventh centuries had a lot of ground to make up.

The need to assert that saints and their relics had always been present can be seen clearly in Gregory of Tours. His writings of course are the major source of information on the attitudes of sixth-century Gaul toward its Christian past.[52] For many saints of Gaul, their first formal biography was in Gregory's "Lives of the Fathers," a work in which the majority were either connected with the dioceses he knew best (especially Clermont and Tours) or were indeed his relatives.[53] He filled his pages with saints and miracle-working relics, but his accounts need to be understood as a response to what he felt was a serious gap: saints who evidently (to him) required *vitae* had not earlier received them.

Many of the saints he discussed had tombs that had long been neglected. The martyrs had lived and died in a past that seemed quite distant, and yet he had to account for why they had possessed no cult in the intervening centuries. That is, they were beginning to be venerated in the sixth century, yet they had been killed in the second or third, and those missing centuries required an explanation. Moreover, as well as glorifying the saints, Gregory urged that they not be forgotten again; the expansion of the cult of the saints was recent enough that it was still in danger of receding. For example, Gregory discussed the martyr Benignus, whose basilica was erected by Gregory's own great-grandfather, Bishop Gregory of Langres. In this account, the location of the great sarcophagus where Benignus was buried was lost after his third-century martyrdom at Dijon. However, rumor of it persisted into the sixth century, when the bishop of Langres decided to search for it. It was discovered by the local countryfolk because it was leaking wax, but it was guarded by a great serpent. The combination of the countryfolk and the serpent certainly gave an impression of a location far out in the hinterlands, not in Dijon, but the bishop quickly built an appropriate basilica in the city and translated the relics there.[54]

Similarly, in telling the story of Amarandus, who had been martyred at Albi, Gregory said that "for a long time his tomb lay hidden by brambles and thorn bushes." But then, miraculously, "the crypt in which he lay was revealed and shone brightly." But Amarandus was soon forgotten again because the local Christians moved away. The second time the saint was discovered, however, by new inhabitants of the area, his memory stayed alive. His tomb would itself kindle candles that were placed upon it without anyone striking a light. Thus the saint showed his power to those who came to his burial site, both through the miraculously reappearing tomb itself and through the ritual of lighting candles for the dead. The spontaneously igniting candles, Gregory noted, persisted only until the region was built up enough that finding a fire was no longer difficult—and until a settled population assured that their saint would not be forgotten a third time.[55] Gregory's account is not focused on either the life or death of Amarandus; he does even say how he came to be martyred, instead commenting, "buried, he lives in glory." Rather, it is a story of Christians discovering a forgotten tomb and being rewarded with relics and spectacular miracles.

Martyrologies

Part of the expanded commemoration of saints was the need for a list of all the saints and the dates on which they should be remembered. A few saints could be easily venerated; multiple saints needed lists and calendars to keep them all straight. Martyrologies had a long history, but the most important for Gaul was the so-called *Martyrologium Hieronymianum*, given that name because it is often found with a dedicatory letter supposedly addressed to Jerome. It included many early saints from Antioch and Cappadoccia, but these were intermingled with ones from the West.[56] A day-by-day calendar listed all the saints the compilers knew who had done something memorable on that day: generally die, but sometimes receive burial or translation, or even occasionally be born. There are today dozens of martyrology manuscripts whose texts (and sometimes whose very parchment) date from the seventh or eighth century, none identical although they all bear a strong family resemblance.

The *Martyrologium Hieronymianum* is usually assumed to have begun in Italy near the end of the sixth century and then sent to Auxerre, where it was rewritten and augmented by a local scribe, to include not just universal and Italian saints but saints from the Auxerrois.[57] This scribe's first step was doubtless to add his region's own saints to the margins and blank spaces—as scribes at Auxerre were still doing in the twelfth century to an eleventh-century copy of this martyrology.[58] The whole text would then have been copied out cleanly. In all the manuscripts, a greater number of local saints from Auxerre appear than from any other diocese. The *Martyrologium* includes thirty saints and bishops from Auxerre, especially striking given the paucity of Auxerrois saints a century earlier. Only two other dioceses have anywhere near as many local listings as does Auxerre: Lyon has twenty-six, Autun twenty-five.[59] No other diocese in Gaul has more than eight entries in the *Martyrologium*, and most have only one or two. Even in the cases of Lyon and Autun, almost all of the entries are for bishops, not for local saints, and the episcopal lists are essentially complete. It seems most likely, therefore, that the original compiler had the lists of bishops of the two most important other dioceses of his region before him but either did not know or care about their local martyrs as he did about Auxerre's.[60]

The martyrology doubtless arrived in Auxerre at the same time as a collection of Ambrose's treatises, known to have reached there at the end of the sixth century, most likely sent from Rome by Pope Pelagius II (579–90).[61] These treatises include a copy of Victricius of Rouen's "De laude sanctorum," the first theological discussion in Gaul of the value of relics. The martyrology must have acquired its Gallic saints around the year 600, because Bishop Aunarius of Auxerre (d. 604) is the last bishop chronologically to have an entry, and significantly it is an entry for his birth, not his death. In addition, Pope Pelagius is known to have written to Bishop Aunarius, congratulating him on founding so many "new churches" and responding to the bishop's request for relics for them. Aunarius also made a number of liturgical innovations, including the establishment of a daily rota of diocesan churches where services would be held, making him a good candidate for the regular listing of saints and bishops that the martyrology represented.[62] There are only a few other entries for a birthday in the martyrology besides his; one is for Syragrius, bishop of Autun, who died in 600, and he is given a birthday in some versions of the *Martyrologium Hieronymianum* and a burial date in others. Bishop Avitus of the Auvergne, a friend of Gregory of Tours who died in 592, is listed by date of burial but not date of birth.[63] It thus seems most likely that the martyrology was put together shortly before 600, with final emendations made between 600 and 604.[64]

Although this original martyrology is long gone,[65] it proved enormously influential. When other regions of Gaul made their own martyrologies, they relied not on the original Italian version but on one that incorporated the saints of Auxerre. Indeed, all copies of this martyrology made in Francia and the Rhineland in the Carolingian and later periods derived ultimately from the Auxerre version of the very end of the sixth century, into which scribes of other localities incorporated their own regional saints as marginal additions.[66] The influence of the version of c. 600 indicates that it was only at this period that those in Gaul became serious about compiling such lists of their saints and the days on which they should be commemorated.[67]

Within a century and a half, Auxerre had gone from commemorating no local saints at all, back when Germanus was bishop, to having thirty men and women worth commemorating around the year 600—and the majority of these dated from *before* the age of Germanus. Of Auxerre's thirty entries in the martyrology, about half were bishops, the rest local martyrs and confessors. Even though most of the bishops were not saints, the episcopal list is essentially complete; all but two of the bishops whom the cathedral canons of the ninth century included in their history of the see also appear in the martyrology from three centuries earlier, and those two were probably products of ninth-century misreadings.[68] The writers of c. 600 thus shaped a memory that persisted in the following centuries of the history of their diocese and its martyrs, bishops, and saints.

By the time of the funeral of Bishop Audoin of Rouen in the seventh century, it was taken for granted that the holy dead were full members of the living Christian community and that their bodies had significance and power. The body of the man who had assiduously collected relics became a relic itself once he had died. But while he and his contemporaries assumed that Christianity had always been centered on such loci of supernatural power, saints and their relics were a relatively new phenomenon in late antique Gaul.

In early Christianity, the dead had been remembered, especially the martyrs whose spectacular deaths were the center of a narrative of persecution and eventual triumph. But only in the final years of the fourth century was the initially controversial decision made to put relics of martyrs into a church. During the fifth century, even while relics slowly became more common, they remained unusual. During the course of the sixth century, however, relics became necessary for all churches, and the wave of discoveries of the lost tombs of the now extremely numerous early martyrs of Gaul meant that such relics were readily available.

But those writing in the late sixth and seventh centuries did not remember a past without saints and their relics. They reimagined their past so that the fourth century, which appears very different from the sixth to modern scholars, was instead not different at all. The scribe at Auxerre who put together the Gallic version of the *Martyrologium Hieronymianum* took it for granted that his see had always had a great many saints, including its early bishops and third-century martyrs. The well-established, comfortably institutionalized church of the year 600 could look back over the centuries to martyrs killed by pagan Romans, but for the previous two hundred years, they assumed, the church and its saints had always taken the same form—or, if not, they certainly should have done so.

Conclusion

The saints and ancestors who were remembered, rewritten, and reconceptualized between the sixth century and the twelfth all had one significant aspect in common: they were dead. The living, too, were worthy of memory, as Anselm of St.-Remy made clear in the eleventh century when he recorded the events of the Council of Reims. But control of memory principally meant control of the dead. Even before the development of a unified liturgy of Christian death in the late ninth century,[1] the dead were a crucial part of the community of the faithful, perhaps the most important part, and how they were remembered shaped the living present.

When chroniclers and cartulary scribes worked in the high Middle Ages, re-creating the histories of their houses, placing them in the history of the world as a whole (or at least the part they knew), or organizing, trying to make sense of, and copying charters that had been accumulating in the archives for as long as six centuries, they wrote of those long dead. But those who had come before had constant relevance for the present, a relevance that could indeed be improved with judicious reinterpretation. The dead were thus a crucial element in the early medieval construction of memory.[2] Because their predecessors had created the past that thinkers assumed ought to shape contemporary experience, and because the dead continued to be present, the distinction between long ago and right now could easily be blurred.

Overcoming death through resurrection of the body had of course been a central tenet of Christianity since its earliest days.[3] The dead were thus not to be feared but rather to be embraced, and the presence of human remains was not a reminder of mortality but a marker of immortality. Once early Christianity had made the transition, in Alan Bernstein's terms, from death as a neutral event to death as a moral event, and the choice between heaven and hell loomed large for the dying,[4] it is not surprising that Christians preferred burial at churches. By making tombs of stone, Merovingian-era Christians were assuring that these tombs could be quite literally incorporated into their churches.

The crypts of ancient churches from Arles in southern France to St.-Laurent of Grenoble in the Alps to St.-Germain of Auxerre in Burgundy to St.-Denis outside of Paris to Diekirch in Luxembourg not only are full of Merovingian sarcophagi but are in fact partially constructed of these sarcophagi.

The biographer of Bishop Caesarius of Arles, writing in the middle of the sixth century, described the saint paying for stone sarcophagi with which he covered the floor of a basilica in Arles so that the nuns he had established there would be "relieved of concern" for how they would be buried.[5] Excavations at the church of St.-Laurent of Grenoble have revealed a fifth-century stone mausoleum where the tapered sarcophagi were neatly lined up to fill all available space. By the early seventh century it was a fully developed cruciform church, with altars and sacristy—and hundreds of tombs. The Christians of Grenoble were buried in the church itself, and subsequent rebuildings of the church, in first Carolingian and eventually the present Romanesque styles, all preserved the layers of crypts from previous centuries.[6] In church for mass, baptism, or ordination, medieval people were always reminded of the continuing presence of the dead.

But nearly as important as the bodies of those who had gone before were what had been written by or about them. Charters and *vitae* were not just historical artifacts but living testimony to events still highly important. Times and dates, the starting point for understanding history for modern scholars, were much more flexible in early medieval thought. Indeed, one of the purposes of memory was to bridge the gaps that time might create. Thus the creation of a cartulary took the individual charters out of their temporal context and reordered them in a way that corresponded to the needs or perceptions of the cartulary scribe and his contemporaries. Even the universal chroniclers who recounted several thousand years of history, in order, viewed the past teleologically: biblical history led up to the atonement, and a monastery's history of foundation, difficulties, and even destruction led up to its present glory. Only those documents that could not be interpreted to meet a community's present needs, most notably the polyptyques, were allowed to disappear quietly.

Dead ancestors helped define royal families just as dead monks and monastic donors helped define monasteries. The rise of the Carolingians was accompanied by a deliberate if uneasy effort by the royal family themselves as well as the publicists of their court to reconstruct their history as that of a true dynasty that self-evidently deserved to rule. Presenting the accomplishments of Charlemagne and his relatives also required the creation of a straight-line set of ancestors. The difficulty of remembering his predecessors in this way, a novel act of memory, is reflected in the substantial differences between the various family trees constructed for him at the royal court within a generation of each other. Neither the Robertians/Capetians nor the relatives of Count Hugh of Tours managed to remember their ancestors any further back than the time of Charlemagne, a further indication that dynasty itself was an act of memory, not simply biological descent.

The Carolingians' extensive accomplishments, as celebrated by the publicists of their court, shaped the later memory of the relationship between the kings and the church. The serious problems posed by the granting of *precaria*, seizures of property, and the imposition of lay abbots in the eighth and ninth centuries are well documented and indeed caused some monks to look back regretfully to better times under the Merovingians. Yet the golden glow the publicists successfully attached to all memories of the Carolingians inspired thinkers, from the eleventh and twelfth centuries to very recent times, to assume that their age must have been a high point for the Frankish churches.

The churches of the ninth century, which did not share this vision, fought back against interference from kings and other powerful laymen by creating their own memory of the past, through manipulation of the written word. Most notably at Le Mans, churchmen confected mounds of forged documents to try to argue their case against the king. The contemporary Pseudo-Isidorian decretals similarly attempted to create a memory of eight centuries of episcopal independence, both from laymen and from other bishops—who at the time were often backed by kings.

In part this widespread effort at forgery was a reaction to uncertainty. The eighth century had been a difficult period for many west Frankish monasteries, and although they might retain some of their Merovingian-era documents, demonstrating that the kings then had been—at least some of the time— reliable supporters of the church, the ninth-century landscape was very different from that of the seventh or early eighth century. Gaps in the records of these houses, sometimes over two generations long, hint at a loss of regular claustral life, as do later retrospective accounts of Saracens or pagans. With a drop in urban population and lay literacy, lay notaries also disappeared, taking with them many monasteries' early records.

It was not enough to reestablish both a regular life and monastic archives. The monks of the ninth century—and for that matter the seventh and eighth—wanted clear accounts of the early days of their houses. The model that was usually settled on was the normal pattern from the seventh century onward: foundation by a powerful layman, sometimes a king, who granted an unambiguous foundation charter spelling out the property that now belonged to the monks. Flavigny, whose 717 foundation was the last in Burgundy for another century and a half,[7] actually was founded in this way. In memory, so were all the other religious houses of the three previous centuries. The story of early monasticism that historians can now construct, of an oratory attracting a hermit and eventually a small body of followers, of bishops confirming the religious communities under their direction, and of churches served only intermittently by groups of men following a rule, was not the story that later monks wanted to hear. They wanted founders, foundation charters, and unbroken histories.[8]

They also wanted relics, both of regional martyrs and of universal saints, and the memory they created was of events leading seamlessly from third-century martyrdoms to well-established monasteries built over those saints' bones. Such a memory left out all the changes that took place between the third century and the seventh in the ways that saints were revered. The very first monastery in Gaul, Saint Martin's house in Tours, and the very first insertion of saints' relics into an altar had both taken place shortly before 400, and for the next century and a half both local saints and local monasteries had been unusual, but that was not how later writers wanted to remember the Christianization of the region.

Late sixth-century writers like Gregory of Tours, looking back over centuries when martyrs had not been the defining center of the Christian cult and when churches had not collected saints' bones, had to explain this apparent lack by indicating that it had not in fact happened. For Gregory martyrs, like the martyrs of Lyon, had *always* been revered, and if there had been plenty of lost tombs to be rediscovered, these were to be explained by carelessness, not a change in Christian practice and belief. The modern critic may look at such examples as Saint Benignus, whose body we are told was discovered by Gregory's great-grandfather in a forgotten tomb and assigned the name and story of the Greek Saint Menignos, and conclude that virtually none of the martyr saints revered in the Merovingian era had any claim to historical authenticity. But for sixth-century Christians modern definitions of historical accuracy were irrelevant; Benignus was to be remembered as one of those who originally brought Christianity to Gaul, and thus his body formed a crucial part of their current community.

Saints' *vitae* provide one of the clearest examples of malleable memory, being used to keep the dead up-to-date, as saints from Martin to Radegund had the stories of their lives told and retold, with each iteration serving the changing needs of the community that remembered and revered the saint. Such saints, including Martin and Germanus, were frequently attached to monasteries in the seventh century, but in later generations the memory of the transition, from saint to basilica to group of hermits to regular monastery, was smoothed out to indicate that, from the time of the saint to the present, a recognizable monastic life had been followed at the sites of their veneration—and their bones.

For those living in late Roman Gaul and for the succeeding Merovingian, Carolingian, and Capetian periods, the past and the memory of the past were more than historical concerns. Rather, the lives of dead saints, clerics, and kings remained as important as those of their successors. Thus the past was not simply an exemplary tableau of venerated predecessors and their actions but something that continued to live in the present. For this to be so, however, regular updating and reworking were always necessary to keep the past current and intelligible.

Appendix I

Monasteries in Burgundy and Southern Champagne

This handlist of the monasteries in the Burgundy–southern Champagne region (within the medieval dioceses of Autun, Auxerre, Chalon-sur-Saône, Châlons-sur-Marne, Langres, Mâcon, Nevers, Sens, and Troyes) illustrates the discussion of monasticism in Chapters 8 and 11. The list is arranged by approximate date of the establishment of monks. It includes the principal houses founded before the year 1000 but not the smaller ones about which essentially nothing is known or which may have had monks or nuns for only a few years.[1] The annotations principally cover the houses' foundations or refoundations.[2] In these appendixes, briefer references to primary sources are given in parentheses.

St.-Marien of Auxerre

The oldest monastery in the region, founded by Bishop Germanus in the first half of the fifth century; see Appendix II.

Moûtier-St.-Jean (Reomaus)

Founded as a hermitage in the first half of the sixth century by Saint John, who also was supposed to have been the teacher of Saint Sequanus (see below). His *vita* from a century later suggests that his house originally followed the institutes of Lérins. Bishop Sigoald issued a privilege in the mid-seventh century.[3] Abbot Waldo attended the 760/2 Council of Attigny ("Consilium Attiniacense," MGH Concilia 2:73). Apollinaris, abbot of St.-Bénigne of Dijon and Flavigny, headed Reomaus at the beginning of the ninth century (Hugh of Flavigny, *Chronicon*, MGH SS 8:352). In 819 Louis the Pious received *dona* and military service from the monks.[4] The house lost its regular life in the ninth century and was given to Bishop Geylo of Langres by Charles the Fat in the 880s.[5] In the early tenth century, Bishop Agrin, Duke Richard le Justicier, and Count Manasses gave the *abbatia* to St.-Bénigne, although it became independent again almost immediately. In 984 Bishop Bruno of Langres requested a reforming abbot from Cluny; Heldric, the new abbot, also served as abbot of Flavigny and St.-Germain. The monastery then passed under the direction of Abbot William of St.-Bénigne. A house of black monks in the 1130s.[6]

St.-Bénigne of Dijon

Founded as a basilica in the early sixth century by Bishop Gregory of Langres. The later *Chronicle* adds the spurious detail that monks were established at the same time.[7] King Chlothar III in the 660s recalled earlier gifts from King Guntram in the later sixth century, by which time there were almost certainly monks there.[8] Under episcopal authority in the ninth century, until Bishop Isaac of Langres rebuilt the church in 869 and reformed the monastic life under Saro, already abbot of Pouthières.[9] In an association of prayers with the other monasteries of Burgundy still following a regular life at the end of the ninth century. It maintained its regularity at least into the 920s.[10] In 990, however, Bishop Bruno of Langres asked the abbot of Cluny for a reforming abbot, William, who soon became a reformer of other Burgundian monasteries as well, including St.-Vivant of Vergy, Bèze, Moûtier-St.-Jean, St.-Michel of Tonnerre, and Molosmes; all of these had their own abbots again after his death.[11]

St.-Remi of Sens

Claimed foundation in the sixth century. The early eighth-century *vita* of the early seventh-century Bishop Lupus of Sens calls it both a basilica and a monastery.[12] Monks were reestablished under episcopal authority in the *cella* of St.-Remi in 822, then moved out of town to Vareilles in 833, to a larger location. Charles the Bald confirmed this move two decades later.[13]

St.-Jean of Sens

Founded in the sixth century as a nunnery. The bishop reestablished the monastic life in the *cella* in 822.[14]

St.-Marcel-lès-Chalon

Founded in the late sixth century (traditionally 584) by King Guntram, one of the last Frankish monasteries before the 590 arrival of Irish-influenced monasticism under Columbanus. The king granted immunities to the basilica "and those serving God there" in the 583/5 Council of Valence.[15] Originally the monks followed the institutes of Agaune. By the 770s the house was headed by laymen. Hucbertus, a *magnificus vir*, held office under Charlemagne, and the house, with canons rather than monks, was then governed by provosts under lay abbots until the late tenth century.[16] Reformed as a priory of Cluny by Adelaide, countess of Chalon, with her second husband, Count Geoffrey Greymantle of Anjou, and with the consent of Duke Henry of Burgundy.[17]

St.-Symphorien of Autun

Originally founded as a basilica in the middle of the fifth century (Gregory of Tours, *Hist* 2.15, p. 64). King Guntram granted immunities to the basilica of St.-Symphorien "and to those serving God there" in the 583/5 Council of Valence, at the same time as to St.-Marcel; see above (Gislemarus, "Vita Droctovei abbatis Parisiensis" 7, MGH SSRM 3:539). A community of monks in the 670s ("Passio Leudegarii episcopi Augustodunensis" 10, MGH SSRM 5:292). In 866 Count Adalard of Autun was lay abbot.[18] Associated in prayers with St.-Martin of Autun at the end of the ninth century. A house of secular canons in the tenth century, it was reformed with canons regular by the early twelfth century.[19]

St.-Seine

The sixth-century Saint Sequanus had a shrine in the second half of the century at which Gregory of Tours said that miracles were worked, although he did not mention monks there.[20] Sequanus had been a pupil of Saint John, founder of Moûtier-St.-Jean,[21] and it is most likely that St.-Seine, like that house, began as a hermitage. Owed Louis the Pious *dona* in 819.[22] Charles the Fat confirmed the possessions of the monks, under Abbot Boniface, in 886 (MGH DD regum Germaniae ex stirpe Karolinorum 2:225–27, no. 140). Associated in prayer with St.-Martin of Autun at the end of the ninth century.[23] A house of black monks in the eleventh and twelfth centuries.[24]

St.-Germain of Auxerre

Founded as a basilica in the early sixth century; had monks by the late sixth or early seventh century; see Appendix II.

Notre-Dame of Autun

Founded as a nunnery at the very end of the sixth century by Queen Brunhildis and Bishop Syagrius.[25] Probably the same as the urban nunnery known as St.-Andoche in the ninth century, into which Bishop Jonas put Benedictine nuns in 858, replacing the canonesses who had been there.[26]

St.-Martin of Autun

Founded at the very end of the sixth century by Queen Brunhildis and Bishop Syagrius, at the same time as Notre-Dame of Autun. In 602, Lupus was "abbot and priest," but there was no sign of monks.[27] Brunhildis was considered to have been buried there. The monastery then disappears from the sources until 843, when Charles the Bald confirmed the bishop of Autun's authority over the house. In 855 Robert the Strong was lay abbot. Restored, under Abbot Arnulf, in 875.[28] At the end of the ninth century, an association of prayers was formed between St.-Martin and the other churches of Burgundy still following a regular life: Flavigny, St.-Bénigne, St.-Seine, Corbigny, St.-Pierre of Chalon, and St.-Symphorien of Autun.[29] The monks' possessions were confirmed by King Raoul in 924, but they soon lost their regularity of life, for the house had to be reestablished in 949 by the Burgundian counts Hugh the Black and Giselbert, with the assistance of monks from Cluny.[30] St.-Martin had its own abbot in 1034. In 1058, Pope Nicholas took the house under the papacy's direct jurisdiction.[31]

St.-Pierre of Melun

Although it later claimed a foundation in the sixth century, it was probably a basilica then, not a monastery.[32] It owed Louis the Pious prayers but not *dona*.[33] Rebuilt with a community of monks, under Abbot Walter, by Archbishop Seguin of Sens in the 990s, with the confirmation of Hugh Capet.[34]

St.-Julien of Auxerre

Originally founded as a monastery at the beginning of the seventh century, then refounded as a nunnery within two generations; see Appendix II.

St.-Pierre-le-Vif of Sens

A twelfth-century chronicler dated St.-Pierre's foundation to the time of Clovis and his supposed daughter Theuchildis, although it is more likely that the house was founded in the early seventh century. A Theuchildis *regina* was buried there, according to a mid-seventh-century charter, probably the source for making her the founder.[35] Queen Balthildis called St.-Pierre one of the "senior basilicas" of the realm ("Vita S. Balthildis" 9, MGH SSRM 2:493). In 822 Louis the Pious granted authority over the house, now called a *cella*, to the archbishop of Sens, saying it had long since lost its monks. It had monks again a decade later, however, when the abbot of St.-Wandrille included them in his testament.[36] The house was dominated by the archbishops of Sens until 891, when the archbishop agreed to let the monks choose their own abbots. It was a house of black monks, under Abbot Raynard, at the end of the tenth century.[37]

Ferrières

First appears in the *vita* of the seventh-century Bishop Eligius of Noyon ("Vita Eligii episcopi Noviomagensis" 1.10, MGH SSRM 4:678). In the twelfth century the monks asserted foundation by Duke Wandelbert (GC 12:15–16, no. 15). Charlemagne made Alcuin the abbot in 782 ("Vita Alcuini" 9, MGH SS 15:190). The house owed Louis the Pious *dona* and military service. Louis did, however, grant the monks the right to free election, a privilege repeated by Charles the Bald in 841.[38]

St.-Loup of Troyes

A basilica outside of town had been dedicated to the sainted fifth-century bishop of Troyes by the middle of the sixth century. It had an abbot by the early seventh century, according to the early eighth-century *vita* of Bishop Lupus of Sens.[39] Charlemagne made Alcuin the abbot in 782, at the same time as he became abbot of Ferrières ("Vita Alcuini" 9, MGH SS 15:190). Destroyed by the Vikings in the 880s. Rebuilt within the city of Troyes in 890 by Adalem, count of Troyes, who also acted as abbot. First the counts and then, in the eleventh century, the lords of Chappes acted as lay abbots until the monastery was made an independent house of secular canons by Lord Clarembald of Chappes in 1114. These canons were replaced by Augustinian canons in 1135. Meanwhile, St.-Loup's original church was refounded as a house of canons dedicated to St.-Martin.[40]

Bèze

Founded, according to its twelfth-century chronicle, in the seventh century by the couple Amalgarius and Aquilina, parents of Waldalenus, the first abbot, although the authenticity of its founding documents has been cast into doubt.[41] It initially followed the "rule of St. Columbanus or of St. Benedict." The monastery lost its regularity in the eighth century. Though Bishop Alberic reestablished a body of monks in 830, the house was sacked by the Vikings in 888. A new restoration by the bishop in 890 was followed by a sack by the Magyars in 936/7. Under the direction of Abbot William of St.-Bénigne at the end of the tenth century, although it had its own abbots after his death.[42]

St.-Etienne of Nevers

Originally founded as a house of nuns in the early seventh century, under the influence of Columbanus (Jonas of Bobbio, "Vita Columbani" 2, MGH SSRM 4:129). However, it then disappears from the records until the eleventh century. It was deserted in 1063 when Bishop Hugh gave it to his cathedral chapter. Count William of Nevers rebuilt it and gave it to Cluny as a priory in 1097.[43]

Ste.-Colombe of Sens

A basilica in the first decades of the seventh century, when Bishop Desiderius of Auxerre mentioned it in his testament.[44] It was a monastery by 660, with an abbot and brothers, when Bishop Emmo of Sens gave it a privilege of immunity.[45] Abbot Wideradus attended the 760/2 Council of Attigny ("Consilium Attiniacense," MGH Concilia 2:73). In the first decades of the ninth century it served as a refuge for the monks of St.-Riquier, fleeing the Vikings, and the leader of the St.-Riquier monks became archbishop of Sens and assumed authority over the house. Served by canons in the 830s when it received a privilege from Louis the Pious, specifying that the brothers could choose their own abbot, rather than being subject to the archbishop of Sens.[46] In 847, it once again had monks rather than canons, even though it also had a secular *rector*, when Charles the Bald confirmed the brothers as following the Benedictine Rule.[47] In 891, Richard le Justicier served as lay abbot.[48] It had its own abbot, Guntio, in 988 when Hugh Capet confirmed the monks' privileges.[49]

Montier-en-Der

Founded in 666 at the site of the hermitage of Bercharius, who became the first abbot, originally following variously the rules of Lérins, Luxeuil, Agaune, and Benedict. The monks received privileges from Childeric II and Theoderic III.[50] In the eighth century, the monks were replaced by canons. Although the Benedictine Rule was established by Louis the Pious around 830, lay abbots and rectors governed the house in the following decades,[51] and in the later ninth century the monks had to flee from the Vikings to the Jura. They soon returned, but an eleventh-century author said that they fell into decadence under Abbot Benzo and were only reformed in 935 by the arrival of monks from St.-Evre of Toul (itself recently reformed on the model of Fleury), under Abbot Alberic.[52]

St.-Georges of Couches

This little monastery in the diocese of Autun, probably founded in the seventh century, had its own abbot in the first decades of the ninth century.[53] In 1018 the bishop, saying that it had long been deserted, gave it to the monastery of Flavigny to reform to the Benedictine Rule, but by the 1080s it had become a simple *ecclesia*.[54]

Montier-la-Celle

Founded in the middle of the seventh century in "Insula Germanus," outside of Troyes, by a recluse named Frodbert.[55] Queen Balthildis and her husband, Clovis II, granted the monks some fisc land, which their son Clothar III confirmed in the 650s.[56] It was a house of regular monks in the middle of the eighth century.[57] It received gifts and a confirmation of its possessions from Charles the Bald.[58] In 935, Benzo, formerly abbot of Montier-en-Der, was driven out of there and settled instead at Montier-la-Celle. The house was following a monastic life in 1048, when Count Theobold of Troyes took monks from there to reestablish the regular life in a church in Provins.[59]

Poulangy

Founded in the seventh century as a house of nuns. In the ninth through early twelfth centuries it was an *abbatiola* dependent on the bishops of Langres. In the twelfth century it became a house of nuns associated with Cîteaux.[60]

Puellemontier

Founded in 693 as a nunnery, dependent on Montier-en-Der.[61]

St.-Andoche of Saulieu

Established as a monastery by the first decades of the eighth century, when Wideradus remembered it in his testament, at the same time as he founded Flavigny. In 843, Charles the Bald confirmed the bishop of Autun's authority over it.[62]

Flavigny

Founded in 717;[63] originally followed a "mixed rule" containing elements of the rules of Lérins, Luxeuil, and Agaune but almost immediately adopted the Benedictine Rule. Abbot Manasses attended the 760/2 Council of Attigny ("Consilium Attiniacense," MGH Concilia 2:73). Owed Louis the Pious *dona* and military service. Count Warin was lay abbot (*rector*) in the 840s, and Bishop Adalgar became abbot in 877.[64] Joined the association of prayers with St.-Martin of Autun at the end of the ninth century, but bishops of Autun continued to hold the office of abbot of Flavigny, ruling through rectors, until the 990s, when Bishop Walter reformed the house by subjecting it to Abbot Heldric of St.-Germain.[65] In the eleventh and twelfth centuries it elected its own abbots.

Nesle

Claimed origins in the sixth century, although there is no evidence for a foundation before the eighth century.[66] Owed Louis the Pious *dona* and military service. In 841 the emperor Lothar confirmed the monastery's possessions and granted the monks the right to elect their abbot freely, saying that Louis the Pious had made a similar grant of immunity.[67]

St.-Etienne of Dijon

Claimed foundation in the seventh century, although it is only definitively attested in the eighth century. It was a house of canons around the year 800 when Bishop Betto of Langres made the house gifts.[68] Under episcopal control in the ninth century. An *ecclesia*, not a monastery, in 889. A house of secular canons in the early twelfth century.[69] These were replaced by Augustinian canons between 1113 and 1116.[70]

Molosmes

A monastery dependent on the bishop of Langres in the ninth century, with the implication that it had long been a monastery. Owed Louis the Pious prayers but not *dona*.[71] Its abbot attended a council at Langres in 858. Put under the direction of Abbot William of St.-Bénigne at the end of the tenth century.[72]

Sts.-Géosmes

A monastery dependent on the bishop of Langres in the ninth century, with the implication that it had long been a monastery. Hosted a council in 858.[73]

Montiéramey

Founded in 837 by Count Aledram and Bishop Adalbert of Troyes as a cell for the hermit Adremar, for whom the house is named (GC 12:247, no. 2). Charles the Bald confirmed the foundation. In the 850s this former hermitage had Benedictine monks.[74] Kings Odo and Raoul confirmed the monks' rights in the 890s and 920s, respectively. It continued as a house of Benedictine monks in the eleventh and twelfth centuries.[75]

Tournus

Originally a basilica dedicated St.-Valérien, in honor of a local martyr. Refounded by Charles the Bald in 875 as a home for the monks of St.-Philibert (Noirmoutier), who were fleeing the Vikings. The church at Tournus was rededicated as St.-Philibert. It managed to maintain itself as a regular monastery throughout the tenth and eleventh centuries.[76]

St.-Pierre of Chalon

Associated in prayers with St.-Martin of Autun at the end of the ninth century.[77] Abbot Seinfred attended a reform council in 1064 (GC 12:328, no. 36). St.-Pierre had black monks throughout the eleventh and twelfth centuries.[78]

Vézelay

Founded in 858/9 by Count Girard and his wife, Bertha. They intended it to be a house of nuns, but at some point between 863 and 878 the nuns were forced to flee, and the house instead acquired Benedictine monks.[79] Beginning in 1058, the house was regularly listed as an *abbatia* subject to Cluny in that house's papal bulls, even though it retained its own abbot.[80]

Pouthières

Founded in 858/9 by Count Girard and Countess Bertha at the same time as Vézelay; the couple was buried at Pouthières.[81] The abbot of the house was accused of gross irregularities at the 1049 Council of Reims and forced to resign.[82] Unlike its sister house of Vézelay, the monastery of Pouthières was never associated with Cluny and had its own abbot in the twelfth century.[83]

Corbigny

Founded in 864 by Abbot Eygilo of Flavigny, as a house of Benedictine monks, headed by Abbot Wulfrid.[84] Taken by Bishop Adalgar of Autun along with Flavigny in 877; see above. Associated in prayers with St.-Martin of Autun at the end of the ninth century.[85] Reformed and placed under the authority of the bishop of Autun in 1034 (GC 4:78–79, no. 42). During the following decades the monks of Corbigny sought to establish their independence both from the bishops of Autun and from Flavigny.[86]

St.-Martin of Nevers

Bishop Herman of Nevers put canons in the church in 849 (GC 12:301–3, no. 4), then in 886 Bishop Emmenus replaced the canons with nuns (MGH DD regum Germaniae ex stirpe Karolinorum 2:221–22, no. 138).[87] Refounded as a house of canons in the first decades of the twelfth century (GC 12:338–39, no. 47).

St.-Sauveur/Notre-Dame of Nevers

Bishop Herman put nuns in the church in 849 (GC 12:301–3, no. 4; "Annales Nivernenses" 858, MGH SS 13:89). In 1045, after it had "lost the Rule of Saint Benedict," the bishop of Nevers gave it to Cluny as a priory.[88]

St.-Urbain of Châlons

Bishop Erchenraus of Châlons established the monastery in the 860s, having obtained for the purpose some relics of Pope Urban I from the monks of St.-Germain of Auxerre.[89]

Charlieu

Founded in 872 by Robert, bishop of Valence, who appointed the first abbot. Boso, count and later king of Provence, was an early benefactor.[90] The pope gave it to Cluny in 932, at the request of King Hugh of Italy, and it may perhaps be considered the first abbey subjected to Cluny. It topped the list of Cluny's dependencies in the 954 confirmation of Pope Agapitus and remained a Cluniac priory in the eleventh and twelfth centuries.[91]

St.-Michel of Tonnerre

Most likely founded in the ninth century.[92] In the 880s Bishop Theobold of Langres gave the monks some churches, saying they were rich in edifices but poor in income. Under the control of the bishop of Langres in the 930s, when the bishop gave it to one Teuto, his *miles* and faithful follower. In 980, the bishop of Langres and the count of Tonnerre set out together to rebuild the house and submit it to a monastic rule; the count had controlled much of its income.[93] It was put under Abbot William of St.-Bénigne, who, however, made one of his monks abbot of St.-Michel.[94] In the eleventh century, the house freed itself from the bishops of Langres, wishing to elect its own abbots (GC 4:143–45, nos. 19, 21). In the twelfth century the house became dependent on Molesme.[95]

St.-Vivant/Notre-Dame of Vergy

Founded around 900 by Count Manasses of Autun, along with his wife, Ermengard, son Giselbert, and brother Walo, bishop of Autun. At the end of the tenth century, Duke Henry of Burgundy subjected the house to William, abbot of St.-Bénigne of Dijon.[96] As of 1095, the abbots were elected with the approval of the abbot of Cluny,[97] but the house quickly became a Cluniac priory, which it remained throughout the twelfth century.

Cluny

Founded in 909/10 by Duke William of Aquitaine.[98] At the end of the tenth century, several monasteries of the region, including St.-Bénigne of Dijon and St.-Germain of Auxerre, were reformed by having monks from Cluny settle there. Initially these houses retained their independence, but from about 1000 on it became more common to make a house a Cluniac priory in order to reform it. By the beginning of the twelfth century many of the other monasteries of the region had come under Cluny's direction, including St.-Germain of Auxerre and Vézelay (which kept their own abbots though listed as dependencies of Cluny in papal bulls) and the priories of St.-Marcel-lès-Chalon, Paray-le-Monial, St.-Sauveur of Nevers, St.-Etienne of Nevers, and St.-Vivant of Vergy.[99]

Paray-le-Monial

Founded in 973 by Lambert, count of Chalon. Given to Cluny in 999 by Lambert's son, Count Hugh, it became a priory.[100]

St.-Pierre of Châlons

There is no record of a monastic life until the house was rebuilt by Bishop Roger of Châlons, with the consent of King Robert II, in 1021; at this time the house was said to have been founded by Memmius, the first bishop of Châlons (GC 10:152-53, no. 5).

Appendix II

Churches in Auxerre

The following list of all the churches in Auxerre (whether or not they were monasteries), arranged roughly in order of foundation, is intended to illustrate the establishment of commemoration of the see's Christian past. The single most informative source is the *Gesta* of the bishops, originally composed in the 870s and added to over subsequent centuries.[1]

The "Basilica of Lord Valerian"/St.-Pèlerin

Doubtless Auxerre's original church, located near the river. Called Lord Valerian's basilica at the end of the sixth century (*Gesta*, 1:77).[2] Assuming, as seems most likely, that Peregrinus was not in fact Auxerre's first bishop in spite of the *Gesta* and that Bishops Valerius and Valerian were the same man, then Valerian was the second bishop of Auxerre and the builder of its first real church. The church now known as St.-Pèlerin was doubtless built on its site.[3] It was not listed as one of the churches of Auxerre whose abbots or archpriests were expected to say mass at the cathedral at the end of the seventh century (*Gesta*, 1:119); that listing included only the nine churches I give here after the cathedral. The ecclesiastics of Auxerre long seem to have considered this their city's original church, although it is first called the church of St.-Pèlerin in the third quarter of the eleventh century. Then Bishop Geoffrey, calling it a "chapel," recovered it from "usurpers" and restored it (*Gesta*, 1:273).[4]

St.-Etienne

The cathedral, built at the end of the fourth century on top of Auxerre's central hill, in the center of the old Gallo-Roman *civitas*, to replace the original basilica as Auxerre's principal church (*Gesta*, 1:27). Dedicated to Saint Stephen by the second half of the sixth century (*Gesta*, 1:75). It was surrounded by a complex of small churches, as follows.

St.-Alban

Founded by Bishop Germanus in the first half of the fifth century, to house relics he brought back from Britain (*Gesta*, 1:39), but it never became more than a small church inside the city walls.[5] The only church in the city to escape the destructive fire of the beginning of the eleventh century (*Gesta*, 1:253).[6] St.-Alban and the following three were all minor churches in the cathedral complex.

St.-Remi

A house of monks in the 830s,[7] it had a short life as an independent house. In the middle of the ninth century Bishop Heribald, calling it a *cella*, gave it to the canons of his cathedral (*Gesta*, 1:151).

St.-Jean

Bishop Heribald rebuilt this church, most likely the original baptistry, in the second quarter of the ninth century. The *Gesta* say that it was a very old church, which had collapsed from age (*Gesta*, 1:151, 171, 199).

Ste.-Marie

Part of the cathedral complex from the early ninth century on (*Gesta*, 1:144, 171, 199, 261).

St.-Marien

A monastery founded by Bishop Germanus in the first half of the fifth century, across the river from the cathedral, and originally dedicated to Saints Cosme and Damien (*Gesta*, 1:37).[8] It acquired a dedication to Marien, a local saint, by the end of the sixth century (*Gesta*, 1:51, 73). Auxerre's first monastery, it was the only church of Auxerre called a *monasterium* in a late sixth-century listing (*Gesta*, 1:73, 77). The *abbatia* was taken over by the bishop of Auxerre at the beginning of the ninth century (*Gesta*, 1:143). Long abandoned in the 1130s, it was refounded as a house of Premonstratensian canons.[9]

St.-Germain

Originally a basilica dedicated to Saint Maurice of Agaune, established by Bishop Germanus in the first half of the fifth century (*Gesta*, 1:39).[10] The bishop was buried there, and the basilica then became known by his name. According to Heiric, a monk of St.-Germain, Queen Clotildis rebuilt the basilica in sumptuous style in the early sixth century. Gregory of Tours visited it as a youth.[11] It was still listed as a basilica, not a monastery, in the second half of the sixth century (*Gesta*, 1:73). By the first quarter of the seventh century, however, it had an abbot, mentioned in the testament of Bishop Desiderius (d. 632) (*Gesta*, 1:103). In the middle of the seventh century, according to her *vita*, Queen Balthildis considered it one of the "senior basilicas" of the realm and praised the brothers who followed a "regular order" there.[12] Abbot Lantfrid attended the 760/2 Council of Attigny ("Consilium Attiniacense," MGH Concilia 2:73). In the ninth and tenth centuries, although Louis the Pious granted the monks the right to elect their own abbot, the house was ruled by a series of lay abbots: Hugh "the Abbot" of the powerful Welf family; Lothair, young son of Charles the Bald; Count Boso, future king of Burgundy; Boso's brother Richard le Justicier; and Hugh the Great, father of Hugh Capet.[13] Yet the monastery continued to have monks, and provosts directed the house's affairs. The house prospered in spite of the lay abbots, and the church and crypt were rebuilt in the ninth century, but the tenth century was more difficult. The Benedictine Rule, including the monks' right to elect their own abbot, was reestablished there in 994, at the instigation of Duke Henry of Burgundy—who also seems to have been lay abbot—under Heldric, a monk of Cluny who was simultaneously abbot of St.-Germain, Flavigny, and Moûtier-St.-Jean (*Gesta*, 1:233–35).[14] In the 1090s it was reformed again, again by an abbot from Cluny although at the instigation of the bishop of Auxerre. Though retaining its own abbot, it was regularly listed among Cluny's *abbatiae* in papal bulls from the twelfth century.[15]

St.-Amâtre

Erected over the Gallo-Roman cemetery on Mont Artre, where the bishops of Auxerre were all buried before Germanus.[16] The dedication is to Bishop Amator, buried there in the early fifth century. A basilica was established there by the beginning of the sixth century when Ursus, a holy man who was soon made bishop, established a cell as an anchorite (*Gesta*, 1:55, 73). It is not clear when it acquired a body of monks. This *abbatia* was taken over by the bishops at some point, then, according to the later episcopal *Gesta*, given to a "tyrant" in benefice, who in turn granted it "by the law of heredity" to his own son, the bishop of Autun (*Gesta*, 1:271).[17] But Bishop Geoffrey finally recovered the house for the bishops of Auxerre in the third quarter of the eleventh century. Bishop Hugh refounded it as a priory of Augustinian canons around 1130.[19]

St.-Pierre

A basilica in the later sixth century, located in the "suburb" of Auxerre (*Gesta*, 1:75, 105).[19] Bishop Humbaud established canons regular there at the beginning of the twelfth century, with the approval of the pope (*Gesta*, 2:65–69).

St.-Martin

A basilica in the second half of the sixth century (*Gesta*, 1:75). It may have originally been dedicated to the local saint Mammertinus.[20] By the early seventh century it had become a house of nuns, associated with St.-Marien and its monks (*Gesta*, 1:105). In the eighth century it was "usurped" by laymen, according to the *Gesta*, but returned to the control of the bishop by Charlemagne (*Gesta*, 1:141). Around 1140 Bishop Hugh gave this church, which had long been abandoned, to the Premonstratensian canons of St.-Marien.[21]

St.-Julien

First mentioned as a basilica within the city in the second half of the sixth century (*Gesta*, 1:75).[22] It acquired a small body of monks by the beginning of the seventh century, and in the first quarter of the century it had an abbot (*Gesta*, 1:105). In 631, Bishop Palladius moved the house outside the city walls and made it into a house of nuns (*Gesta*, 1:113).[23] Louis the Pious made Count Hugh of Tours lay abbot in the early ninth century, although it was a nunnery at the time. It continued to have both nuns and a lay abbot; Hugh "the Abbot," of the family of the Welfs, headed it a generation later.[24] By the 1040s, however, it had its own abbess, Emma.[25]

St.-Gervais/St.-Protais/St.-Nazaire

Originally constructed as a basilica in the first quarter of the seventh century, under episcopal direction (*Gesta*, 1:107). In the eighth century it was "usurped" by laymen, according to the *Gesta*, but Charlemagne returned it to the control of the bishop (*Gesta*, 1:141). It had an abbot in the early ninth century (*Gesta*, 1:143). The brothers lived there "regularly" at the beginning of the tenth century (*Gesta*, 1:185). In the 1140s Bishop Hugh made it a priory of Molesme.[26]

St.-Eusèbe

Established as a basilica, with a body of monks, by Bishop Palladius in the second quarter of the seventh century (*Gesta*, 1:113). In the eighth century it was "usurped" by laymen, according to the *Gesta*, but was returned to the control of the bishop by Charlemagne (*Gesta*, 1:141). According to an eleventh-century entry in the *Gesta*, it was originally a house of canons but had been almost completely destroyed before Bishop Geoffrey reestablished it with a body of canons and an abbot, in the third quarter of the eleventh century (*Gesta*, 1:271). Bishop Humbaud replaced these secular canons with canons regular at the beginning of the twelfth century (*Gesta*, 2:69).[27]

Notre-Dame-la-Dehors

Bishop Vigilius founded the monastery by testament in the final quarter of the seventh century (*Gesta*, 1:115).[28] This and the eight preceding churches were listed at the end of the seventh century as the principal churches of Auxerre (*Gesta*, 1:119). Recovered by Bishop Geoffrey from the bishop of Autun and restored at the same time as St.-Amâtre; see above. In the 1140s it had a body of canons, whom Bishop Hugh turned out, saying "their way of life was not honorable"; he gave the church instead to the Premonstratensians of St.-Marien.[29]

Abbreviations

AASS	Acta Sanctorum
Arch. Aube	Troyes, Archives départementales de l'Aube
Arch. Côte-d'Or	Dijon, Archives départementales de la Côte-d'Or
Arch. Haute-Marne	Chaumont, Archives départementales de la Haute-Marne
Arch. Haute-Saône	Vesoul, Archives départementales de la Haute-Saône
Arch. Marne	Châlons-en-Champagne [-sur-Marne], Archives départementales de la Marne
Arch. Saône-et-Loire	Mâcon, Archives départementales de Saône-et-Loire
Arch. Yonne	Auxerre, Archives départementales de l'Yonne
Bibl. mun.	Bibliothèque municipale
BnF	Paris, Bibliothèque nationale de France
CCCM	Corpus Christianorum Continuatio Mediaevalis
CCSL	Corpus Christianorum Series Latina
ChLA	*Chartae Latinae Antiquiores*; cited by document number, volume, and pages
CSEL	Corpus Scriptorum Ecclesiasticorum Latinorum
GC	*Gallia Christiana in provincias ecclesiasticas distributas*; cited by column of the *instrumenta*
Gesta	*Gesta pontificum Autissiodorensium*
Gregory of Tours, *Hist*	Gregory of Tours, *Historia*, ed. Bruno Krusch and Wilhelm Levison, MGH SSRM I/I
KdG	*Karl der Grosse: Lebenswerk und Nachleben*, ed. Wolfgang Braunfels
Mansi	J. D. Mansi, ed., *Sacrorum conciliorum nova et amplissima collecta*

MGH	Monumenta Germaniae Historica
AA	Auctores antiquissimi
Capit.	Legum sectio II, Capitularia regum Francorum
Concilia	Legum sectio III, Concilia
DD	Diplomata
DD Burgundiae	Diplomata regum Burgundiae e stirpe Rudolfina
Epp.	Epistolae
Formulae	Legum sectio V, Formulae Merowingici et Karolini aevi
Poetae	Poetae Latini aevi Carolini
SS	Scriptores
SSRL	Scriptores rerum Langobardicarum
SSRM	Scriptores rerum Merovingicarum
NCMH	*The New Cambridge Medieval History*
PL	J.-P. Migne, ed., *Patrologiae cursus completus*, series Latina

Notes

NOTES ON TERMINOLOGY

1. Pippin of Herstal, Charlemagne's great-grandfather, received power and property from both his presumed paternal grandfather, Arnulf of Metz, and his maternal grandfather, Pippin I. I shall restrict the label "Pippinid" to Pippin of Herstal's maternal ancestry. The term "Arnulfing" becomes seriously problematic if one removes Arnulf from the family tree, as discussed in Chapter 7, but I have nonetheless kept the term, as sanctioned by scholarly tradition.

INTRODUCTION

1. Anselm of St.-Remy, "Histoire de la dédicace de Saint-Remy," Prologue, p. 200; *Chronique de l'abbaye de Saint-Bénigne de Dijon, suivie de la Chronique de Saint-Pierre de Bèze*, ed. E. Bougaud and Joseph Garnier, p. 327.

2. This point was perhaps made most boldly by Walter Ullman, *The Growth of Papal Government in the Middle Ages*, pp. 359–60. Karl F. Morrison, however, suggests tradition and authority were often contradictory; *Tradition and Authority in the Western Church*.

3. Esther Cohen, "Introduction," in *Medieval Transformations*, ed. Esther Cohen and Mayke B. de Jong, pp. 1–2.

4. Celia Chazelle and Felice Lifshitz, "Early Medieval Studies in Twenty-First-Century America," in *Paradigms and Methods in Early Medieval Studies*, ed. Celia Chazelle and Felice Lifshitz, p. 10; Chris Wickham, *Framing the Early Middle Ages*, pp. 8–9.

5. Giles Constable, "Forgery and Plagiarism in the Middle Ages"; idem, "Forged Letters in the Middle Ages," in *Fälschungen im Mittelalter*, 5:11–37.

6. Mark Mersiowsky, "Towards a Reappraisal of Carolingian Sovereign Charters," in *Charters and the Use of the Written Word in Medieval Society*, ed. Karl Heidecker, pp. 17–20.

7. Elizabeth A. R. Brown, "*Falsitas pia sive reprehensibilia*: Medieval Forgers and Their Intentions," in *Fälschungen im Mittelalter*, 1:101–19; Ernst Pitz, "Erschleichung und Anfechtung von Herrscher- und Papsturkunden vom 4. bis 10. Jahrhundert," in *Fälschungen im Mittelalter*, 3:69–113.

8. Gabrielle M. Spiegel, "History, Historicism, and the Social Logic of the Text in the

Middle Ages"; eadem, *The Past as Text*, pp. 3–28; Guy Halsall, "The Sources and Their Interpretation," *NCMH*, 1:56–90. Even German medievalists, coming out of a tradition that invented positivist history, have long discussed the attitudes and expectations of the authors they study; Timothy Reuter, *Germany in the Early Middle Ages*, pp. 14–15.

9. Matthew Innes, "Introduction," in *The Uses of the Past in the Early Middle Ages*, ed. Yitzhak Hen and Matthew Innes, pp. 1–8.

10. Walter Goffart, *The Narrators of Barbarian History*; Patrick J. Geary, *Phantoms of Remembrance*; Mary Carruthers, *The Book of Memory*; eadem, *The Craft of Thought*.

11. Among recent examples, see Susan Boynton, *Shaping a Monastic Identity*; Margot E. Fassler, *The Virgin of Chartres*; Amy G. Remensnyder, *Remembering Kings Past*; *Medieval Concepts of the Past*, ed. Gerd Althoff, Johannes Fried, and Patrick J. Geary; Rosamond McKitterick, *Perceptions of the Past in the Early Middle Ages*; Karine Ugé, *Creating the Monastic Past in Medieval Flanders*; Samantha Kahn Herrick, *Imagining the Sacred Past*; Ellen F. Arnold, *Negotiating the Landscape*; and Constance B. Bouchard, "Episcopal *Gesta* and the Creation of a Useful Past." See also Patrick J. Geary, "Monastic Memory and the Mutation of the Year Thousand," in *Monks and Nuns, Saints and Outcasts*, ed. Sharon Farmer and Barbara H. Rosenwein, pp. 25–36.

12. Hagiography has entered the twenty-first century with an online database of medieval saints; Guy Philippart and Michel Trigalet, "Latin Hagiography Before the Ninth Century: A Synoptic View," in *The Long Morning of Medieval Europe*, ed. Jennifer R. Davis and Michael McCormick, pp. 111–29.

13. Anneke B. Mulder-Bakker, "The Invention of Saintliness: Texts and Contexts," in *The Invention of Saintliness*, ed. Anneke B. Mulder-Bakker, pp. 4–7. A cogent argument for seeing saints' lives as more than the naive expression of half-pagan popular culture is made by Raymond Van Dam, "Images of Saint Martin in Late Roman and Early Merovingian Gaul." An indication of how far the field has advanced in the last two decades is how unnecessary his (entirely valid) arguments now seem. See also Constance B. Bouchard, "Reconstructing Sanctity and Refiguring Saints in Early Medieval Gaul."

14. Patrick J. Geary, *Furta Sacra*. This book, which received a number of scathing reviews when it first appeared in 1978, was reissued for classroom use in the 1990s, the earlier furor forgotten—perhaps itself an incident of creative memory.

15. Thomas Head, *Hagiography and the Cult of Saints*; Sharon Farmer, *Communities of Saint Martin*; Felice Lifshitz, *The Norman Conquest of Pious Neustria*; Catherine Cubitt, "Memory and Narrative in the Cult of Early Anglo-Saxon Saints," in *The Uses of the Past*, pp. 29–66; Elizabeth A. Castelli, *Martyrdom and Memory*; Mathew Kuefler, *The Making and Unmaking of a Saint*. See also Julia M. H. Smith, "Early Medieval Hagiography in the Late Twentieth Century"; and Patrick J. Geary, *Living with the Dead in the Middle Ages*, pp. 9–10.

16. The pioneering study was by Paul Fouracre, "Merovingian History and Merovingian Hagiography." Very influential has been the volume of translated *vitae*, *Sacred Women of the Dark Ages*, ed. and trans. Jo Ann McNamara and John E. Halborg (Durham, N.C., 1992). Among many recent monographs, see Lynda L. Coon, *Sacred Fictions*; and John Kitchen, *Saints' Lives and the Rhetoric of Gender*.

17. John B. Freed, "Artistic and Literary Representations of Family Consciousness," in *Medieval Concepts of the Past*, pp. 233–52.

18. M. T. Clanchy, *From Memory to Written Record*, pp. 7–11; Patrick J. Geary, "Oblivion Between Orality and Textuality in the Tenth Century," in *Medieval Concepts of the Past*, pp. 111–22; Walter Goffart, "Conspicuously Absent: Martial Heroism in the *Histories* of Gregory of Tours and Its Likes," in *The World of Gregory of Tours*, ed. Kathleen Mitchell and Ian Wood, pp. 387–93; Wolfert S. van Egmond, *Conversing with the Saints*, pp. 4–6. Elisabeth van Houts links oral memory especially to women; *Memory and Gender in Medieval Europe*, pp. 1–5.

19. Karine Ugé, "Relics as Tools of Power: The Eleventh-Century *Inventio* of St. Bertin's Relics and the Assertion of Abbot Bovo's Authority," in *Negotiating Secular and Ecclesiastical Power*, ed. Henk Teunis, Andrew Wareham, and Arnoud-Jan A. Bijsterveld, pp. 51–71.

20. The promotion of patriotism in the nineteenth and twentieth centuries is now understood as involving the creation of a shared past; Eric Hobsbawm, "Inventing Traditions." See also Dominique Barthélemy, *L'an mil et la paix de Dieu*; and Patrick J. Geary, *The Myth of Nations*.

21. Constance Brittain Bouchard, *Sword, Miter, and Cloister*; eadem, *Holy Entrepreneurs*; eadem, *"Every Valley Shall be Exalted."*

22. Constance Brittain Bouchard, *"Those of My Blood."*

CHAPTER I

1. Arch. Marne G 462, fol. 1r. The cartulary was printed by P. Pélicier, "Cartulaire de Saint-Etienne de Châlons." Warin does not seem to have been concerned about the late antique distinction between royal *precepta* and private *cartae*, on which see Georges Declercq, "Originals and Cartularies: The Organization of Archival Memory (Ninth-Eleventh Centuries)," in *Charters and the Use of the Written Word in Medieval Society*, ed. Karl Heidecker, p. 151.

2. One of the documents is also found in the cartulary of Montier-en-Der, composed twenty years later; see Chapter 2.

3. Declercq, "Originals and Cartularies," p. 148.

4. It was used in this sense by a ninth-century author at Le Mans; *Gesta domni Aldrici Cenomannicae urbis episcopi*, ed. R. Charles and L[ouis] Froger, p. 34: "cartulas et privilegia in cartelario suae sedis aecclesiae invenit." The new edition is in *Geschichte des Bistums Le Mans von der Spätantike bis zur Karolingerzeit*, ed. Margarete Weidemann, 1:133.

5. Paul Bertrand, Caroline Bourlet, and Xavier Hélary, "Vers une typologie des cartulaires médiévaux," in *Les cartulaires méridionaux*, ed. Daniel Le Blévec, pp. 14–15.

6. Isabelle Vérité, "Les entreprises françaises de recensement des cartulaires (XVIIIe–XXe siècles)," in *Les cartulaires*, ed. Olivier Guyotjeannin, Laurent Morelle, and Michel Parisse, pp. 179–213. The first repertory of French cartularies has appeared, covering the

southeast. For England, see Jean-Philippe Genet, "Cartulaires, registres et histoire: L'exemple anglais," in *Le métier d'historien au moyen âge*, ed. Bernard Guenée, pp. 95–138.

7. Patrick Geary, "Entre gestion et *gesta*," in *Les cartulaires*, pp. 13–24.

8. Constance B. Bouchard, "Monastic Cartularies: Organizing Eternity," in *Charters, Cartularies, and Archives*, ed. Adam J. Kosto and Anders Winroth, pp. 22–32.

9. Theodore Evergates, "The Earliest Comital Cartulary from Champagne," in *Charters, Cartularies, and Archives*, pp. 128–36; Robert-Henri Bautier, "Cartulaires de chancellerie et recueils d'actes des autorités laïques et ecclésiastiques," in *Les cartulaires*, pp. 363–77; Pierre Chastang, "La préface du *Liber instrumentorum memorialis* des Guilhem de Montpellier ou les enjeux de la rédaction d'un cartulaire laïque méridional," in *Les cartulaires méridionaux*, pp. 91–92; Hélène Débax, "Un cartulaire, une titulature et un sceau: Le programme politique du vicomte Roger II (Trencavel) dans les années 1180," in *Les cartulaires méridionaux*, pp. 125–26; Adam J. Kosto, "The *Liber feudorum maior* of the Counts of Barcelona."

10. Theodore Evergates, "The Chancery Archives of the Counts of Champagne."

11. Dietrich Lohrmann, "Evolution et organisation interne des cartulaires rhénans du moyen âge," in *Les cartulaires*, pp. 79–90.

12. *Urkundenbuch des Klosters Fulda*, ed. Edmund E. Stengel; Geary, *Phantoms of Remembrance*, pp. 87–90; Rosamond McKitterick, *History and Memory in the Carolingian World*, pp. 157–58; Janneke Raaijmakers, *The Making of the Monastic Community of Fulda*, pp. 198–206.

13. *Traditiones Wizenburgenses*, ed. Karl Glöckner and Anton Doll.

14. *Codex Laureshamensis*, ed. Karl Glöckner; Matthew Innes, *State and Society in the Early Middle Ages*, pp. 14–15. Lorsch has so many documents in its cartulary, some three thousand, that the editor, Glöckner, felt compelled to abbreviate heavily.

15. *Codex Carolinus*, ed. W. Gundlach, MGH Epp. 3:469–657; Mary Garrison, "The Franks as the New Israel? Education for an Identity from Pippin to Charlemagne," in *The Uses of the Past in the Early Middle Ages*, ed. Yitzhak Hen and Matthew Innes, pp. 125–29; Detlev Jasper and Horst Fuhrmann, *Papal Letters in the Early Middle Ages*, p. 104. See, most recently, the massive study by Achim Thomas Hack, *Codex Carolinus*.

16. *Urkundenbuch der Abtei Sanct Gallen*, ed. Hermann Wartmann; Matthew Innes, "Archives, Documents and Landowners in Carolingian Francia," in *Documentary Culture and the Laity in the Early Middle Ages*, ed. Warren C. Brown, Marios Costambeyes, Matthew Innes, and Adam J. Kosto, pp. 155–73.

17. Declercq, "Originals and Cartularies," pp. 148–49; Geary, *Phantoms of Remembrance*, pp. 81–82.

18. Monique Bourin, "Conclusion," in *Les cartulaires méridionaux*, pp. 259–60; Clanchy, *From Memory to Written Record*, pp. 101–2; Boynton, *Shaping a Monastic Identity*, p. 20.

19. Declercq, "Originals and Cartularies," pp. 152–53. The best-known example is the so-called "cartulary" of St.-Calais, a dossier the monks of that house put together in the 860s (see Chapter 5). It consisted not of everything in the monastery's archives but rather

of the privileges that freed them from the authority of the bishop; *Cartulaire de l'abbaye de Saint-Calais*, ed. L[ouis] Froger.

20. *Chronique des abbés de Fontenelle*, ed. Pascal Pradié. See also John Howe, "The Hagiography of Saint-Wandrille (Fontenelle) (Province of Haute-Normandie)," in *L'hagiographie du haut moyen âge du Gaule du nord*, ed. Martin Heinzelmann, pp. 127–92. The ninth-century *Gesta* of Bishop Aldric of Le Mans included complete copies of charters, but many were forgeries, not documents already in the archives. *Gesta domni Aldrici*, ed. Charles and Froger; ed. Weidemann, *Geschichte des Bistums Le Mans*.

21. "Gesta Dagoberti I regis Francorum," MGH SSRM 2:396–425.

22. Ugé, *Creating the Monastic Past in Medieval Flanders*, pp. 61–71; *Le polyptyque de l'abbaye de Saint-Bertin*, ed. François-Louis Ganshof, Françoise Godding-Ganshof, and Antoine de Smet, pp. 1–2. See also Robert F. Berkhofer, *Day of Reckoning*, pp. 79–80.

23. Michel Parisse, "Ecriture et réécriture des chartes," pp. 258–59.

24. Declercq, "Originals and Cartularies," pp. 160–69.

25. Olivier Guyotjeannin, "*Penuria scriptorum*," pp. 32–33.

26. Geary, *Phantoms of Remembrance*, pp. 84–87.

27. Constance B. Bouchard, "Merovingian, Carolingian, and Cluniac Monasticism." See also Guyotjeannin, "*Penuria scriptorum*," p. 42.

28. The same was true in Brittany, where Redon's cartulary, though containing nearly three hundred ninth-century charters, was composed only in the second half of the eleventh century; Wendy Davies, "The Composition of the Redon Cartulary."

29. *Chartes de l'abbaye de Saint-Etienne de Dijon*, ed. J. Courtois.

30. It certainly dates to before 1035, because it does not include a privilege that King Henry issued to the abbey in that year; Arch. Yonne, H 32. It must indeed be even earlier, for it also does not include (now lost) grants that Henry's charter said were made by his own father, Robert II (996–1031).

31. Portions are now found both in Auxerre and in Metz; the Auxerre folia (Arch. Yonne, H 167), few in number, were originally located between the first and second gatherings of a manuscript now in Metz (Bibl. mun., MS 1161). The Auxerre fragments, dated to around the year 1000 by the editors, are printed in *Chronique de Saint-Pierre-le-Vif*, ed. Robert-Henri Bautier and Monique Gilles, pp. 237–51. Metz 1161 includes copies of charters on fol. 9r—continuing from the leaves now in Auxerre—and on fols. 102r–104v. See also Rudolf Pokorny, "Ein übersehenes Diplom Karls des Kahlen und der 'verloren' *Liber vetus* von Saint-Pierre-le-Vif/Sens."

32. Hugh of Flavigny, *Chronicon*, MGH SS 8:280–502; *The Cartulary of Flavigny*, ed. Constance Brittain Bouchard, "Introduction," pp. 4–10. Patrick Healy is mistaken in suggesting that Hugh was responsible for the cartulary; *The Chronicle of Hugh of Flavigny*, p. 75. Hugh had already been gone from Flavigny for a decade when the twelfth-century cartulary was composed.

33. Jean Mabillon, *Acta sanctorum ordinis S. Benedicti*, 2nd ed., vol. 3 (Venice, 1734), pp. 632–35. Although the twelfth-century cartulary, with its Merovingian attachments, was lost at the time of the French Revolution, an early eighteenth-century scribe working for

Dom Plancher copied it all; for this scribe, see Marie-Louise Auger, *La collection de Bourgogne*, pp. 61–64.

34. BnF, nouv. acq. lat. 1497. The printed edition of all of Cluny's tenth- to thirteenth-century documents is *Recueil des chartes de l'abbaye de Cluny*, ed. Auguste Bernard and Alexander Bruel. The original organization of the cartularies is not immediately evident from the printed edition. Barbara H. Rosenwein, *To Be the Neighbor of Saint Peter*, pp. 15–16; Dominique Iogna-Prat, "La confection des cartulaires et l'historiographie à Cluny (XIe–XIIe siècles)," in *Les cartulaires*, pp. 27–42; Matthew Innes, "On the Material Culture of Legal Documents: Charters and Their Preservation in the Cluny Archive, Ninth to Eleventh Century," in *Documentary Culture and the Laity*, pp. 295–96.

35. Dijon, Bibl. mun., MS 591.

36. *Chartes de Saint-Etienne de Dijon.* St.-Marcel's cartulary, BnF, nouv. acq. lat. 496, is edited as *The Cartulary of St.-Marcel-lès-Chalon*, ed. Constance Brittain Bouchard. The cartulary of Bèze, BnF, MS lat. 4997, was written around 1130, although documents were subsequently copied into it throughout the twelfth century. It is edited in *Chronique de l'abbaye de Saint-Bénigne de Dijon, suivie de la Chronique de Saint-Pierre de Bèze*, ed. Bougaud and Garnier. See also Theo Kölzer, *Merowingerstudien*, 2:1–17. Montier-en-Der's cartulary, Arch. Haute-Marne, 7 H 1, is edited as *The Cartulary of Montier-en-Der*, ed. Constance Brittain Bouchard. *Le cartulaire de Marcigny-sur-Loire*, ed. Jean Richard. Vézelay's cartulary is in Auxerre, Bibl. mun., MS 227, fols. 22r–63v. It is edited in *Monumenta Vizeliacensia*, ed. R. B. C. Huygens.

37. *Le premier cartulaire de l'abbaye cistercienne de Pontigny*, ed. Martine Garrigues. The unedited cartulary of Theuley is in private hands, but a microfilm is in the Arch. Haute-Saône, 1 Mi-3 (R1).

38. Cîteaux's early thirteenth-century cartulary is Arch. Côte-d'Or, 11 H 64; about half the documents are edited by J. Marilier, *Chartes et documents concernant l'abbaye de Cîteaux*. The two-volume cartulary of Clairvaux is Arch. Aube, 3 H 9–10 and is partially edited by Jean Waquet, Jean-Marc Roger, and Laurent Veyssière, *Recueil des chartes de l'abbaye de Clairvaux*. St.-Seine's unedited cartulary is Arch. Côte-d'Or, 10 H 6, pp. 245–76.

39. Arch. Haute-Marne, 2 G 921. *Cartulaire du chapitre cathédral de Langres*, ed. Hubert Flammarion, "Introduction," pp. 7–10. See also Hubert Flammarion, "Une équipe de scribes au travail."

40. Auxerre, Bibl. mun., MS 161. The cartulary is unedited, though many of its charters have been printed, especially those from kings and popes. A catalogue of its contents is provided by Noëlle Deflou-Leca, *Saint-Germain d'Auxerre et ses dépendances*, pp. 648–72.

41. *Premier et second livres des cartulaires de l'abbaye Saint-Serge et Saint-Bach d'Angers*, ed. Yves Chauvin, 1:v.

42. Arch. Haute-Marne, 7 H 2. *Cartulaires de l'abbaye de Molesme*, ed. Jacques Laurent. Similarly, the monks of St.-Victor of Marseille composed their original cartulary around 1080, added to it during the twelfth century, and created a second cartulary in the thirteenth century; Monique Zerner, "L'abbaye de Saint-Victor de Marseille et ses cartulaires: Retour aux manuscrits," in *Les cartulaires méridionaux*, pp. 163–210. St.-Victor's

charters are printed in *Cartulaire de l'abbaye de Saint-Victor de Marseille*, ed. [Benjamin Edme Charles] Guérard.

43. Cîteaux's late thirteenth-century cartulary is in the Arch. Côte-d'Or, 11 H 63. Longué's two cartularies are bound together in the Arch. Haute-Marne, 6 H 2. Fontenay's two cartularies are bound together in the Arch. Côte-d'Or, 15 H 9. For Pontigny, see *Le premier cartulaire de Pontigny*, pp. 50–52.

44. Constance B. Bouchard, "Forging Papal Authority"; Laurent Morelle, "Examen de trois privilèges pontificaux du XIe siècle en faveur de Montier-en-Der."

45. See also Berkhofer, *Day of Reckoning*, pp. 46–47.

46. Hartmut Atsma and Jean Vezin, "Les faux sur papyrus de l'abbaye de Saint-Denis," p. 676.

47. Geary, *Phantoms of Remembrance*, pp. 107–13.

48. BnF, MS nouv. acq. lat. 326; Atsma and Vezin, "Les faux sur papyrus," p. 678.

49. The cartulary scribe referred to the "Clausula de Pippino," written at St.-Denis in the 760s; MGH SSRM 1/2:15–16.

50. When the monks of St.-Denis composed their next cartulary, early in the thirteenth century, they included the privileges from their eleventh-century cartulary in it; Rolf Grosse, "Remarques sur les cartulaires de Saint-Denis aux XIIIe et XIVe siècles," in *Les cartulaires*, pp. 280–89.

51. Clanchy, *From Memory to Written Record*, pp. 1–2, 154–62.

52. Dominique Barthélemy, who once proposed such a mutation, later retracted it; "Une crise de l'écrite?" p. 99, n. 24, and p. 116.

53. Guyotjeannin, *"Penuria scriptorum,"* pp. 12–13; Hartmut Atsma and Jean Vezin, "Autour des actes privés du chartrier de Cluny," pp. 50–51; Barthélemy, "Une crise de l'écrite?" pp. 99–102.

54. Brigitte Miriam Bedos-Rezak, "The Bishop Makes an Impression: Seals: Authority and Episcopal Identity," in *The Bishop*, ed. Sean Gilsdorf, pp. 137–54; Declercq, "Originals and Cartularies," p. 147; Charles Hiegel, "Les sceaux de l'évêque de Metz Adalbéron III (1047–1072)," in *Retour aux sources*, pp. 167–78; Jean-Luc Chassel, "L'essor du sceau au XIe siècle," in *Negotiating Secular and Ecclesiastical Power*, ed. Henk Teunis, Andrew Wareham, and Arnoud-Jan A. Bijsterveld, pp. 221–34.

55. Guyotjeannin, *"Penuria scriptorum,"* pp. 11–13.

56. Arch. Saône-et-Loire, H 142.

57. Constance B. Bouchard, "High Medieval Monks Contemplate Their Merovingian Past."

58. Barbara H. Rosenwein, *Negotiating Space*, pp. 5–8.

59. Betto's complaint was long taken as proof of a Saracen sack of Burgundy in 725 or 731, an event on which Hervé Mouillebouche has recently cast doubt; "Un autre mythe historiographique."

60. *Cartulaire général de l'Yonne*, ed. Maximilien Quantin, 1:26–28, no. 13. Robert-Henri Bautier argues that at base this is an authentic charter but that late in the ninth century the bishop of Langres falsified it by adding a long list of property; *Chartes, sceaux*

et chancelleries, 1:213–15. The seventh-century formulary of Marculf included a sample letter to ask a king to confirm a church's possessions after enemies had burned it and its charters were lost. "Marculfi formulae" 1.34, MGH Formulae, pp. 64–65.

61. Constance Brittain Bouchard, *Holy Entrepreneurs*, pp. 14–16; Hubert Flammarion, "Remarques sur quelques pancartes épiscopales du diocèse de Langres au XIIe siècle," in *Pancartes monastiques*, ed. M. Parisse, P. Pégeot, and B.-M. Tock, pp. 115–17.

62. Michel Parisse, "Les pancartes: Etude d'un type d'acte diplomatique," in *Pancartes monastiques*, p. 26; idem, "Ecriture et réécriture," p. 248.

63. Indeed, scholars have debated whether to call a pancarte an "original," because it is generally the earliest written record of an event, or a "copy," because its format, of multiple transactions recorded together, looks much more like copies such as are found in cartularies; Parisse, "Les pancartes," pp. 11, 39.

64. Parisse calls some pancartes "précartulaires"; "Ecriture et réécriture," pp. 252, 262. He is followed by Bertrand, Bourlet, and Hélary, "Vers une typologie des cartulaires," pp. 10–12.

65. For parallels, see Benoît-Michel Tock, "La diplomatique sans pancarte: L'exemple des diocèses de Thérouanne et Arras, 1000–1120," in *Pancartes monastiques*, pp. 144–47.

66. Isabelle Vérité, "Des pancartes dans les fonds des prieurés de Marmoutier? L'exemple des prieurés poitevins," in *Pancartes monastiques*, p. 92. Parisse suggests unconvincingly that such originals had previously existed but were then deliberately destroyed; "Les pancartes," 38.

67. *Recueil des pancartes de l'abbaye de La Ferté-sur-Grosne*, ed. Georges Duby.

68. The pancarte that records Auberive's foundation, Arch. Haute-Marne, 1 H 7 bis, begins the house's two thirteenth-century cartularies: Arch. Haute-Marne, 1 H 3, fols. 3r–4r; and 1 H 4, fols. 1r–4r.

69. Although in most of France it was the bishop who drew up monastic pancartes, in eleventh-century Normandy the monasteries sought them from the dukes; David Bates, "Les chartes de confirmation et les pancartes normandes du règne de Guillaume le Conquérant," in *Pancartes monastiques*, pp. 100–101.

70. Bouchard, *Holy Entrepreneurs*, p. 14. For parallels, see Bates, "Les chartes de confirmation," p. 97; and Parisse, "Ecriture et réécriture," p. 252.

71. Parisse, "Ecriture et réécriture," pp. 249–50. For Flemish parallels, see Tock, "La diplomatique sans pancarte," pp. 152–57.

72. Bouchard, *Holy Entrepreneurs*, p. 16; Arch. Côte-d'Or, series 12 H. La Bussière's first cartulary was not composed until the fourteenth century; BnF, MS lat. 5463.

73. Dependent priories were less likely to have episcopally sealed pancartes than were the mother-house. At Marmoutier, for example, the long lists of minor donations to its priories were normally left unconfirmed and unsealed. Vérité, "Des pancartes de Marmoutier?" pp. 75, 90.

CHAPTER 2

1. *Gesta*, 1:265–67.

2. *Le premier cartulaire de Pontigny*, ed. Garrigues, pp. 9–10. See also Guyotjeannin, "*Penuria scriptorum*," pp. 15–17.

3. *The Cartulary of Montier-en-Der*, ed. Bouchard, "Introduction," p. 10. See also Laurent Morelle, "Des moines face à leur chartrier: Etude sur le premier cartulaire de Montier-en-Der (vers. 1127)," in *Les moines du Der*, ed. Patrick Corbet, pp. 223–24.

4. Berkeley, Boalt Hall, Robbins Collection MS 48, ed. Constance Brittain Bouchard, *Three Cartularies from Thirteenth-Century Auxerre*.

5. *Cartulaire de l'abbaye de Saint-Père de Chartres*, ed. [Benjamin Edme Charles] Guérard, 1:119.

6. Laurent Morelle, "De l'original à la copie: Remarques sur l'évaluation des transcriptions dans les cartulaires médiévaux," in *Les cartulaires*, ed. Guyotjeannin, Morelle, and Parisse, pp. 95–97.

7. Hartmut Atsma and Jean Vezin, "Originaux et copies: La reproduction des éléments graphiques des actes des Xe et XIe siècles dans le cartulaire de Cluny," in *Charters, Cartularies, and Archives*, ed. Kosto and Winroth, pp. 113–26.

8. See, for example, Jean Dufour, "Etat et comparisons des actes faux ou falsifiés intitulés au nom des Carolingiens français (840–987)," in *Fälschungen im Mittelalter*, 4:169.

9. The ninth-century author of the *Actus* of the bishops of Le Mans complained that a great many documents in the archives could be read only partially if at all "because of age or negligence"; *Actus pontificum Cenomannis in urbe degentium*, ed. G. Busson and A. Ledru, p. 276. The new edition is in *Geschichte des Bistums Le Mans von der Spätantike bis zur Karolingerzeit*, ed. Margarete Weidemann, 1:106.

10. Arch. Haute-Marne, 7 H 1; *The Cartulary of Montier-en-Der*, ed. Bouchard, pp. 45–52, nos. 1–3.

11. Alain Dierkens, "La fondation et le premier siècle des monastères du Der," in *Les moines du Der*, pp. 31–36.

12. *The Cartulary of Montier-en-Der*, "Introduction," pp. 11–15. The *vita* of Bercharius was written by Adso of Der, *Opera hagiographica*, ed. Monique Goullet, pp. 305–32.

13. *Chronique de Saint-Bénigne de Dijon, suivie de la Chronique de Bèze*, ed. Bougaud and Garnier, pp. 233–35, 357.

14. Arch. Yonne, H 1667. A sixteenth-century copy of the cartulary, H 1668, faithfully reproduced everything, including this marginal comment, which led later scholars to assume mistakenly that the original documents still existed in the early modern period.

15. See also Morelle, "Des moines face à leur chartrier," pp. 231–33.

16. The original is Arch. Haute-Marne 2 G 166. The cartulary is Arch. Haute-Marne 2 G 921, fol. 58r. It is printed in *Cartulaire de Langres*, ed. Flammarion, pp. 165–66, no. 143; and in *Recueil des actes d'Henri le Libéral, comte de Champagne*, ed. John Benton and Michel Bur, pp. 174–75, no. 130. Indeed, the thirteenth-century scribe was at least as accurate as

Flammarion, who gives Symon for Simon, mistakenly substitutes *erat* for *esset*, and misspells the place-name Monteranponis as Monteramponis.

17. The original is Arch. Haute-Marne G 6. It is on fol. 57r in the cartulary and printed in *Cartulaire de Langres*, pp. 160–61, no. 139. Since the "e-cedilla" had completely dropped out of use in the thirteenth century, its absence should not be surprising.

18. Arch. Haute-Marne, G 537. Cartulary fol. 60r–v; *Cartulaire de Langres*, pp. 171–73, no. 150. For parallels, see *Le premier cartulaire de Pontigny*, p. 54.

19. Julia M. H. Smith, "*Aedificatio sancti loci*: The Making of a Ninth-Century Holy Place," in *Topographies of Power in the Early Middle Ages*, ed. Mayke de Jong and Frans Theuws, pp. 373–74; Matthew Innes, "Archives, Documents and Landowners in Carolingian Francia," in *Documentary Culture and the Laity*, ed. Brown et al., pp. 155–64. See also Atsma and Vezin, "Les faux sur papyrus," p. 675.

20. Arch. Côte-d'Or, series 15 H.

21. Michel Parisse, "Les cartulaires: Copies ou sources originales?" in *Les cartulaires*, pp. 507–8; Berkhofer, *Day of Reckoning*, pp. 78–80.

22. For German parallels, see Dietrich Lohrmann, "Evolution et organisation interne des cartulaires rhénans du moyen âge," in *Les cartulaires*, pp. 86–87.

23. *The Cartulary and Charters of Notre-Dame of Homblières*, ed. Theodore Evergates and William Mendel Newman, p. 22; Auxerre, Bibl. mun., MS 161. Similarly, the cartulary of the counts of Barcelona, composed in the 1190s, was organized geographically and left blank folia after each section for later additions; Kosto, "The *Liber feudorum maior* of the Counts of Barcelona."

24. *Cartulaire de Langres*, "Introduction," pp. 9–10; Charles Lalore, ed., *Collection des principaux cartulaires du diocèse de Troyes*, vol. 6.

25. Arch. Haute-Marne, 6 H 2. See also Bouchard, *Holy Entrepreneurs*, p. 17.

26. Dominique Barthélemy, "Note sur les cartulaires de Marmoutier (Touraine) au XIe siècle," in *Les cartulaires*, pp. 247–58.

27. Georges Declercq, "Originals and Cartularies: The Organization of Archival Memory (Ninth–Eleventh Centuries)," in *Charters and the Use of the Written Word in Medieval Society*, ed. Heidecker, p. 152; Morelle, "Des moines face à leur chartrier," pp. 224–28. See also Patrick Geary, "Entre gestion et *gesta*," in *Les cartulaires*, p. 13.

28. As in the twelfth-century cartulary of the Bavarian house of Reichersberg; Alexander Hecht, "Between *Memoria*, Historiography and Pragmatic Literacy: The *Liber Delegacionum* of Reichersberg," in *Charters and the Use of the Written Word*, pp. 205–7.

29. Stephen D. White, *Custom, Kinship, and Gifts to Saints*, pp. 170–76; Rosenwein, *To Be the Neighbor of Saint Peter*.

30. For parallels, see Boynton, *Shaping a Monastic Identity*, pp. 36–37.

31. Arch. Haute-Marne, 7 H 1, fols. 4r–6v; Arch. Marne, G 462, fols. 30r–33r. See the comparisons in *The Cartulary of Montier-en-Der*, pp. 52–58, no. 4.

32. Hans-Werner Goetz, "The Concept of Time in the Historiography of the Eleventh and Twelfth Centuries," in *Medieval Concepts of the Past*, ed. Althoff, Fried, and Geary, pp. 139–65.

33. Benoît-Michel Tock, "Les textes non diplomatiques dans les cartulaires de la province de Reims," in *Les cartulaires*, p. 52; Pascale Bourgain and Marie-Clotilde Hubert, "Latin et rhétorique dans les préfaces de cartulaire," ibid., pp. 115–36.

34. BnF, MS nouv. acq. lat. 1497. The preface is edited by Ernst Sackur, *Die Cluniacenser in ihrer kirchlichen und allgemeinschichtlichen Wirksamkeit*, 1:377.

35. *Le cartulaire de Marcigny-sur-Loire*, ed. Richard, p. 6. See also Declercq, "Originals and Cartularies," p. 167.

36. *Cartulaire de Saint-Père de Chartres*, 1:3–4.

37. Ibid., 1:15. See also Guyotjeannin, "*Penuria scriptorum*," p. 12.

38. Brigitte Bedos, "Signes et insignes du pouvoir royal et seigneurial au moyen âge."

39. Michel Parisse, "Les pancartes: Etude d'un type d'acte diplomatique," in *Pancartes monastiques*, ed. Parisse, Pégeot, and Tock, p. 12.

40. *Cartulaire de Langres*, pp. 285–86, no. 287. Cluny's copy is printed in *Recueil des chartes de l'abbaye de Cluny*, ed. Bernard and Bruel, 5:743–44, no. 4384.

41. For parallels, see Jean-Philippe Genet, "Cartulaires, registres et histoire: L'exemple anglais," in *Le métier d'historien au moyen âge*, ed. Guenée, pp. 96–105.

42. Jean-Loup Lemaître, "Les actes transcrits dans les livres liturgiques," in *Les cartulaires*, pp. 59–78.

43. *Cartulary and Charters of Homblères*, pp. 167–71, no. 88; the charters were rearranged chronologically for the printed edition. *The Cartulary of St.-Marcel-lès-Chalon*, ed. Bouchard, pp. 17–25, nos. 1–3.

44. McKitterick, *History and Memory in the Carolingian World*, p. 156.

45. Raymund Kottje, "Schriftlichkeit im Dienst der Klosterverwaltung und des klösterlichen Lebens unter Hrabanus Maurus," in *Kloster Fulda in der Welt der Karolinger und Ottonen*, ed. Gangolf Schrimpf, pp. 181–83; Raaijmakers, *The Making of the Monastic Community of Fulda*, pp. 179–213.

46. This volume, unedited, is in Chaumont, Bibl. mun. ("Les silos"), MS 38. The cartulary has been separated from it and is now in Arch. Haute-Marne, 2 G 921.

47. *Cartulaire de Langres*, "Introduction," p. 8.

48. Declercq, "Originals and Cartularies," p. 150.

49. *Cartulaire de Saint-Vincent de Mâcon*, ed. M.-C. Ragut.

50. *Three Cartularies from Thirteenth-Century Auxerre*. A seventeenth-century inventory of the bishop's titles—now Paris, BnF, MS fr. 18692—lists only one original charter from before 1300 (although it notes the cartulary and its contents), and that charter, in which King Philip II remitted regalian rights, was crucial enough that it was also copied into the *Gesta* of the bishops; *Gesta*, 2:217.

51. *Cartulary of St.-Marcel*, "Introduction," p. 3.

52. Brigitte Bedos-Rezak, "Towards an Archaeology of the Medieval Charter: Textual Production and Reproduction in Northern French *Chartriers*," in *Charters, Cartularies, and Archives*, pp. 43–60.

53. *Cartulaire de Langres*, pp. 37–40, no. 17.

54. For a similar case, see Benoît-Michel Tock, "Une notice en deux exemplaires à Tours en 1002," in *Retour aux sources*, pp. 193–206.

55. Laurent Morelle, "The Metamorphosis of Three Monastic Charter Collections in the Eleventh Century (Saint-Amand, Saint-Riquier, Montier-en-Der)," in *Charters and the Use of the Written Word in Medieval Society*, p. 172.

56. Arch. Haute-Marne, 7 H 3–6.

57. *Cartulary of Montier-en-Der*, "Introduction," p. 32.

58. *The Cartulary of Flavigny*, ed. Bouchard, "Introduction," p. 8.

59. *Premier et second cartulaires de Saint-Serge et Saint-Bach d'Angers*, ed. Chavin, 1:iv.

CHAPTER 3

1. Gregory the Great, *Moralia in Job* 23.3.7, PL 76:672. See also Patrick J. Geary, "Oblivion Between Orality and Textuality in the Tenth Century," in *Medieval Concepts of the Past*, ed. Althoff, Fried, and Geary, p. 112.

2. BnF, MS lat. 17090, pp. 98–99.

3. McKitterick, *Perceptions of the Past in the Early Middle Ages*.

4. Auxerre, Bibl. mun., MS 212; *Chronique de Saint-Pierre-le-Vif*, ed. Bautier and Gilles. The editors state that a new, separate chronicle began with the seventh century, but in the manuscript there is no distinction between the universal chronicle and that part of the chronicle in which events from Sens feature prominently.

5. Alberic de Trois-Fontaines, *Chronica*, MGH SS 23:674–950.

6. Odorannus of Sens, *Opera omnia*, ed. Robert-Henri Bautier and Monique Gilles.

7. Similarly, scholars have often tried to separate charters and narrative materials in their editions, even if in the medieval manuscripts they are intermingled. This is the case with the modern editions both of the *Gesta* of the abbots of St.-Bertin and of the bishops of Le Mans. Berkhofer, *Day of Reckoning*, pp. 171–74; Bouchard, "Episcopal *Gesta* and the Creation of a Useful Past," p. 3, n. 12.

8. *Chronique de Saint-Bénigne*, ed. Bougaud and Garnier. For parallels, see Boynton, *Shaping a Monastic Identity*, pp. 20–21.

9. *Cartulaire de Saint-Père de Chartres*, ed. Guérard, 1:3–54, 94.

10. Hugh of Flavigny, *Chronicon*, MGH SS 8:280–502.

11. Auxerre, Bibl. mun., MS 227. Edited in *Monumenta Vizeliacensia*, ed. Huygens, 1:xiii. See also John O. Ward, "Parchment and Power in Abbey and Cathedral: Chartres, Sherborne and Vézelay, c. 1000–1150," in *Negotiating Secular and Ecclesiastical Power*, ed. Henk Teunis, Andrew Wareham, and Arnoud-Jan A. Bijsterveld, pp. 159–61.

12. *Monumenta Vizeliacensia*, 2:2.

13. Bouchard, "High Medieval Monks Contemplate Their Merovingian Past."

14. Herrick, *Imagining the Sacred Past*, pp. 112–31.

15. The brothers of St.-Maximin of Trier decided that their house had been founded by the Empress Helen in the fourth century, doubtless to claim precedence over houses

with sixth-century origins, but they were unusual. Heinrich Beyer, ed., *Urkundenbuch zur Geschichte der mittelrheinischen Territorien*, 1:1, no. 2. See also Theo Kolzer, "Zur den Fälschungen für St. Maximin in Trier," in *Fälschungen im Mittelalter*, 3:315–26.

16. Metz, Bibl. mun., MS 1161, fols. 102r–103r. It is printed from a seventeenth-century copy in *Cartulaire général de l'Yonne*, ed. Quantin, 1:10–13, no. 6; Constance B. Bouchard, "Queen Theuchildis of Sens."

17. *Chronique de Saint-Pierre-le-Vif* 503, p. 36.

18. Gregory of Tours, *Liber in gloria martyrum* 50, MGH SSRM 1/2:72–73; *Chronique de Saint-Bénigne*, pp. 15–16.

19. Hugh of Flavigny, *Chronicon*, pp. 323, 339; *The Cartulary of Flavigny*, ed. Bouchard, "Introduction," pp. 14–15.

20. GC 4:228, no. 9.

21. *Concilia Galliae, A. 511–A. 695*, ed. Charles de Clercq, pp. 282, 314. The *episcopus* Palladius was doubtless the priest in charge of the basilica, usually called *abbas* elsewhere. It is highly unlikely, as Jean Marilier asserted, that Losne was ever a diocese; "Les privilèges épiscopaux de l'église de Losne."

22. *Chronique de Saint-Bénigne*, pp. 336–37, 353.

23. An exception was Paray-le-Monial, founded by Count Lambert of Chalon in 973. Lambert's son Hugh, bishop of Auxerre, gave it to Cluny to become a priory in 999. *Cartulaire du prieuré de Paray-le-Monial*, ed. Ulysse Chevalier, pp. 2–3, no. 2; *Recueil des chartes de l'abbaye de Cluny*, ed. Bernard and Bruel, 3:562–66, no. 2848. See also Constance B. Bouchard, "The Aristocratic Bishop: The Case of Hugh of Chalon," in *The Bishop*, ed. Gilsdorf, pp. 37–49.

24. *Chronique de Saint-Bénigne*, p. 278.

25. Bouchard, "Merovingian, Carolingian, and Cluniac Monasticism," pp. 369–73.

26. *Chronique de Saint-Bénigne*, p. 138.

27. *Chronique de Saint-Pierre-le-Vif* 675, p. 42.

28. *Cartulaire de l'Yonne*, 1:10–13, no. 6. For the context of this grant of immunity, see Rosenwein, *Negotiating Space*, pp. 80–81.

29. "Vita S. Balthildis" 9, MGH SSRM 2:493.

30. *Chronique de Saint-Pierre-le-Vif* 715, pp. 44–46.

31. Bouchard, *Sword, Miter, and Cloister*, pp. 225–46; eadem, "High Medieval Monks Contemplate Their Merovingian Past," p. 52.

32. Documents 1–2, in *Chronique de Saint-Pierre-le-Vif*, pp. 239–43.

33. Constance Brittain Bouchard, *Spirituality and Administration*, pp. 37–67.

34. *Chronique de Saint-Pierre-le-Vif* 865, pp. 60–64.

35. The relics of these brother-sister martyrs were received at Sens by the chronicler Odorannus himself at the beginning of the eleventh century; *Opera omnia*, p. 112.

36. Similarly, in eleventh-century Normandy the Viking attacks were reconceptualized as positive because they led to reform and renewal of the churches; Herrick, *Imagining the Sacred Past*.

37. *Chronique de Saint-Pierre-le-Vif*, p. 74. The chronicle suggests that Abbot Odo of

Cluny was behind the reform, but this is far from certain and may be more informative about twelfth-century views of Cluny than tenth-century events. See Isabelle Rosé, *Construire une société seigneuriale*, pp. 324–26.

38. *Chronique de Saint-Pierre-le-Vif*, pp. 82–86.

39. *Cartulaire de Saint-Père de Chartres*, 1:5–11. See also Fassler, *The Virgin of Chartres*, pp. 8–10.

40. For Hugh's career, see Mathias Lawo, *Studien zu Hugo von Flavigny*, pp. 1–40; and Patrick Healy, *The Chronicle of Hugh of Flavigny*, pp. 63–88. Most of the latter book focuses on Hugh's attitude toward the Investiture Conflict.

41. For a detailed study of Hugh's many sources, see Lawo, *Studien zu Hugo von Flavigny*, pp. 93–281.

42. Hugh of Flavigny, *Chronicon*, p. 288.

43. "Invenitur etiam scriptis in gestis." Hugh of Flavigny, *Chronicon*, p. 327. He and other monks of St.-Vanne of Verdun were in exile in Dijon when he began his chronicle, and they had doubtless brought their library with them; Healy, *The Chronicle of Hugh of Flavigny*, p. 101.

44. Hugh of Flavigny, *Chronicon*, pp. 348–51.

45. Ibid., p. 351; *Cartulary of Flavigny*, pp. 34–36, no. 4.

46. Hugh of Flavigny, *Chronicon*, pp. 322–23; *Cartulary of Flavigny*, pp. 19–28, no. 1. Hugh was referring to the cartulary's first charter, not the later reconfirmation, because he specifies that it was done at Semur. Hugh interpreted the royal monogram, reproduced in the cartulary, as a seal.

47. Hugh of Flavigny, *Chronicon*, p. 339; *Cartulary of Flavigny*, pp. 33–34, 38–41, nos. 3, 6, 7.

48. Hugh of Flavigny, *Chronicon*, p. 352; *Cartulary of Flavigny*, pp. 48–49, no. 13. It is of course possible that the charter actually did say Carloman and that the twelfth-century cartulary scribe mistakenly substituted Charlemagne.

49. Hugh of Flavigny, *Chronicon*, p. 355. Hugh knew about Corbigny's foundation from the cartulary; *Cartulary of Flavigny*, pp. 125–28, no. 52.

50. Hugh of Flavigny, *Chronicon*, p. 475.

51. Ibid., pp. 476–80.

52. Ibid., pp. 477–79.

53. Ibid., pp. 481–92. See also Healy, *The Chronicle of Hugh of Flavigny*, pp. 76–82.

54. Charles Pietri, "Remarques sur la topographie chrétienne des cités de la Gaule entre Loire et Rhin (des origines au VIIe siècle)," in *La christianisation des pays entre Loire et Rhin*, ed. Pierre Riché, pp. 189–204.

55. Bouchard, "Reconstructing Sanctity and Refiguring Saints in Early Medieval Gaul," pp. 95–99; eadem, "Episcopal *Gesta* and the Creation of a Useful Past," pp. 15–25.

56. Sharon Farmer, *Communities of Saint Martin*. See also Luce Pietri, "Bâtiments et sanctuaires annexes de la basilique Saint-Martin de Tours, à la fin du VIe siècle," in *La christianisation des pays entre Loire et Rhin*, pp. 223–34.

57. Michael Borgolte, "Fiktive Gräber in der Historiographie Hugo von Flavigny und die sepultur der Bischöfe von Verdun," in *Fälschungen im Mittelalter*, 1:205–40.

58. Richard Landes, *Relics, Apocalypse, and the Deceits of History*.

59. Lifshitz, *The Norman Conquest of Pious Neustria*, pp. 184–85.

60. Odile Wilsdorf-Colin, "Recherche sur les pouvoirs de justice des évêques de Langres aux Xe et XIe siècles," in *Langres et ses évêques*, pp. 194–95.

CHAPTER 4

1. For an introduction to the genre, see Robert Fossier, *Polyptyques et censiers*; and Yoshiki Morimoto, "Etat et perspectives des recherches sur les polyptyques carolingiens."

2. Pierre Gasnault, ed., *Documents comptables de Saint-Martin de Tours à l'époque mérovingienne*. A few extra folia from this manuscript have recently been discovered; Shoichi Sato, "The Merovingian Account Documents of Tours."

3. "Capitulare de villis," MGH Capit. 1:82–91; Adriaan Verhulst, *The Carolingian Economy*, pp. 37–41.

4. Walter Goffart, *Rome's Fall and After*, pp. 193–96, 233–53.

5. *Das Polyptychon von Saint-Germain-des-Prés*, ed. Dieter Hägermann; Jean-Pierre Devroey, "St.-Germain-des-Prés et le polyptyque d'Irminon," in *La Neustrie*, ed. Hartmut Atsma, 1:441.

6. Ugé, *Creating the Monastic Past in Medieval Flanders*, pp. 61–71; Y. Morimoto, "Problèmes autour du polyptyque de Saint-Bertin (844–859)," in *Le grand domaine aux époques mérovingienne et carolingienne/Die Grundherrschaft im frühen Mittelalter*, ed. Adriaan Verhulst, p. 126.

7. Fossier, *Polyptyques et censiers*, pp. 31–32. For Marmoutier, see Sato, "The Merovingian Account Documents of Tours," p. 152.

8. Robin Fleming, *Domesday Book and the Law*, pp. 1–7.

9. At Montier-en-Der, polyptyque entries for villas even a few kilometers apart gave different names for the surveyors who *iurauerunt et dictauerunt*. *The Cartulary of Montier-en-Der*, ed. Bouchard, pp. 314–34, no. 164.

10. Morimoto, "Etat et perspectives des recherches," pp. 115–17. Even the ninth-century manuscript of the polyptyque of St.-Germain includes duplications and non-uniform entries; Devroey, "St.-Germain-des-Prés," p. 452.

11. For example, Ferdinand Lot, "Note sur la date du polyptyque de Montierender."

12. J.-P. Devroey, "Les premiers polyptyques rémois, VIIe–IXe siècles," in *Le grand domaine/Die Grundherrschaft*, p. 78; idem, "Les services de transport à l'abbaye de Prüm," p. 543. The polyptyque of Prüm is sometimes treated as an exception, all composed at one time (893), but Yoshiki Morimoto argues for extensive additions in the three centuries after it was initially composed, before the existing copy was made; *Etudes sur l'économie rurale du haut Moyen Age*, pp. 246–60, 291–308.

13. *Cartulary of Montier-en-Der*, "Introduction," pp. 28–29.

14. Morimoto, *Etudes sur l'économie rurale*, pp. 354–58.

15. See also Michel Bur, "A propos du chapitre xxxviii du polyptyque de Montier-en-Der"; Guyotjeannin, "*Penuria scriptorum*," pp. 28–29; and Morimoto, "Etat et perspectives des recherches," pp. 115–17.

16. Fossier, *Polyptyques et censiers*, pp. 56–57. Sometimes we have an even later copy of a copy. For the modern edition of the polyptyque of St.-Remi, the editor attempted to reconstruct what the eighteenth-century copyist might have had before him; *Le polyptyque et les listes de cens de l'abbaye de Saint-Remi de Reims*, ed. Jean-Pierre Devroey.

17. See also Laurent Morelle, "Des moines face à leur chartrier: Etude sur le premier cartulaire de Montier-en-Der (vers 1127)," in *Les moines du Der*, ed. Corbet, p. 231.

18. For a convenient list of terms in polyptyques and their definitions—at least at one monastery—see Louis Richard, *Le polyptyque de Montier-en-Der*, pp. 32–65.

19. Or so most scholars assume. The editors of the polyptyque of St.-Bertin, however, put *servi* into a higher social category than *mancipia*; *Le polyptyque de l'abbaye de Saint-Bertin*, ed. François-Louis Ganshof, Françoise Godding-Ganshof, and Antoine de Smet, p. 31.

20. Adriaan Verhulst, "Quelques remarques à propos des corvées de colons à l'époque du Bas-Empire et du Haut Moyen Age," in *D'une déposition à un couronnement*, ed. Institut des Hautes Etudes de Belgique, pp. 89–95; Etienne Renard, "Les *mancipia* carolingiens étaient-ils des esclaves? Les donnés du polyptyque de Montier-en-Der dans le contexte documentaire du IXe siècle," in *Les moines du Der*, pp. 179–209; idem, "Lectures et relectures d'un polyptyque carolingien," pp. 388–90, 406–24. The differences (or similarities) between *mancipia* and *coloni* are even more unclear if, as Hans-Werner Goetz suggests, *mancipia* was a collective word, *servus* being the normal singular; "Serfdom and the Beginnings of a 'Seigneurial System' in the Carolingian Period," p. 40.

21. Most notably Jean Durliat, *Les finances publiques de Dioclétien aux Carolingiens*, esp. pp. 240–51. He suggests, p. 244, that the polyptyques do not show "public" dues because the monks would not have wanted to preserve the record of what they owed the state. See also Elisabeth Magnou-Nortier, "La gestion publique en Neustrie: Les moyens et les hommes (VIIe–IXe siècles)," in *La Neustrie*, 1:271–320. These ideas are accepted uncritically by Berkhofer, *Day of Reckoning*, p. 12. They are dismissed, however, by Verhulst, *Carolingian Economy*, p. 45; see also Goetz, "Serfdom," p. 44, n. 136.

22. *Cartulary of Montier-en-Der*, pp. 77–88, nos. 14, 16, 17.

23. Renard, "Lectures et relectures," p. 382; Morimoto, "Problèmes autour du polyptyque de Saint-Bertin," pp. 144–49.

24. See also Richard, *Le polyptyque de Montier-en-Der*, pp. 145–46.

25. Morimoto, for example, attempts to fit the elements of the St.-Bertin polyptyque into the "classic" ninth-century manor; "Problèmes autour du polyptyque de Saint-Bertin," pp. 130, 141–42.

26. Jean-Pierre Devroey discusses these difficulties; "Les méthodes d'analyse démographique des polyptyques du haut moyen âge," in his *Etudes sur le grand domaine carolingien*.

27. *Cartulaire de Saint-Père de Chartres*, ed. Guérard, 1:43.

28. *Cartulary of Montier-en-Der*, pp. 91–93, 331, nos. 20, 164.xlviii.

29. Similarly, adding up the figures for the individual entries in the polyptyque of St.-Remi does not yield the *summa* asserted by the polyptyque itself; *Le polyptyque de Saint-Remi*, "Introduction," pp. xxxix–xl.

30. Both C. D. Droste and Ganshof rely far too much on the reliability of the figures in the polyptyque—and of the likelihood that ninth-century measures can be accurately translated into modern hectares. Droste, "Die Grundherrschaft Montiérender im 9. Jahrhundert," in *Le grand domaine/Die Grundherrschaft*, pp. 101–11; *Le polyptyque de St.-Bertin*, pp. 135–36.

31. *Cartulaire de Saint-Père de Chartres*, 1:14.

32. Ibid., 1:35–43.

33. See also Berkhofer, *Day of Reckoning*, pp. 31–33.

34. *Das Prümer Urbar*, ed. Ingo Schwab, pp. 158–59. For Caesarius, see Dieter Hägermann, "Eine Grundherrschaft des 13. Jh. im Spiegel des Frühmittelalters." See also Morimoto, *Etudes sur l'économie rurale*, pp. 236–41.

35. *Das Prümer Urbar*, pp. 164–65. See also Morimoto, *Etudes sur l'économie rurale*, pp. 261–75.

36. Many of the entries in the Prüm polyptyque, however, do specify three days' service; Morimoto, *Etudes sur l'économie rurale*, pp. 276–77.

37. Scholars have tended to take him literally, arguing that these *mansi* indicate land originally belonging to the royal fisc and that they were much larger than most *mansi*. See Morimoto, *Etudes sur l'économie rurale*, pp. 278–82. It is possible, however, that Caesarius mistakenly equated *ingenuilis* with *regalis*. See Renard, "Lectures et relectures," pp. 388–90. He may simply not have recognized the word *ingenuilis*, no longer used after the end of the tenth century; Benoît-Michel Tock, "Les mutations de vocabulaire latin des chartes au XIe siècle," p. 124.

38. *Das Prümer Urbar*, pp. 168–69.

39. *Le polyptyque de Saint-Bertin*, p. 13, no. 15. See also Renard, "Lectures et relectures," p. 406.

40. *Cartulary of Montier-en-Der*, "Introduction," p. 28. Unlike Yoshiki Morimoto, I cannot agree that the royal diploma can be used to date either the granting of *precaria* or the polyptyque itself; Morimoto, "Le polyptyque de Montier-en-Der: Historiographie et état des questions," in *Les moines du Der*, p. 174 and n. 40.

41. *Das Prümer Urbar*, p. 259.

42. Even modern scholars are troubled by words that may appear in one polyptyque but nowhere else, such as *ladmen*, owed by female tenants of St.-Bertin; *Le polyptyque de Saint-Bertin*, p. 13, no. 16; commentary, pp. 32–33.

43. M.-J. Tits-Dieuaide, "Grands domaines, grandes et petites exploitations en Gaule mérovingenne: Remarques et suggestions," in *Le grand domaine/Die Grundherrschaft*, pp. 23–50; and, more broadly, Devroey, *Etudes sur le grand domaine carolingien*. See also Verhulst, *Carolingian Economy*, pp. 31–37.

44. For example, Chris Wickham stops his early medieval economic history at 800; *Framing the Early Middle Ages.* Michael McCormick stops his at 900; *Origins of the European Economy.*

45. Goetz assumes without discussion that Carolingian seigneurialism was also the seigneurialism of two or three centuries later; "Serfdom."

46. Robert Fossier, "Rural Economy and Country Life," in *NCMH* 3:29 (for the quote), 41–45.

47. The most thorough discussion is that by Dominique Barthélemy, *La mutation de l'an mil a-t-elle eu lieu?* See also Jeffrey A. Bowman, *Shifting Landmarks*, esp. pp. 211–28; and Richard E. Barton, *Lordship in the County of Maine.*

48. For example, Verhulst, *Carolingian Economy*, p. 135.

CHAPTER 5

1. See also Ugé, *Creating the Monastic Past in Medieval Flanders*, pp. 10–11.

2. Carlrichard Brühl, "Die Entwicklung der diplomatischen Methode im Zusammenhang mit dem Erkennen vom Fälschungen," in *Fälschungen im Mittelalter*, 3:11–12.

3. Jean Dufour attempts to distinguish four categories between completely true and completely false documents: interpolated, rewritten, reworked, and *subreptice*, a real document with false contents (e.g., obtained under false pretenses); "Etat et comparisons des actes faux ou falsifiés intitulés au nom des Carolingiens français (840–987)," in *Fälschungen im Mittelalter*, 4:169.

4. Geoffrey Koziol also sees the ninth century as an especially active period for forgery, although his approach is quite different; *The Politics of Memory and Identity in Carolingian Royal Diplomas*, pp. 315–99.

5. Dieter Hägermann, "Die Urkundenfälschungen auf Karl der Großen," in *Fälschungen im Mittelalter*, 3:435–36; Dufour, "Etat et comparisons des actes faux," pp. 208–9.

6. Constable, "Forgery and Plagiarism in the Middle Ages," pp. 11–23.

7. Koziol argues that creating a forgery was a way to assert power: if a forgery were accepted, then one had won; *The Politics of Memory*, p. 358.

8. For example, one of the earliest authentic documents from the Rhineland, a testament dating to the early seventh century, survives only because it was recopied in the Carolingian era; Wilhelm Levison, "Das Testament des Diakons Adalgisel-Grimo," p. 71.

9. John B. Wickstrom, *The Life and Miracles of Saint Maurus.* See also Head, *Hagiography and the Cult of Saints*, pp. 23–24.

10. Rosamond McKitterick, *The Carolingians and the Written Word.*

11. *Gesta domni Aldrici*, ed. Charles and Froger, pp. 21, 56, 130. The new edition is in *Geschichte des Bistums Le Mans*, ed. Weidemann, 1:131, 133, 154. Deplorably, the new edition of these texts puts the narrative material and the documents into separate volumes.

12. *Gesta domni Aldrici*, ed. Charles and Froger, p. 134; ed. Weidemann, 1:155. "Vidimus

quod iste episcopus vester Aldricus habet suas auctoritates et praecepta regalia tam genitoris vestri quam et aliorum antecessorum vestrorum videlicet regum Francorum."

13. *Gesta domni Aldrici*, ed. Charles and Froger, pp. 144–47; ed. Weidemann, 1:158–59.

14. Walter Goffart, *The Le Mans Forgeries*, pp. 24, 274.

15. *Decretales Pseudo-Isidorianae et capitula Angilramni*, ed. Paul Hinschius, pp. 249–54; *The Treatise of Lorenzo Valla on the Donation of Constantine*, ed. Christopher B. Coleman (New Haven, Conn., 1922).

16. Horst Fuhrmann, "The Pseudo-Isidorian Forgeries," in Detlev Jasper and Horst Fuhrmann, *Papal Letters in the Early Middle Ages*, pp. 171–72. See also Goffart, *The Le Mans Forgeries*, pp. 66–69.

17. Philippe Le Maître, "Evêques et moines dans le Maine, IVe–VIIe siècle," in *La christianisation des pays entre Loire et Rhin*, ed. Riché, p. 91.

18. For this genre, see Michel Sot, *Gesta episcoporum, gesta abbatum*.

19. Margarete Weidemann, "Das Testament des Bischofs Aldricus von Le Mans—Eine Falschung?" in *Fälschungen im Mittelalter*, 4:237–63.

20. Compare the *Gesta* of Le Mans to those composed at Auxerre a generation or so later; Bouchard, "Episcopal *Gesta* and the Creation of a Useful Past in Ninth-Century Auxerre."

21. *Cartulaire de l'abbaye de Saint-Calais*, ed. Froger, pp. 27–35, nos. 17–20; the last also in *Recueil des actes de Charles II le Chauve*, ed. Georges Tessier, Arthur Giry, and Maurice Prou, 1:463–65, no. 176. See also Goffart, *The Le Mans Forgeries*, pp. 136–41.

22. *Recueil des actes de Charles le Chauve*, 2:81–86, no. 258; Goffart, *The Le Mans Forgeries*, p. 82.

23. *Gesta domni Aldrici*, ed. Charles and Froger, pp. 130–48; ed. Weidemann, 1:154–60.

24. "Vita Carilefi abbatis Anisolensis," MGH SSRM 3:389–94.

25. Vultrogoda is the correct name of the wife of Childebert I; Gregory of Tours, *Hist* 4.20, p. 152. Venantius Fortunatus wrote a poem in her honor; Carmen 6.6, in *Poèmes*, ed. Marc Reydellet, 2:76. See also Ian Wood, *The Merovingian Kingdoms*, p. 353; and A. H. M. Jones and J. R. Martindale, *The Prosopography of the Later Roman Empire*, 3:1391. The author of this *vita* may have seen a charter to which the *Actus* author also refers, in which Queen Vultrogoda established a monastery dedicated to Saint George; *Actus pontificum Cenomannis in urbe degentium*, ed. G. Busson and A. Ledru, p. 195; ed. Weidemann, 1:81.

26. *Actus pontificum Cenomannis*, ed. Busson and Ledru, p. 40; ed. Weidemann, 1:38; Goffart, *The Le Mans Forgeries*, pp. 61–65.

27. The relevant parts of the *vita* of Turibius are edited by Goffart, *The Le Mans Forgeries*, p. 357.

28. *Actus pontificum Cenomannis*, ed. Busson and Ledru, pp. 56–57; ed. Weidemann, 1:50–51.

29. *Actus pontificum Cenomannis*, ed. Busson and Ledru, pp. 59–69; ed. Weidemann, 2:362–68, nos. 66F–68F.

30. *Actus pontificum Cenomannis*, ed. Busson and Ledru, pp. 89–91, 162–65, 182–84; ed. Weidemann, 2:365–70, 378–80, 381–83, nos. 69F, 74F, 76F. Appropriate royal documents of confirmation followed each of these in the *Actus*, purportedly issued by Kings Chilperic and Dagobert; *Actus pontificum Cenomannis*, ed. Busson and Ledru, pp. 91–93, 165–66, 184–86; ed. Weidemann, 2:370–72, 380–81, 383–85, nos. 70F, 75F, 77F. Also in MGH DD imperii, pp. 131–32, 166, 200–201, spuria nos. 15, 48, 86; and in MGH DD regum Francorum e stirpe Merovingica, pp. 56–58, 96–97, 401–2, nos. 20, 35, 161.

31. *Gesta domni Aldrici*, ed. Charles and Froger, pp. 112–15; ed. Weidemann, 2:317–20, no. 55. See also Goffart, *The Le Mans Forgeries*, pp. 310–12, no. 65.

32. *Cartulaire de Saint-Calais*, pp. 3–5, no. 2.

33. Goffart, *The Le Mans Forgeries*, p. 80, suggests that the land listed in it corresponded to what St.-Calais held in the ninth century. Doubt should also be raised about Childebert I's, Chilperic I's, and Theoderic I's charters in which they took Calais's monastery—here called Anisola—under their protection. *Cartulaire de Saint-Calais*, pp. 5–8, nos. 2–4; also in MGH DD imperii, pp. 6–7, 12–13, 45–46, nos. 4, 9, 50; and in MGH DD regum Francorum e stirpe Merovingica, pp. 35–36, 55–56, 298–99, nos. 9, 19, 116. All these nearly identical charters, supposedly from the sixth century (if Theoderic I is meant, although the MGH editors assign the "Theoderic" document to a later king), couple the terms *emunitas* and *tuitio*, otherwise not seen together for another two centuries; Rosenwein, *Negotiating Space*, p. 111.

34. Venantius Fortunatus, "Vita Sancti Paterni" 10, MGH AA 4/2:36; Gregory of Tours, *Hist* 5.14, p. 207. See also Friedrich Prinz, *Frühes Mönchtum in Frankreich*, p. 155.

35. *Actus pontificum Cenomannis*, ed. Busson and Ledru, pp. 66–69; ed. Weidemann, 2:367–68, no. 68F. Also in MGH DD imperii, pp. 124–25, spuria no. 8; and in MGH DD regum Francorum e stirpe Merovingica, pp. 37–38, no. 10.

36. *Actus pontificum Cenomannis*, ed. Busson and Ledru, pp. 93–95; ed. Weidemann, 2:200–202, no. 3. Also in MGH DD imperii, pp. 122–23, spuria no. 6; dated 541; and in MGH DD regum Francorum e stirpe Merovingica, pp. 68–70. The nineteenth-century MGH editors assumed its falsity primarily because of Le Mans's reputation for forgery. Its authenticity is now widely accepted; Goffart, *The Le Mans Forgeries*, p. 261.

37. MGH DD Karolinorum 1:4–5, 19–20, nos. 2, 14. Also in *Cartulaire de Saint-Calais*, pp. 13–16, nos. 8–9.

38. *Gesta domni Aldrici*, ed. Charles and Froger, pp. 148–58; ed. Weidemann, 1:164–69, and 2:315–16, nos. 53, 54. Philippe Le Maître concludes that one of these Louis the Pious documents is authentic and the others interpolated; "L'oeuvre d'Aldric du Mans et sa signification," pp. 62–63.

39. *Actus pontificum Cenomannis*, ed. Busson and Ledru, pp. 245, 258, 263; ed. Weidemann, 1:90–91, 93.

40. *Actus pontificum Cenomannis*, ed. Busson and Ledru, p. 337. This addition to the *Actus* is not edited by Weidemann.

41. *Cartulaire de Saint-Calais*, pp. 18–26, nos. 11–16. Also in MGH DD Karolinorum 1:90–91, 178–79, nos. 62, 128; and *Recueil des actes de Charles le Chauve*, 1:336–39, nos. 127–28.

42. Nicholas I, *Epistolae* 109–13, 159, MGH Epp. 6:624–29, 680–83. Except for two letters addressed to the bishop of Le Mans, the pope's correspondence was copied into the *Cartulaire de Saint-Calais*, pp. 40–50, nos. 22–25.

43. *Cartulaire de Saint-Calais*, pp. 1–5, no. 1; also in MGH DD imperii, pp. 3–5, no. 2; and in MGH DD regum Francorum e stirpe Merovingica, pp. 29–33, no. 7.

44. *Cartulaire de Saint-Calais*, pp. 8–11, nos. 5–6. Also in MGH DD regum Francorum e stirpe Merovingica, pp. 352–54, 367–69, nos. 140, 146; the first of these is also in MGH DD imperii, p. 56, no. 63.

45. *Cartulaire de Saint-Calais*, p. 47, no. 25; also Nicholas I, *Epistola* 159, MGH Epp. 6:681.

46. Goffart, *The Le Mans Forgeries*, pp. 79–81.

47. *Recueil des actes de Charles le Chauve*, 2:86–89, no. 259.

48. *Gesta domni Aldrici*, ed. Charles and Froger, pp. 156–57; ed. Weidemann, 1:168–69.

49. *Actus pontificum Cenomannis*, ed. Busson and Ledru, pp. 244–45; ed. Weidemann, 1:90; Le Maître, "Evêques et moines," pp. 100–101.

50. One of the earliest examples is from the 770s, when Charlemagne declared the monastery of Salonnes free from the authority of its diocesan bishop (Metz); Rosenwein, *Negotiating Space*, pp. 115–34.

51. *Recueil des chartes de l'abbaye de Cluny*, ed. Bernard and Bruel, 1:124–28, no. 112.

52. *Cartulary of Flavigny*, ed. Bouchard, pp. 62, 69–72, nos. 19, 23. St.-Germain received a similar immunity from Charles the Bald. Yves Sassier argues that these are forgeries, dating from the reform of these houses to Cluny's *ordo* around 1000, but the wording is different from that of Cluny's foundation charter, and they look very much like ninth-century productions; Sassier, "Quelques remarques sur les diplômes d'immunité octroyés par les Carolingiens à l'abbaye de Saint-Germain d'Auxerre," pp. 46–48.

53. *Monumenta Vizeliacensia*, ed. Huygens, 1:243–48, no. 1; Rosenwein, *Negotiating Space*, p. 158.

54. The best introduction is by Fuhrmann, "The Pseudo-Isidorian Forgeries," pp. 135–95.

55. Schafer Williams, "Pseudo-Isidore from the Manuscripts," pp. 58–61. Williams, who had hoped to reedit the false decretals but was never able to do so, called the Hinschius edition a "mishmash that is virtually useless"; ibid., pp. 61–62. Some other manuscripts have been identified since his study; Lotte Kéry, *Canonical Collections of the Early Middle Ages*, pp. 100–108. A provisional version of a new edition by Karl-Georg Schon and Klaus Zechiel-Eckes is available online: http://www.pseudoisidor.mgh.de/ (accessed December 11, 2012).

56. Detlev Jasper, "The Beginning of the Decretal Tradition," in Jasper and Fuhrmann, *Papal Letters*, pp. 1–87.

57. Williams, "Pseudo-Isidore," pp. 62–64. See also Fuhrmann, "The Pseudo-Isidorian Forgeries," pp. 184–85.

58. Abigail Firey, "Lawyers and Wisdom," pp. 189–214.

59. Kéry, *Canonical Collections*, pp. 108–17; Horst Fuhrmann, *Einfluß und Verbreitung der pseudoisidorischen Fälschungen*, 1:1–63; Ullman, *The Growth of Papal Government in the Middle Ages*, pp. 180–84; Nicolás Alvarez de las Asturias, "Lanfranc of Bec's Version of Decretals in a Canonistic Context."

60. Uta-Renate Blumenthal, "Fälschungen bei Kanonisten der Kirchenreform des 11. Jahrhunderts," in *Fälschungen im Mittelalter*, 2:241–62.

61. *Decretales Pseudo-Isidorianae*, pp. 128, 132, 190, 467, 488. See also Firey, "Lawyers and Wisdom," pp. 193–94.

62. *Decretales Pseudo-Isidorianae*, p. 145.

63. Ibid., pp. 143–46.

64. According to Peter Brown, this way of thinking about church property developed only in the sixth century; *Through the Eye of a Needle*.

65. Ibid., pp. 73, 179–80. Pope Anaclete was the fifth pope according to the *Liber Pontificalis*, although he is now considered identical with Cletus, the third pope.

66. Notker the Stammerer, *Gesta Karoli imperatoris*, MGH SS 2:726–63; Simon MacLean, *Kingship and Politics in the Late Ninth Century*, pp. 211–12.

67. *Decretales Pseudo-Isidorianae*, pp. 17–18, 42.

68. Bouchard, "Episcopal *Gesta* and the Creation of a Useful Past."

69. Fuhrmann, "The Pseudo-Isidorian Forgeries," pp. 155, 162–63.

70. *Decretales Pseudo-Isidorianae*, pp. 249–54.

71. Firey, "Lawyers and Wisdom," p. 212.

72. Fuhrmann, "The Pseudo-Isidorian Forgeries," pp. 140–42.

73. Council of Quierzy, MGH Concilia 3:393–94. See also Fuhrmann, "The Pseudo-Isidorian Forgeries," pp. 175–76.

74. For this quarrel, see Fuhrmann, "The Pseudo-Isidorian Forgeries," pp. 177–81; idem, *Einfluß der pseudoisidorischen Fälschungen*, 1:219–24.

75. Fuhrmann, *Einfluß der pseudoisidorischen Fälschungen*, 2:237–353.

76. The decretals of Benedictus *levita* have not been properly edited since the seventeenth century, but a new edition is forthcoming. For this work in progress, including the texts of both the old edition and the new, as well as articles about Benedictus, see http://www.benedictus.mgh.de/haupt.htm (accessed March 8, 2011). I am grateful to Karl Ubl for alerting me to this collection.

77. See also Giles Constable, "Forged Letters in the Middle Ages," in *Fälschungen im Mittelalter*, 5:11–12.

78. *Annales Bertiniani* 878, ed. Félix Grat, Jeanne Vielliard, and Suzanne Clémencet, pp. 227–28. For this case, see also Dufour, "Etat et comparisons des actes faux," p. 167.

79. *Recueil des actes de Charles le Chauve*, 2:354, no. 381. See also *Cartulary of Flavigny*, p. 147.

CHAPTER 6

1. Pierre Riché, *Les Carolingiens*; Alessandro Barbero, *Charlemagne, Father of a Continent*. Although doubt was implied by the subtitle of the 1979 Spoleto conference, the papers themselves were much less cautious; *Nascita dell'Europa ed Europa carolingia: Un'equazione da verificare*. See also Richard E. Sullivan, "The Carolingian Age."

2. For example, McKitterick, *History and Memory in the Carolingian World*; Roger Collins, "Frankish Past and Carolingian Present in the Age of Charlemagne," in *Am Vorabend der Kaiser Krönung*, ed. Peter Godman, Jörg Jarnut, and Peter Johanek, pp. 301–22; and Yitzhak Hen, "The Annals of Metz and the Merovingian Past," in *Uses of the Past*, ed. Hen and Innes, pp. 175–90. See also Paul Fouracre, "Frankish Gaul to 814," in *NCMH*, 2:85; and Roger Collins, *Charlemagne*, pp. 1–6.

3. This issue is addressed by many of the articles in the volume *La chanson de geste et le mythe carolingien*. See also Patrick J. Geary, *The Myth of Nations*; Matthew Gabriele, *An Empire of Memory*; and Constance B. Bouchard, "Images of the Merovingians and Carolingians," pp. 8–11.

4. "Karolus magnus et Leo papa," MGH Poetae 1:366–79; Robert Morrissey, *Charlemagne and France*, p. 9. The authorship is disputed; see Francesco Stella, "Autore et attribuzioni del 'Karolus Magnus et Leo Papa,'" in *Am Vorabend der Kaiser Krönung*, pp. 19–33.

5. Rosamond McKitterick has identified a ninth-century manuscript in Vienna, in which their political and family history is embedded in an ecclesiastical context; "L'idéologie politique dans l'historiographie carolingienne," in *La royauté et les élites dans l'Europe carolingienne*, ed. Régine Le Jan, pp. 59–70.

6. Ildar H. Garipzanov, *The Symbolic Language of Authority in the Carolingian World*, pp. 43–73; Rosamond McKitterick, "Royal Patronage of Culture in the Frankish Kingdoms Under the Carolingians: Motives and Consequences," in her *The Frankish Kings and Culture in the Early Middle Ages*.

7. Gerd Tellenbach, "Die geistigen und politischen Grundlagen der Karolingischen Thronfolge."

8. "Admonitio generalis," MGH Capit. 1:53; Peter Brown, *The Rise of Western Christendom*, pp. 440–41; Rob Meens, "Religious Instruction in the Frankish Kingdoms," in *Medieval Transformations*, ed. Cohen and de Jong, pp. 51–67.

9. MGH DD Karolinorum 1:33, 65, nos. 24, 45. See also Rosenwein, *Negotiating Space*, pp. 99–100; and Bautier, *Chartes, sceaux et chancelleries*, 2:46.

10. *Codex Carolinus*, ed. W. Gundlach, MGH Epp. 3:469–657;. Achim Thomas Hack, *Codex Carolinus*; Mary Garrison, "The Franks as the New Israel? Education for an Identity from Pippin to Charlemagne," in *The Uses of the Past*, pp. 125–29; Jasper and Fuhrmann, *Papal Letters*, p. 104.

11. *Opus Caroli regis contra synodum (Libri Carolini)*, ed. Ann Freeman, MGH Concilia 2, suppl. 1; Thomas F. X. Noble, *Images, Iconoclasm, and the Carolingians*, pp. 158–206.

12. Ann Freeman, "Carolingian Orthodoxy and the Fate of the Libri Carolini"; J. M. Wallace-Hadrill, *The Frankish Church*, pp. 219–20; Donald A. Bullough, *Alcuin*, pp. 402–4; Chazelle, *The Crucified God in the Carolingian Era*, pp. 39–52.

13. The "Mirrors for Princes," discussions of what good kings were like, which began to be written in the early ninth century, stressed the ruler's religiosity. Alain Dubreucq, "La littérature des *Specula*: Délimitation du genre, contenu, destinaires et réception," in *Guerriers et moines*, ed. Michel Lauwers, pp. 17–39; Raffaele Savigni, "Les laïcs dans l'ecclésiologie carolingienne: Normes statuaires et idéal de 'conversion,'" ibid., pp. 63–92; Rachel Stone, *Morality and Masculinity in the Carolingian Empire*, pp. 42–46. The classic study is by Hans Hubert Anton, *Fürstenspiegel und Herrscherethos in der Karolingerzeit*, pp. 132–68.

14. Wolfgang Braunfels, "Karolingischer Klassizismus als politisches Programm und karolingischer Humanismus als Lebenshaltung," in *Nascita dell'Europa ed Europa carolingia*, 2:821–42; Michael McCormick, *Eternal Victory*, pp. 347–84.

15. Kathleen Mitchell, "Marking the Bounds: The Distant Past in Gregory's History," in *The World of Gregory of Tours*, ed. Mitchell and Wood, pp. 295–99; McKitterick, *Perceptions of the Past in the Early Middle Ages*, pp. 35–61.

16. Bernard S. Bachrach, "Charlemagne's Military Responsibilities am Vorabend der Kaiserkrönung," in *Am Vorabend der Kaiser Krönung*, pp. 231–55.

17. David Ganz, "Visions of Carolingian Education, Past, Present, and Future," in *"The Gentle Voices of Teachers,"* ed. Richard E. Sullivan, pp. 261–83; Lawrence Nees, "Carolingian Art and Politics," ibid., pp. 186–87; Celia Chazelle, "'Romanness' in Early Medieval Culture," in *Paradigms and Methods in Early Medieval Studies*, ed. Chazelle and Lifshitz, pp. 81–98.

18. Uwe Lobbedey, "Carolingian Royal Palaces," pp. 134–35; Janet L. Nelson, "Aachen as a Place of Power," in *Topographies of Power in the Early Middle Ages*, ed. de Jong and Theuws, pp. 217–41; Matthias Untermann, "'Opere mirabili constructa': Die Aachener 'Residenz' Karls des Großen," in *799*, ed. Christoph Stiegemann and Matthias Wemhoff, 3:152–64; Walter Kaemmerer, "Die Aachener Pfalz Karls des Grossen in Anlage und Überlieferung," in *KdG*, 1:322–48; Janet L. Nelson, "La cour impériale de Charlemagne," in *La royauté et les élites*, pp. 177–91; John Beckwith, "Byzantine Influence on Art at the Court of Charlemagne," in *KdG*, 3:288–300.

19. Ildar H. Garipzanov, "The Image of Authority in Carolingian Coinage"; idem, *The Symbolic Language of Authority*, pp. 182–88; Bernd Kluge, "Nomen imperatoris und Christiana religio: Das Kaisertum Karls des Großen und Ludwigs des Frommen im Licht der numismatischen Quellen," in *799*, 3:82–90.

20. Helmut Beumann, "Grab und Thron Karls des Großen zu Aachen," in *KdG*, 4:9–34; Robert Melzak, "Antiquarianism in the Time of Louis the Pious and its Influence on the Art of Metz," in *Charlemagne's Heir*, ed. Peter Godman and Roger Collins, pp. 630–31; Theun-Mathias Schmidt, "Prosperina-Sarkophag," in *799*, 2:758–63; idem, "Fragmente eines Sarkophags mit dem Durchzug der Israeliten durch das Rote Meer," ibid., 2:763–66.

21. Ermoldus Nigellus, *Carmina* 4, MGH SS 2:504–6. I am grateful to Irving Lavin for pointing out the significance of this passage. See also Janet L. Nelson, "The Merovingian Church in Carolingian Retrospective," in *The World of Gregory of Tours*, pp. 247–48.

22. Similarly, Loup of Ferrières wrote to Charles the Bald urging him to contemplate the Roman emperors Trajan and Theodosius. Loup of Ferrières, Letter 37, *Correspondance*, ed. Léon Levillain, 1:164.

23. Thomas F. X. Noble, "Tradition and Learning in Search of Ideology: The *Libri Carolini*," in *"The Gentle Voices of Teachers,"* p. 245.

24. Paul Edward Dutton, *Charlemagne's Mustache and Other Cultural Clusters of a Dark Age*, pp. 24–26. See also Roger Collins, "Frankish Past and Carolingian Present in the Age of Charlemagne," in *Am Vorabend der Kaiser Krönung*, pp. 320–21.

25. Einhard, *Vie de Charlemagne* 7, 15, ed. Louis Halphen, pp. 26, 42. On this work, see Matthias M. Tischler, *Einharts "Vita Karoli."*

26. Einhard, *Vie de Charlemagne* 1, p. 8.

27. See also Janet L. Nelson, *The Frankish World*, pp. xvii–xxii; and Garipzanov, *The Symbolic Language of Authority*, pp. 262–66.

28. Einhard, *Vie de Charlemagne* 3, 22, 23, pp. 14, 16, 68. *Vestito patrio, id est Francico, utebatur.*

29. "Vita Hludowici imperatoris" 3, ed. Ernst Tremp, MGH SS rerum Germanicarum (1995), p. 290. For the Astronomer, see Philippe Depreux, *Prosopographie de l'entourage de Louis le Pieux*, pp. 113–14, no. 37.

30. BnF, MS lat 1, fol. 423r. For Vivien, count of Tours, who is seen in this image presenting the Bible to Emperor Charles, see André Moisan, "Le fuite de Charles le Chauve devant les Bretons d'Erispoé et la mort du comte Vivien de Tours," in *La chanson de geste*, 1:85–100.

31. The fullest study of this Bible is by Paul Edward Dutton and Herbert L. Kessler, *The Poetry and Paintings of the First Bible of Charles the Bald*. The authors edit the poems as well as discussing the visual images. They argue (p. 73) that the way that Charles is portrayed is intended to suggest Theodosius.

32. The two weapons-bearers are slightly obscured in the presentation miniature because of other figures in the foreground; it is hard to get a good sense of the round shield. The weapons-bearers may be seen more easily in the Psalms frontispiece (fol. 215v), where identical figures stand on either side of David.

33. For the importance the Franks gave their weapons, see Régine Le Jan, *Femmes, pouvoir et société dans le haut Moyen Age*, pp. 171–82; and Nelson, *Frankish World*, pp. 80–85.

34. Gregory of Tours, *Hist* 7.33, p. 353. David Harry Miller attempts unconvincingly to make the lance a pagan symbol; "Sacral Kingship, Biblical Kingship, and the Elevation of Pepin the Short," in *Religion, Culture, and Society in the Early Middle Ages*, ed. Thomas F. X. Noble and John J. Contreni, p. 134.

35. "Vita Hludowici imperatoris" 4, p. 294. See also Thilo Offergeld, *Reges pueri*, pp. 310–11.

36. Mary Garrison, "The Franks as the New Israel? Education for an Identity from Pippin to Charlemagne," in *The Uses of the Past*, p. 120.

37. Nees, "Carolingian Art and Politics," pp. 209–12.

38. See also Lifshitz, *The Norman Conquest of Pious Neustria*, pp. 61–62; and Nelson, *Frankish World*, pp. 102–3, 108–10.

39. "Admonitio generalis," MGH Capit. 1:54; Jennifer R. Davis, "A Pattern for Power: Charlemagne's Delegation of Judicial Responsibilities," in *The Long Morning of Medieval Europe*, ed. Davis and McCormick, pp. 235–46; Le Jan, *Femmes, pouvoir et société*, pp. 149–70; Rosamond McKitterick, *The Frankish Kingdoms Under the Carolingians*, pp. 77–105; François Louis Ganshof, "Charlemagne et l'administration de la justice dans la monarchie franque," in *KdG*, 1:394–419; Stone, *Morality and Masculinity*, pp. 159–73.

40. Karl Ferdinand Werner, "*Hludovicus Augustus*: Gouverner l'empire chrétien—Idées et réalités," in *Charlemagne's Heir*, pp. 76–82; Geneviève Bührer-Thierry, "Episcopat et royauté dans le monde carolingien," in *Le monde carolingien*, ed. Wojciech Falkowski and Yves Sassier, pp. 143–55.

41. Stuart Airlie, "Towards a Carolingian Aristocracy," in *Der Dynastiewechsel von 751*, ed. Matthias Becher and Jörg Jarnut, pp. 109–27.

42. Bernard S. Bachrach, *Early Carolingian Warfare*, pp. 1–50.

43. Stuart Airlie, "*Semper Fideles*? Loyauté envers les Carolingiens comme constituant de l'identité aristocratique," in *La royauté et les élites*, pp. 130–31; Le Jan, *Femmes, pouvoir et société*, pp. 108–18; Jurgen Hannig, *Consensus Fidelium*, pp. 200–285.

44. See also Richard E. Sullivan, "The Context of Cultural Activity in the Carolingian Age," in *"The Gentle Voices of Teachers,"* pp. 63–66: the constant celebration of Carolingian achievements at the time "has the unmistakeable odor of a noble family never quite certain of its hold on a usurped crown" (p. 66).

45. Josef Semmler, *Der Dynastiewechsel von 751 und die fränkische Königssalbung*; Arnold Angenendt, "Pippins Königserhebung und Salbung," in *Der Dynastiewechsel*, ed. Becher and Jarnut, pp. 179–209; Constance Brittain Bouchard, "The Carolingian Creation of a Model of Patrilineage," in *Paradigms and Methods*, pp. 139–40.

46. For example, Wallace-Hadrill, *The Frankish Church*, pp. 166–70; and Riché, *Les Carolingiens*, pp. 74–78. It has even been argued that in 751 no more happened than that a dynasty supported by the ritual of pagan religion was replaced by one supported by the ritual of the Christian religion; Miller, "Sacral Kingship," p. 131.

47. Fredegar, *The Fourth Book of the Chronicle with its Continuations* cont.33, ed. J. M. Wallace-Hadrill, p. 102. For Fredegar and his continuators, see Roger Collins, *Die Fredegar-Chroniken*; he dates the continuators about two decades later than have most scholars. See also Roger Collins, "Pippin III as Mayor of the Palace: The Evidence," in *Der Dynastiewechsel*, ed. Becher and Jarnut, pp. 75–78.

48. Robert-Henri Bautier, "Sacres et coronnements sous les Carolingiens et les premiers Capétiens: Recherches sur la genèse du sacre royal français," in his *Recherches sur l'histoire de la France medieval*; Arnold Angenendt, "Pippins Königshebung und Salbung," in *Der Dynastiewechsel*, ed. Becher and Jarnut, pp. 179–209.

49. "Clausula de Pippino," MGH SSRM 1/2:15–16. For its authenticity, see Bautier, "Sacres et coronnements," p. 12, n. 13; and Olaf Schneider, "Die Königserhebung Pippins 751 in der Erinnerung der karolingischen Quellen," in *Der Dynastiewechsel*, ed. Becher and Jarnut, pp. 254, 268–75.

50. *Annales regni Francorum* 749, 750, ed. Friedrich Kurze, pp. 8–10. See also Schneider, "Die Königshebung Pippins," pp. 243–68; McKitterick, *History and Memory*, pp. 141–42; Collins, "Pippin III," pp. 76–78; and Semmler, *Der Dynastiewechsel*, p. 15.

51. Marios Costambeys, Matthew Innes, and Simon MacLean, *The Carolingian World*, pp. 2, 33.

52. Einhard, *Vie de Charlemagne* 1–2, pp. 8–14. The story of the deposition of the last Merovingian and Pippin's accession reached Byzantium, in rather confused form, around the same time as Einhard wrote. The chronicler Theophanes echoed Einhard's account of weakling kings; *The Chronicle of Theophanes* 6216, trans. Harry Turtledove, p. 94.

53. Constance B. Bouchard, "Childeric III and the Emperors Drogo Magnus and Pippin the Pious," pp. 12–16.

54. Brown, *The Rise of Western Christendom*, pp. 428–30; Thomas F. X. Noble, "Topography, Celebration, and Power: The Making of a Papal Rome in the Eighth and Ninth Centuries," in *Topographies of Power*, pp. 75–79.

55. Fredegar, *The Fourth Book* cont.22, p. 96.

56. *Annales regni Francorum* 754, p. 12. The recently discovered remains of a royal palace at St.-Denis appear to date to the eighth century and may have been built by Pippin; Lobbedey, "Carolingian Royal Palaces," p. 148.

57. See also Janet L. Nelson, "Bertrada," in *Der Dynastiewechsel*, ed. Becher and Jarnut, pp. 102–3.

58. Einhard, *Vie de Charlemagne* 1, p. 8. McKitterick postulates that only Stephen actually agreed to Pippin's deposition of the last Merovingian and that Zacharias, the pope of 751, was added to the story later; *History and Memory*, pp. 137–50.

59. *Pace* Janet L. Nelson, who downplays the novelty of the anointing; *Politics and Ritual in Early Medieval Europe*, pp. 289–91.

60. "Clausula de Pippino," pp. 15–16. Wallace-Hadrill sees the "other family" against which the pope warned as Carolingian cousins; *Frankish Church*, p. 169.

61. *Codex Carolinus* 11, MGH Epp. 3:505. Alain J. Stoclet, about the last scholar to argue against the authenticity of the "Clausula," makes an unconvincing effort to explain away this blessing of Pippin's wife and children; "La 'Clausula de unctione Pippini regis,'" pp. 34–35.

62. *Codex Carolinus* 60, p. 586. See also Walter Goffart, "Paul the Deacon's *Gesta episcoporum Mettensium* and the Early Design of Charlemagne's Succession," pp. 60–61.

63. "Vita Hludowici imperatoris" 4, pp. 292–94. See also Semmler, *Der Dynastiewechsel*, p. 52.

64. Perhaps the most enthusiastic supporter of this view was Ferdinand Lot, *The End of the Ancient World and the Beginnings of the Middle Ages*. This book, originally published in French in 1927, was reprinted in English in 2000, showing its continued influence.

65. This cart might really have been, as some scholars have suggested, a traditional marker of royal rule, but for Einhard it was a sign of decay. Already in the sixth century a Merovingian king had humiliated an enemy by sending him home in a cart (*plaustrum*), "an indignity worse than death" according to Gregory of Tours; *Hist* 6.35, p. 306. Miller unconvincingly asserts that the cart was a pagan symbol of fertility; "Sacral Kingship," pp. 137–38. It is counterproductive at best to label the Merovingians "pagan" two and a half centuries after they considered themselves Christian.

66. Einhard, *Vie de Charlemagne* 1, pp. 8–10. For Carolingian efforts to remove hair as a marker of kingship, see Dutton, *Charlemagne's Mustache*, pp. 3–24.

67. Yitzhak Hen, *Culture and Religion in Merovingian Gaul*, pp. 197–206; idem, "Paganism and Superstition in the Time of Gregory of Tours: *Une question mal posée!*" in *The World of Gregory of Tours*, pp. 229–40.

68. *Annales Mettenses priores* 691, ed. B. de Simson, p. 12. See also Richard A. Gerberding, *The Rise of the Carolingians and the "Liber historiae Francorum*,*"* pp. 92–93. The Battle of Tertry is not considered as significant a turning point by modern scholars as it was by historians at Charlemagne's court; see Paul J. Fouracre, "Observations on the Outgrowth of Pippinid Influence in the 'Regnum Francorum' After the Battle of Tertry"; idem, *The Age of Charles Martel*, pp. 48–49.

69. Bouchard, "Images of the Merovingians and Carolingians"; Patrick J. Geary, *Before France and Germany*, pp. 221–25.

70. Theo Kölzer, while not accepting the image of feeble-minded Merovingians, still insists on their political weakness as justifying the term *fainéant*; "Die letzten Merowingerkönige: Rois fainéants?" in *Der Dynastiewechsel*, ed. Becher and Jarnut, pp. 33–60.

71. Even J. M. Wallace-Hadrill, the pioneering Anglophone scholar of Merovingian studies, took Einhard at his word, believing that he could not possibly have had any motivation for making a mockery of a "dynasty so long defunct"; *The Long-Haired Kings*, pp. 231–33.

72. Roger Collins suggests that any criticism of Charlemagne that surfaced after his death was due to trying to present a strong program of moral reform while having human flaws; "Charlemagne and His Critics, 814–829," in *La royauté et les élites*, pp. 193–211.

73. Rosamond McKitterick, *Charlemagne*, pp. 1–7; Morrissey, *Charlemagne and France*; Costambeys, Innes, and MacLean, *The Carolingian World*, pp. 6–7.

74. See also Koziol, *The Politics of Memory*, pp. 324–25.

75. Gregory of Tours, *Hist* 2.42, p. 93. For Gregory as satirist, see Goffart, *The Narrators of Barbarian History*, pp. 197–208.

76. Yitzhak Hen, *Roman Barbarians*, pp. 94–123.

77. Fredegar, *Chronica* 3.12, MGH SSRM 2:97. See also Wallace-Hadrill, *Long-Haired Kings*, p. 84.

78. *Liber Historiae Francorum* 44, MGH SSRM 2:316; "Vita S. Balthildis" 4, MGH SSRM 2:486–87.

79. The 1,500th anniversary of the baptism of Clovis inspired a number of scholars to

look again at Merovingian materials; see especially *Clovis: Histoire et mémoire*, ed. Michel Rouche.

80. Janet L. Nelson, "Rituals of Power," in *Rituals of Power from Late Antiquity to the Early Middle Ages*, ed. Frans Theuws and Janet L. Nelson, p. 479.

81. A colloquium devoted to the difficulties of the fifth century avoided giving any prominence to 476; *Fifth-Century Gaul*, ed. John Drinkwater and Hugh Elton. Guy Halsall, who would put the real end of the western Empire in 480, notes that no one set out to destroy it; rather, he says, "it accidentally committed suicide"; *Barbarian Migrations and the Roman West*, pp. 276–83 (quote on p. 283).

82. William M. Daly, "Clovis: How Barbaric, How Pagan?"; Wickham, *Framing the Early Middle Ages*, pp. 80–82; Ian Wood, "The Governing Class of the Gibichung and Early Merovingian Kingdoms."

83. Gregory of Tours, *Hist* 2.38, pp. 88–89; McCormick, *Eternal Victory*, pp. 328–47; Yitzhak Hen, "The Christianisation of Kingship," in *Der Dynastiewechsel*, ed. Becher and Jarnut, pp. 165–66; Kevin Uhalde, "The Quasi-Imperial Coinage and Fiscal Administration in Merovingian Provence," in *Society and Culture in Late Antique Gaul*, ed. Ralph W. Mathisen and Danuta Shanzer, pp. 134–65; S. Fanning, "Clovis Augustus and Merovingian *imitatio imperii*," in *The World of Gregory of Tours*, pp. 321–35. Although Fanning is convincing on the widespread Merovingian use of imperial titles and attributes, I disagree with his assumption that Charlemagne was inspired by Clovis's example.

84. Anton, *Fürstenspiegel und Herrscherethos*, pp. 179–89.

85. Hildegar, "Vita Faronis episcopi Meldensis" 78, MGH SSRM 5:193. See also Nelson, *Frankish World*, pp. xix, 185.

86. Camillus Wampach, ed., *Urkunden- und Quellenbuch zur Geschichte der altluxemburgischen Territorien bis zur burgundischen Zeit*, 1:18–26, no. 19. The Carolingian-era compilation is known from a twelfth-century copy. Wampach argues convincingly that if one leaves out the mention of Dagobert, then everything else suggests an authentic testament from the 730s.

87. Eduard Hlawitschka, "Die Vorfahren Karls des Grossen," in *KdG*, 1:75–76. Interestingly, Adela's (probable) mother was also identified in the same compilation as a "daughter of Dagobert."

88. Reinhold Kaiser, "Les évêques neustriens du Xe siècle dans l'exercice de leur pouvoir temporel d'après l'historiographie médiévale," in *Pays de Loire et Aquitaine de Robert le Fort aux premiers Capétiens*, ed. Olivier Guillot and Robert Favreau, p. 119. More broadly, see Goffart, *The Le Mans Forgeries*.

89. Charles Vulliez, "L'abbaye de Micy-Saint-Mesmin et Clovis dans la tradition et l'histoire," in *Clovis*, 2:129–46; Head, *Hagiography and the Cult of Saints*, pp. 202–3.

90. Similarly, the authors of the *Gesta* of the bishops of Auxerre, writing in the 870s, spoke nostalgically of the Merovingian kings; Bouchard, "Episcopal *Gesta* and the Creation of a Useful Past," pp. 33–34.

91. "Vita Leutfredi," AASS June 5:95. This edition, although older, is to be preferred to the abbreviated version in MGH SSRM 7:7–16. For the date, see Lifshitz, *The Norman*

Conquest of Pious Neustria, p. 51, n. 99. See also Hans-Werner Goetz, "Karl Martell und die Heiligen: Kirchenpolitik und Maiordomat im Spiegel der Spätmerowingischen Hagiographie," in *Karl Martell in seiner Zeit*, ed. Jörg Jarnut, Ulrich Nonn, and Michael Richter, p. 113.

1. Paul the Deacon, "Gesta episcoporum Mettensium," MGH SS 2:264–65; Bouchard, "Images of the Merovingians and Carolingians," pp. 6–8.

2. Camillus Wampach, ed., *Geschichte der Grundherrschaft Echternach im Frühmittelalter*, 2:4–8. See also Constance Brittain Bouchard, "The Carolingian Creation of a Model of Patrilineage," in *Paradigms and Methods*, ed. Chazelle and Lifshitz, p. 137.

3. Fredegar, *Chronica* 3.9, MGH SSRM 2:95; Einhard, *Vie de Charlemagne* 1, ed. Halphen, p. 8.

4. Wallace-Hadrill, *Long-Haired Kings*, pp. 155–231.

5. Fredegar, *The Fourth Book* 27, 36, ed. Wallace-Hadrill, pp. 18, 24. Fredegar based his account of the second incident on the slightly earlier "Vita Columbani" 19 of Jonas of Bobbio, MGH SSRM 4:87. See also Albrecht Diem, "Monks, Kings, and the Transformation of Sanctity," pp. 531–32.

6. *Liber Historiae Francorum* 43, MGH SSRM 2:316. Richard A. Gerberding argues that this event took in 651, not 656 as usually thought. His thoughtful discussion assumes, as I do not, that Grimoald tried to put his own son on the throne; *The Rise of the Carolingians and the "Liber historiae Francorum,"* pp. 47–66.

7. See, for example, the letters of Bishop Desiderius of Cahors, asking for Grimoald's kind affection and entrusting a newly founded monastery to his protection; PL 87:249, 251, nos. 2, 6.

8. Mayke de Jong argues that such enforced stays in monasteries were ways for someone to remain safe while both sides kept their options open; "Monastic Prisoners or Opting Out? Political Coercion and Honour in the Frankish Kingdoms," in *Topographies of Power*, ed. de Jong and Theuws, pp. 293–94, 318.

9. The question of the relationship between Grimoald and Childebert *adoptivus* has generated considerable attention. The two major competing theories are that Childebert was really a Merovingian, Sigibert's son, and adopted by Grimoald, or else really a Pippinid, Grimoald's own son, adopted by Sigibert and renamed with a Merovingian name. A serious flaw with the second alternative—which, however, is usually adopted by scholars—is that it requires that the phrase, *Childebertus adoptivus filius Grimoaldi*, not be read in what would seem to be its clear sense, "Childebert, the adopted son of Grimoald," but rather as "Childebert 'the Adopted,' son of Grimoald" or even "the son of Grimoald, who took the name Childebert when adopted." See Matthias Becher, "Der sogenannte Staatsstreich Grimoalds," in *Karl Martell in seiner Zeit*, ed. Jarnut, Nonn, and Richter, pp. 119–47; and Thilo Offergeld, *Reges pueri*, pp. 253–57. The first alternative, argued by Becher, is much more

plausible. The early eighth-century *vita* of Bishop Bonitus of Clermont refers to Sigibert as having sons, in the plural, and a later charter of Chilperic II refers to Childebert as his *consobrinus*, a cousin; "Vita Boniti episcopi Arverni" 3, MGH SSRM 6:120; MGH DD imperii, pp. 79–80, no. 90; also in MGH DD regum Francorum e stirpe Merovingica, pp. 441–43, no. 178. If young Childebert had been adopted as his heir by Sigibert, then it would be difficult to explain why Grimoald, the boy's champion, would have been detested and eventually executed, according to the *Liber Historiae Francorum*, as one who "went to war against his lord."

10. Gregory of Tours, *Hist* 7.5–7, pp. 328–30; Fredegar, *The Fourth Book* 3, p. 5.

11. Modern historians, as thorough legitimists as early medieval chroniclers, do not designate Childebert as Childebert III, as he is assumed not to be a Merovingian by blood. But he was king of Austrasia for at least a few years and was recalled in the ninth century as having made, as *rex*, a grant of immunity to the bishop of Reims around 660, at the same time as Grimoald, *vir illustris*, also made a gift for his soul; "Vita Nivardi episcopi Remensis," MGH SSRM 5:163–64. The man now called Childebert III (d. 711) should be renumbered as Childebert IV.

12. Paul Fouracre, "Forgetting and Remembering Dagobert II: The English Connection," in *Frankland*, ed. Paul Fouracre and David Ganz, pp. 70–89.

13. See also Ian Wood, "Usurpers and Merovingian Kingship," in *Der Dynastiewechsel von 751*, ed. Becher and Jarnut, pp. 15–16, 27–31.

14. Fouracre, *The Age of Charles Martel*, pp. 157–58; Becher, "Der Staatsstreich Grimoalds," p. 144; Martina Hartmann, "*Pater incertus?*"; Bouchard, "Carolingian Creation of Patrilineage," p. 139.

15. Bouchard, "Childeric III and the Emperors Drogo Magnus and Pippin the Pious."

16. Bouchard, *"Those of My Blood,"* pp. 76–85; Stuart Airlie, "The Nearly Men: Boso of Vienne and Arnulf of Bavaria," in *Nobles and Nobility in Medieval Europe*, ed. Anne J. Duggan, pp. 25–41. See also Franz Staab, who attempts to identify Boso with another man most scholars (including me) identify as his uncle; "Jugement moral et propagande: Boson de Vienne vu par les élites du royaume de l'Est," in *La royauté et les élites*, ed. Le Jan, pp. 365–81.

17. Simon MacLean, "The Carolingian Response to the Revolt of Boso."

18. Bouchard, *"Those of My Blood,"* pp. 100–108; Janet L. Nelson, "Les reines carolingiennes," in *Femmes et pouvoirs des femmes à Byzance et en Occident*, ed. Stéphane Lebecq, Alain Dierkens, Régine Le Jan, and Jean-Marie Sansterre, pp. 121–32. Guy Halsall suggests that the Merovingians preferred lowborn or foreign-born wives because they could thus avoid giving Frankish aristocrats power through their sisters; *Barbarian Migrations and the Roman West*, p. 492.

19. Einhard, *Vie de Charlemagne* 2, pp. 10–12. For Charlemagne's family tree, see Eduard Hlawitschka, "Die Vorfahren Karls des Grossen," in *KdG*, 1:51–82; and Christian Settipani, *La préhistoire des Capétiens*, pp. 139–87.

20. Fredegar, *The Fourth Book* cont.8, p. 87; Josef Semmler, "Zur pippinidisch-karolingischen Sukzessionskrise."

21. *Liber Historiae Francorum* 48, p. 323; *Chronique des abbés de Fontenelle* 2.2, ed. Pradié, p. 30. For Drogo, see also Josef Semmler, "Die Aufrichtung der Karolingischen Herrschaft im nördlichen Burgund im VIIIe Jahrhundert," in *Langres et ses évêques*, p. 23. Grifo is not mentioned by Hlawitschka, "Die Vorfahren." Grifo was, however, probably real, because the author of the *Gesta* of Fontenelle wrote with a charter of Pippin's before him, from which he copied the names of Pippin's and Plectrudis's sons. In addition, a brother of Charles Martel by this name would explain why the memorial book of Remiremont lists *two* men named Grifo in association with Charles ("Grifonis, item Grifonis"), one of whom would be his brother, one his son; *Liber memorialis von Remiremont*, ed. Eduard Hlawitschka, Karl Schmid, and Gerd Tellenbach, p. 4. Settipani does not mention Grifo but instead proposes a brother of Charles Martel named Pippin, who died young, though the evidence is weak; *La préhistoire*, pp. 156–58.

22. MGH DD imperii, p. 96, no. 7; also in *Die Urkunden der Arnulfinger*, ed. Ingrid Heidrich, pp. 71–75, no. 8; *Chronique de Fontenelle* 4.1, pp. 58–60.

23. Fredegar, *The Fourth Book* cont.20, 24, pp. 94, 97. Hildebrand is called the *germanus* of Charles Martel and *avunculus* of Pippin the Short. He was most likely Charles Martel's full brother, the most common meaning then of *germanus*—the continuations of Fredegar refer to Pippin the Short's full brother Carloman as his *germanus*. Woltraud Joch, however, makes Hildebrand the son of Pippin of Herstal by a concubine; "Karl Martell: Ein minderberechtiger Erbe Pippins?" in *Karl Martell in seiner Zeit*, p. 162. Hildebrand was a powerful figure at court, holding the office of duke and sponsoring the continuations of Fredegar's chronicle, and he was the ancestor of the "historic Nibelungen"; see Bouchard, *"Those of My Blood,"* pp. 141–42. According to Josef Semmler, he may have assisted in the accession to the throne of his nephew Pippin the Short; *Der Dynastiewechsel von 751 und die fränkische Königssalbung*, pp. 1–15.

24. *Liber Historiae Francorum* 47, p. 321. See also Horst Ebling, *Prosopographie der Amtsträger des Merowinger reiches*, pp. 159–61, nos. 187–88. He divides Giselmar into two different people.

25. Bercharius, like Drogo, married a daughter of Waratto and Ansfletis; Fredegar, *The Fourth Book* cont.5, p. 85. See also Ebling, *Prosopographie*, pp. 77–78, 234–35, nos. 69, 308. Pippin of Herstal defeated Bercharius at the battle of Tertry. Scholars have usually assumed that Drogo married Bercharius's widow, following the *Annales Mettenses priores* 693, ed. de Simson, p. 16. However, an original charter from Tussonval refers to Bercharius as *socer* of Drogo; ChLA 581, 14:32–35. Based on this charter, Ingrid Heidrich argues that Drogo was son-in-law of Bercharius, not of Waratto; "Maires du palais, agents du roi, abbés," in *La Neustrie*, ed. Atsma, 1:224. This charter also gives the name of Drogo's wife as Adaltrudis, whereas the *Annales Mettenses priores* call Bercharius's widow Anstrudis. Rather than making Drogo either the husband of Bercharius's widow or the son-in-law of Bercharius, it makes more sense to conclude that the scribe, whose grasp of classical Latin was rather shaky, meant *socerio* and that Drogo and Bercharius were brothers-in-law, having married sisters.

26. *Liber Historiae Francorum* 51–53, pp. 325–27. See also Ebling, *Prosopographie*, pp.

206–8, no. 265; and Régine Hennibicque-Le Jan, "Prosopographica Neustrica: Les agents du roi en Neustrie de 639 à 840," in *La Neustrie*, 1:262, no. 239.

27. Fredegar, *The Fourth Book* 52, p. 43.

28. Bouchard, "Carolingian Creation of Patrilineage," pp. 140–41.

29. Paul the Deacon, *Historia Langobardorum* 4.37, MGH SSRL, pp. 131–32. Rosamond McKitterick argues that this work ought to be seen as aimed at a Frankish rather than a Lombard audience; "Paul the Deacon and the Franks."

30. Walter Goffart argues that the work should be seen as an effort to prefigure the division of the Frankish realm among Charlemagne's heirs which, it was believed in the 780s, would become necessary; "Paul the Deacon's *Gesta episcoporum Mettensium* and the Early Design of Charlemagne's Succession."

31. The only women in Paul's *Gesta* of the bishops of Metz are the Carolingian princesses whose epitaphs his work recorded—and the epitaphs are not in the earliest manuscript of his *Gesta*; Michel Sot, "Faut-il rééditer le *Livre des évêques de Metz* de Paul Diacre?" in *Retour aux sources*, pp. 971–77. For the women in Charlemagne's family tree, see Bouchard, *"Those of My Blood,"* pp. 100–108.

32. Paul the Deacon, "Gesta episcoporum Mettensium," MGH SS 2:264–65. Goffart points out that this overly simplified family tree has many parallels with Paul's episcopal lists in the same work; "Paul the Deacon's *Gesta*," pp. 81–82.

33. MGH DD imperii, pp. 93–95, nos. 4–6; *Die Urkunden der Arnulfinger*, ed. Heidrich, pp. 61–69, nos. 4–6.

34. A charter of Pippin of Herstal, in which he refers to his grandfather Bishop Arnulf, comes to us only through late copies of the cartulary of St.-Arnulf of Metz and is accompanied by a brief history of Pippin's family that appears derived from Paul the Deacon; MGH DD imperii, p. 92, no. 2. See also Ingrid Heidrich, "Titular und Urkunden der arnulfingischen Hausmeier," p. 248, no. A Metz 1. Curiously, in her new edition of the charter, Heidrich places it in the *echte Urkunden* and calls Arnulf Pippin's *maternal* grandfather; *Die Urkunden der Arnulfinger*, pp. 55–58, no. 2.

35. Fredegar, *The Fourth Book* cont.3, p. 83.

36. Paul Fouracre and Richard A. Gerberding, *Late Merovingian France*, pp. 311, 339; Collins, *Charlemagne*, pp. 24–25.

37. "Vita S. Arnulfi" 1, 5, MGH SSRM 2:432–33. For the copying of the *vita* by Jerome, see p. 429.

38. Jonas of Bobbio, "De vita Bertulfi abbatis," MGH SSRM 4:144.

39. It is also possible that Charlemagne believed Clodulf and Arnulf were in his family tree because Pippin of Herstal had confirmed gifts from a mayor of the palace Clodulf with his son Aunulf, and it was easy to assume that these must be relatives and must be connected to the bishops of Metz. Pippin's confirmation does not survive but is referred to in a document of Otto I; MGH DD regum et imperatorum germaniae 1:183, no. 101.

40. Paul the Deacon, "Gesta episcoporum Mettensium," p. 267. Clodulf plays a bigger role in the *vita* of Saint Trond, commissioned by the same bishop of Metz who commissioned Paul the Deacon; Donatus, "Vita Trudonis confessoris Hasbaniensis," MGH SSRM

6:273–98. Clodulf is not, however, made the son of Arnulf or the uncle of Pippin of Herstal in this *vita*. See also Rosenwein, *Negotiating Space*, p. 127.

41. Aigradus, "Vita Ansberti episcopi Rotomagensis" 22, MGH SSRM 5:635. For the date around 700, see Lifshitz, *The Norman Conquest of Pious Neustria*, p. 39, n. 73. Ian Wood rejects the possibility of this connection; "Genealogy Defined by Women: The Case of the Pippinids," in *Gender in the Early Medieval World*, ed. Leslie Brubaker and Julia M. H. Smith, p. 251. The ninth-century *Gesta* of the abbots of Fontenelle, relying in part on Merovingian-era saints' lives, made Wandregesil and Pippin first cousins, sons respectively of the brothers Waltchisus and Anschisus (the name of Pippin's father as given by Paul the Deacon); *Chronique de Fontenelle* 1.2, p. 4. Christian Settipani speculates that Wandregesil and Pippin were second cousins once removed, related through Pippin's mother; "L'apport de l'onomastique dans l'étude des généalogies carolingiennes," in *Onomastique et parenté dans l'Occident médiéval*, ed. K. S. B. Keats-Rohan and C. Settipani, pp. 214–17.

42. Ian Wood, "Saint-Wandrille and Its Hagiography," p. 10. Nearly the only exceptions are historians of St.-Wandrille, for example, Jacques Fontaine, "La culture carolingienne dans les abbayes normandes: L'exemple de Saint-Wandrille," in *Aspects du monachisme en Normandie*, ed. Lucien Musset, p. 33.

43. Levison, "Das Testament des Diakons Adalgisel-Grimo"; Fredegar, *The Fourth Book* 75, 77, 87, pp. 63–64, 73; Ebling, *Prosopographie*, pp. 30–31, no. 5.

44. Another possible group of relatives, overlooked by modern scholars because not acknowledged by Charlemagne's publicists, includes seventh-century Lombard kings; Bouchard, "Carolingian Creation of Patrilineage," pp. 144–46.

45. Fredegar, *Chronica* 2.4, MGH SSRM 2:45; Eugen Ewig, "Le mythe troyen et l'histoire des Francs," in *Clovis*, ed. Rouche, 1:817–47; McKitterick, *History and Memory in the Carolingian World*, p. 125.

46. Paul the Deacon, *Historia Langobardorum* 6.16, p. 170. See also Rosamond McKitterick, "Political Ideology in Carolingian Historiography," in *Uses of the Past*, ed. Hen and Innes, p. 166.

47. Paul the Deacon, "Gesta episcoporum Mettensium," pp. 264–65.

48. Bouchard, "Childeric III," p. 14.

49. Yitzhak Hen, "The Annales of Metz and the Merovingian Past," in *Uses of the Past*, pp. 175–90.

50. Bouchard, "Carolingian Creation of Patrilineage," pp. 141–43.

51. As we might as well call the author of the Annals, even though he—or she—most likely did not write at Metz. Rosamond McKitterick suggests that the author may have been Charlemagne's sister Gisela, a nun at Chelles; *Charlemagne*, pp. 61–62.

52. Wood, "Genealogy Defined by Women," pp. 234–56.

53. *Annales Mettenses priores* 688, pp. 1–2. For the couple Pippin I and Itta, see the seventh-century "Vita S. Geretrudis" 1, MGH SSRM 2:454. Saint Gertrude was said by her *vita* to be one of their daughters; Begga was another, according to the *virtutes* of Gertrude; "De virtutibus S. Geretrudis" 10, MGH SSRM 2:469. The only detail not given in the

Gertrude material is that Begga married Ansegesil. Fouracre and Gerberding, *Late Merovingian France*, pp. 309–11.

54. *Annales Mettenses priores* 688, pp. 2–3.

55. Fredegar, *The Fourth Book* 85–86, pp. 71–72. See also Gerberding, *The Rise of the Carolingians*, p. 65.

56. *Annales Mettenses priores* 688, p. 3.

57. Besides Arnulf and Hugh, Drogo most likely had sons named Gottfried and Pippin. They appear only in a charter of Hugh's once considered a forgery but now accepted as authentic. MGH DD imperii, pp. 214–15, no. 7; *Die Urkunden der Arnulfinger*, ed. Heidrich, p. 73, no. 8; Heidrich, "Titular und Urkunden," pp. 251–52, no. A Metz 4. See also Hlawitschka, "Die Vorfahren," p. 80, no. 39.

58. Pippin the Short himself made no effort to conceal the existence of his uncles; he confirmed in 753 what his *avunculus* Grimoald II had earlier granted St.-Denis. ChLA 598, 15:16; also in MGH DD Karolinorum 1:10, no. 6.

59. *Annales Mettenses priores* 693, 708, 714, pp. 16–20.

60. MGH DD imperii, pp. 91–96, nos. 2–6; *Die Urkunden der Arnulfinger*, ed. Heidrich, pp. 55–69, nos. 2–6.

61. Fredegar, *The Fourth Book* cont.5–6, pp. 85–86. The story that Alpaidis was a concubine dates from the ninth century. It is argued against by Waltraud Joch, *Legitimität und Integration*, pp. 11–24; and by Gerberding, *Rise of the Carolingians*, pp. 117–18.

62. Suzanne Fonay Wemple, *Women in Frankish Society*, pp. 39–40; Isabelle Réal, *Vies de saints, vie de famille*, pp. 280–83.

63. Or possibly he had a first wife, from whom he separated for a second marriage, before returning eventually to the original wife after the second's death; Hartmann, "*Pater incertus?*" p. 3, n. 9.

64. Pope Stephen III had referred around 770 to Charlemagne's first consort, Himiltrudis, as a legitimate wife; *Codex Carolinus*, ed. Gundlach, MGH Epp. 3:561, no. 45. Only in the late 770s, when Himiltrudis was in a nunnery and Charlemagne had had four sons by Hildegard, did it become necessary to discredit his first union. Pippin was first accused of illegitimacy in the 780s but not called a hunchback until Einhard wrote, after Pippin was dead; Carl L. Hammer, "'Pipinus Rex.'" Charlemagne had the pope baptize his third son, originally named Carloman, as Pippin in 781, and Pippin the Hunchback's desperate rebellion in the 790s finished any chance for recognition he might once have had. See also Mayke de Jong, *The Penitential State*, pp. 14–17; and Bouchard, "Childeric III," pp. 9–12.

65. *Liber Historiae Francorum* 48–50, MGH SSRM 2:323–25; *Chronique de Fontenelle* 3.4, p. 50; MGH DD imperii, p. 99, no. 11; *Die Urkunden der Arnulfinger*, ed. Heidrich, p. 86, no. 12. According to both the "Annales Petaviani" and the "Annales Alamannici," Theodoald was killed—though the annals do not say by whom—in the same year his uncle Charles Martel died; MGH SS 1:11, 26. See also Roger Collins, "Deception and Misrepresentation in Early Eighth Century Frankish Historiography: Two Case Studies," in *Karl Martell in seiner Zeit*, pp. 229–35; and Joch, *Legitimität und Integration*, pp. 92–102.

66. *Annales Mettenses priores* 750, p. 42; "Vita Eucherii episcopi Aurelianensis," MGH SSRM 7:48.

67. "Chronicon Moissiacense," MGH SS 1:292.

68. Matthias Becher, "Drogo und die Königserhebung Pippins"; Bouchard, "Childeric III."

69. Fouracre, *The Age of Charles Martel*, p. 171; Janet L. Nelson, "Bertrada," in *Der Dynastiewechsel*, ed. Becher and Jarnut, pp. 99–100; Fredegar, *The Fourth Book* cont.30, pp. 100–101. Drogo signed a charter of his father's, MGH DD imperii, p. 102, no. 15; *Die Urkunden der Arnulfinger*, ed. Heidrich, p. 94, no. 15.

70. It is, however, possible that Drogo continued to serve his uncle Pippin the Short; a Drogo appears among Pippin's *fideles* in charters from 753 and 762, in the latter with the title *comes*. MGH DD Karolinorum 1:10, 24, nos. 6, 16; the former still exists as an original, *ChLA* 598, 15:16. See also Settipani, *La préhistoire*, pp. 180–81.

71. The "Annales Petaviani," however, say that he felt great remorse for the many men he had killed; MGH SS 1:11.

72. *Annales Mettenses priores* 741, p. 31; Einhard, *Vie de Charlemagne* 2–3, 18, pp. 12–16, 54. There may also have been suspicion at the time about the 754 death of Pippin's monastic brother Carloman, at whose death Pippin's wife was present; Nelson, "Bertrada," p. 104.

73. Brigitte Kasten, *Königssöhne und Königsherrschaft*, pp. 102–10.

74. Grifo, interestingly, is not mentioned in the continuations of Fredegar that were composed shortly after 751, perhaps as complicating the story of Pippin's accession; Roger Collins, "Pippin III as Mayor of the Palace: The Evidence," in *Der Dynastiewechsel*, ed. Becher and Jarnut, pp. 77–78, 86–87.

75. Fredegar, *The Fourth Book* cont.35, p. 103; *Annales Mettenses priores* 741, p. 32. For his death, see "Annales Alamannici" 752, MGH SS 1:26; and *Chronique de Fontenelle* 11.1, pp. 128–30—the latter source indeed links Grifo's death with the tonsuring of the sons of Pippin's late brother Carloman. Grifo is also mentioned by the late eighth-century "Vita Leutfredi"; AASS June 5:95. Grifo's mother was probably a wife, not a concubine; see Rudolf Schieffer, "Karl Martell und seiner Familie," in *Karl Martell in seiner Zeit*, pp. 310–11.

76. *Codex Carolinus*, MGH Epp. 3:519, 553, nos. 19, 41; *Chronique de Fontenelle* 8.2, p. 100; *Annales Fuldenses* 754, ed. G. H. Pertz and Friedrich Kurze, p. 7.

77. Settipani, however, identifies Jerome as a count, the ancestor of counts of Rouen and of the Bosonids; *La préhistoire*, pp. 359–62.

78. For Wala and Adalhard, see Depreux, *Prosopographie de l'entourage de Louis le Pieux*, pp. 76–79, 390–93, nos. 8, 269.

79. "Genealogiae comitum Flandriae," MGH SS 9:302; "Ex vitis Adalhardi et Walae abbatum Corbeiensium" 7, 32–33, 61, MGH SS 2:525, 527, 530. See also Hlawitschka, "Die Vorfahren," p. 80, no. 42.

80. "Vita Hludowici imperatoris" 21, ed. Ernst Tremp, MGH SS rerum Germanicarum, p. 346.

81. Jörg Jarnut, "Chlodwig und Chlothar"; Bouchard, *"Those of My Blood,"* p. 101.

82. Paul the Deacon, "Gesta episcoporum Mettensium," pp. 264–65.

83. Flodoard of Reims, *Historia Remensis ecclesiae* 2.17, MGH SS 36:170–71; Anne Prache, "La tombe du roi Carloman à Saint-Remi de Reims," in *Clovis*, 2:777–84.

84. Michel Bur, "Aux origines de la 'religion de Reims.' Les sacres carolingiens: Un réexamen du dossier (751–1131)," in *Clovis*, 2:45–72.

85. "Commemoratio genealogiae domni Karoli gloriosissimi imperatoris," MGH SS 13:245–46. This gives Arnulf's father as Arnoald, oldest son of Ansbertus (of senatorial origins), who had married Blitildis, daughter of King Clothar. King Clothar I would be roughly right chronologically, and the name Blitildis or Bilchildis is indeed found among Merovingian women, but almost no modern scholar has accepted this account. See also Roger Collins, "Frankish Past and Carolingian Present in the Age of Charlemagne," in *Am Vorabend der Kaiser Krönung*, ed. Godman, Jarnut, and Johanek, pp. 318–19.

86. "Domus Carolingicae genealogia," MGH SS 2:308–9. The one scholar who gives this account credence is Jörg Jarnut, *Agiolfingerstudien*. For these efforts to make the Arnulfings' ancestors Gallo-Roman senators, see Settipani, *La préhistoire*, pp. 139–46.

87. Riché, *Les Carolingiens*, p. 162.

88. Eugen Ewig, *Spätantikes und fränkisches Gallien*, 1:114–230.

89. Fredegar, *The Fourth Book* cont.23, p. 97.

CHAPTER 8

1. Alcuin, "Vita Willibrordi archiepiscopi Traiectensis" 5, 23, MGH SSRM 7:121, 133–34. See also Lifshitz, *The Norman Conquest of Pious Neustria*, pp. 84–85.

2. Wallace-Hadrill, *The Frankish Church*, pp. 229–31; Riché, *Les Carolingiens*, pp. 274–75; McKitterick, *The Frankish Kingdoms Under the Carolingians*, pp. 109–24; Friedrich Prinz, "Der fränkische Episkopat zwischen Merowinger- und Karolingerzeit," in *Nascita dell'Europa ed Europa carolingia*, 1:117–18; Josef Semmler, "Karl der Grosse und das fränkische Mönchtum," in *KdG*, 2:255–67.

3. Amy G. Remensnyder, *Remembering Kings Past*, pp. 116–49.

4. Pope Pius XI declared as much in 1923. This topos was ultimately derived from a misreading of Columbanus's *vita;* Lifshitz, *The Norman Conquest of Pious Neustria*, pp. 73–78.

5. Boniface, Letter 50, ed. Michael Tangl, MGH Epp. Selectae 1:82. Timothy Reuter argues that Boniface was concerned with doctrine, not church institutions; "'Kirchenreform' und 'Kirchenpolitik' im Zeitalter Karl Martells: Begriff und Wirchlichkeit," in *Karl Martell in seiner Zeit*, ed. Jarnut, Nonn, and Richter, pp. 35–51. However, Boniface clearly addressed church structure and organization: he used the phrase *de ecclesiastica religione* (not simply *de religione*) and added that a chief symptom was an absence of synods.

6. See the discussion of this perception by Karl Ferdinand Werner, "Le rôle de l'aristocratie dans la christianisation du nord de la Gaule," in *La christianisation des pays entre Loire et Rhin*, ed. Pierre Riché, pp. 53–54.

7. Yitzhak Hen, "Martin of Braga's *De correctione rusticorum* and Its Uses in Frankish

Gaul," in *Medieval Transformations*, ed. Cohen and de Jong, pp. 35–49; Werner, "Le rôle de l'aristocratie," p. 52.

8. John Howe, "The Hagiography of Saint-Wandrille (Fontenelle) (Province of Haute-Normandie)," in *L'hagiographie du haut moyen âge du Gaule du nord*, ed. Heinzelmann, p. 190.

9. As is done, for example, by Joachim Wollasch, "Monasticism: The First Wave of Reform," in *NCMH*, 3:163–65.

10. Jean Heuclin, "Les abbés des monastères neustriens, 650–850," in *La Neustrie*, ed. Hartmut Atsma, 1:321–26; Reinhold Kaiser, "Royauté et pouvoir épiscopal," ibid., 1:143–60; Karl Ferdinand Werner, *Vom Frankenreich zur Entfaltung Deutschlands und Frankreichs*, pp. 114–20.

11. Janet L. Nelson states that Charlemagne was "too canny to disburse much property"; "The Merovingian Church in Carolingian Retrospective," in *The World of Gregory of Tours*, ed. Kathleen Mitchell and Ian Wood, pp. 248–50. Hans J. Hummer argues that Carolingian immunities must "imply . . . additional donations"; *Politics and Power in Early Medieval Europe*, pp. 61–62. See also Mayke de Jong, "Carolingian Monasticism: The Power of Prayer," in *NCMH*, 2:622–36; and Nelson, *Frankish World*, pp. 145–48.

12. Susan Wood is one of the few modern scholars to characterize the Carolingians as seizing monastic property; *The Proprietary Church in the Medieval West*, pp. 211–35.

13. *Cartulaire de l'Yonne*, ed. Quantin, 1:26–28, no. 13; *Chronique de Saint-Bénigne*, ed. Bougaud and Garnier, p. 278; Bautier, *Chartes, sceaux et chancelleries*, pp. 213–15. Hervé Mouillebouche argues that attributions of disaster to the Saracens were a result of churchmen not feeling safe in attributing them to the real cause, Charles Martel; "Un autre mythe historiographique."

14. This victory may need to be dated a year or two later, based on the Arabic sources; Wood, *The Merovingian Kingdoms*, p. 283.

15. "Annales Petaviani" 740, MGH SS 1:9. See also Ulrich Nonn, "Das Bild Karl Martells im Mittelalterlichen Quellen," in *Karl Martell in seiner Zeit*, p. 9.

16. Fredegar, *The Fourth Book* cont.47, ed. Wallace-Hadrill, p. 115.

17. It is still robust in Gerd Althoff, *Family, Friends and Followers*, p. 113.

18. Bernard S. Bachrach, "Charles Martel, Mounted Shock Combat, the Stirrup, and Feudalism"; Herwig Wolfram, "Karl Martell und das fränkische Lehenswesen," in *Karl Martell in seiner Zeit*, pp. 61–78; Fouracre, *The Age of Charles Martel*, pp. 2–3, 145–54.

19. Nonn, "Das Bild Karl Martells," pp. 10–17; Hans-Werner Goetz, "Karl Martell und die Heiligen: Kirchenpolitik und Maiordomat im Spiegel der Spätmerowingischen Hagiographie," in *Karl Martell in seiner Zeit*, pp. 101–18; Alain Dierkens, "Carolus monasteriorum multorum eversor et ecclesiarum pecuniarum in usos proprios commutator? Notes sur la politique monastique du maire du palais Charles Martel," ibid., pp. 277–94; Fouracre, *The Age of Charles Martel*, pp. 122–25.

20. Durliat, *Les finances publiques de Dioclétien aux Carolingiens*, p. 149. In contrast, Wood argues that Arnulfing control of monasteries was "a practical power, not a legal

right"; *The Proprietary Church*, p. 213. Hummer attempts to clear Charles Martel from the accusation of secularizing church property, saying that while he and his successors were "quick to help themselves to the landed wealth accumulating in monasteries," it was only appropriate that the monks make grants to them in return for protection; *Politics and Power*, pp. 76–77.

21. "Vita Leutfredi," AASS June 5:95.

22. Fredegar, *The Fourth Book* cont.14, p. 91. Wallace-Hadrill incorrectly translates *infideles* as followers of pagan practices; the use of *fidelibus* in the next line to mean Charles's followers clearly indicates that the issue was whether they were faithful to *him*.

23. Raaijmakers, *The Making of the Monastic Community of Fulda*, pp. 19–40; Wallace-Hadrill, *Frankish Church*, pp. 150–52; Fouracre, *The Age of Charles Martel*, pp. 130–32; Josef Semmler, "Bonifatius, die Karolinger und 'die Franken.'"

24. Boniface, Letter 73, p. 153 n. "Carolus monasteriorum multorum eversor et ecclesiasticarum pecuniarum in usos proprios commutator." This rather incendiary sentence is not found in all the manuscripts, but its authenticity is argued by Reuter, "'Kirchenreform' und 'Kirchenpolitik,'" pp. 51–58. This comment, unlike others in the eighth century, found no echo in the ninth century; Nonn, "Das Bild Karl Martells," p. 15. Fouracre, however, asserts that this phrase was concocted in the twelfth century, from ninth-century sources; *The Age of Charles Martel*, pp. 134–36.

25. Boniface, Letter 78, pp. 169–70. The term "murderer of the poor" dated to the sixth century, used for someone who seized church property, which was supposed to support the poor; Brown, *Through the Eye of a Needle*, p. 508.

26. "Vita Eucherii episcopi Aurelianensis," MGH SSRM 7:51 n. The story was retold around 1100, with many dramatic flourishes, by Hugh of Flavigny; *Chronicon*, MGH SS 8:343. Lester K. Little argues that this story of Charles Martel's tomb dates to a good century later; *Benedictine Maledictions*, pp. 100–101.

27. Wolfram, "Karl Martell und das Lehenswesen," p. 75; Fouracre, *The Age of Charles Martel*, pp. 125, 136–37.

28. Wood, *The Proprietary Church*, pp. 181–90.

29. Gregory of Tours, *Hist* 7.7, 7.19, pp. 330, 338–39. See also Martin Heinzelmann, *Gregory of Tours*, pp. 53–56.

30. Bobolenus, "Vita Germani abbatis Grandivallensis" 10–12, MGH SSRM 5:37–39.

31. Fredegar, *The Fourth Book* cont.6, p. 86.

32. *ChLA* 581, 14:32–35. See also Rosenwein, *Negotiating Space*, pp. 91–96. She interprets the case differently, calling it a "fictive dispute."

33. Gregory of Tours, *Hist* 6.9, p. 279; Wood, *The Proprietary Church*, p. 118; Gregory I. Halfond, *The Archaeology of Frankish Church Councils*, pp. 108–22.

34. Jean Heuclin, *Hommes de Dieu et fonctionnaires du roi en Gaule du Nord*, pp. 246–52.

35. Matthew Innes, "'Immune from Heresy': Defining the Boundaries of Carolingian Christianity," in *Frankland*, ed. Paul Fouracre and David Ganz, pp. 101–25. See also Franz J. Felten, *Äbte und Laienäbte im Frankenreich*, p. 99.

36. Caesarius of Arles, Sermon 54.5, in *Opera omnia*, ed. Germain Morin, 1/1:229. See also William E. Klingshirn, *Caesarius of Arles: The Making of a Christian Community*, pp. 273–74. Boniface mistakenly attributed Caesarius's quote to Augustine.

37. Boniface was probably referring to the Council of Autun, which took place in the 660s or 670s; *Concilia Galliae, A. 511–A. 695*, ed. Charles de Clercq, pp. 318–20. This was the last major Merovingian synod, although Theoderic III did hold a synod at his palace a few years later, attended by five bishops; ibid., p. 322. The Auxerre synod of the 690s seems to have been purely local; ibid., pp. 264–72.

38. Boniface, Letter 50, p. 82. The pope agreed that Carloman should hold the synod, although it seems to have been held already by the time that Boniface received the pope's letter; Boniface, Letter 51, p. 87; Goffart, *The Le Mans Forgeries*, p. 8.

39. Halfond, *Archaeology of Frankish Councils*, pp. 198–202.

40. Heuclin, *Hommes de Dieu et fonctionnaires du roi*, pp. 168–69.

41. For an overview, see Laurent Morelle, "Les 'actes de précaire,' instruments de transferts patrimoniaux." Hummer argues that *precaria* may have had their start in early eighth-century Alsace and that the payment of a rent became part of a precarial arrangement only toward the end of the eighth century; *Politics and Power*, pp. 78–79, 84–94.

42. MGH Capit. 1:24–26.

43. MGH Capit. 1:26–28.

44. Fouracre, *The Age of Charles Martel*, pp. 137–38; Ian Wood, "Teutsind, Witlaic and the History of Merovingian *Precaria*," in *Property and Power in the Early Middle Ages*, ed. Wendy Davies and Paul Fouracre, pp. 43–47.

45. Indeed, Hummer argues that churches knew that precarial grants they made would pass to the recipient's heirs and then to *their* heirs, in perpetuity; *Politics and Power*, pp. 20–21. Nonetheless, he asserts that such grants were "a painless way for Carolingian rulers both to endow [secular] supporters and to respect ecclesiastical rights"; ibid., p. 79, and cf. p. 109.

46. These *precaria* had been granted to *him*, not to his followers. Fouracre mistakenly says that the *precaria* would be held "by men who performed military service"; *The Age of Charles Martel*, p. 139. The text does not support such a reading. Halfond, following Fouracre, makes the same error; *Archaeology of Frankish Councils*, p. 123.

47. Goffart puts a much sunnier interpretation on this canon, seeing it as indicating that the Carolingians intended to ensure that all churches had at least the minimum "basic requirements"; *The Le Mans Forgeries*, pp. 9–11.

48. *Actus pontificum Cenomannis in urbe degentium*, ed. G. Busson and A. Ledru, pp. 244–45, 254–56. The new edition is *Geschichte des Bistums Le Mans von der Spätantike bis zur Karolingerzeit*, ed. Margarete Weidemann, 1:90–91, 2:265–66, no. 31. For the charter's authenticity, see Goffart, *The Le Mans Forgeries*, p. 259. See also Philippe Le Maître, "L'oeuvre d'Aldric du Mans et sa signification," p. 45.

49. MGH DD imperii 1:103, no. 16; also in *Die Urkunden der Arnulfinger*, ed. Ingrid Heidrich, pp. 95–98, no. 16. Heuclin, *Hommes de Dieu et fonctionnaires du roi*, p. 163. For the abbeys, see Ellen F. Arnold, *Negotiating the Landscape*.

50. Wolfram, "Karl Martell und das Lehenswesen," p. 76.

51. Patrick J. Geary, "Die Provence zur Zeit Karl Martells," in *Karl Martell in seiner Zeit*, pp. 381–92. Geary reprints the relative documents from Marseille in his article.

52. Fredegar, *The Fourth Book* cont.53, p. 120.

53. Heuclin, *Hommes de Dieu et fonctionnaires du roi*, p. 293.

54. "Formulae Morbacenses" 4, MGH Formulae, pp. 350–51.

55. I here disagree with Hummer, who tries to downplay the seriousness of Murbach's complaints; *Politics and Power*, pp. 106–8.

56. "Formulae Turonenses" 7, MGH Formulae, p. 139.

57. MGH Capit. 1:50.

58. MGH Concilia 2/1:293, no. 51. See also Morelle, "Les 'actes de précaire,'" pp. 613–15; and Hummer, *Politics and Power*, pp. 102–4. Hummer asserts that this was not a problem for the monasteries because they had become "fabulously well-endowed."

59. *Gesta domni Aldrici*, ed. R. Charles and L[ouis] Froger, pp. 174–77. The new edition is by Weidemann, *Geschichte des Bistums Le Mans*, 2:305–6, 313–15, nos. 47, 52; she treats the charters as authentic. Le Maître, however, calls both forgeries; "L'oeuvre d'Aldric du Mans," pp. 62–63.

60. "Admonitio generalis," MGH Capit. 1:53–54.

61. John J. Contreni, "The Pursuit of Knowledge in Carolingian Europe," in *"The Gentle Voices of Teachers,"* ed. Sullivan, pp. 107–8.

62. Canon 22, MGH Concilia 2:278.

63. Canons 114–15, MGH Concilia 2:394–97. The Rule of Aachen is edited by Jerome Bertram, *The Chrodegang Rules*, pp. 96–131. "Vita Hludowici imperatoris" 28, ed. Ernst Tremp, MGH SS rerum Germanicarum (1995), p. 374; Alain Dierkens, "La Christianisation des campagnes de l'Europe de Louis le Pieux," in *Charlemagne's Heir*, ed. Godman and Collins, p. 309.

64. For example, Peter King, *Western Monasticism*, pp. 103–12.

65. "Capitulare de villis," MGH Capit. 1:82–91.

66. "Annales Alamannici" 751, MGH SS 1:26; *Chronique de Fontenelle* II.3, ed. Pradié, p. 132; Fossier, *Polyptyques et censiers*, pp. 25–26.

67. *Traditiones Wizenburgenses*, ed. Karl Glöckner and Anton Doll, pp. 270–71, no. 69.

68. *Recueil des actes de Charles le Chauve*, ed. Tessier, Giry, and Prou, 1:9–12, 74–77, nos. 3, 30; Loup of Ferrières, *Correspondance*, ed. Léon Levillain, 1:174–78, no. 42. For Count Odulf as dangerously greedy, see 1:148, no. 82. I only hint here at a long, complex series of claims, where Charlemagne originally gave the cell to Alcuin, then Louis the Pious confirmed that it belonged to Ferrières, then first Lothar I and then Charles the Bald granted it to their followers, and Lupus finally recovered it.

69. *Corpus consuetudinum monasticarum*, vol. 1, ed. Kassius Hallinger, pp. 493–99. The old edition is MGH Capit. 1:350–52, no. 17. See also Wood, *The Proprietary Church*, pp. 269–71.

70. Hincmar of Reims, *Collectio de ecclesiis et capelis*, ed. Martina Stratmann, MGH

Fontes iuris Germanici antiqui 14:120. See also Nelson, *Politics and Ritual in Early Medieval Europe*, pp. 117–32.

71. Rosenwein, *Negotiating Space*, pp. 74–81.

72. "Vita S. Balthildis" 9, MGH SSRM 2:493.

73. François Louis Ganshof, "Charlemagne et les institutions de la monarchie franque," in *KdG*, 1:383–88. He does not note Merovingian-era immunities.

74. Hummer describes this protection as positive, saying that the Carolingians earned the "gratitude" of the monks while safeguarding the property of local landowners. But even so he immediately adds that the effect was to allow the kings to "project their authority into localities"; *Politics and Power*, p. 24.

75. Rosenwein, *Negotiating Space*, pp. 97, 111. Timothy Reuter blurs the distinction, saying that late eighth-century monasteries sought immunity and protection, implying that the king only extended such *tuitio* when asked; Reuter, *Germany in the Early Middle Ages*, p. 43.

76. "Marculfi formulae" 1.24, MGH Formulae, p. 58. For Marculf, see, most recently, Alice Rio, *Legal Practice and the Written Word in the Early Middle Ages*; and Wood, *The Proprietary Church*, pp. 230–31.

77. For the novelty of these charters of protection, see Ingrid Heidrich, "Titular und Urkunden," pp. 122–23.

78. Marios Costambeys argues that Willibrord, not the Arnulfings, should be given credit for the establishment of Echternach and its property; "An Aristocratic Community on the Northern Frankish Frontier." Richard A. Gerberding argues that Charles Martel's success was partly due to Willibrord; "716: A Crucial Year for Charles Martel," in *Karl Martell in seiner Zeit*, pp. 205–16.

79. MGH DD imperii, pp. 94–95, no. 5; also in *Die Urkunden der Arnulfinger*, ed. Heidrich, pp. 4–66, no. 5. See also Rosenwein, *Negotiating Space*, pp. 109–10.

80. *Gesta Aldrici*, ed. Charles and Froger, pp. 131–32; ed. Weidemann, 1:154–55.

81. *Gesta Aldrici*, ed. Charles and Froger, pp. 133–34, 143; ed. Weidemann, 1:155.

82. *Gesta Aldrici*, ed. Charles and Froger, pp. 137–39; ed. Weidemann, 1:157.

83. Felten, *Äbte und Laienäbte*, pp. 129–35; Gerberding, *The Rise of the Carolingians*, p. 97.

84. Notker the Stammerer, *Gesta Karoli imperatoris* 13, MGH SS 2:736.

85. For Notker, see Matthew Innes, "'He Never Allowed His White Teeth to Be Bared in Laughter': The Politics of Humour in the Carolingian Renaissance," in *Humour, History and Politics in Late Antiquity and the Early Middle Ages*, ed. Guy Halsall, pp. 131–32; Paul Kershaw, "Laughter After Babel's Fall: Misunderstanding and Miscommunication in the Ninth-Century West," ibid., pp. 191–94; Morrissey, *Charlemagne and France*, pp. 27–38; and MacLean, *Kingship and Politics in the Late Ninth Century*, pp. 199–229.

86. Gerberding, *The Rise of the Carolingians*, pp. 95–115 and n. 20.

87. Robert F. Berkhofer, for example, characterizes as "reform" the Carolingian practice of dividing abbot's and monks' portions of a monastery's holdings and then giving the

abbot's portion to a layman; *Day of Reckoning*, pp. 13–22. A notable exception is Wood, *The Proprietary Church*, pp. 215–17, 312–18.

88. The historiography is discussed by Felten, *Äbte und Laienäbte*, pp. 5–17.

89. Anne-Marie Helvétius, "L'abbatiat laïque comme relais du pouvoir royal aux frontières du royaume: Le cas du nord de la Neustrie au IXe siècle," in *La royauté et les élites*, ed. Le Jan, pp. 285–99.

90. See Anne-Marie Helvétius, *Abbayes, évêques et laïques*, pp. 197–204, for this process in one region.

91. Hummer, *Politics and Power*, pp. 214–15.

92. Albert Bruckner, *Regesta Alsatiae aevi Merovingici et Karolini*, 1:225–27, no. 354.

93. *Recueil des actes de Charles le Chauve*, 1:411–13, no. 156; 2:377–80, no. 396.

94. Alain Dierkens, *Abbayes et chapitres entre Sambre et Meuse*, pp. 78–79.

95. Goffart, "Paul the Deacon's *Gesta*," pp. 90–91. Several other dioceses in northern Francia were vacant throughout Charlemagne's entire reign, including Chartres and most of the dioceses in the province of Rouen, while others, including Reims and Nevers, experienced lengthy vacancies; Heuclin, *Hommes de Dieu et fonctionnaires du roi*, pp. 325–31.

96. "Vita Hludowici imperatoris" 36, pp. 414–16.

97. *Actus pontificum Cenomannis*, ed. Busson and Ledru, pp. 271–72; ed. Weidemann, 1:104–5.

98. MGH DD Karolinorum 1:171–73, no. 123.

99. "Vita Alcuini" 9, MGH SS 15:190; Hugh of Flavigny, *Chronicon*, MGH SS 8:352; idem, "Series abbatum Flaviniacensium," MGH SS 8:502–3. See also Bullough, *Alcuin*, pp. 341–42.

100. Hugh of Flavigny, *Chronicon*, MGH SS 8:352.

101. "Vita Hludowici imperatoris" 3, p. 290.

102. Rosenwein, *Negotiating Space*, pp. 101–2.

103. "Vita Hludowici imperatoris" 19, pp. 334–36.

104. Riché, *Les Carolingiens*, p. 149. This view has been disputed for the last generation; see, most recently, Eric J. Goldberg, "Louis the Pious and the Hunt."

105. Rudolf Schieffer says that he was also bishop of Lisieux and Avranches and abbot of St.-Denis, although it is not clear on what grounds; "Karl Martell und seine Familie," in *Karl Martell in seiner Zeit*, p. 308.

106. *Chronique de Fontenelle* 4.1, pp. 58–60. For the St.-Wandrille sources, see the extensive analysis by Howe, "The Hagiography of Saint-Wandrille," pp. 127–92.

107. I here disagree with Jacques Fontaine, who sees the *Gesta* of St.-Wandrille as showing the transition from the "nadir" of culture in the seventh century to the creativity and originality of the Carolingian Renaissance; "La culture carolingienne dans les abbayes normandes: L'exemple de Saint-Wandrille," in *Aspects du monachisme en Normandie*, ed. Musset, pp. 31–32.

108. Aigradus, "Vita Ansberti episcopi Rotomagensis" 22, MGH SSRM 5:635; *Chronique de Fontenelle* 1.2, p. 4.

109. This creative addition to the Arnulfing line has not generally been accepted by

modern scholars and seems to reveal more of ninth-century ideas about name elements within a family group than actual knowledge of the royal family tree. Ian Wood, "Saint-Wandrille and Its Hagiography," p. 10. For the names, see Le Jan, *Femmes, pouvoir et société*, pp. 224–38.

110. *Chronique de Fontenelle* 1.2, 1.4, pp. 4, 10.

111. This case is discussed extensively by Wood, "Teutsind, Witlaic and Merovingian *Precaria*," pp. 35–51. He attempts to absolve Charles Martel from blame for the monastery's loss of its property.

112. *Chronique de Fontenelle* 6.1–2, pp. 74–80. The original grant is also described in the early ninth-century "Vita Lantberti abbatis Fontanellensis" 3, MGH SSRM 5:610–11. Both the author of the *Gesta* and the author of the slightly earlier "Vita" doubtless had the original seventh-century royal charter before them.

113. *Chronique de Fontenelle* 1.7, 2.1, pp. 20–24, 28.

114. Wood, "Saint-Wandrille," p. 1; Gerberding, *The Rise of the Carolingians*, pp. 97–98.

115. Aigradus, "Vita Ansberti episcopi Rotomagensis" 7, 18, 21–34, pp. 623–24, 630–31, 634–40. See also Lifshitz, *The Norman Conquest of Pious Neustria*, pp. 38–41.

116. Joseph van der Straeten, ed., "La vie inédite de S. Hughes, évêque de Rouen," p. 235; *Chronique de Fontenelle* 4, pp. 58–66. See also John Howe, "The Hagiography of Jumièges (Province of Haute-Normandie)," in *L'hagiographie du haut moyen âge*, p. 123.

117. "Gesta Dagoberti I regis Francorum," MGH SSRM 2:396–425. For the date, see Atsma and Vezin, "Les faux sur papyrus," p. 675.

118. See also McKitterick, *Charlemagne*, pp. 74–75.

119. Laurent Theis dismisses its content as "legendary"; "Dagobert, Saint-Denis et la royauté française au moyen âge," in *Le métier d'historien au moyen âge*, ed. Bernard Guenée, pp. 19–30.

120. "Gesta Dagoberti" 1, p. 401.

121. Ibid., 2, 5, pp. 401–2. Fredegar does mention Dagobert's father's grief at the death of his wife Bertetrudis, *The Fourth Book* 46, p. 39. The *Gesta* author's identification of her as Dagobert's mother does, therefore, seem plausible. It is accepted by Theis, "Dagobert," p. 20. More recently, however, Eugen Ewig has argued that Dagobert was the son of Clothar II's first wife, named Haldetrudis; "Die Namengebung bei den Ältesten Franken Königen und im Merowingischen Königshaus," p. 64, no. 48.

122. "Gesta Dagoberti" 17–20, 23, 26, 29, 33–34, 37, 39–42, 49–52, pp. 406–7, 409–11, 413–21, 423–25; Atsma and Vezin, "Les faux sur papyrus," p. 675.

123. Ulrich Nonn, "Das Bild Karl Martells im Mittelalterlichen Quellen," in *Karl Martell in seiner Zeit*, pp. 15–16.

124. *Cartulaire de Saint-Père de Chartres*, ed. Guérard, 1:4–6.

125. *Chronique de Saint-Bénigne*, pp. 248–49, 278.

CHAPTER 9

1. Richard Hodges and David Whitehouse, *Mohammed, Charlemagne and the Origins of Europe*; Paolo Delogu, "Reading Pirenne Again," in *The Sixth Century*, ed. Richard Hodges and William Bowden, pp. 15–40; T. N. Bisson, "The 'Feudal Revolution.'"

2. Sullivan, "The Carolingian Age." A colloquium on early medieval transitions assumed that whatever transitions were going to take place were over by the time of Charlemagne's imperial coronation; *D'une déposition à un couronnement*.

3. The "mutations" of the year 1000 have become a historiographic issue in themselves; Bouchard, *"Those of My Blood,"* pp. 175–80. Recently scholars have convincingly argued that the evidence for a feudal revolution has been overstated.

4. For example, *La Neustrie*, ed. Atsma; and *The Long Eighth Century*, ed. Inge Lyse Hansen and Chris Wickham.

5. Wickham, *Framing the Early Middle Ages*, pp. 519–88. This argument is echoed by Joachim Henning, "Strong Rulers—Weak Economy? Rome, the Carolingians and the Archaeology of Slavery in the First Millennium AD," in *The Long Morning of Medieval Europe*, ed. Davis and McCormick, pp. 33–53.

6. Scholars have demonstrated that literacy was more prevalent in Carolingian court circles than was once thought, so it should not be surprising to find it in the Merovingian era. McKitterick, *The Carolingians and the Written Word*; Hen, *Culture and Religion in Merovingian Gaul*; Dutton, *Charlemagne's Mustache*, pp. 69–92.

7. Hen, *Culture and Religion in Merovingian Gaul*, pp. 29–42; Rosamond McKitterick, "The Written Word and Oral Communication: Rome's Legacy to the Franks," in her *The Frankish Kings and Culture*; Julia M. H. Smith, *Europe After Rome*, pp. 40–50; Jacques Fontaine, "Education and Learning," in *NCMH*, 1:735–59; Ian Wood, "Administration, Law, and Culture in Merovingian Gaul."

8. Venantius Fortunatus, "Vita Sanctae Radegundis regina" 2, MGH SSRM 2:365.

9. Gregory of Tours, *Hist* 5.44, 6.46, pp. 254, 320.

10. Judith M. George, *Venantius Fortunatus*, pp. 48–57. George reedits and translates the panegyric on pp. 198–207.

11. Ulrich Nonn, "Merowingische Testamente."

12. *Chronique de Fontenelle* 1.7, ed. Pradié, pp. 20–22. "Cuius auctoritas largitionis adhuc in scriniis privilegiorum nostri coenobii conservata tenetur."

13. MGH DD imperii, p. 174, no. 56. Although included among the *diplomata spuria* in the MGH edition, this testament is now generally considered genuine.

14. "Marculfi formulae" 2.7–38, MGH Formulae, pp. 79–98; Alice Rio, "Charters, Law Codes, and Formulae: The Franks Between Theory and Practice," in *Frankland*, ed. Fouracre and Ganz, pp. 7–27; eadem, *Legal Practice and the Written Word*, pp. 85–88.

15. Warren C. Brown, "Laypeople and Documents in the Frankish Formula Collections," in *Documentary Culture and the Laity*, ed. Brown et al., pp. 133–36.

16. Michel Banniard, "Seuils et frontières langagières dans la Francia romane du VIIIe siècle," in *Karl Martell in seiner Zeit*, ed. Jarnut, Nonn, and Richter, pp. 171–91; Hen,

Culture and Religion in Merovingian Gaul, pp. 21–25; Brown, *The Rise of Western Christendom*, pp. 446–48.

17. Guy Halsall, *Settlement and Social Organization*, pp. 262–70.

18. *ChLA* 581, 14:32–35. ". . . se talis epistulas commutacionis exinde inter se ficissent aut se ipsas in nostri presencia presentare potibat. Sed ipsi strumentum exinde nullatenus presentauit nec nulla euidenti potuit tradere." For this case, see also Chapter 8.

19. Carlo Bertelli, "The Production and Distribution of Books in Late Antiquity," in *The Sixth Century*, pp. 41–60; Hen, *Culture and Religion in Merovingian Gaul*, pp. 25–29. Augustine even apologized at one point for using parchment for a letter rather than papyrus; Letter 15.1, PL 33:80–81.

20. Geary, *Phantoms of Remembrance*, pp. 81–114.

21. David Ganz, "Corbie and Neustrian Monastic Culture, 661–874," in *La Neustrie*, 2:339. The monks of St.-Denis preserved their early charters by later confecting forged Merovingian privileges from the papyrus; see Chapter 1.

22. Julia M. H. Smith, "*Aedificatio sancti loci*: The Making of a Ninth-Century Holy Place," in *Topographies of Power*, ed. de Jong and Theuws, pp. 371–73. For the municipal archives, see, most recently, Warren C. Brown, "On the *Gesta municipalia* and the Public Validation of Documents in Frankish Europe"; and Nicholas Everett, "Lay Documents and Archives in Early Medieval Spain and Italy, c. 400–700," in *Documentary Culture and the Laity*, pp. 70–82.

23. *Cartulary of Flavigny*, ed. Bouchard, pp. 19–33, 135–44, nos. 1–2, 57–58.

24. Matthew Innes, "People, Place and Power in Carolingian Society," in *Topographies of Power*, p. 407.

25. The records of Wissembourg were all drawn up by secular notaries in the seventh and eighth centuries, yet they were there in the archives in the ninth century when the monks created their first cartulary; Régine Le Jan, "À la recherche des élites rurales."

26. *Cartulary of Flavigny*, pp. 19–33, 135–44, nos. 1–2, 57–58. For the dates of Wideradus's testaments, see the "Introduction," pp. 13–16.

27. Nonn, "Merowingische Testamente," pp. 33–34; Patrick J. Geary, *Aristocracy in Provence*, pp. 27–29.

28. *Cartulary of Flavigny*, pp. 20, 135, nos. 1, 57; Wickham, *Framing the Early Middle Ages*, pp. 70, 110–11; Rio, *Legal Practice and the Written Word*, pp. 177–82.

29. Earlier editors of Wideradus's testament were often confused by this term and have mistakenly given *infancidia*, infanticide.

30. Wood, *The Merovingian Kingdoms*, pp. 204–5.

31. *Cartulary of Flavigny*, pp. 38–41, 43–44, nos. 6, 7, 9.

32. Ibid., pp. 33–34, 41–47, nos. 3, 8, 10–12. He was Charles Martel's brother.

33. Ibid., pp. 34–36, 48–49, nos. 4, 13.

34. BnF, MS lat. 2123. A description and detailed list of contents is given by Rio, *Legal Practice and the Written Word*, p. 252. See also Brown, "Laypeople and Documents," pp. 125–51. He argues that this manuscript is a slightly later copy of a lost original.

35. "Formulae collectionis Sancti Dionysii," MGH Formulae, pp. 493–511. See also

Atsma and Vezin, "Les faux sur papyrus," p. 675; and Rio, *Legal Practice and the Written Word*, pp. 141–44.

36. Rosamond McKitterick, "The Scriptoria of Merovingian Gaul: A Survey of the Evidence," in *Columbanus and Merovingian Monasticism*, ed. H. B. Clarke and Mary Brown, p. 207, n. 109. McKitterick, however, attributes more books to Flavigny than the house indeed produced by interpreting references to St.-Germer of Fly as references to Flavigny; eadem, "The Diffusion of Insular Culture in Neustria Between 650 and 850: The Implications of the Manuscript Evidence," in *La Neustrie*, 2:403–4.

37. Autun, Bibl. mun., MS 4, fol. 115r. Uncial was standard for Bibles at this time; see Patrick McGurk, "The Oldest Manuscripts of the Latin Bible," p. 5; and Bernhard Bischoff, *Latin Palaeography*, p. 71. This manuscript is described and catalogued as number 717a–b by E. A. Lowe, *Codices Latini antiquiores*, vol. 6, *France*. Lowe reads the anagram as LIBER S[AN]C[T]I PETRI FLAUINIACENSIS, but at the time the gospels were copied the monastery was still normally referred to as dedicated to Saint Prix (Preiectus), in preference to Saint Peter.

38. Autun, Bibl. mun., MS 3. This earlier manuscript was copied by a scribe named Gundohinus in the 750s at an unidentified monastery; see Lawrence Nees, *The Gundohinus Gospels*, p. 167. These two manuscripts, now together in the library of Autun, had previously been together in the cathedral of Autun and before then doubtless at Flavigny, from which the bishops of Autun acquired them in the ninth century, when they took over direction of the abbey. See *Voyage litteraire de deux réligieux Bénédictins de la congrégation de Saint Maur* [Martène and Durand], vol. 1, p. 1.151. For other eighth-century manuscripts from Flavigny now in the Bibl. mun. of Autun, see Jacques Madignier, *Diocèse d'Autun*, p. 62.

39. *Cartulary of Flavigny*, pp. 33–34, no. 3; Jean Marilier, "Le scriptorium de l'abbaye de Flavigny au VIIIe siècle." For the use of ivory, see also Danielle Gaborit-Chopin, "Les trésors de Neustrie du VIIe au IXe siècle d'après les sources écrites: Orfèvrerie et sculpture sur ivoire," in *La Neustrie*, 2:277–79; Robert Melzak, "Antiquarianism in the Time of Louis the Pious and Its Influence on the Art of Metz," in *Charlemagne's Heir*, ed. Peter Godman and Roger Collins, pp. 638–40; Bertelli, "The Production and Distribution of Books," pp. 47–48; and Lawrence Nees, "Carolingian Art and Politics," in *"The Gentle Voices of Teachers,"* ed. Sullivan, pp. 195–202.

40. Orléans, Bibl. mun., MS 82.

41. MGH Formulae, pp. 476–77, 480–81; *Cartulary of Flavigny*, pp. 135–44, nos. 57–58. For the relationship between the testaments and the formulary, see Nonn, "Merowingische Testamente," pp. 110–21; and Rio, *Legal Practice and the Written Word*, pp. 117–21.

42. Brown sees this formulary as indicating that the monks assumed continued lay literacy; "Laypeople and Documents," pp. 138, 150.

43. Brown indicates that in the late Empire transactions were publicly validated before witnesses before being recorded in the municipal *gesta*; "On the *Gesta municipalia*," pp. 349–53. By the ninth century, only the first of these processes was followed.

44. *Urkundenbuch der Abtei Sanct Gallen*, ed. Wartmann.

45. *Cartulary of Flavigny*, pp. 73–75, no. 24.

46. Ibid., pp. 102–4, no. 40.

47. Hebr. 13:14; 1 Cor. 15:53; Matt. 10:42; Ecclesiasticus 3:33. For such quotations, see Bouchard, *Sword, Miter, and Cloister*, pp. 225–27.

48. J. Percival, "The Fifth-Century Villa: New Life or Death Postponed?" in *Fifth-Century Gaul*, ed. John Drinkwater and Hugh Elton, pp. 156–64; Gisela Ripoll and Javier Arce, "The Transformation and End of Roman *Villae* in the West (Fourth–Seventh Centuries): Problems and Perspectives," in *Towns and Their Territories Between Late Antiquity and the Early Middle Ages*, ed. G. P. Brogiolo, N. Gauthier, and N. Christie, p. 63.

49. Nancy Gauthier, "From the Ancient City to the Medieval Town: Continuity and Change in the Early Middle Ages," in *The World of Gregory of Tours*, ed. Mitchell and Wood, pp. 47–48.

50. *Cartulary of Flavigny*, p. 20, no. 1.

51. I am indebted to the scholars who have traced the ancient forms of many place-names through Latin and Old French in late medieval and modern documents. Alphonse Roserot, *Dictionnaire topographique du département de la Haute-Marne*; idem, *Dictionnaire topographique du département de la Côte-d'Or*; Maximilien Quantin, *Dictionnaire topographique du département de l'Yonne*; Georges de Soultrait, *Dictionnaire topographique du département de la Nièvre*.

52. Compare the cartulary scribe's version of Wideradus's original charter with the Merovingian original itself; *Cartulary of Flavigny*, pp. 23, 137, nos. 1, 57.

53. See also Edward James, "Archaeology and the Merovingian Monastery," in *Columbanus and Merovingian Monasticism*, p. 47.

54. Jacques Harmand, *Alesia*.

55. Constantius of Lyon, *Vie de Saint Germain d'Auxerre* 4.22, ed. René Borius, p. 164. See also E. A. Thompson, *Saint Germanus of Auxerre and the End of Roman Britain*, p. 78.

56. J. Le Gall and J. Marilier, "L'apport d'Alésia à l'histoire du christianisme en Gaule du IVe au IXe siècle," in *La christianisation des pays entre Loire et Rhin*, ed. Riché, pp. 253–54. For parallels, see S. T. Loseby, "Marseille and the Pirenne Thesis, II: 'Ville morte,'" in *The Long Eighth Century*, pp. 167–93.

57. *Cartulary of Flavigny*, pp. 36–37, no. 5.

58. Ibid., pp. 69–72, 82–86, nos. 23, 28.

59. Ibid., pp. 50–52, 61–63, 82–86, nos. 14, 19, 28.

60. *The Cartulary of St.-Marcel*, ed. Bouchard, pp. 25–27, no. 4.

61. *Chartes et documents de Saint-Bénigne de Dijon*, ed. Georges Chevrier and Maurice Chaume, 1:67–68, 70–71, nos. 31, 36. St.-Bénigne has ten surviving eighth-century documents in its cartulary and a large number dating from after its restoration by Louis the Pious.

62. *Chronique de Saint-Bénigne*, ed. Bougaud and Garnier, p. 253.

63. *The Cartulary of Montier-en-Der*, ed. Bouchard, pp. 64–66, 334–37, nos. 7, 165. See also Josiane Barbier, "Rois et moines et Perthois pendant le haut moyen âge: A propos des

origines et du temporel de Montier-en-Der," in *Les moines du Der*, ed. Patrick Corbet, pp. 61–62.

64. Alain Dierkens, *Abbayes et chapitres entre Sambre et Meuse*, pp. 76, 318.

65. Hélène Noizet, "Le centre canonial de Saint-Martin de Tours et ses domaines péripheriques en val de Loire," pp. 12–16.

66. For these wars, see Ado of Vienne, "Chronicon," MGH SS 2:318–19; and, more generally, Gerberding, *The Rise of the Carolingians*, pp. 132–44.

67. Helena Hamerow, *Early Medieval Settlements*, pp. 86–88, 191–94; Wickham, *Framing the Early Middle Ages*, pp. 262–65, 280–92; Halsall, *Settlement and Social Organization*, pp. 276–78; Pierre Demolon, "Villes et villages dans le nord-est de la Neustrie du VIe au IXe siècle," in *La Neustrie*, 2:435–36.

68. Wickham, however, argues that demographic decline should be seen as a result of political crisis, not a cause of social change; *Framing the Early Middle Ages*, pp. 547–50.

69. McCormick, *Origins of the European Economy*, pp. 27–41; Georges Duby, *The Early Growth of the European Economy*, pp. 6–10.

70. *Chronicon Sancti Petri Vivi Senonensis* 503, in *Chronique de Saint-Pierre-le-Vif*, ed. Bautier and Gilles, p. 36; "Vita S. Balthildis" 9, MGH SSRM 2:493. See also Bouchard, "Queen Theuchildis of Sens."

71. McCormick, *Origins of the European Economy*, pp. 290–93.

72. Documents 1–2 of St.-Pierre, in *Chronique de Saint-Pierre-le-Vif*, pp. 239–43.

73. "Formulae Senonenses," in MGH Formulae, pp. 190–91, 198–99, nos. 14, 31. See also the comparison of texts in *Chronique de Saint-Pierre-le-Vif*, pp. 245–46.

74. *Cartulaire de l'Yonne*, ed. Quantin, 1:33–35, no. 17.

75. McCormick, *Origins of the European Economy*, pp. 308–9.

76. Prinz, *Frühes Mönchtum in Frankreich*, Map XII.C. Because the cut-off for this map is the year 690, it excludes such houses as Flavigny, founded in the first two decades of the eighth century, which might better belong in the earlier period, before the consolidation of Charles Martel's power.

77. Rudolf Schieffer, "Fulda, Abtei der Könige und Kaiser," in *Kloster Fulda in der Welt der Karolinger und Ottonen*, ed. Schrimpf, pp. 39–55.

78. Wampach, *Geschichte der Grundherrschaft Echternach im Frühmittelalter*, pp. 39–43, nos. 14–15. Also in MGH DD imperii, pp. 93–94, nos. 4–5; and in *Die Urkunden der Arnulfinger*, ed. Ingrid Heidrich, pp. 61–66, nos. 4–5. For the authenticity of these charters, see Heidrich, "Titular und Urkunden," pp. 238–39, nos. A3–4.

79. Heinrich Beyer, ed., *Urkundenbuch zur Geschichte der mittelrheinischen Territorien*, 1:10–11, no. 8; MGH DD Karolinorum 1:21–25, no. 16.

80. Hummer, *Politics and Power*, pp. 57–63, 102.

81. *Traditiones Wizenburgenses*, ed. Karl Glöckner and Anton Doll, pp. 185–87, nos. 10–11.

82. *Urkundenbuch der Abtei Sanct Gallen*. The St.-Gall documents fill the first two volumes of *ChLA*.

83. Stéphane Lebecq, "The Role of the Monasteries in the Systems of Production and

Exchange of the Frankish World Between the Seventh and the Beginning of the Ninth Centuries," in *The Long Eighth Century*, pp. 121–24; Bouchard, "Merovingian, Carolingian, and Cluniac Monasticism." An extreme example is the region of Hainaut, where no new monasteries were founded for close to three hundred years, from the seventh century to the first half of the tenth; Helvétius, *Abbayes, évêques et laïques*, pp. 290–91.

84. McKitterick, *Charlemagne*, p. 297.

85. *Gesta domni Aldrici*, ed. Charles and Froger, pp. 68, 73; also in *Geschichte des Bistums Le Mans*, ed. Weidemann, 1:136, 142. *Actus pontificum Cenomannis* ed. Busson and Ledru, p. 261; also in *Geschichte des Bistums Le Mans*, ed. Weidemann, 1:93.

86. J.-Gabriel Bulliot, *Essai historique sur l'abbaye de Saint-Martin d'Autun*, 2:22–24, no. 9.

87. *Monumenta Vizeliacensia*, ed. Huygens, 1:259–61, no. 4.

88. Barbara H. Rosenwein, *Rhinoceros Bound*; Bouchard, *"Those of My Blood,"* pp. 93–94.

89. Friedrich Prinz, "Schenkungen und Privilegien Karls des Grossen," in *KdG*, 1:488.

90. MGH DD imperii, pp. 94–95, no. 5; *Die Urkunden der Arnulfinger*, ed. Heidrich, pp. 64–66, no. 5; *Urkundenbuch des Klosters Fulda*, ed. Edmund E. Stengel, pp. 1–6, no. 4; *Das Prümer Urbar*, ed. Ingo Schwab, p. 180; *Cartulaire de l'abbaye de Gorze*, ed. A. d'Herbomez, pp. 1–4, no. 1. See also Rosenwein, *Negotiating Space*, pp. 102–3.

91. Paul the Deacon, "Gesta episcoporum Mettensium," MGH SS 2:267. For Chrodegang as a patron of reform, see M. A. Claussen, *The Reform of the Frankish Church*; and Eugen Ewig, *Spätantikes und fränkisches Gallien*, 2:220–59.

92. *Codex Laureshamensis*, ed. Karl Glöckner, 1:266. Claussen doubts, however, that Chrodegang was a relative; *Reform of the Frankish Church*, p. 22. For the relationship between Lorsch and Charlemagne's court, see Matthew Innes, "Kings, Monks and Patrons: Political Identities and the Abbey of Lorsch," in *La royauté et les élites*, ed. Le Jan, pp. 301–24.

93. *Codex Laureshamensis*, 1:267, no. 1; 1:270–71.

94. MGH Concilia 2:60–62. See Rosenwein's comparison of Chrodegang's privilege with the formulary for privileges developed in the Merovingian era; *Negotiating Space*, pp. 103–6, 221–24.

95. Bruckner, *Regesta Alsatiae aevi Merovingici et Karolini*, 1:97–100, no. 166. See also Rosenwein, *Negotiating Space*, pp. 105–6; and Ewig, *Spätantikes und fränkisches Gallien*, 2:224.

96. MGH DD Karolini 1:105–6, no. 72.

97. Wampach, *Geschichte der Grundherrschaft Echternach*, 2:4–5; MGH DD regum Germaniae ex stirpe Karolinorum 3:150–52, no. 103. By the next year Arnulf was asserting that his chaplain had been freely elected by the monks; ibid., pp. 162–63, no. 110.

98. Claussen, *Reform of the Frankish Church*, pp. 30–33.

99. Wilhelm Störmer, "Bischöfe von Langres aus Alemannien und Bayern," in *Langres et ses évêques*, pp. 45–47; Jean Marilier, "L'origine de quelques évêques de Langres aux VIIIe et IXe siècles," ibid., pp. 81–88; Bautier, *Chartes, sceaux et chancelleries*, pp. 209–42.

100. See also Geneviève Bührer-Thierry, "L'épiscopat en Francie orientale et occidentale à la fin du IXe siècle," in *La royauté et les élites*, pp. 347–64.

CHAPTER 10

1. Wickham, *Framing the Early Middle Ages*, p. 168. There are only one or two exceptions, and these are from Armenia.

2. Ulrich Nonn, "Merowingische Testamente"; Josiane Barbier, "La reine fait le roi: Une révision de la datation du 'testament de *Leodebodus*,'" in *Retour aux sources*, pp. 31–42.

3. Margarete Weidemann, *Das Testament des Bischofs Bertramn von Le Mans*, pp. 7–49, especially pp. 16, 24, 34, 36, 42. For the extent of his property, see the map on p. 84. See also Wickham, *Framing the Early Middle Ages*, pp. 186–87.

4. *Gesta*, 1:65–67.

5. *The Cartulary of Montier-en-Der*, ed. Bouchard, pp. 50–52, no. 3. See also Alain Dierkens, "La fondation et le premier siècle des monastères de Der," in *Les moines du Der*, ed. Patrick Corbet, pp. 27–44.

6. In the edition of Flavigny's cartulary, I identified St.-Férreol as being in Besançon; *Cartulary of Flavigny*, ed. Bouchard, p. 2. However, it seems more likely that this basilica was the heart of the monastic complex located at Grigny, on the west bank of the Rhône across from Vienne. See Ian Wood, "A Prelude to Columbanus: The Monastic Achievement in the Burgundian Territories," in *Columbanus and Merovingian Monasticism*, ed. H. B. Clarke and Mary Brown, p. 7. The bones of Saint Férreol were brought across the river into Vienne by Archbishop Wilicarius in 737, twenty years after Wideradus's testament; Ado of Vienne, "Chronicon," MGH SS 2:319.

7. Saint Praeiectus had been martyred in Clermont some two generations before Flavigny's foundation; see Fouracre and Gerberding, *Late Merovingian France*, pp. 254–70. According to the twelfth-century chronicler Hugh of Flavigny, the monastery translated his relics from Volvic in the second half of the eighth century; Hugh of Flavigny, *Chronicon*, MGH SS 8:351–52.

8. *Cartulary of Flavigny*, pp. 19–33, 135–44, nos. 1–2, 57–58.

9. Although there is no direct evidence, it is tempting to see him as related to the Abbot Wideradus of Ste.-Colombe of Sens who held office a generation later; "Consilium Attiniacense," MGH Concilia 2:73.

10. Josef Fleckenstein, "Fulrad von Saint-Denis und der fränkische Ausgriff in den süddeutschen Raum," in *Studien und Vorarbeiten zur Geschichte des grossfränkischen und frühdeutschen Adels*, ed. Gerd Tellenbach, pp. 9–39.

11. Geary, *Aristocracy in Provence*; for Abbo's family, see pp. 114–15.

12. "De SS. Prisco et Cotto aliisque plurimis martyribus," AASS May 6:364.

13. Jean Marie Pardessus, ed., *Diplomata, chartae, epistolae, leges*, 2:250–53, nos. 448–50. Although the document refers to itself as a *testamentum*, Nonn argues that it is not really

a testament but rather a donation *a die presente*; "Merowingische Testamente," p. 32. Once considered a later forgery, this document's authenticity is now generally accepted.

14. *ChLA* 592, 14:72–79. Also printed in Pardessus, *Diplomata, chartae*, 2:255–58, no. 452. For this testament, see Ulrich Nonn, "Erminethrud."

15. For the significance of these names, see Le Jan, *Femmes, pouvoir et société*, pp. 225–26.

16. *ChLA* 569, 13:80–89. Also printed in Pardessus, *Diplomata, chartae*, 2:211–12, no. 413. For Idda's son, see also Wickham, *Framing the Early Middle Ages*, p. 188. He draws no connection with Erminethrudis.

17. Franz Irsigler, "On the Aristocratic Character of Early Frankish Society," in *The Medieval Nobility*, ed. and trans. Timothy Reuter, pp. 105–36. The idea is dismissed by Karl Ferdinand Werner, "Important Noble Families in the Kingdom of Charlemagne: A Prosopographical Study of the Relationship Between King and Nobility in the Early Middle Ages," ibid., pp. 142–46.

18. Wickham, *Framing the Early Middle Ages*, pp. 168, 178–86. Hans J. Hummer argues that with the breakdown of urban culture, new rural aristocracies were established; *Politics and Power*, pp. 28–29.

19. The idea of ninth-century princes as "stem dukes," descendants of old clan leaders, was refuted by Gerd Tellenbach, *Königtum und Stamme in der Werdezeit des deutschen Reiches*, pp. 1, 22–29, 41, 74–84. Werner rejects the idea that the Merovingian-era aristocracy ended when the Carolingians replaced them with their own men; "Important Noble Families," pp. 146–49. See also Geary, *Aristocracy in Provence*, pp. 2–5; and John B. Freed, "Reflections on the Medieval German Nobility," pp. 573–75. Tremendously influential was J. Dhondt, *Etudes sur la naissance des principautés territoriales en France*. He called for regional studies, to show how individual principalities took on the identities they would maintain until the end of the ancien régime, a program that occupied French medievalists for the second half of the twentieth century.

20. Régine Hennibicque-Le Jan, "Prosopographica Neustrica: Les agents du roi en Neustrie de 639 à 840," in *La Neustrie*, ed. Atsma, 1:231–34.

21. Constance Brittain Bouchard, "The Carolingian Creation of a Model of Patrilineage," in *Paradigms and Methods*, ed. Chazelle and Lifshitz, pp. 135–51.

22. The basic studies of this group of relatives remain those of Franz Vollmer, "Die Etichonen: Ein Beitrag zur Frage der Kontinuität früher Adelsfamilien," in *Studien und Vorarbeiten zur Geschichte*, pp. 137–84; and Christian Wilsdorf, "Les Etichonides aux temps carolingiens et ottoniens." Although I do not draw the same conclusions as they do from the history of this group, and indeed disagree with much of Vollmer's reconstruction of the family tree, I am still indebted to their footnotes. See also Hummer, *Politics and Power*, pp. 46–55.

23. Ebling, *Prosopographie*, pp. 137–39, no. 156. Erchenoald appears as the *clarissimus* governor of the royal palace in the "Vita S. Balthildis," written perhaps a generation later; MGH SSRM 2:483–85.

24. Fredegar, *The Fourth Book* 46–47, 84, ed. Wallace-Hadrill, pp. 39, 46–47. The

somewhat later "Gesta Dagoberti" calls Dagobert's mother Bertetrudis; cap. 2, MGH SSRM 2:401. The question of her identity has, however, been debated by modern scholars; Wood, *The Merovingian Kingdoms*, p. 357.

25. An undated charter of St.-Denis speaks of the late Erchenoald, mayor of the palace, but does not specify any such office for his son, Leudesius; *ChLA* 557, 13:32–35. Ebling dates Leudesius's short reign as mayor of the palace to 675; *Prosopographie*, p. 181, no. 226.

26. *Liber Historiae Francorum* 45, MGH SSRM 2:317–19. See also Fredegar, *The Fourth Book* cont.2, pp. 80–81. For Liutsinda, see "Virtutes Fursei abbatis Latiniacensis" 20, MGH SSRM 4:447.

27. Fredegar, *The Fourth Book* 52, p. 43.

28. *Liber Historiae Francorum* 45, MGH SSRM 2:319; Fredegar, *The Fourth Book* cont.2, p. 82.

29. The thirteenth-century chronicle of Ebersheim made this identification; "Chronicon Ebersheimense" 4–5, MGH SS 23:434. Ebling does not make this connection; *Prosopographie*, pp. 33–37, no. 8.

30. Wilsdorf begins his study with Adalric, apparently not wishing to speculate on his descent from Erchenoald; "Les Etichonides," pp. 1–5. Hummer follows him; *Politics and Power*, pp. 46–47.

31. *ChLA* 674, 19:20–21; "Vita Odilae abbatissae Hohenburgensis" 1, MGH SSRM 6:37; MGH DD imperii, p. 43, no. 46; also in MGH DD regum Francorum e stirpe Merovingica, pp. 306–8, no. 120. Bobolenus, "Vita Germani abbatis Grandivallensis " 10, MGH SSRM 5:37; *Chronique de Saint-Bénigne*, ed. Bougaud and Garnier, p. 240. Werner doubts Adalricus's membership in the family that founded Bèze; "Important Noble Families," p. 158. Ebling makes the Adalricus in Bèze's chronicle someone else; *Prosopographie*, pp. 32–33, no. 7. Hummer makes this Adalricus the father of the Duke Adalricus whom he treats as the first of the Etichonids, even though the sources do not support making Adalricus into two people; *Politics and Power*, p. 47.

32. MGH DD Karolini 1:280–82, no. 210; "Chronicon Ebersheimense" 6, MGH SS 23:434. The chronicle goes on to say that Bersuindis was the sister of Childeric II's queen, but no scholar accepts this identification.

33. "Passio Leudegarii" 26, MGH SSRM 5:307. See also Fouracre and Gerberding, *Late Merovingian France*, p. 242, n. 192.

34. "Vita Odilae" 2, 19, pp. 38, 47; MGH DD imperii, pp. 84–86, no. 95; p. 106, no. 20; also in MGH DD regum Francorum e stirpe Merovingica, pp. 468–71, no. 188, called false. *Traditiones Wizenburgenses*, ed. Glöckner and Doll, pp. 185–86, no. 10; Pardessus, *Diplomata, chartae*, 2:337–38, nos. 524–25; 2:458, no. 55; Bruckner, *Regesta Alsatiae aevi Merovingici et Karolini*, 1:56, 189, nos. 113, 302.

35. *Traditiones Wizenburgenses*, pp. 173, 188, 214–25, nos. 2, 12, 35; *ChLA* 670, 19:2–4; Bruckner, *Regesta Alsatiae*, pp. 67–68, no. 127; "Annales Guelferbytani" 747, MGH SS 1:27; these annals are most likely from Murbach. For Liutfrid and Ebrohard, see also Ebling, *Prosopographie*, pp. 129–31, 182–84, nos. 148, 229.

36. Hummer argues for a much more extensive family tree for the early Etichonids,

based on a genealogy in a fifteenth-century cartulary from Honau; *Politics and Power*, pp. 53, 64. Even if one accepts that the monks of Honau were working from now-lost charters, one should note that this genealogy, concentrating on collateral branches, takes the family only one generation further and provides no connection to the ninth-century Etichonids.

37. Thegan, "Vita Hludowici imperatoris" 28, ed. Ernst Tremp, MGH SS rerum Germanicarum (1995), p. 216. For this biography, see, more broadly, Ernst Tremp, *Studien zu den Gesta Hludowici imperatoris des Trierer Chorbischofs Thegan*.

38. Einhard, *Annales* 811, MGH SS 1:198; MGH DD Karolinorum 1:274–75, no. 205; *Cartulaire de l'Yonne*, ed. Quantin, 1:30–31, no. 15. See also Depreux, *Prosopographie de l'entourage de Louis le Pieux*, pp. 262–64, no. 164.

39. Wilsdorf says rather airily that the Etichonids "reappeared on the scene" after sixty years; "Les Etichonides," p. 7. Vollmer, who attempts to demonstrate continuity of the lineage from the seventh century to the tenth, still recognizes that there is a major gap in the documentation in the second half of the eighth century; "Die Etichonen," pp. 147–54, 163. Even scholars who cite Vollmer uncritically discuss either the seventh- and early eighth-century Etichonids or the ninth-century Etichonids, but not both.

40. See also Régine Le Jan, *Famille et pouvoir dans le monde franc*, p. 42. Although Le Jan relies on Vollmer's work for the Etichonid family tree, she quietly eliminates all his seventh- and eighth-century family members and begins the lineage in the ninth century with Hugh of Tours, pp. 208–10.

41. Bouchard, "Carolingian Creation of Patrilineage," pp. 146–47.

42. Another example is provided by the ancestors of the dukes of Aquitaine and Septimania; Bouchard, *"Those of My Blood,"* pp. 185–88.

43. Richer, *Historia* 1.5, ed. Robert Latouche, 1:16. For Richer, see, most recently, Jason Glenn, *Politics and History in the Tenth Century*. See also Karl Ferdinand Werner, "Les premiers Robertiens et les premiers Anjou (IXe siècle–début Xe siècle)," in *Pays de Loire et Aquitaine de Robert le Fort aux premiers Capétiens*, ed. Olivier Guillot and Robert Favreau, pp. 10–12. I earlier discussed what comments such as Richer's reveal of high medieval beliefs about the origins of the nobility of the Carolingian era; Bouchard, *"Those of My Blood,"* pp. 14, 20. Strangely, some have misread me as subscribing to Richer's views.

44. *Recueil des actes de Charles le Chauve*, ed. Tessier, Giry, and Prou, 1:213, 388, nos. 75, 147. Philippe Baccou has made the argument, ingenious if not entirely convincing, that the Robert who held Marmoutier in the 850s and the Robert who was killed fighting the Vikings in 866 (i.e., Robert the Strong) were two different people; "Les débuts de Robert le Fort."

45. *Recueil des actes d'Eudes*, ed. Robert-Henri Bautier, p. 216, no. 55; *Recueil des actes de Robert Ier et de Raoul*, ed. Jean Dufour, p. 66, no. 15.

46. "Historia Francorum Senonensis" 750, 987, MGH SS 9:364, 368; "Hic defecit progenies Clodovei regis. . . . Hic deficit regnum Karoli Magni."

47. Bernd Schneidmüller, "Constructing the Past by Means of the Present: Historiographical Foundations of Medieval Institutions, Dynasties, People, and Communities," in *Medieval Concepts of the Past*, ed. Althoff, Fried, and Geary, pp. 168–74.

48. Werner, "Les premiers Robertiens," p. 14. The pioneering study was by K. Glöckner, "Lorsch und Lothringen, Robertiner und Capetinger."

49. MGH Capit 1:308; Einhard, "Epistolae" 7, MGH Epp. 5:112. Robert also appeared in 820 in a charter for Wissembourg, which Louis the Pious confirmed; *Traditiones Wizenburgenses*, pp. 270–71, no. 69. See also Hennibicque-Le Jan, "Prosopographica Neustrica," p. 254, no. 166; and Depreux, *Prosopographie de l'entourage de Louis le Pieux*, pp. 366–67, no. 235.

50. *Codex Laureshamensis*, ed. Glöckner, 2:467, no. 1826; Beyer, *Urkundenbuch zur Geschichte der mittelrheinischen Territorien*, 1:72–73, no. 64.

51. *Codex Laureshamensis*, 2:469, no. 1835; Regino of Prüm, *Chronicon* 892, ed. Friedrich Kurze, p. 140. Le Jan assumes without discussion that Megingoz was Robert the Strong's brother-in-law; *Famille et pouvoir*, pp. 185, 187. Matthew Innes prefers to leave the exact relationship unspecified; *State and Society in the Early Middle Ages*, pp. 217, 264.

52. Regino of Prüm, *Chronicon* 892, p. 139. According to Regino, Adelhelm had a son named Walter. *Adelelmus comes* is mentioned in a 864 charter of Charles the Bald as having been made rector of St.-Bavo of Ghent; *Recueil des actes de Charles le Chauve*, 2:116, no. 274. An eighth-century Adelhelm in Robert the Strong's ancestry, as indicated below, may suggest that this ninth-century count was his brother rather than brother-in-law. Eduoard de Saint-Phalle makes him a half brother, son of the same father; "Comtes de Troyes et de Poitiers au IXe siècle: Histoire d'un double échec," in *Onomastique et parenté dans l'Occident médiéval*, ed. Keats-Rohan and Settipani, pp. 154–70.

53. Glöckner, "Lorsch," p. 307, is followed by Le Jan, *Famille et pouvoir*, p. 440. Werner is vaguer about how all the various "Rupertiners" were related; "Les premiers Robertiens," pp. 17–18.

54. *Codex Laureshamensis*, 2:3–4, 423, nos. 167–68, 1541. The name Cancor is very unusual. A count with this name appears a generation earlier in the documents of St.-Gall; *Urkundenbuch der Abtei Sanct Gallen*, ed. Hermann Wartmann, 1:13, no. 11. The bishop of Würzburg in the mid-eighth century was named Megingoz, which may or may not be significant; he attended the 760/2 Council of Attigny. "Consilium Attiniacense," MGH Concilia 2:73. A Megingoz, perhaps the same, was bishop of an unidentified see, probably in or near Alsace, in 748; Pardessus, *Diplomata, chartae*, 2:411, no. 596.

55. *Codex Laureshamensis*, 1:267–68, no. 1. For the necrology, ibid., 1:265, n. 4.

56. *Codex Laureshamensis*, 1:266.

57. Werner, "Les premiers Robertiens," p. 18. See also Matthew Innes, "Kings, Monks and Patrons: Political Identities and the Abbey of Lorsch," in *La royauté et les élites*, pp. 301–24.

58. Paul the Deacon, "Gesta episcoporum Mettensium," MGH SS 2:267. The story that Landrada was sister of Pippin the Short dates only from the tenth century and has not received much credence; "Vita Chrodegangi episcopi Mettensis," MGH SS 10:556.

59. Eugen Ewig suggests that Chrodegang's mother, Landrada, could have been sister of Cancor's father, Robert, seeing the name element *Land-* as evoking Lambert; *Spätantikes und fränkisches Gallien*, 2:234–35.

60. Pardessus, *Diplomata, chartae*, 2:379, no. 562; "Vita Eucherii episcopi Aurelianensis," MGH SSRM 7:50; "Annales Alamannici" 748, MGH SS 1:26. See also Ebling, *Prosopographie*, pp. 116–17, no. 129.

61. MGH DD imperii, pp. 214–15, no. 7; also in *Die Urkunden der Arnulfinger*, ed. Heidrich, p. 74, no. 8. Although long considered a forgery, this document is now considered authentic, if somewhat reworked; Heidrich, "Titular und Urkunden," pp. 251–52, no. A Metz 4.

62. *ChLA* 589, 14:65. Although I identify him with the other Roberts who acted during the mayorship of Charles Martel, other scholars usually identify him rather with the *referendarius* of a quarter century earlier; see, for example, Hennibicque-Le Jan, "Prosopographica Neustrica," p. 254, no. 164.

63. MGH DD imperii, p. 99, no. 11; also in *Die Urkunden der Arnulfinger*, ed. Heidrich, p. 86, no. 12. *Chronique de Fontenelle* 3.5, ed. Pradié, p. 54. See also Ebling, *Prosopographie*, pp. 115–16, no. 128.

64. "Vita Hrodberti episcopi Salisburgensis," MGH SSRM 6:157–62.

65. *ChLA* 576, 14:12.

66. Pardessus, *Diplomata, chartae*, 2:131, no. 348. Also in *Chronique de Saint-Bénigne*, p. 242. "Vita Lantberti abbatis Fontanellensis" 1, MGH SSRM 5:608. See also Ebling, *Prosopographie*, p. 115, no. 127; and Hennibicque-Le Jan, "Prosopographica Neustrica," p. 254, no. 162.

67. Aigradus, "Vita Ansberti episcopi Rotomagensis" 2, MGH SSRM 5:620–21. For the dates of the *vitae* of Lambert and Ansbert, see Lifshitz, *The Norman Conquest of Pious Neustria*, pp. 42–43.

68. *ChLA* 674, 19:20–21; "Passio Leudegarii" 33, MGH SSRM 5:315. Ebling, however, distinguishes the count of the palace of the 670s from the contemporary count of Alsace; *Prosopographie*, pp. 113–15, nos. 125–26.

69. "Vita S. Balthildis" 5, MGH SSRM 2:487. See also Martin Heinzelmann, "L'aristocratie et les évêchés entre Loire et Rhin jusqu'à la fin du VIIe siècle," in *La christianisation des pays entre Loire et Rhin*, ed. Riché, p. 83.

70. MGH DD imperii, p. 15, no. 13, also in MGH DD regum Francorum e stirpe Merovingica, pp. 101–4, no. 38; Fredegar, *The Fourth Book* 68, p. 57.

71. MGH DD imperii, p. 106, no. 21; also in *Die Urkunden der Arnulfinger*, ed. Heidrich, p. 110, no. 21. Clothar's document is *ChLA* 552, 13:16–19; also in MGH DD imperii, p. 13, no. 10; and MGH DD regum Francorum e stirpe Merovingica, pp. 75–77, no. 28. Ebling does not identify the duke who fought the Wends with any of the other Roberts of the 620s; *Prospographie*, p. 112, no. 122.

72. Ingrid Heidrich, "Maires du palais, agents du roi, abbés," in *La Neustrie*, 1:217–18.

73. Hennibicque-Le Jan, "Prosopographica Neustrica," p. 233.

74. Eduard Hlawitschka, "Die Vorfahren Karls des Grossen," in *KdG*, 1:51–82; Karl Ferdinand Werner, "Die Nachkommen Karls des Großen bis um das Jahr 1000 (1.–8. Generation)," in *KdG*, 4:403–82.

CHAPTER 11

1. Of course, there has never been a generally accepted definition of what is "true Christianity," and in the sixth century as the twenty-first, one person's Christianity is another's paganism. Lifshitz, *The Norman Conquest of Pious Neustria*, pp. 1–11; R. A. Markus, *Gregory the Great and His World*, pp. 80–82; Brown, *Through the Eye of a Needle*.

2. Daniel Caner, *Wandering, Begging Monks*; Peter Brown, *Authority and the Sacred*, pp. 50–51.

3. Jean Heuclin, *Aux origines monastiques de la Gaule du Nord*, pp. 91–96.

4. Council of Chalcedon, canons 4, 8, Mansi 7:374–75; Rosenwein, *Negotiating Space*, pp. 32–36.

5. Farmer, *Communities of Saint Martin*, pp. 13–16.

6. Marilyn Dunn, *The Emergence of Monasticism from the Desert Fathers to the Early Middle Ages*, pp. 82–84; Elie Griffe, *La Gaule chrétienne à l'époque romaine*, 3:332–41.

7. Prinz, *Frühes Mönchtum in Frankreich*, pp. 88–117; Barbara H. Rosenwein, "One Site, Many Meanings: Saint-Maurice d'Agaune as a Place of Power in the Early Middle Ages," in *Topographies of Power*, ed. de Jong and Theuws, pp. 273–77; Brown, *Through the Eye of a Needle*, pp. 411–32.

8. Klingshirn, *Caesarius of Arles: The Making of a Christian Community*, pp. 22–23. See also Bouchard, "Reconstructing Sanctity and Refiguring Saints in Early Medieval Gaul," pp. 102–5.

9. Jacques Biarne, "État du monachisme en Gaule à la fin du Ve siècle," in *Clovis*, ed. Rouche, 1:115–26; Brown, *The Rise of Western Christendom*, pp. 220–21.

10. Wood, *The Merovingian Kingdoms*, pp. 181–89; Frederick S. Paxton, "Power and the Power to Heal," pp. 101–6; Régine Le Jan, "Convents, Violence, and Competition for Power in Seventh-Century Francia," in *Topographies of Power*, pp. 243–44; Karl Ferdinand Werner, "Le rôle de l'aristocratie dans la christianisation du nord de la Gaule," in *La christianisation des pays entre Loire et Rhin*, ed. Riché, pp. 63–72; Wood, *The Proprietary Church*, p. 111.

11. Jean-Charles Picard, "Les églises d'Auxerre au temps de Saint Germain (418–448?)," in *Saint Germain d'Auxerre*, p. 3.

12. Similarly, in Hainaut the first monastic foundations date to the middle of the seventh century; Helvétius, *Abbayes, évêques et laïques*, pp. 54–59.

13. Geary, *Living with the Dead in the Middle Ages*, pp. 36–39; Bailey Young, "Sacred Topography: The Impact of the Funerary Basilica in Late Antique Gaul," in *Society and Culture in Late Antique Gaul*, ed. Ralph W. Mathisen and Danuta Shanzer, pp. 171–80.

14. Hartmut Atsma, "Klöster und Mönchtum im Bistum Auxerre," pp. 13–14; Wood, *The Proprietary Church*, p. 109.

15. Bonnie Effros, "Monuments and Memory: Repossessing Ancient Remains in Early Medieval Gaul," in *Topographies of Power*, pp. 93–94; Biarne, "État du monachisme," p. 120; Brown, *The Rise of Western Christendom*, pp. 222–23.

16. Bishop Aunarius included them all in his liturgical institutes at the end of the

century; *Gesta*, 1:71–77. See also Bouchard, "Episcopal *Gesta* and the Creation of a Useful Past," pp. 25–27, 32.

17. Jean-Charles Picard, "Les églises d'Auxerre à la fin du VIe siècle," in *Saint Germain d'Auxerre*, p. 7.

18. Diem, "Monks, Kings, and the Transformation of Sanctity."

19. MGH DD imperii, pp. 125–26, spuria no. 9; also in MGH DD regum Francorum e stirpe Merovingica, pp. 47–49, no. 15.

20. Julia M. H. Smith, "Women at the Tomb: Access to Relic Shrines in the Early Middle Ages," in *The World of Gregory of Tours*, ed. Mitchell and Wood, pp. 163–80; Prinz, *Frühes Mönchtum*, pp. 157–58; Elizabeth A. Clark, "Claims on the Bones of Saint Stephen," p. 141.

21. Gregory of Tours, *Liber in gloria martyrum* 50, MGH SSRM 1/2:72–73.

22. Gregory of Tours, *Hist* 9.39, 9.42, pp. 460–63, 470–74. For Radegund, see also Bouchard, "Reconstructing Sanctity and Refiguring Saints in Early Medieval Gaul," pp. 105–9.

23. Pardessus, *Diplomata, chartae*, 1:107, no. 140; Ado of Vienne, "Chronicon" 575, MGH SS 2:317; Werner, "Le rôle de l'aristocratie," p. 63.

24. Fredegar, *The Fourth Book* 1, 14, ed. Wallace-Hadrill, pp. 4, 10. Wallace-Hadrill incorrectly translates *Sequanum*, "Saône," as "Seine."

25. *The Cartulary of St.-Marcel*, ed. Bouchard, pp. 31–32, no. 7.

26. Remensnyder, *Remembering Kings Past*, pp. 100–103, 116–49.

27. Gregory of Tours, *Liber in gloria martyrum* 52, MGH SSRM 1/2:75. A few years before the establishment of a monastery at St.-Marcel, King Guntram had held a synod there; Gregory of Tours, *Hist* 5.27, p. 233.

28. William E. Klingshirn, *Caesarius of Arles: Life, Testament, Letters*, pp. 10–11.

29. Fredegar, *The Fourth Book* 1, p. 10; Gregory of Tours, *Hist* 3.5, p. 100; Barbara H. Rosenwein, "Perennial Prayer at Agaune," in *Monks and Nuns, Saints and Outcasts*, ed. Farmer and Rosenwein, pp. 37–56.

30. Marius of Avenches, *La Chronique* 574, ed. Justin Favrod, p. 84. Marius says that a "Frankish army" defeated the Lombards. Fredegar, who wrote a century later, adds the detail that Guntram killed the Lombard leaders; *Chronica* 3.68, MGH SSRM 2:111. See also Paxton, "Power and the Power to Heal," p. 107.

31. Nelson, *Politics and Ritual in Early Medieval Europe*, pp. 31–43; Heuclin, *Hommes de Dieu et fonctionnaires du roi*, pp. 159–62; Wemple, *Women in Frankish Society*, pp. 67–69.

32. "Vita S. Balthildis" 9, MGH SSRM 2:493. The editor mistakenly identifies St.-Germain of Auxerre as St.-Germain-des-Prés (Paris).

33. Her chemise is still preserved in a reliquary at Chelles; Janet L. Nelson, "Gendering Courts in the Early Medieval West," in *Gender in the Early Medieval World*, ed. Brubaker and Smith, pp. 188–89.

34. Wood assumes "senior basilicas" meant churches that had received large endowments from the Merovingian kings; *The Proprietary Church*, pp. 221–22.

35. For the spike in foundations of nunneries in the seventh century, see Bruce L. Venarde, *Women's Monasticism and Medieval Society*, p. 8.

36. Bouchard, "Merovingian, Carolingian, and Cluniac Monasticism," p. 368. In Champagne, two-thirds of the monasteries in existence in the year 1000 were founded before 700; Jackie Lusse, "Le monachisme en Champagne," p. 25. Hartmut Atsma estimates that more than eight hundred monasteries had been founded in Gaul before 751, two-thirds of them in the century and a half preceding Pippin's coronation; "Les monastères urbains du nord de la Gaule," in *La christianisation des pays entre Loire et Rhin*, pp. 165, n. 6, 168.

37. Lucien Musset, "Monachisme d'époque franque et monachisme d'époque ducale en Normandie: Le problème de la continuité," in *Aspects du monachisme en Normandie*, ed. Musset, pp. 55–74; Lifshitz, *The Norman Conquest of Pious Neustria*, pp. 100–136; Herrick, *Imagining the Sacred Past*.

38. Atsma, "Les monastères urbains," p. 183; Prinz, *Frühes Mönchtum*, Map XII.A–C.

39. *Chronique de Saint-Bénigne*, ed. Bougaud and Garnier, pp. 243–45. Also in MGH DD imperii, pp. 39–41, nos. 42–43; and in MGH DD regum Francorum e stirpe Merovingica, pp. 234–37, 273–75, nos. 91, 106.

40. Ebling, *Prosopographie*, pp. 112–13, no. 123. See also Wood, *The Proprietary Church*, p. 136.

41. Rosenwein, *Negotiating Space*, pp. 62–63; Friedrich Prinz, "Der fränkische Episkopat zwischen Merowinger- und Karolingerzeit," in *Nascita dell'Europa ed Europa carolingia*, 1:105–6.

42. "Vita Audoini episcopi Rotomagensis" 5, MGH SSRM 5:556–57. The biographer wrote within a generation or so of the bishop's death; Fouracre and Gerberding, *Late Merovingian France*, p. 133.

43. Wampach, *Geschichte der Grundherrschaft Echternach*, vol. 2, *Quellenband*, pp. 19–20, no. 3. Also in Pardessus, *Diplomata, chartae*, 2:250–52, nos. 448–49. See also Ian Wood, "Teutsind, Witlaic and the History of Merovingian *Precaria*," in *Property and Power in the Early Middle Ages*, ed. Davies and Fouracre, pp. 32–33.

44. Venantius Fortunatus, "Vita Sancti Paterni" 3–9, MGH AA 4/2:34–35.

45. David Ganz, "The Ideal of Sharing: Apostolic Community and Ecclesiastical Property in the Early Middle Ages," in *Property and Power*, pp. 17–30; Caner, *Wandering, Begging Monks*, p. 2; Brown, *Through the Eye of a Needle*, pp. 498–502.

46. Aigradus, "Vita Ansberti episcopi Rotomagensis" 6, MGH SSRM 5:622–23; Jerome, Letter 125.15, ed. Jérôme Labourt, *Lettres*, vol. 7 (Paris, 1961), p. 127.

47. Sidonius Apollinaris, Letter 3.1, *Poems and Letters*, ed. W. B. Anderson, 2:2–6.

48. Philippe Jobert, *La notion de donation*, pp. 205–25; Arnoud-Jan A. Bijsterveld, "The Medieval Gift as Agent of Social Bonding and Political Power: A Comparative Approach," in *Medieval Transformations*, ed. Cohen and de Jong, pp. 128–29; Brown, *The Rise of Western Christendom*, pp. 226–27; Florin Curta, "Merovingian and Carolingian Gift Giving," p. 674. Arnold Angenendt argues that Irish influence was crucial; "*Pro vivis et defunctis*: Histoire et influence d'une oraison de messe," in *Retour aux sources*, pp. 563–71; idem,

"*Donationes pro anima:* Gift and Countergift in the Early Medieval Liturgy," in *The Long Morning of Medieval Europe,* ed. Davis and McCormick, pp. 135–41.

49. Yitzhak Hen, "The Christianisation of Kingship," in *Der Dynastiewechsel von 751,* ed. Becher and Jarnut, pp. 168–72.

50. Gregory of Tours, *Hist* 8.30, p. 395. See also Chris Wickham, "Topographies of Power," in *Topographies of Power,* pp. 1–8; and Hervé Oudart, "Le roi franc et l'idée de justice aux époques mérovingienne et carolingienne," in *Le monde carolingien,* ed. Wojciech Falkowski and Yves Sassier, pp. 59–60.

51. Gregory of Tours, *Hist* 5.14, pp. 207–9.

52. Gregory of Tours, *Hist* 6.46, pp. 319–21.

53. Gregory of Tours, *Hist* 5.47, p. 257.

54. Guy Halsall, "Nero and Herod? The Death of Chilperic and Gregory's Writing of History," in *The World of Gregory of Tours,* pp. 337–50; Goffart, *The Narrators of Barbarian History,* pp. 223–24. See also Edward James, *The Franks,* pp. 165–68.

55. Jonas of Bobbio, "Vita Columbani" 1.18–19, MGH SSRM 4:86–87; Fredegar, *The Fourth Book* 36, pp. 23–26. See also Rosenwein, *Negotiating Space,* pp. 70–72.

56. Jonas of Bobbio, "Vita Columbani" 1.19, pp. 88–89; Fredegar, *The Fourth Book* 36, pp. 25–28. See also Diem, "Monks, Kings," pp. 531–35.

57. *Liber Historiae Francorum* 32, MGH SSRM 2:296. See also Gerberding, *The Rise of the Carolingians,* p. 155.

58. Clovis had ordained how churches were to use the money saved by such royal immunities from fees: for the upkeep of priests and the poor or for redemption of captives. 511 Council of Orléans, *Concilia Galliae, A. 511–A. 695,* ed. de Clercq, p. 6, no. 5.

59. *Codice diplomatico del monasterio di S. Colombano di Bobbio,* ed. Carlo Cipolla, 1:100–103, no. 10. This exemption is also mentioned by Jonas of Bobbio, "Vita Columbani" 2.23, p. 145.

60. For the distinction between Roman immunities from taxes and exemptions against entry, see Rosenwein, *Negotiating Space,* pp. 27–32. Elisabeth Magnou-Nortier, in contrast, treats them together; "Remarques sur la genèse du *Pactus Legis Salicae* et sur le privilège d'immunité," in *Clovis,* 1:513–35.

61. The royal and episcopal privileges for Rebais are edited by V. Leblond and Maurice Lecomte, *Les privilèges de l'abbaye de Rebais-en-Brie,* pp. 51–56, nos. 1–2. The first is also in MGH DD imperii, pp. 16–18, no. 15, and MGH DD regum Francorum e stirpe Merovingica, pp. 126–28, no. 49, called false; the second is also in Pardessus, *Diplomata, chartae,* 2:39–41, no. 275. See Eugen Ewig, *Spätantikes und fränkisches Gallien,* 2:456–76; and Rosenwein, *Negotiating Space,* pp. 66–70.

62. "Marculfi formulae" 1.1–2, MGH Formulae, pp. 39–43. It is often argued that the Rebais exemptions must have been based on the formulary of Marculf and thus cannot date to the 630s, before Marculf worked; see, for example, Rio, *Legal Practice and the Written Word,* pp. 83–84, nn. But the Marculf formulary was not created out of thin air; it seems much more likely that it was based on the model of the Rebais privileges (both episcopal and royal).

63. *The Cartulary of Montier-en-Der*, ed. Bouchard, pp. 341–42, no. 167. The privilege for Luxeuil is known only from this cartulary; the founding abbot of Der, Bercharius, had spent time at Luxeuil. Because the manuscript version breaks off in the middle of a sentence, earlier printed versions added material from later privileges (from as late as the eleventh century), making them unreliable witnesses to the seventh century.

64. For St.-Denis, see Pardessus, *Diplomata, chartae*, 2:95–97, no. 320. This privilege, known only from later copies, is assumed to have been reworked, but the confirmation by King Clovis II still exists; *ChLA* 558, 13:36–37. For the privileges at Sens, see *Cartulaire de l'Yonne*, ed. Quantin, 1:10–17, nos. 6–7. For Corbie, see Pardessus, *Diplomata, chartae*, 2:126–28, no. 345; and MGH DD imperii, p. 35, no. 38; also in MGH DD regum Francorum e stirpe Merovingica, pp. 246–48, no. 96.

65. "Vita S. Balthildis" 9, p. 493.

66. Pardessus, *Diplomata, chartae*, 2:128–29, no. 346; *ChLA* 570, 579, 13:90–91, 14:23; *The Cartulary of Montier-en-Der*, pp. 52–58, no. 4. See also Rosenwein, *Negotiating Space*, pp. 81–96; and Alain Dierkens, "La fondation et le premier siècle des monastères du Der," in *Les moines du Der*, ed. Corbet, pp. 35–44.

67. Scholars have categorically distinguished between a *grosse Freiheit*, which included the monks' freedom to seek consecration from whatever bishop they wanted, and a *kleine Freiheit*, which lacked this aspect. Ewig, *Spätantikes und fränkisches Gallien*, 2:418–20; Rosenwein, *Negotiating Space*, pp. 35–36. Such categories seem overly restrictive; no one in the seventh century spoke of monasteries receiving "greater" or "lesser" privileges.

68. Rosenwein, *Negotiating Space*, pp. 64–67. For the older view, see Wallace-Hadrill, *Frankish Church*, p. 66; and Nancy Gauthier, "Le reseau de pouvoirs de l'évêque dans la Gaule du haut moyen-âge," in *Towns and Their Territories Between Late Antiquity and the Early Middle Ages*, ed. Brogiolo, Gauthier, and Christie, pp. 181–82.

69. Rosenwein, *Negotiating Space*, p. 81.

70. Council of Carthage, in *Concilia Africae, A. 345–A. 525*, ed. C. Munier, pp. 280–81. Augustine's "Sermones" 355 and 356 are both headed, "De vita et moribus clericorum," PL 39:1568–81. Their content was the necessity of monks giving away their property and living in common, like the original Apostles.

71. *Cartulaire de l'Yonne*, 1:10–13, no. 6.

72. Rosenwein, *Negotiating Space*, pp. 32–35; eadem, "Inaccessible Cloisters: Gregory of Tours and Episcopal Exemption," in *The World of Gregory of Tours*, pp. 181–82.

73. "Marculfi formulae" 1.1, p. 39.

74. Jonas, "Vita Columbani" 1.26, p. 100; Rosenwein, *Negotiating Space*, pp. 70–72.

75. Council of Arles, *Concilia Galliae, A. 314–A. 506*, ed. C. Munier, pp. 131–34. For this quarrel, see Ralph W. Mathisen, *Ecclesiastical Factionalism and Religious Controversy in Fifth-Century Gaul*, pp. 193–98.

76. Council of Valence, *Concilia Galliae*, ed. de Clercq, p. 235. See also Rosenwein,

Negotiating Space, pp. 42–52. Pope Gregory I used similar language some twenty years later in privileges for three churches at Autun, saying no bishop or royal power should dare to take any of the possessions Queen Brunhildis had given; *Registrum epistolarum* 13.9–11, ed. Dag Norberg, 2:1004–11.

77. Rosenwein, "One Site, Many Meanings," pp. 272–77.

78. Fredegar's account of the council says that St.-Marcel was established following the *instar* of Agaune's institutions; *The Fourth Book* 1, p. 4.

CHAPTER 12

1. Diem, "Monks, Kings," p. 559; Peter Brown, *The Cult of the Saints,* pp. 1–24.

2. Raymond Van Dam, *Saints and Their Miracles in Late Antique Gaul,* pp. 116–47.

3. Elizabeth A. Clark, "Claims on the Bones of Saint Stephen"; R. A. Markus, *The End of Ancient Christianity,* pp. 98–99, 148–49; Alan Thacker, "*Loca sanctorum*: The Significance of Place in the Study of the Saints," in *Local Saints and Local Churches in the Medieval West,* ed. Alan Thacker and Richard Sharpe, pp. 12–14.

4. Marianne Sághy, "*Scinditur in partes populus.*" More broadly, see Candida Moss, *The Myth of Persecution.*

5. Sulpicius Severus, *Vita Sancti Martini,* ed. Jacques Fontaine; Van Dam, "Images of Saint Martin in Late Roman and Early Merovingian Gaul."

6. Bouchard, "Reconstructing Sanctity and Refiguring Saints in Early Medieval Gaul"; Coon, *Sacred Fictions,* pp. xv–xvi. For Genovefa, see, most recently, Lisa M. Bitel, *Landscape with Two Saints,* pp. 3–96.

7. Sulpicius Severus, *Chroniques* 32.1, ed. Ghislaine de Senneville-Grave, p. 298.

8. AASS Aug. 4:491–98. For the date of the *vita,* see Wolfert S. van Egmond, *Conversing with the Saints,* p. 83.

9. Gregory of Tours, *Hist* 2.15, p. 64; *Concilia Galliae, A. 511–A. 695,* ed. de Clercq, p. 235.

10. Gislemarus, "Vita Droctovei abbatis Parisiensis," MGH SSRM 3:539.

11. Jones and Martindale, *The Prosopography of the Later Roman Empire,* 2:115–18; Henry Chadwick, *The Church in Ancient Society,* pp. 642–46. Later, in the tenth century, Sidonius's own city of Clermont had churches and altars dedicated to nearly a hundred saints; Ian Wood, "Constructing Cults in Early Medieval France: Local Saints and Churches in Burgundy and the Auvergne, 400–1000," in *Local Saints,* p. 165.

12. Raymond Van Dam, *Leadership and Community in Late Antique Gaul,* pp. 157–65; J. D. Harries, "Sidonius Apollinaris, Rome and the Barbarians: A Climate of Treason?" in *Fifth-Century Gaul,* ed. Drinkwater and Elton, pp. 298–308.

13. Sidonius Apollinaris, Letters 2.8, 3.12, in *Poems and Letters,* ed. W. B. Anderson, 1:446–48, 2:40–46. For funerary inscriptions, see also Barbara H. Rosenwein, *Emotional Communities in the Early Middle Ages,* pp. 57–78.

14. Sidonius Apollinaris, Letter 1.1, 1:330. For the uneasy dead, see Constantius of Lyon, *Vie de Saint Germain d'Auxerre* 2.10, ed. René Borius, pp. 138–42.

15. Wood, "Constructing Cults," p. 155; Felice Lifshitz, "The Martyr, the Tomb, and the Matron: Constructing the (Masculine) 'Past' as a Female Power Base," in *Medieval Concepts of the Past*, ed. Althoff, Fried, and Geary, pp. 311–17; Van Dam, *Leadership and Community*, pp. 165–72.

16. See also Head, *Hagiography and the Cult of Saints*, pp. 1–2.

17. "Deeds" of saints may have been systematically assembled for the first time in this period; the sixth-century *Liber Pontificalis* said third-century popes collected such *gesta*, but Gregory the Great at the end of the century could not find such a collection. Barbara H. Rosenwein, "*In gestis emendatioribus*: Gregory the Great and the *Gesta martyrum*," in *Retour aux sources*, pp. 842–48.

18. Joseph van der Straeten, "Les actes des martyrs d'Aurélien en Bourgogne." This article includes both an edition of the "Acta" and an extensive commentary. See also Wood, "Constructing Cults," pp. 155–56, 162.

19. Jones and Martindale, *The Prosopography of the Later Roman Empire*, 3:491–92.

20. Privatus never developed much of a cult. Gregory of Tours, however, mentioned him in his *vita* of Saint Julien as a saint especially feared by demons; *Liber de virtutibus S. Iuliani* 30, MGH SSRM 1/2:126.

21. MGH AA 4/1:185, no. 8.3.

22. Arnold Angenendt assumes the importance of relics from the second century on; "Relics and Their Veneration in the Middle Ages," in *The Invention of Saintliness*, ed. Mulder-Bakker, pp. 29–32. Michael McCormick's discussion of the relic trade takes their frequency in the Carolingian period as the early medieval norm; *Origins of the European Economy*, pp. 283–90.

23. Brown, *Cult of the Saints*, p. 9.

24. Sulpicius Severus, *Chroniques* 32.2, 34.1–2, pp. 298, 302–4.

25. Castelli, *Martyrdom and Memory*.

26. Gillian Clark, "Translating Relics"; Thacker, "*Loca sanctorum*," pp. 5–12.

27. Augustine, *Sermones* 336.1, 337.2, PL 38:1471, 1476; Markus, *The End of Ancient Christianity*, pp. 139–45; Peter Brown, "Enjoying the Saints in Late Antiquity"; idem, *Cult of the Saints*, pp. 36–37; Clark, "Translating Relics," p. 174.

28. Caroline Walker Bynum, *The Resurrection of the Body in Western Christianity*, pp. 104–6.

29. Victricius of Rouen, "De laude sanctorum," ed. J[acques] Mulders and R. Demeulenaere.

30. Clark, "Translating Relics," pp. 174–76; Bynum, *Resurrection of the Body*, pp. 107–8.

31. *Gesta*, 1:39, 47; Bouchard, "Episcopal *Gesta* and the Creation of a Useful Past," p. 16.

32. René Louis, "L'église d'Auxerre et ses évêques avant Saint Germain," in *Saint Germain d'Auxerre et son temps*, ed. Société des sciences historiques et naturelles de l'Yonne, pp.

45–49; Jean-Charles Picard, "Espace urbain et sépultures épiscopales à Auxerre," in *La chris-tianisation des pays entre Loire et Rhin*, ed. Riché, pp. 206–12; Richard Burgess, "The Gallic Chronicle of 452: A New Critical Introduction with a Brief Introduction," in *Society and Culture in Late Antique Gaul*, ed. Mathisen and Shanzer, pp. 67, 68, 72, 78.

33. Sidonius Apollinaris, Letter 7.1, 2:286–92.

34. Picard, "Espace urbain et sépultures épiscopales," pp. 205–22. Similarly at Reims, the old Roman cemetery received the bodies of numerous Christians, over which a cluster of churches was built, less than a kilometer beyond the city walls. Walter Berry and Robert Neiss, "La découverte du baptistère paléochrétien de Reims," in *Clovis*, ed. Rouche, 2:870–71.

35. Stephen Africanus, "Vita S. Amatoris Autissiodorensis episcopi" 3.21, 5.32, ed. L.-M. Duru, *Bibliothèque historique de l'Yonne*, 1:150, 157.

36. The account of the conversion of Mamertinus was inserted into the earlier *vita* of Germanus; ed. Duru, *Bibliothèque historique*, 1:59–63. See also Louis, "L'église d'Auxerre," pp. 70–74.

37. The Auxerre connection was stressed much more in the sixth-century version of the *vita* of Germanus than in the original, fifth-century version; van Egmond, *Conversing with the Saints*, p. 119.

38. See also Michel Sot, "Organisation de l'espace et historiographie épiscopale dans quelques cités de la Gaule carolingienne," in *Le métier d'historien au moyen âge*, ed. Bernard Guenée, pp. 36–37; and Noëlle Deflou-Leca, *Saint-Germain d'Auxerre et ses dépendances*, pp. 62–67.

39. The traditional date of 177 is open to question; T. D. Barnes, "Eusebius and the Date of the Martyrdom," in *Les martyrs de Lyon*, pp. 137–43.

40. R. M. Grant, "Eusebius and the Martyrs of Gaul," in *Les martyrs de Lyon*, pp. 130–31; Griffe, *La Gaule chrétienne à l'époque romaine*, 1:27–43. Eusebius's account was known in the west through Rufinus's somewhat reworked Latin version, AASS June 1:157–63. Louis Neyrand, "Le récit de la passion des martyrs de Lyon dans la traduction de Rufin," in *Les martyrs de Lyon*, pp. 289–97.

41. Eusebius Gallicanus, *Collectio Homiliarum* 11, ed. Iohannes Leroy, p. 134. Griffe argues that "Eusebius Gallicanus" should be identified with Bishop Faustus of Riez, a con-temporary of Sidonius; *La Gaule chrétienne*, 1:323–35.

42. Some of the names may in fact have been *cognomina*, not recognized as such in a period when the single name was rapidly becoming the rule; for example, Pomponia Rhodana as a single name is more plausible than one woman being named Pomponia and another named for the river. See also Garth Thomas, "La condition sociale de l'Eglise de Lyon en 177," in *Les martyrs de Lyon*, p. 97.

43. Gregory of Tours, *Liber in gloria martyrum* 48, pp. 71–72.

44. Conrad Leyser, "The Temptations of Cult."

45. Kathleen Mitchell, "Marking the Bounds: The Distant Past in Gregory's History," in *The World of Gregory of Tours*, pp. 298–99.

46. *Gesta*, 1:69–71; Bouchard, "Episcopal *Gesta* and the Creation of a Useful Past," pp. 25–27.

47. "Vita Audoini episcopi Rotomagensis" 6, MGH SSRM 5:557. For the date, see Lifshitz, *The Norman Conquest of Pious Neustria*, pp. 39–40 and n. 73.

48. "Vita Audoini" 10, 13, pp. 559–60, 562. For the conflicts to which the biographer refers, see also the *Liber Historiae Francorum* 48, MGH SSRM 2:322–23. For holy thefts, see Geary, *Furta Sacra*.

49. "Vita Audoini" 16–17, pp. 564–65.

50. Bouchard, "Episcopal *Gesta* and the Creation of a Useful Past," p. 16. See also Hen, *Culture and Religion in Merovingian Gaul*, p. 99.

51. For sixth-century cemeteries—increasingly built inside cities—see Heinrich Härke, "Cemeteries as Places of Power," in *Topographies of Power*, ed. de Jong and Theuws, pp. 9–30.

52. There have recently been efforts to see Gregory as a historian who shaped his material for his own purposes, to counteract the old picture of him as a rather naive recorder of events. Heinzelmann, *Gregory of Tours*; Goffart, *The Narrators of Barbarian History*; Kathleen Mitchell, "Saints and Public Christianity in the *Historiae* of Gregory of Tours," in *Religion, Culture, and Society in the Early Middle Ages*, ed. Noble and Contreni, pp. 77–94.

53. Thomas J. Hefferman, *Sacred Biography*, pp. 3–4.

54. Gregory of Tours, *Liber in gloria martyrum* 50, pp. 72–73. See also Wood, "Constructing Cults," pp. 161–64.

55. Gregory of Tours, *Liber in gloria martyrum* 56, pp. 76–77.

56. *Martyrologium Hieronymianum*, ed. Jean-Baptiste de Rossi and Louis Duchesne. An extensive discussion of the text and its purpose is given by Felice Lifshitz, *The Name of the Saint*. She does not agree with most of the conclusions of previous scholars, some of which I adopt below.

57. Lifshitz, however, argues that there was no sixth-century Italian version and that it was not put together at Auxerre; *The Name of the Saint*, pp. 13–15, 133–38.

58. The martyrology is now in two parts, with a few folios missing between them; Paris, BnF MS lat. 894, and MS lat. 5253.

59. The editors of the *Martyrologium Hieronymianum* helpfully separate out the listings for Auxerre, Lyon, and Autun; pp. xl–xlii. For their argument for the origins of the *Martyrologium* in Auxerre, see pp. xlii–xliii.

60. Lifshitz argues for Luxeuil, rather than Auxerre, primarily on the basis of the inclusion of Saint Columbanus (d. 615) in all the earliest manuscripts; *The Name of the Saint*, pp. 13–15. The large number of Auxerrois saints, however, is difficult to ignore. My own conjecture is that the martyrology was sent from Auxerre to Luxeuil shortly after its compilation, and all existing early manuscripts derive from a Luxeuil copy—to which the name of Columbanus would naturally have been added. See also van Egmond, *Conversing with the Saints*, pp. 71–74.

61. For the relationship of the martyrology to Ambrose's treatises, see the editors' introduction to the *Martyrologium Hieronymianum*, pp. 59–60.

62. *Gesta*, 1:69–77.

63. *Martyrologium Hieronymianum*, pp. II, 98, III, II5.

64. The bishops and local saints who figured in Auxerre's martyrology of c. 600 were carefully added in the late ninth century to Auxerre's copy of a martyrology drawn up by Archbishop Ado of Vienne; *Le martyrologie d'Adon*, ed. Jacques Dubois and Geneviève Renaud. For Ado, see McKitterick, *Perceptions of the Past in the Early Middle Ages*, pp. 52–54.

65. Lost too is the "thousand-year-old" manuscript of the martyrology found at St.-Germain of Auxerre in the early eighteenth century, which must have been copied locally from the martyrology of c. 600. For an edition of this probable eighth-century manuscript, see the "Martyrologium vetus," ed. Edmund Martène and Ursin Durand, cols. 1547–64.

66. Louis, "L'église d'Auxerre," pp. 57–61; Atsma, "Klöster und Mönchtum im Bistum Auxerre," pp. 10–11; Hen, *Culture and Religion in Merovingian Gaul*, p. 97.

67. The number and varieties of martyrologies ballooned in the ninth through twelfth centuries—usually combined with computational charts for determining days of the week, phases of the moon, and Easter. *Der karolingische Reichskalender und seine Überlieferung*, ed. Arno Borst.

68. Bouchard, "Episcopal *Gesta* and the Creation of a Useful Past," pp. 8, II.

CONCLUSION

1. Frederick S. Paxton, *Christianizing Death*.

2. Bonnie Effros, *Caring for Body and Soul*. See also Geary, *Living with the Dead in the Middle Ages*, pp. 77–92; and Paul Binski, *Medieval Death*.

3. Bynum, *Resurrection of the Body*.

4. Alan E. Bernstein, *The Formation of Hell*.

5. Klingshirn, *Caesarius of Arles: Life, Testament, Letters*, p. 38.

6. Jean-François Reynaud, "Text and Excavation: Some Problems in the Theory and Practice of Late Antique Monumental Archaeology," in *Spaces of the Living and the Dead*, ed. Catherine E. Karkov, Kelley M. Wickham-Crowley, and Bailey K. Young, pp. 28–29.

7. *The Cartulary of Flavigny*, ed. Bouchard, pp. 19–33, 135–44, nos. 1–2, 57–58.

8. See also Bouchard, "Queen Theuchildis of Sens."

APPENDIX I

1. For example, I do not include St.-Pierre-le-Moûtier, in the diocese of Nevers, whose first appearance is as an *abbatia* in an apparently forged charter of Charles the Fat and about which essentially nothing else is known until it became a priory of St.-Martin of Autun in the twelfth century. MGH DD regum Germaniae ex stirpe Karolinorum 2:311–12, no. 186; BnF, Coll. Bourgogne III.

2. An earlier such listing is given in Bouchard, "Merovingian, Carolingian, and Cluniac Monasticism," pp. 382–88. See also Lusse, "Le monachisme en Champagne."

3. Gregory of Tours, *Liber in gloria confessorum* 85, MGH SSRM 1/2:353 n. According to his *vita*, John was the son of the noble couple Hilary and Quieta; Jonas, "Vita Iohannis abbatis Reomaensis" 1, MGH SSRM 3:507. The privilege does not survive, but a twelfth-century summary says that it concerned consecration of the abbot and correction of erring brothers, suggesting that it was of the type issued in the seventh century; GC 4:158, no. 35.

4. *Corpus consuetudinum monasticarum*, vol. 1, ed. Hallinger, p. 493 n.

5. MGH DD regum Germaniae ex stirpe Karolinorum 2:206–7, no. 129. For Bishop Geylo and his diocese, see Bautier, *Chartes, sceaux et chancelleries*, pp. 216–29.

6. *Chronique de Saint-Bénigne*, ed. Bougaud and Garnier, pp. 116–17, 135; Petrus Roverius, *Reomaus*, p. 174; Document 23 of St.-Pierre-le-Vif, in *Chronique de Saint-Pierre-le-Vif*, ed. Bautier and Gilles, p. 277.

7. Gregory of Tours, *Liber in gloria martyrum* 50, MGH SSRM 1/2:72–73; *Chartes et documents de Saint-Bénigne de Dijon*, ed. Chevrier and Chaume, 1:44, no. 2.

8. MGH DD imperii, pp. 38–39, no. 41; the new edition is MGH DD regum Francorum e stirpe Merovingica, pp. 264–68, no. 103, called false. Although King Guntram's donation charter does not survive, the twelfth-century chronicler refers to it; *Chronique de Saint-Bénigne*, pp. 29–31. Its reference to the establishment of the observances of St.-Maurice d'Agaune suggests authenticity. See also Prinz, *Frühes Mönchtum*, pp. 160–61.

9. *Chronique de Saint-Bénigne*, pp. 105–6; *Chartes et documents de Saint-Bénigne*, 1:111–12, 115–16, nos. 82, 85.

10. Bulliot, *Essai historique sur l'abbaye de Saint-Martin d'Autun*, 2:22, no. 9; *Recueil des actes de Robert Ier et de Raoul*, ed. Dufour, pp. 41–46, no. 11.

11. *Chronique de Saint-Bénigne*, pp. 135–36. For William, see Niethard Bulst, *Untersuchungen zu den Klosterreform Wilhelms von Dijon*.

12. "Vita Lupi episcopi Senonici," MGH SSRM 4:182–83.

13. GC 12:2–6, nos. 2–3; *Recueil des actes de Charles le Chauve*, ed. Tessier, Giry, and Prou, 2:389–94, no. 148.

14. *Cartulaire de l'Yonne*, ed. Quantin, 1:33–35, no. 17.

15. Fredegar, *The Fourth Book* 1, 14, ed. Wallace-Hadrill, pp. 4, 10; *Concilia Galliae, A. 511–A. 695*, ed. de Clercq, p. 235. See also Prinz, *Frühes Mönchtum*, p. 160.

16. *The Cartulary of St.-Marcel*, ed. Bouchard, pp. 23–27, nos. 3–4. In 924 Countess Ermengard of Autun directed the monastery; ibid., pp. 53–54, no. 28.

17. *Recueil des chartes de l'abbaye de Cluny*, ed. Bernard and Bruel, 3:562–66, no. 2484; 4:429–31, no. 3341; *The Cartulary of St.-Marcel*, pp. 29–31, no. 6; Bouchard, *"Those of My Blood,"* pp. 149–53.

18. *Recueil des actes de Charles le Chauve*, 2:146–49, no. 293.

19. Bulliot, *Essai historique sur Saint-Martin*, 2:23–24, no. 9; *Recueil des actes de Robert Ier et de Raoul*, pp. 29–31, 34–38, nos. 6, 8; *Recueil des actes du prieuré de Saint-Symphorien d'Autun*, ed. André Déléage, pp. 54–55, no. 22.

20. Gregory of Tours, *Liber in gloria confessorum* 86, p. 354.

21. Jonas, "Vita Iohannis abbatis Reomaensis" 14, MGH SSRM 3:512–13. See also Prinz, *Frühes Mönchtum*, p. 298.

22. *Corpus consuetudinum monasticarum*, 1:494.

23. Bulliot, *Essai historique sur Saint-Martin*, 2:22, no. 9.

24. *Chartes et documents de Saint-Bénigne*, 2:124, no. 344. See also Bouchard, *Sword, Miter, and Cloister*, pp. 428–29; and *Cartulary of Flavigny*, ed. Bouchard, p. 5, n. 5.

25. Gregory I, *Registrum epistolarum* 13.10, ed. Norberg, 2:1007. Gregory of Tours mentions it; *Hist* 9.40, p. 466. See also Prinz, *Frühes Mönchtum*, pp. 161–62.

26. GC 4:51–54, no. 13; *Recueil des actes de Charles le Chauve*, 1:58, no. 23.

27. Gregory I, *Registrum epistolarum* 13.11, 2:1009.

28. *Recueil des actes de Charles le Chauve*, 1:58, 2:340–42, nos. 23, 175, 377; MGH DD regum Germaniae ex stirpe Karolinorum 2:191–93, no. 121.

29. Bulliot, *Essai historique sur Saint-Martin*, 2:22–24, no. 9. Confusingly, the editor does not include St.-Symphorien in the document's brief header and adds that St.-Germain of Auxerre, Moûtier-St.-Jean, Pouthières, and Fleury-sur-Loire were all included, even though they do not appear in the text.

30. *Recueil des actes de Robert Ier et de Raoul*, pp. 19–22, no. 3; *Recueil des actes de Louis IV, roi de France*, ed. Philippe Lauer, pp. 78–79, no. 33.

31. *Cartulary of Flavigny*, p. 121, no. 49; Bulliot, *Essai historique sur Saint-Martin*, pp. 30–33, no. 13.

32. Hartmut Atsma, "Les monastères urbains du nord de la Gaule," in *La christianisation des pays entre Loire et Rhin*, ed. Riché, p. 175.

33. *Corpus consuetudinum monasticarum*, 1:496. This house is incorrectly identified in a footnote as Moûtiers in the diocese of Auxerre.

34. GC 12:12–13, no. 11. See also Odorannus of Sens, *Opera omnia*, ed. Bautier and Gilles, p. 96.

35. Clarius of Sens, *Chronicon Sancti Petri Vivi Senonensis* 503, in *Chronique de Saint-Pierre-le-Vif*, p. 36; *Cartulaire de l'Yonne*, 1:10–13, no. 6; Bouchard, "Queen Theuchildis of Sens"; Prinz, *Frühes Mönchtum*, pp. 162–63.

36. *Cartulaire de l'Yonne*, 1:33–35, no. 17; *Chronique de Fontenelle* 13.7, ed. Pradié, p. 178.

37. *Cartulaire de l'Yonne*, 1:127–28, no. 64; Document 3 of St.-Pierre-le-Vif, in *Chronique de Saint-Pierre-le-Vif*, pp. 252–54.

38. *Corpus consuetudinum monasticarum*, 1:493; *Recueil des actes de Charles le Chauve*, 1:9–12, no. 3.

39. Gregory of Tours, *Liber in gloria confessorum* 66, p. 337; "Vita Lupi episcopi Senonici," MGH SSRM 4:183. See also Isabelle Crété-Protin, *Eglise et vie chrétienne dans le diocèse de Troyes*, pp. 201–5.

40. Lalore, ed., *Collection des principaux cartulaires du diocèse de Troyes*, 1:2–5, no. 1.

41. *Chronique de Saint-Bénigne*, pp. 232–46; MGH DD imperii, pp. 39–41, nos. 42–43; also in MGH DD regum Francorum e stirpe Merovingica, pp. 234–37, 273–75, nos. 91,

106. Prinz, *Frühes Mönchtum*, p. 179. For its Merovingian-era charters, see Kölzer, *Merowingerstudien*, 2:1–17.

42. *Cartulaire de l'Yonne*, 1:27, no. 13; *Recueil des actes d'Eudes*, ed. Bautier, p. 70, no. 15; *Chronique de Saint-Bénigne*, pp. 135, 278, 282–83, 286–87; MGH Concilia 2:681–82.

43. GC 12:326–29, no. 36; *Recueil des chartes de Cluny*, 5:67–74, no. 3724; René de Lespinasse, ed., "Les chartes de Saint-Etienne de Nevers," pp. 76–77, no. 2; Paschal II, *Epistola* 31, PL 163:52.

44. *Gesta*, 1:106. Bishop Lupus of Sens, a contemporary of Desiderius, was buried in the basilica according to his *vita* from a century later; "Vita Lupi episcopi Senonici," MGH SSRM 4:186.

45. *Cartulaire de l'Yonne*, 1:14–17, no. 7. See also Paul Deschamps, "Critique du privilège épiscopal accordé par Emmon de Sens à l'abbaye de Sainte-Colombe"; and Ewig, *Spätantikes und fränkisches Gallien*, 2:485–506.

46. *Cartulaire de l'Yonne*, 1:44–46, 49–51, nos. 22, 25.

47. *Recueil des actes de Charles le Chauve*, 1:265–74, nos. 100–102. The first two of these three documents, all given on the same day, still exist as originals. The third is sometimes considered a forgery because it refers to the rules of Lérins, Luxeuil, and Agaune, which one would not expect a Carolingian to mention. This anomaly is easily explained, however; the monks must have presented Charles with the privilege of Bishop Emmo for confirmation. See also Loup of Ferrières, Letter 71, *Correspondance*, ed. Levillain, 2:8–10.

48. *Recueil des actes d'Eudes*, pp. 113–19, no. 25. The editor casts doubt on this charter, saying its provision of a postern through which the monks could flee was probably a fourteenth-century invention. The detail that Richard le Justicier was abbot, however, was unlikely to have been fabricated.

49. *Cartulaire de l'Yonne*, 1:150–52, no. 78.

50. *The Cartulary of Montier-en-Der*, ed. Bouchard, pp. 45–52, nos. 1–3. See also Prinz, *Frühes Mönchtum*, p. 182.

51. *The Cartulary of Montier-en-Der*, pp. 67–70, 72–74, 77–80, nos. 9, 11, 14.

52. "Miracula S. Bercharii," AASS Oct. 7:1020–22. See also Michel Parisse, "L'abbaye de Gorze dans le contexte politique et religieux lorraine," p. 63.

53. *Chronique de Saint-Bénigne*, p. 259.

54. *Cartulary of Flavigny*, pp. 109–12, 133–34, nos. 43, 56.

55. His *vita* was written in the tenth century; Adso of Der, "Vita Frodoberti," in *Opera hagiographica*, ed. Goullet, pp. 23–52.

56. MGH DD imperii, pp. 31–32, no. 33; the new edition is MGH DD rerum Francorum e stirpe Merovingica, pp. 237–39, no. 92. See also Prinz, *Frühes Mönchtum*, p. 172; and Crété-Protin, *Eglise et vie chrétienne*, pp. 222–29.

57. Lalore, *Collection des cartulaires de Troyes*, 6:1–4, no. 1.

58. *Recueil des actes de Charles le Chauve*, 1:512–14, 2:291–93, nos. 201, 356.

59. "Miracula S. Bercharii," p. 1022; Lalore, *Collection des cartulaires de Troyes*, 6:189–91, no. 185.

60. *Cartulaire de Langres*, ed. Flammarion, pp. 20–22, no. 4; "Chronicon Clareval-lense" 1184, PL 185:1250.

61. *The Cartulary of Montier-en-Der*, pp. 52–58, no. 4. Curiously, Crété-Protin puts its foundation before rather than after that of Montier-en-Der; *Eglise et vie chrétienne*, pp. 241–42. Adso, writing a *vita* of Bercharius at the end of the tenth century, was confused by an early charter in Montier-en-Der's archives that referred to an unsuccessful effort to establish a nunnery at *villa Gauchiacus* and said that the nuns originally settled at *Mangisvillare*. Adso of Der, "Vita Sancti Bercharii" 14, in *Opera hagiographica*, p. 324; *The Cartulary of Montier-en-Der*, p. 388, no. 166.

62. *Cartulary of Flavigny*, p. 22, no. 1; *Recueil des actes de Charles le Chauve*, 1:58, no. 23. See also Jean Emile Courtois, "L'église Saint-Andoche de Saulieu et la légende de sa fondation par Charlemagne," in *La chanson de geste*, 2:1175–98.

63. *Cartulary of Flavigny*, pp. 19–28, no. 1.

64. *Corpus consuetudinum monasticarum*, 1:494; *Cartulary of Flavigny*, pp. 61–63, 69–72, nos. 19, 23.

65. Bulliot, *Essai historique sur Saint-Martin*, 2:22, no. 9; *Cartulary of Flavigny*, pp. 82–86, 131–32, nos. 28, 55.

66. Crété-Protin, *Eglise et vie chrétienne*, pp. 342–46. The sixth-century claim was doubtless based on the monks reading the privilege of Lothar I, son of Louis the Pious, as given by Clothar, son of Clovis.

67. *Corpus consuetudinum monasticarum*, 1:493; MGH DD Karolinorum 3:175–77, no. 65.

68. GC 4:128–29, no. 4. See also Jean Marilier, "L'origine de quelques évêques de Langres aux VIIIe et IXe siècles," in *Langres et ses évêques*, p. 83.

69. *Recueil des actes d'Eudes*, p. 70, no. 15; *Cartulaire de Langres*, ed. Flammarion, pp. 20–22, no. 4.

70. *Chartes de l'abbaye de Saint-Etienne de Dijon*, ed. Adrien Bièvre Poulalier, pp. 25–28, 31–34, nos. 22, 24.

71. Lusse considers Molosmes a seventh-century foundation; "Le monachisme," Map 3, pp. 30–31; *Cartulaire de l'Yonne*, 1:27, no. 13; *Recueil des actes d'Eudes*, p. 70, no. 15; *Corpus consuetudinum monasticarum*, 1:496.

72. *Cartulaire de l'église d'Autun*, ed. A. de Charmasse, p. 34, no. 21; *Chronique de Saint-Bénigne*, p. 136.

73. *Cartulaire de l'Yonne*, 1:27, no. 13; *Recueil des actes d'Eudes*, p. 70, no. 15; *Cartulaire de l'église d'Autun*, p. 34, no. 21.

74. *Recueil des actes de Charles le Chauve*, 1:452–53, no. 171. See also Crété-Protin, *Eglise et vie chrétienne*, pp. 347–59.

75. *Recueil des actes d'Eudes*, pp. 134–35, no. 30; *Recueil des actes de Robert Ier et de Raoul*, pp. 38–40, no. 9; *Chronique de Saint-Bénigne*, pp. 373–74; Lalore, *Collection des cartulaires de Troyes*, 7:52, no. 29.

76. *Recueil des actes de Charles le Chauve*, 2:342–44, no. 378; Pierre Juénin, *Nouvelle histoire de l'abbaïe de Saint-Filibert et de la ville de Tournus*, 2:120, 125, 130–31, 139–40.

77. Bulliot, *Essai historique sur Saint-Martin*, 2:23, no. 9.

78. *Recueil des chartes de Cluny*, 5:697–99, no. 4333; *Cartulaire de l'abbaye de Saint-André-le-Bas de Vienne*, ed. C.-U.-J. Chevalier, pp. 265–66, no. 54.

79. *Monumenta Vizeliacensia*, ed. Huygens, 1:244–48, 259–61, nos. 1, 4. See also René Louis, *Girart, comte de Vienne*, pp. 59–66.

80. Stephen IX, "Epistola" 8, PL 143:883. See also Bouchard, "Merovingian, Carolingian, and Cluniac Monasticism," p. 379; and Dietrich W. Poeck, *Cluniacensis Ecclesia*, pp. 111–13.

81. *Monumenta Vizeliacensia*, 1:244–48, no. 1; "Annales Vizeliacenses," in *Monumenta Vizeliacensia*, 1:211.

82. Anselm of St.-Remy, "Histoire de la dédicace de Saint-Remy" 27, ed. Hourlier, in *La Champagne bénédictine*, p. 240.

83. *Chronique de Saint-Bénigne*, p. 423.

84. *Cartulary of Flavigny*, pp. 48–49, 125–28, nos. 13, 52.

85. Bulliot, *Essai historique sur Saint-Martin*, 2:23, no. 9.

86. "Chartes de l'abbaye de Corbigny," ed. Anatole de Charmasse, 4–6, nos. 1–2.

87. Although this house appears in the records only from the mid-ninth century on, Merovingian-era sarcophagi have been found below it, suggesting it had earlier been a basilica; Nancy Gauthier and Jean-Charles Picard, eds., *Topographie chrétienne des cités de la Gaule*, 8:150.

88. *Recueil des chartes de Cluny*, 4:159–60, no. 2961; Paschal II, *Epistola* 31, PL 163:52.

89. *Recueil des actes de Charles le Chauve*, 2:67–70, no. 248; Heiric, *Miracula Sancti Germani* 2.3, PL 124:1262–63.

90. E. Fournial, ed., "Documents inédits des IXe, Xe, XIe and XIIe siècles relatifs à l'histoire de Charlieu," pp. 107–8, no. 1; *Recueil des actes des rois de Provence*, ed. René Poupardin, pp. 33–34, no. 18.

91. Harald Zimmerman, ed., *Papsturkunden*, 1:111–12, 229–31, nos. 67, 130.

92. Lusse, however, dates its foundation to the sixth century; "Le monachisme," Map 3, pp. 30–31. This seems unlikely, for Gregory of Tours mentions Tonnerre, but only as a *castrum*, not a location with a monastery; *Liber in gloria confessorum* 11, p. 304. Similarly, the seventh-century *vita* of Abbot John of Reomaus speaks of Tonnerre but with no indication that there was another monastery in the region besides John's; Jonas, "Vita Iohannis abbatis Reomaensis," pp. 505–17.

93. *Cartulaire de l'Yonne*, 1:119–20, 141–42, 146–48, nos. 60, 73, 76.

94. *Chronique de Saint-Bénigne*, pp. 136, 149.

95. *Cartulaires de l'abbaye de Molesme*, ed. Laurent, 2:269, no. 2.17.

96. "Vita S. Viventii" 8, AASS Jan. 2:95. For the family, see Bouchard, *"Those of My Blood,"* pp. 145–47. *Chronique de Saint-Bénigne*, p. 135.

97. Bull of Urban II, BnF, Coll. Bourgogne 179, no. 161. The edition in PL 151:410, no. 137, incorrectly changes Vergy, *Verziaco*, to read *Vizeliaco*, Vézelay.

98. *Recueil des chartes de Cluny*, 1:124–28, no. 112. For its early years, see Rosenwein, *Rhinoceros Bound*.

99. The most extensive study of Cluny's priories, dependent abbeys, and cells is by Poeck, *Cluniacensis Ecclesia*.

100. *Cartulaire du prieuré de Paray-le-Monial*, ed. Chevalier pp. 2–3, no. 2; *Recueil des chartes de Cluny*, 3:562–66, no. 2848. See also Constance Brittain Bouchard, "The Aristocratic Bishop: The Case of Hugh of Chalon," in *The Bishop*, ed. Gilsdorf, pp. 37–49.

APPENDIX II

1. The most thorough modern studies are those by Atsma, "Klöster und Mönchtum im Bistum Auxerre"; Jean-Charles Picard, "Les églises d'Auxerre au temps de Saint Germain (418–448?)," "Les églises d'Auxerre à la fin du VIe siècle," and "Auxerre à la fin du VIIe siècle," all in *Saint-Germain d'Auxerre*, pp. 3–11; and Gauthier and Picard, *Topographie chrétienne*, 8:47–65. For the Merovingian-era *vitae* of the Auxerrois saints, see van Egmond, *Conversing with the Saints*.

2. According to Gauthier and Picard, *Topographie chrétienne*, 8:61, this designation refers rather to a church built over the bishop's tomb at Mont Artre. Atsma says that nothing can be known for sure about "Valerian's basilica"; "Klöster und Mönchtum im Bistum Auxerre," pp. 23–24. René Louis, however, believed, as do I, that this designated Auxerre's first Christian church; "L'église d'Auxerre et ses évêques avant Saint Germain," in *Saint Germain d'Auxerre et son temps*, p. 49.

3. Louis, "L'église d'Auxerre," pp. 39–45, 49, 74–80, 88 n. 118. The first sign in the sources of Saint Peregrinus is his *vita*, probably from the sixth century; his remains were translated to St.-Denis in the seventh century. Gauthier and Picard cast doubt on this location because it is outside the Roman *civitas*; *Topographie chrétienne*, 8:53–54. Jean-Charles Picard argues that if Auxerre's first church were outside the Roman walls it would be unique in Gaul; *Evêques, saints et cités en Italie et en Gaule*, pp. 265–74. Yet other cathedrals, including Mâcon, were located on the margins of the Roman city; see also Nancy Gauthier, "From the Ancient City to the Medieval Town: Continuity and Change in the Early Middle Ages," in *The World of Gregory of Tours*, ed. Mitchell and Wood, p. 57. It would have been precisely because of its location outside the *civitas* that the cathedral was relocated in the fourth century.

4. Recent archaeological excavations have found no remains that can be definitively dated before the later eleventh century; Fabrice Henrion, "L'ancienne église Saint-Pèlerin d'Auxerre." But Bishop Geoffrey's identification of this church as Peregrinus's and the bishop's desire to restore it indicate there was some sort of oratory on the site before the Romanesque church was built.

5. Picard proposes it as Auxerre's original, fourth-century cathedral; *Evêques, saints et cités*, pp. 271–75.

6. St.-Alban seems to have been incorporated into the count's castle in the eleventh century; *Cartulaire de l'Yonne*, 1:382–83, no. 238. See also Gauthier and Picard, *Topographie chrétienne*, 8:56.

7. *Chronique de Fontenelle* 13.7, p. 180.

8. See also Atsma, "Klöster und Mönchtum im Bistum Auxerre," pp. 30–40.

9. Robert of St.-Marien, *Chronicon*, MGH SS 26:231–34. See also Bouchard, *Spirituality and Administration*, pp. 56–57.

10. For this house, see Deflou-Leca, *Saint-Germain d'Auxerre et ses dépendances;* and Atsma, "Klöster und Mönchtum im Bistum Auxerre," pp. 12–20.

11. Heiric, *Miracula Sancti Germani* 1.4, PL 124:1225–27; Gregory of Tours, *Liber in gloria confessorum* 40, p. 323.

12. "Vita S. Balthildis" 9, MGH SSRM 2:493. The editors mistakenly identify the church of St.-Germain as St.-Germain-des-Prés. Deflou-Leca argues that monks became established at St.-Germain only at Balthildis's insistence, thus in the second half of the seventh century; *Saint-Germain d'Auxerre et ses dépendances*, pp. 67–70.

13. *Recueil des actes de Charles le Chauve*, 1:411–13, no. 156; 2:106, 137, nos. 269, 288; *Cartulaire de l'Yonne*, 1:46–47, 87, 133–34, 139, 161, nos. 23, 45, 68, 72, 84.

14. In the late thirteenth century, the monks of St.-Germain wrote the history of their abbots and began with Heldric; *Gesta abbatum Sancti Germani Autissiodorensis*, ed. Noëlle Deflou-Leca and Yves Sassier, pp. 8–18; Yves Sassier, *Recherches sur le pouvoir comtal en Auxerrois*, pp. 19–23; *Cartulaire de l'Yonne*, 1:157–59, no. 82; Roverius, *Reomaus*, p. 174.

15. *Gesta*, 2:65, 77; Paschal II, *Epistola* 31, PL 163:52. See also Bouchard, *Spirituality and Administration*, pp. 26–28.

16. See also Atsma, "Klöster und Mönchtum im Bistum Auxerre," pp. 21–22.

17. The "tyrant" may be the unnamed father of Bishop Adalgar of Autun (d. 894), who also took over the abbey of Flavigny; Bouchard, *Sword, Miter, and Cloister*, p. 341. See also *Cartulary of Flavigny*, p. 147. Or the bishop of Autun may have been one of Adalgar's two immediate successors, Walo (d. 919) and Hervé (d. 935), uncle and nephew, the first the son of an unnamed lord, the second son of Count Manasses I of Autun; Bouchard, *"Those of My Blood,"* p. 144.

18. *Cartulaire de l'Yonne*, 1:284–86, no. 164.

19. See also Atsma, "Klöster und Mönchtum im Bistum Auxerre," pp. 22–23.

20. Louis, "L'église d'Auxerre," p. 48, n. 17. Atsma, however, rejects this possibility of confusion between Martin and Mammertinus; "Klöster und Mönchtum im Bistum Auxerre," p. 26.

21. *Cartulaire de l'Yonne*, 2:145, no. 134. See also Bouchard, *Spirituality and Administration*, pp. 56–57.

22. For this house, see also Atsma, "Klöster und Mönchtum im Bistum Auxerre," pp. 26–29.

23. See also *Three Cartularies from Thirteenth-Century Auxerre*, ed. Bouchard, pp.185–89, no. 2.

24. *Cartulaire de l'Yonne*, 1:30–31, no. 15; *Recueil des actes de Charles le Chauve*, 2:377–80, no. 396. Hugh "the Abbot" was grandson of Hugh of Tours; Louis, *Girart, comte de Vienne*, pp. 33–34.

25. *Three Cartularies*, pp. 191–92, no. 4.

26. *Cartulaire de l'Yonne*, 2:54–55, no. 49.

27. See also Bouchard, *Spirituality and Administration*, pp. 28–29.

28. In the seventeenth century the scholar Dom Viole transcribed Vigilius's testament from the original; *Cartulaire de l'Yonne*, 1:17–21, no. 8.

29. *Gesta*, 2:103–5; Robert of St.-Marien, *Chronicon*, MGH SS 26:234; *Cartulaire de l'Yonne*, 1:382–83, no. 238. See also Bouchard, *Spirituality and Administration*, pp. 56–57.

Bibliography

MANUSCRIPTS

Autun, Bibliothèque municipale, MS 3 (mid-eighth-century "Gundohinus" gospels).
———, MS 4 (late eighth-century gospels from Flavigny).
Auxerre, Arch. Yonne, H 32 (privilege of King Henry I for St.-Pierre-le-Vif).
———, H 167 (fragments of the eleventh-century cartulary of St.-Pierre-le-Vif).
———, H 1667 (late thirteenth-century cartulary of St.-Julien of Auxerre).
———, H 1668 (sixteenth-century copy of the cartulary of St.-Julien).
Auxerre, Bibliothèque municipale, MS 142 (twelfth-century copy of the *Gesta pontificum Autissiodorensium*).
———, MS 161 (thirteenth-century cartulary of St.-Germain of Auxerre).
———, MS 212 (twelfth-century chronicle of St.-Pierre-le-Vif).
———, MS 227 (twelfth-century chronicle and cartulary of Vézelay).
Berkeley, Boalt Hall, Robbins Collection MS 48 (thirteenth-century cartulary of the bishopric of Auxerre).
Châlons-en-Champagne [-sur-Marne], Arch. Marne G 462 (early twelfth-century cartulary of St.-Etienne of Châlons).
Chaumont, Arch. Haute-Marne, 2 G 921 (thirteenth-century cartulary of the cathedral chapter of Langres).
———, series G and 2G (documents from the cathedral chapter of Langres).
———, 1 H 3–4 (the first and second, early and late thirteenth-century, cartularies of Auberive).
———, series 1 H (documents of Auberive).
———, 6 H 2 (the first and second, early and late thirteenth-century, cartularies of Longué).
———, 7 H 1–2 (the first, early twelfth-century, and second, late thirteenth-century, cartularies of Montier-en-Der).
———, 7 H 3–6 (sixteenth- and seventeenth-century "cartularies" of Montier-en-Der).
Chaumont, Bibliothèque municipale ("Les silos"), MS 38 (thirteenth-century rule and martyrology of the cathedral chapter of Langres).
Dijon, Arch. Côte-d'Or, 10 H 6 (thirteenth-century cartulary of St.-Seine).
———, 11 H 63–64 (respectively late and early thirteenth-century cartularies of Cîteaux).

————, series 12 H (documents of La Bussière).

————, 15 H 9 (early and late thirteenth-century cartularies of Fontenay, bound together).

————, series 15 H (documents of Fontenay).

————, Bibliothèque municipale, MS 591 (eleventh-century cartulary-chronicle of St.-Bénigne).

Mâcon, Arch. Saône-et-Loire, H 142 (records of gifts to St.-Rigaud, made in the 1060s and 1070s).

Metz, Bibliothèque municipale, MS 1161 (eleventh-century formulary/cartulary of St.-Pierre-le-Vif of Sens).

Montpellier, Bibliothèque de la Faculté de Médecine, MS 154 (ninth-century *vitae* of saints; from Auxerre).

Orléans, Bibliothèque municipale [Mediathèque], MS 82 (ninth-century glossed copy of the Pauline letters, done at Flavigny).

Paris, BnF, MS fr. 18692 (inventory of the documents and titles of the bishopric of Auxerre, done in 1642).

————, MS lat. 1 (the "Vivien Bible" presented to Charles the Bald).

————, MS lat. 894 (eleventh-century martyrology from Auxerre—first part).

————, MS lat. 2123 (early ninth-century formulary book of Flavigny).

————, MS lat. 4997 (twelfth-century chronicle of Bèze).

————, MS lat. 5253 (eleventh-century martyrology from Auxerre—second part).

————, MS lat. 5463 (early fourteenth-century cartulary of La Bussière).

————, MS lat. 11743 (includes a forged charter from Sens on fol. 494).

————, MS lat. 17090 (copy made in 1721 of the now-lost fourteenth-century cartulary of the cathedral chapter of Chalon).

————, nouv. acq. lat. 326 (the forgery cartulary of St.-Denis).

————, nouv. acq. lat. 496 (the cartulary of St.-Marcel-lès-Chalon, dating from the 1120s).

————, MS nouv. acq. lat. 1497 (Cluny A, Cluny's first, mid-eleventh-century cartulary).

————, Collection de Bourgogne 111 (documents from St.-Martin of Autun).

————, Collection de Bourgogne 179, no. 161 (bull of Urban II)

Troyes, Arch. Aube, 3 H 9–10 (two-volume thirteenth-century cartulary of Clairvaux).

PRINTED PRIMARY SOURCES

Entries are arranged here by the name of the medieval author rather than the modern editor. Also included here are a few studies useful for the documents printed in them. I have not repeated the monumental collections found in the List of Abbreviations. For both the primary and secondary bibliographies, I do not include a few peripheral sources cited only once.

"Acta S. Victori et S. Victorii." AASS Aug. 5 (1868), pp. 145–47.

Actus pontificum Cenomannis in urbe degentium. Ed. G. Busson and A. Ledru. Archives historiques du Maine 2. Le Mans, 1901.

"Admonitio generalis" [789]. MGH Capit. 1 (1883; rpt. 1984), pp. 55–62.

Ado of Vienne. "Chronicon." MGH SS 2:315–26.

Adso of Der. *Opera hagiographica*. Ed. Monique Goullet. CCCM 198. Turnhout, 2003.

Aigradus. "Vita Ansberti episcopi Rotomagensis." MGH SSRM 5:618–41.

Alberic de Trois-Fontaines. *Chronica*. MGH SS 23:674–950.

Alcuin. "Vita Willibrordi archiepiscopi Traiectensis." MGH SSRM 7:113–41.

"Annales Alamannici." MGH SS 1:22–60.

Annales Bertiniani. Ed. Félix Grat, Jeanne Vielliard, and Suzanne Clémencet. Paris, 1964.

Annales Fuldenses. Ed. G. H. Pertz and Friedrich Kurze. MGH SS rerum Germanicarum in usum scholarum (1891).

"Annales Guelferbytani." MGH SS 1:23–31.

"Annales Lemovicenses." MGH SS 2:251–52.

Annales Mettenses priores. Ed. B. de Simson. MGH SS rerum Germanicarum in usum scholarum (1905).

"Annales Nivernenses." MGH SS 13:88–91.

"Annales Petaviani." MGH SS 1:7–18.

Annales regni Francorum. Ed. Friedrich Kurze. MGH SS rerum Germanicarum in usum scholarum (1895).

Anselm of St.-Remy. "Histoire de la dédicace de Saint-Remy." Ed. Jacques Hourlier. In *La Champagne bénédictine*. Travaux de l'Académie nationale de Reims 160. Reims, 1981. Pp. 179–297.

Astronomer. "Vita Hludowici imperatoris." Ed. Ernst Tremp. MGH SS rerum Germanicarum 64 (1995), pp. 279–555.

Baudonivia. "Vita Sanctae Radegundis regina." MGH SSRM 2:377–95.

Bertram, Jerome. *The Chrodegang Rules: The Rules for the Common Life of the Secular Clergy from the Eighth and Ninth Centuries*. Aldershot, Eng., 2005.

Beyer, Heinrich, ed. *Urkundenbuch zur Geschichte der mittelrheinischen Territorien*. Vol. 1. Coblenz, 1860; rpt. Hildesheim, 1974.

Bobolenus. "Vita Germani abbatis Grandivallensis." MGH SSRM 5:25–40.

Boniface. *Briefe*. Ed. Michael Tangl. MGH Epp. Selectae 1 (1916; rpt. 1978).

Bruckner, Albert. *Regesta Alsatiae aevi Merovingici et Karolini, 496–918*. Vol. 1. *Quellenband*. Strasbourg, 1949.

Bulliot, J.-Gabriel. *Essai historique sur l'abbaye de Saint-Martin d'Autun*. 2 vols. Autun, 1849.

Caesarius of Arles. *Opera omnia*. Ed. Germain Morin. 2 vols. Maredous, 1937–42.

"Capitulare de villis." MGH Capit. 1 (1883; rpt. 1984), pp. 82–91.

Cartulaire de l'abbaye de Gorze. Ed. A. d'Herbomez. Paris, 1898.

Cartulaire de l'abbaye de Saint-André-le-Bas de Vienne. Ed. C.-U.-J. Chevalier. Vienne, 1869.

Cartulaire de l'abbaye de Saint-Calais. Ed. L[ouis] Froger. Mamers, 1888.

Cartulaire de l'abbaye de Saint-Père de Chartres. Ed. [Benjamin Edme Charles] Guérard. 2 vols. Paris, 1840.

Cartulaire de l'abbaye de Saint-Victor de Marseille. 2 vols. Ed. [Benjamin Edme Charles] Guérard. Paris, 1857.

Cartulaire de l'église d'Autun. Ed. A. de Charmasse. Paris, 1865.

"Cartulaire de Saint-Etienne de Châlons." Ed. P. Pélicier. *Mémoires de la Société d'agriculture, commerce, sciences et arts du département de la Marne,* 1895. Pp. 141–96.

Cartulaire de Saint-Vincent de Mâcon. Ed. M.-C. Ragut. Mâcon, 1864.

Cartulaire du chapitre cathédral de Langres. Ed. Hubert Flammarion. Nancy, 1995.

Cartulaire du prieuré de Paray-le-Monial. Ed. Ulysse Chevalier. Paris, 1890.

Cartulaire général de l'Yonne. Ed. Maximilien Quantin. 2 vols. Auxerre, 1854–60.

Cartulaires de l'abbaye de Molesme. 2 vols. Ed. Jacques Laurent. Paris, 1907–11.

Le cartulaire de Marcigny-sur-Loire (1045–1144): Essai de reconstitution d'un manuscrit disparu. Ed. Jean Richard. Dijon, 1957.

The Cartulary and Charters of Notre-Dame of Homblières. Ed. Theodore Evergates and William Mendel Newman. Medieval Academy Books 97. Cambridge, Mass., 1990.

The Cartulary of Flavigny, 717–1113. Ed. Constance Brittain Bouchard. Medieval Academy Books 99. Cambridge, Mass., 1991.

The Cartulary of Montier-en-Der, 666–1129. Ed. Constance Brittain Bouchard. Medieval Academy Books 108. Toronto, 2004.

The Cartulary of St.-Marcel-lès-Chalon, 779–1126. Ed. Constance Brittain Bouchard. Medieval Academy Books 102. Cambridge, Mass., 1998.

Chartae Latinae Antiquiores: Facsimile-Edition of the Latin Charters Prior to the Ninth Century. 49 vols. Ed. Hartmut Atsma, Jean Vezin, and Robert Marichal. Zurich, 1954–98.

"Chartes de l'abbaye de Corbigny." Ed. Anatole de Charmasse. *Mémoires de la Société eduenne* n.s. 17 (1889), 1–39.

Chartes de l'abbaye de Saint-Etienne de Dijon (VIIIe, IXe, Xe et XIe siècles). Ed. J. Courtois. Paris and Dijon, 1908.

Chartes de l'abbaye de Saint-Etienne de Dijon de 1098 à 1140. Ed. Adrien Bièvre Poulalier. Dijon, 1912.

Chartes et documents concernant l'abbaye de Cîteaux, 1098–1182. Ed. J[ean] Marilier. Rome, 1961.

Chartes et documents de Saint-Bénigne de Dijon. Ed. Georges Chevrier and Maurice Chaume. 2 vols. Dijon, 1943–86.

The Chronicle of Theophanes. Trans. Harry Turtledove. Philadelphia, 1982.

"Chronicon Clarevallense." PL 185:1247–52.

"Chronicon Ebersheimense." MGH SS 23:431–53.

"Chronicon Moissiacense." MGH SS 1:280–313.

Chronique de l'abbaye de Saint-Bénigne de Dijon, suivie de la Chronique de Saint-Pierre de Bèze. Ed. E. Bougaud and Joseph Garnier. Dijon, 1875.

Chronique de Saint-Pierre-le-Vif, dite de Clarius. Ed. Robert-Henri Bautier and Monique Gilles. Paris, 1979.

Chronique des abbés de Fontenelle (Saint-Wandrille). Ed. Pascal Pradié. Paris, 1999.

"Clausula de Pippino." MGH SSRM 1/2 (1969), pp. 15–16.

Codex Carolinus. Ed. W. Gundlach. MGH Epp. 3 (1957), pp. 469–657.

Codex Laureshamensis. Ed. Karl Glöckner. 3 vols. Darmstadt, 1929–36.

Codice diplomatico del monasterio di S. Colombano di Bobbio. Ed. Carlo Cipolla. 3 vols. Fonti per la storia d'Italia 52–54. Rome, 1918.

"Commemoratio genealogiae domni Karoli gloriosissimi imperatoris." MGH SS 13:245–46.

Concilia Africae, A. 345–A. 525. Ed. C. Munier. CCSL 149. Turnhout, 1974.

Concilia Galliae, A. 314–A. 506. Ed. C. Munier. CCSL 148. Turnhout, 1963.

Concilia Galliae, A. 511–A. 695. Ed. Charles de Clercq. CCSL 148A. Turnhout, 1963.

"Consilium Attiniacense." MGH Concilia 2 (1904), pp. 72–73.

"Consilium Lingonense." MGH Concilia 2:681–82.

Constantius of Lyon. *Vie de Saint Germain d'Auxerre.* Ed. René Borius. Sources chrétiennes 112. Paris, 1965.

Corpus consuetudinum monasticarum. Vol. 1. Ed. Kassius Hallinger. Siegburg, 1963.

Decretales Pseudo-Isidorianae et capitula Angilramni. Ed. Paul Hinschius. Leipzig, 1863; rpt. Aalen, 1963.

"De SS. Prisco et Cotto aliisque plurimis martyribus." AASS May 6 (1866), 362–65.

"De virtutibus S. Geretrudis." MGH SSRM 2:464–74.

Desiderius of Cahors. "Epistolae." PL 87:247–66.

"Domus Carolingicae genealogia." MGH SS 2:308–9.

Donatus. "Vita Trudonis confessoris Hasbaniensis." MGH SSRM 6:273–98.

Duru, L.-M. *Bibliothèque historique de l'Yonne.* Vol. 1. Auxerre, 1850.

Einhard. *Annales.* MGH SS 1:135–215.

———. "Epistolae." MGH Epp. 5 (1898–99; rpt. 1974), pp. 109–45.

———. *Vie de Charlemagne.* Ed. Louis Halphen. Paris, 1938.

Ermoldus Nigellus. *Carmina.* MGH SS 2:464–516.

Eusebius Gallicanus. *Collectio Homiliarum.* Ed. Iohannes Leroy. CCSL 101/1. Turnhout, 1970.

"Ex vitis Adalhardi et Walae abbatum Corbeiensium." MGH SS 2:524–69.

Flodoard of Reims. *Historia Remensis ecclesiae.* Ed. Martina Stratmann. MGH SS 36 (1998).

"Formulae collectionis Sancti Dionysii." In MGH Formulae (1886; rpt. 1963), pp. 493–511.

"Formulae Morbacenses." In MGH Formulae (1886; rpt. 1963), pp. 46–51.

"Formulae Senonenses." In MGH Formulae (1886; rpt. 1963), pp. 182–211.

"Formulae Turonenses." In MGH Formulae (1886; rpt. 1963), pp. 133–65.

Fournial, E., ed. "Documents inédits des IXe, Xe, XIe and XIIe siècles relatifs à l'histoire de Charlieu." In *Actes des journées d'études d'histoire et d'archéologie à l'occasion du XIe centenaire de la fondation de l'abbaye et de la ville de Charlieu.* Charlieu, 1973.

Fredegar. *Chronica.* MGH SSRM 2 (1888; rpt. 1984), pp. 1–193.

———. *The Fourth Book of the Chronicle with Its Continuations.* Ed. J. M. Wallace-Hadrill. London, 1960.

Gasnault, Pierre, ed. *Documents comptables de Saint-Martin de Tours à l'époque mérovingienne.* Paris, 1975.

"Genealogiae comitum Flandriae." MGH SS 9:302–4.

Geschichte des Bistums Le Mans von der Spätantike bis zur Karolingerzeit: Actus Pontificum Cenomannis in Urbe Degentium und Gesta Aldrici. Ed. Margarete Weidemann. 3 vols. Mainz, 2002.

Gesta abbatum Sancti Germani Autissiodorensis. Ed. Noëlle Deflou-Leca and Yves Sassier. *Les gestes des abbés de Saint Germain d'Auxerre.* Paris, 2011.

"Gesta Dagoberti I regis Francorum." MGH SSRM 2 (1888; rpt. 1984), pp. 396–425.

Gesta domni Aldrici Cenomannicae urbis episcopi. Ed. R. Charles and L[ouis] Froger. Mamers, 1889.

Gesta pontificum Autissiodorensium. Ed. Guy Lobrichon et al. *Les gestes des évêques d'Auxerre.* 3 vols. Paris, 2002–9.

Gislemarus. "Vita Droctovei abbatis Parisiensis." MGH SSRM 3:535–43.

Gregory I. *Registrum epistolarum.* Ed. Dag Norberg. 2 vols. CCSL 140. Turnhout, 1982.

Gregory of Tours. *Historia.* Ed. Bruno Krusch and Wilhelm Levison. MGH SSRM 1/1 (1951).

———. *Liber de virtutibus S. Iuliani.* MGH SSRM 1/2 (1969), pp. 112–34.

———. *Liber in gloria confessorum.* MGH SSRM 1/2 (1969), pp. 294–370.

———. *Liber in gloria martyrum.* MGH SSRM 1/2 (1969), pp. 34–111.

———. *Liber vitae patrum.* MGH SSRM 1/2 (1969), pp. 211–94.

Heiric. *Miracula Sancti Germani.* PL 124:1207–70.

———. *Vita Sancti Germani Autissioderensis.* MGH Poetae 3 (1964), pp. 428–517.

Hildegar. "Vita Faronis episcopi Meldensis." MGH SSRM 5:184–203.

Hincmar of Reims. *Collectio de ecclesiis et capelis.* Ed. Martina Stratmann. MGH Fontes iuris Germanici antiqui 14. Hanover, 1990.

"Historia Francorum Senonensis." MGH SS 9:364–69.

Hugh of Flavigny. *Chronicon.* MGH SS 8:280–502.

———. "Series abbatum Flaviniacensium." MGH SS 8:502–3.

Jonas. "Vita Iohannis abbatis Reomaensis." MGH SSRM 3:505–17.

Jonas of Bobbio. "De vita Bertulfi abbatis." MGH SSRM 4:143–47.

———. "Vita Columbani." MGH SSRM 4 (1902; rpt. 1977), pp. 64–108.

Juénin, Pierre. *Nouvelle histoire de l'abbaïe de Saint-Filibert et de la ville de Tournus.* Vol. 2. *Preuves.* Dijon, 1733.

Der karolingische Reichskalender und seine Überlieferung bis uns 12. Jahrhundert. Ed. Arno Borst. 3 vols. MGH Libri memoriales sectio II. Hanover, 2001.

"Karolus magnus et Leo papa." MGH Poetae 1 (1881), pp. 366–79.

Lalore, Charles, ed. *Collection des principaux cartulaires du diocèse de Troyes.* 7 vols. Paris, 1875–90.

Leblond, V., and Maurice Lecomte. *Les privilèges de l'abbaye de Rebais-en-Brie.* Melun, 1910.

Lespinasse, René de, ed. "Les chartes de Saint-Etienne de Nevers." *Bulletin de la Société nivernaise des lettres, sciences et arts* ser. 3, 12 (1908), 76–130.

Levison, Wilhelm. "Das Testament des Diakons Adalgisel-Grimo vom Jahr 634." *Trierer Zeitschrift* 7 (1932), 69–85.

Liber Historiae Francorum. MGH SSRM 2 (1888; rpt. 1984), pp. 215–328.

Liber memorialis von Remiremont. Ed. Eduard Hlawitschka, Karl Schmid, and Gerd Tellenbach. MGH Libri memoriales 1. Dublin and Zurich, 1970.

Loup of Ferrières. *Correspondance.* Ed. Léon Levillain. 2 vols. Paris, 1927–35.

"Marculfi formulae." MGH Formulae, pp. 36–112.

Marius of Avenches. *La Chronique*. Ed. Justin Favrod. 2nd ed. Lausanne, 1993.

Le martyrologie d'Adon: Ses deux familles, ses trois recensions. Ed. Jacques Dubois and Geneviève Renaud. Paris, 1964.

Martyrologium Hieronymianum. Ed. Jean-Baptiste de Rossi and Louis Duchesne. AASS Nov. 2/1 (1894).

"Martyrologium vetus." Ed. Edmund Martène and Ursin Durand. *Thesaurus novus anecdotorum*. Vol. 3. Paris, 1717; rpt. New York, 1968. Cols. 1547–64.

"Miracula S. Bercharii." AASS Oct. 7 (1869), pp. 1019–31.

Monumenta Vizeliacensia: Textes relatifs à l'histoire de l'abbaye de Vézelay. Ed. R. B. C. Huygens. 2 vols. CCCM 42. Turnhout, 1976–80.

Nicholas I. *Epistolae*. MGH Epp. 6 (1902–25; rpt. 1978), pp. 257–690.

Notker the Stammerer. *Gesta Karoli imperatoris*. MGH SS 2:726–63.

Odorannus of Sens. *Opera omnia*. Ed. Robert-Henri Bautier and Monique Gilles. Paris, 1972.

Opus Caroli regis contra synodum (Libri Carolini). Ed. Ann Freeman. MGH Concilia 2, suppl. 1 (1998).

"Origo gentium Longobardorum." MGH SSRL, pp. 1–6.

Pardessus, Jean Marie, ed. *Diplomata, chartae, epistolae, leges, aliaque instrumenta ad res Gallo-Francicas spectantia*. 2 vols. Paris, 1843–49; rpt. 1969.

Paschal II. *Epistolae et privilegia*. PL 163:31–448.

"Passio Leudegarii episcopi Augustodunensis." MGH SSRM 5:282–322.

Paul the Deacon. "Gesta episcoporum Mettensium." MGH SS 2:261–68.

———. *Historia Langobardorum*. MGH SSRL (1878), pp. 45–187.

Das Polyptychon von Saint-Germain-des-Prés: Studienausgabe. Ed. Dieter Hägermann. Cologne, 1993.

Le polyptyque de l'abbaye de Saint-Bertin (844–859). Ed. François-Louis Ganshof, Françoise Godding-Ganshof, and Antoine de Smet. Paris, 1975.

Le polyptyque et les listes de cens de l'abbaye de Saint-Remi de Reims (IXe–XIe siècles). Ed. Jean-Pierre Devroey. Reims, 1984.

Le premier cartulaire de l'abbaye cistercienne de Pontigny (XIIe–XIIIe siècles). Ed. Martine Garrigues. Paris, 1981.

Premier et second livres des cartulaires de l'abbaye Saint-Serge et Saint-Bach d'Angers (XIe et XIIe siècles). Ed. Yves Chauvin. 2 vols. Angers, 1997.

Prosper of Aquitaine. *Epitoma chronicon*. MGH AA 9 (1892), pp. 341–485.

Das Prümer Urbar. Ed. Ingo Schwab. Rheinische Urbare 5. Düsseldorf, 1983.

Recueil des actes d'Eudes. Ed. Robert-Henri Bautier. Paris, 1967.

Recueil des actes de Charles II le Chauve. Ed. Georges Tessier, Arthur Giry, and Maurice Prou. 3 vols. Paris, 1943–55.

Recueil des actes de Louis IV, roi de France (936–954). Ed. Philippe Lauer. Paris, 1914.

Recueil des actes de Robert Ier et de Raoul. Ed. Jean Dufour. Paris, 1978.

Recueil des actes des rois de Provence (955–928). Ed. René Poupardin. Paris, 1920.

Recueil des actes d'Henri le Libéral, comte de Champagne (1152–1181). Vol. 1. *Chartes*. Ed. John Benton and Michel Bur. Paris, 2009.

Recueil des actes du prieuré de Saint-Symphorien d'Autun de 696 à 1300. Ed. André Déléage. Autun, 1936.

Recueil des chartes de l'abbaye de Clairvaux au XIIe siècle. Ed. Jean Waquet, Jean-Marc Roger, and Laurent Veyssière. Paris, 2004.

Recueil des chartes de l'abbaye de Cluny. Ed. Auguste Bernard and Alexander Bruel. 6 vols. Paris, 1876–1903.

Recueil des pancartes de l'abbaye de La Ferté-sur-Grosne, 1113–1178. Ed. Georges Duby. Aix, 1953.

Regino of Prüm. *Chronicon.* Ed. Friedrich Kurze. MGH SS rerum Germanicarum in usum scholarum (1890; rpt. 1978).

Richer. *Historia.* Ed. Robert Latouche. 2 vols. Paris, 1930–37; rpt. 1964–67.

Robert of St.-Marien. *Chronicon.* MGH SS 26:219–87.

Roverius, Petrus. *Reomaus, seu Historia monasterii S. Joannis Reomaensis.* Paris, 1637.

Sidonius Apollinaris. *Poems and Letters.* Ed. W. B. Anderson. 2 vols. Cambridge, Mass., 1936–65.

Stephen IX. "Epistolae et privilegia." PL 143:869–84.

Stephen Africanus. "Vita S. Amatoris Autissiodorensis episcopi." Ed. L.-M. Duru. *Bibliothèque historique de l'Yonne*, vol. 1. Auxerre, 1850. Pp. 136–58.

Sulpicius Severus. *Chroniques.* Ed. Ghislaine de Senneville-Grave. Paris, 1999.

———. *Vita Sancti Martini.* Ed. Jacques Fontaine. 3 vols. Sources chrétiennes 133–35. Paris, 1967–69.

Thegan. "Vita Hludowici imperatoris." Ed. Ernst Tremp. MGH SS rerum Germanicarum 64 (1995), pp. 167–277.

Three Cartularies from Thirteenth-Century Auxerre. Ed. Constance Brittain Bouchard. Medieval Academy Books 113. Toronto, 2012.

Traditiones Wizenburgenses: Die Urkunden des Klosters Weissenburg, 661–864. Ed. Karl Glöckner and Anton Doll. Darmstadt, 1979.

Urban II. *Epistolae et privilegia.* PL 151:283–558.

Die Urkunden der Arnulfinger. Ed. Ingrid Heidrich. Bad-Münstereifel, 2001.

Urkundenbuch der Abtei Sanct Gallen. Ed. Hermann Wartmann. 2 vols. Zurich, 1863–66; rpt. Frankfurt am Main, 1981.

Urkundenbuch des Klosters Fulda. Ed. Edmund E. Stengel. Marburg, 1956.

van der Straeten, Joseph, ed. "Les actes des martyrs d'Aurélien en Bourgogne." *Analecta Bollandiana* 79 (1961), 115–44, 447–68.

———. "La vie inédite de S. Hughes, évêque de Rouen." *Analecta Bollandiana* 87 (1969), 232–60.

Venantius Fortunatus. *Poèmes.* Ed. Marc Reydellet. 2 vols. Paris, 1994–98.

———. *Vie de Saint Martin.* Ed. Solange Quesnel. Paris, 1996.

———. "Vita Sanctae Radegundis regina." MGH SSRM 2 (1888), pp. 364–77.

———. "Vita Sancti Paterni." MGH AA 4/2 (1885; rpt. 1961), pp. 33–37.

Victricius of Rouen. "De laude sanctorum." Ed. J[acques] Mulders and R. Demeulenaere. In *Foebadius, Victricius, Leporius, Vincentius Lerinensis, Evagrius, Ruricius.* CCSL 64. Turnhout, 1985. Pp. 53–93.

"Virtutes Fursei abbatis Latiniacensis." MGH SSRM 4 (1902; rpt. 1977), pp. 440–49.

"Vita Alcuini." MGH SS 15:184–97.

"Vita Ansberti episcopi Rotomagensis." MGH SSRM 5:618–41.

"Vita Audoini episcopi Rotomagensis." MGH SSRM 5 (1910; rpt. 1979), pp. 536–67.

"Vita Boniti episcopi Arverni." MGH SSRM 6 (1913; rpt. 1979), pp. 119–33.

"Vita Carilefi abbatis Anisolensis." MGH SSRM 3 (1896; rpt. 1977), pp. 389–94.

"Vita Chrodegangi episcopi Mettensis." MGH SS 10:553–72.

"Vita Eligii episcopi Noviomagensis." MGH SSRM 4 (1902; rpt. 1977), pp. 663–742.

"Vita Eucherii episcopi Aurelianensis." MGH SSRM 7 (1920; rpt. 1979), pp. 41–53.

"Vita Genovefae virginis Parisiensis." MGH SSRM 3:215–38.

"Vita Hrodberti episcopi Salisburgensis." MGH SSRM 6:157–62.

"Vita Lantberti abbatis Fontanellensis." MGH SSRM 5:608–12.

"Vita Leutfredi." AASS June 5 (1847), pp. 92–100.

"Vita Lupi episcopi Senonici." MGH SSRM 4 (1902; rpt. 1977), pp. 179–87.

"Vita Nivardi episcopi Remensis." MGH SSRM 5 (1910; rpt. 1979), pp. 157–71.

"Vita Odilae abbatissae Hohenburgensis." MGH SSRM 6 (1913; rpt. 1979), pp. 37–50.

"Vita S. Arnulfi." MGH SSRM 2:432–46.

"Vita S. Balthildis." MGH SSRM 2 (1888; rpt. 1984), pp. 475–508.

"Vita S. Geretrudis." MGH SSRM 2 (1888; rpt. 1984), pp. 453–64.

"Vita S. Germani Autissiodorensis episcopi." Ed. L.-M. Duru. *Bibliothèque historique de l'Yonne*, vol. 1. Auxerre, 1850. Pp. 47–89.

"Vita S. Lupi episcopi Trecensis." MGH SSRM 7:295–302.

"Vita S. Peregrini Autissiodorensis episcopi." Ed. L.-M. Duru. *Bibliothèque historique de l'Yonne*, vol. 1. Auxerre, 1850. Pp. 123–26.

"Vita S. Viventii." AASS Jan. 2:86–95.

Wampach, Camillus, ed. *Geschichte der Grundherrschaft Echternach im Frühmittelalter.* 2 vols. Luxemburg, 1929–30.

———, ed. *Urkunden- und Quellenbuch zur Geschichte der altluxemburgischen Territorien bis zur burgundischen Zeit.* Vol. 1. Luxemburg, 1935.

Weidemann, Margarete. *Das Testament des Bischofs Bertramn von Le Mans vom 27. März 616: Untersuchungen zu Besitz und Geschichte einer frankishen Familie im 6. und 7. Jahrhundert.* Mainz, 1986.

Zimmerman, Harald, ed. *Papsturkunden 896–1046.* 2nd ed. 3 vols. Vienna, 1985–89.

SECONDARY SOURCES

If I cited more than one article from a volume of collected essays, I here give only the volume; individual articles may be found in the notes.

799—Kunst und Kultur der Karolingerzeit: Karl der Große und Papst Leo III. in Paderborn. Ed. Christoph Stiegemann and Matthias Wemhoff. 3 vols. Mainz, 1999.

Airlie, Stuart. "Private Bodies and the Body Politic in the Divorce Case of Lothar II." *Past and Present* 161 (1998), 3–38.

Althoff, Gerd. *Family, Friends and Followers: Political and Social Bonds in Medieval Europe.* Trans. Christopher Carroll. Cambridge, 2004.

Alvarez de las Asturias, Nicolás. "Lanfranc of Bec's Version of Decretals in a Canonistic Context." *Catholic Historical Review* 98 (2012), 649–78.

Am Vorabend der Kaiser Krönung: Das Epos "Karolus Magnus et Leo papa" und der Papstbesuch in Paderborn 799. Ed. Peter Godman, Jörg Jarnut, and Peter Johanek. Berlin, 2002.

Anton, Hans Hubert. *Fürstenspiegel und Herrscherethos in der Karolingerzeit.* Bonn, 1968.

Arnold, Ellen F. *Negotiating the Landscape: Environment and Monastic Identity in the Medieval Ardennes.* Philadelphia, 2013.

Aspects du monachisme en Normandie (IVe–XVIIIe siècles). Ed. Lucien Musset. Paris, 1982.

Atsma, Hartmut. "Klöster und Mönchtum im Bistum Auxerre bis zum Ende des 6. Jahrhunderts." *Francia* 11 (1983), 1–96.

Atsma, Hartmut, and Jean Vezin. "Autour des actes privés du chartrier de Cluny (Xe–XIe siècles)." *Bibliothèque de l'Ecole des chartes* 155 (1997), 45–60.

———. "Les faux sur papyrus de l'abbaye de Saint-Denis." In *Finances, pouvoirs et mémoire: Mélanges offerts à Jean Favier.* Ed. Jean Kerhervé and Albert Rigaudière. Paris, 1999. Pp. 674–99.

Auger, Marie-Louise. *La collection de Bourgogne (mss 1–74) à la Bibliothèque nationale: Une illustration de la méthode mauriste.* Geneva and Paris, 1987.

Baccou, Philippe. "Les débuts de Robert le Fort: Une chronologie à réviser?" *Francia* 36 (2009), 265–76.

Bachrach, Bernard S. "Charles Martel, Mounted Shock Combat, the Stirrup, and Feudalism." *Studies in Medieval and Renaissance History* 7 (1970), 47–75.

———. *Early Carolingian Warfare: Prelude to Empire.* Philadelphia, 2001.

Barbero, Alessandro. *Charlemagne, Father of a Continent.* Trans. Allan Cameron. Berkeley, 2004.

Barthélemy, Dominique. *L'an mil et la paix de Dieu: La France chrétienne et féodale, 980–1060.* Paris, 1999.

———. "Une crise de l'écrite? Observations sur des actes de Saint-Aubin d'Angers (XIe siècle)." *Bibliothèque de l'Ecole des chartes* 155 (1997), 95–117.

———. *La mutation de l'an mil a-t-elle eu lieu? Servage et chevalerie dans la France des Xe et XIe siècles.* Paris, 1997.

Barton, Richard E. *Lordship in the County of Maine, c. 890–1160.* Woodbridge, Eng., 2004.

Bautier, Robert-Henri. *Chartes, sceaux et chancelleries: Etudes de diplomatique et de sigillographie médiévales.* 2 vols. Paris, 1990.

———. *Recherches sur l'histoire de la France médiévale des Mérovingiens aux premiers Capétiens.* Brookfield, Vt., 1991.

Becher, Matthias. "Drogo und die Königserhebung Pippins." *Frühmittelalterliche Studien* 23 (1989), 131–53.

Bedos, Brigitte. "Signes et insignes du pouvoir royal et seigneurial au moyen âge: Le témoinage des sceaux." In Comité des travaux historiques et scientifiques. *Les pouvoirs de commandement jusqu'à 1610*. Actes du 105e Congrès national des sociétés savantes, vol. 1. Paris, 1984.

Berkhofer, Robert F. *Day of Reckoning: Power and Accountability in Medieval France*. Philadelphia, 2004.

———. "Inventaires de biens et proto-compabilités dans le nord de la France (XIe–début du XIIe siècle)." *Bibliothèque de l'Ecole des chartes* 155 (1997), 339–49.

Bernstein, Alan E. *The Formation of Hell: Death and Retribution in the Ancient and Early Christian Worlds*. Ithaca, N.Y., 1993.

Binski, Paul. *Medieval Death: Ritual and Representation*. Ithaca, N.Y., 1996.

Bischoff, Bernhard. *Latin Palaeography: Antiquity and the Middle Ages*. Trans. Dáibhí O Cróinín and David Ganz. Cambridge, 1989.

The Bishop: Power and Piety at the First Millennium. Ed. Sean Gilsdorf. Münster, 2004.

Bisson, T. N. "The 'Feudal Revolution.'" *Past and Present* 142 (1994), 6–42.

Bitel, Lisa M. *Landscape with Two Saints: How Genovefa of Paris and Brigit of Kildare Built Christianity in Barbarian Europe*. Oxford, 2009.

Bouchard, Constance B. "Childeric III and the Emperors Drogo Magnus and Pippin the Pious." *Medieval Prosopography* 28 (2013), 1–16.

———. "Episcopal *Gesta* and the Creation of a Useful Past in Ninth-Century Auxerre." *Speculum* 84 (2009), 1–35.

———. *"Every Valley Shall Be Exalted": The Discourse of Opposites in Twelfth-Century Thought*. Ithaca, N.Y., 2003.

———. "Forging Papal Authority: Charters from the Monastery of Montier-en-Der." *Church History* 69 (2000), 1–17.

———. "High Medieval Monks Contemplate Their Merovingian Past." *Journal of Medieval Monastic Studies* 1 (2012), 41–62.

———. *Holy Entrepreneurs: Cistercians, Knights, and Economic Exchange in Twelfth-Century Burgundy*. Ithaca, N.Y., 1991.

———. "Images of the Merovingians and Carolingians." *History Compass* 4 (2006), 1–15.

———. "Merovingian, Carolingian, and Cluniac Monasticism: Reform and Renewal in Burgundy." *Journal of Ecclesiastical History* 41 (1990), 365–88.

———. "Queen Theuchildis of Sens." *Medieval Prosopography* 26 (2005), 1–12.

———. "Reconstructing Sanctity and Refiguring Saints in Early Medieval Gaul." In *Studies on Medieval Empathies*. Ed. Karl F. Morrison and Rudolph M. Bell. Turnhout, 2013. Pp. 91–114.

———. *Spirituality and Administration: The Role of the Bishop in Twelfth-Century Auxerre*. Speculum Anniversary Monographs 5. Cambridge, Mass., 1979.

———. *Sword, Miter, and Cloister: Nobility and the Church in Burgundy, 980–1198*. Ithaca, N.Y., 1987.

———. *"Those of My Blood": Constructing Noble Families in Medieval Francia*. Philadelphia, 2001.

Bowman, Jeffrey A. *Shifting Landmarks: Property, Proof, and Dispute in Catalonia Around the Year 1000*. Ithaca, N.Y., 2004.

Boynton, Susan. *Shaping a Monastic Identity: Liturgy and History at the Imperial Abbey of Farfa, 1000–1125*. Ithaca, N.Y., 2006.

Brown, Peter. *Authority and the Sacred: Aspects of the Christianisation of the Roman World*. Cambridge, 1995.

———. *The Cult of the Saints: Its Rise and Function in Latin Christianity*. Chicago, 1981.

———. "Enjoying the Saints in Late Antiquity." *Early Medieval Europe* 9 (2000), 1–24.

———. *The Rise of Western Christendom*. 2nd ed. London, 2003.

———. *Through the Eye of a Needle: Wealth, the Fall of Rome, and the Making of Christianity in the West, 350–550 AD*. Princeton, N.J., 2012.

Brown, Warren C. "On the *Gesta municipalia* and the Public Validation of Documents in Frankish Europe." *Speculum* 87 (2012), 345–75.

Bullough, Donald A. *Alcuin: Achievement and Reputation*. Leiden, 2004.

Bulst, Niethard. *Untersuchungen zu den Klosterreform Wilhelms von Dijon (962–1031)*. Bonn, 1973.

Bur, Michel. "A propos du chapitre xxxviii du polyptyque de Montier-en-Der: Aperçu sur la structure et le fontionnement d'un grand domaine du IXe au XIIIe siècle." *Revue du Nord* 72 (1990), 417–28.

Bynum, Caroline Walker. *The Resurrection of the Body in Western Christianity, 200–1336*. New York, 1995.

Caner, Daniel. *Wandering, Begging Monks: Spiritual Authority and the Promotion of Monasticism in Late Antiquity*. Berkeley, 2002.

Carruthers, Mary. *The Book of Memory: A Study of Memory in Medieval Culture*. Cambridge, 1990.

———. *The Craft of Thought: Meditation, Rhetoric, and the Making of Images, 400–1200*. Cambridge, 1998.

Les cartulaires. Ed. Olivier Guyotjeannin, Laurent Morelle, and Michel Parisse. Mémoires et documents de l'Ecole des chartes 39. Paris, 1993.

Les cartulaires méridionaux. Ed. Daniel Le Blévec. Etudes et rencontres de l'Ecole des chartes 19. Paris, 2006.

Castelli, Elizabeth A. *Martyrdom and Memory: Early Christian Culture Making*. New York, 2004.

Chadwick, Henry. *The Church in Ancient Society, from Galilee to Gregory the Great*. Oxford, 2001.

La chanson de geste et le mythe carolingien: Mélanges René Louis. 2 vols. St.-Père-sous-Vézelay, 1982.

Charlemagne's Heir: New Perspectives on the Reign of Louis the Pious. Ed. Peter Godman and Roger Collins. Oxford, 1990.

Charters and the Use of the Written Word in Medieval Society. Ed. Karl Heidecker. Turnhout, 2000.

Charters, Cartularies, and Archives: The Preservation and Transmission of Documents in the Medieval West. Ed. Adam J. Kosto and Anders Winroth. Toronto, 2002.

Chazelle, Celia. *The Crucified God in the Carolingian Era: Theology and Art of Christ's Passion.* Cambridge, 2001.

La christianisation des pays entre Loire et Rhin (IVe–VIIe siècle). Ed. Pierre Riché. Paris, 1993.

Clanchy, M. T. *From Memory to Written Record: England, 1066–1307.* 2nd ed. Oxford, 1993.

Clark, Elizabeth A. "Claims on the Bones of Saint Stephen: The Partisans of Melania and Eudocia." *Church History* 51 (1982), 141–56.

Clark, Gillian. "Translating Relics: Victricius of Rouen and Fourth-Century Debate." *Early Medieval Europe* 10 (2001), 161–76.

Claussen, M. A. *The Reform of the Frankish Church: Chrodegang of Metz and the Regula canonicorum in the Eighth Century.* Cambridge, 2004.

Clovis: Histoire et mémoire. Ed. Michel Rouche. 2 vols. Paris, 1997.

Collins, Roger. *Charlemagne.* Toronto, 1998.

———. *Die Fredegar-Chroniken.* MGH Studien und Texte 44. Hanover, 2007.

Columbanus and Merovingian Monasticism. Ed. H. B. Clarke and Mary Brown. BAR International Series 113. Oxford, 1981.

Constable, Giles. "Forgery and Plagiarism in the Middle Ages." *Archiv für Diplomatik* 29 (1983), 1–41.

Contreni, John J. "'And Even Today': Carolingian Monasticism and the *Miracula Sancti Germani* of Heiric of Auxerre." In *Medieval Monks and Their World, Ideas and Realities: Studies in Honor of Richard E. Sullivan.* Ed. David Blanks, Michael Frassetto, and Amy Livingstone. Leiden, 2006. Pp. 35–48.

Coon, Lynda L. *Sacred Fictions: Holy Women and Hagiography in Late Antiquity.* Philadelphia, 1997.

Costambeys, Marios. "An Aristocratic Community on the Northern Frankish Frontier." *Early Medieval Europe* 3 (1994), 39–62.

Costambeys, Marios, Matthew Innes, and Simon MacLean. *The Carolingian World.* Cambridge, 2011.

Crété-Protin, Isabelle. *Eglise et vie chrétienne dans le diocèse de Troyes du IVe au IXe siècle.* Villeneuve d'Ascq, 2002.

Curta, Florin. "Merovingian and Carolingian Gift Giving." *Speculum* 81 (2006), 671–99.

Daly, William M. "Clovis: How Barbaric, How Pagan?" *Speculum* 69 (1994), 619–64.

Davies, Wendy. "The Composition of the Redon Cartulary." *Francia* 17/1 (1990), 69–90.

De Jong, Mayke. *The Penitential State: Authority and Atonement in the Age of Louis the Pious, 814–840.* Cambridge, 2009.

Deflou-Leca, Noëlle. *Saint-Germain d'Auxerre et ses dépendances (Ve–XIIIe siècle).* St.-Etienne, 2010.

Depreux, Philippe. *Prosopographie de l'entourage de Louis le Pieux (781–840).* Sigmaringen, 1997.

Deschamps, Paul. "Critique du privilège épiscopal accordé par Emmon de Sens à l'abbaye de Sainte-Colombe." *Le moyen âge* 25 (1912), 144–65.

Devroey, Jean-Pierre. *Etudes sur le grand domaine carolingien.* Aldershot, Eng., 1993.

———. "Les services de transport à l'abbaye de Prüm au IXème siècle." *Revue du nord* 61 (1979), 543–69.

Dhondt, J. *Etudes sur la naissance des principautés territoriales en France (IXe–Xe siècles)*. Bruges, 1948.

Diem, Albrecht. *Das monastische Experiment: Die rolle der Keuschheit bei der Entstehung des westlichen Klosterwesens*. Münster, 2005.

———. "Monks, Kings, and the Transformation of Sanctity: Jonas of Bobbio and the End of the Holy Man." *Speculum* 82 (2007), 521–59.

Dierkens, Alain. *Abbayes et chapitres entre Sambre et Meuse (VIIe–XIe siècles)*. Beihefte der Francia 14. Sigmaringen, 1985.

Dierkens, Alain, and Patrick Périn. "Death and Burial in Gaul and Germania, 4th–8th Century." In *Transformation of the Roman World, AD 400–900*. Ed. Leslie Webster and Michelle Brown. London, 1997. Pp. 79–95.

Documentary Culture and the Laity in the Early Middle Ages. Ed. Warren C. Brown, Marios Costambeyes, Matthew Innes, and Adam J. Kosto. Cambridge, 2013.

Duby, Georges. *The Early Growth of the European Economy: Warriors and Peasants from the Seventh to the Twelfth Century*. Trans. Howard B. Clarke. Ithaca, N.Y., 1974.

D'une déposition à un couronnement, 476–800: Rupture ou continuité dans la naissance de l'Occident médiéval. Ed. Institut des Hautes Etudes de Belgique. Brussels, 1975.

Dunn, Marilyn. *The Emergence of Monasticism from the Desert Fathers to the Early Middle Ages*. Oxford, 2000.

Durliat, Jean. *Les finances publiques de Dioclétien aux Carolingiens (284–889)*. Beihefte der Francia 21. Sigmaringen, 1990.

Dutton, Paul Edward. *Charlemagne's Mustache and Other Cultural Clusters of a Dark Age*. New York, 2004.

Dutton, Paul Edward, and Herbert L. Kessler. *The Poetry and Paintings of the First Bible of Charles the Bald*. Ann Arbor, Mich., 1997.

Der Dynastiewechsel von 751: Vorgeschichte, Legitimationsstrategien und Erinnerung. Ed. Matthias Becher and Jörg Jarnut. Münster, 2004.

Ebling, Horst. *Prosopographie der Amtsträger des Merowingerreiches*. Beiheft der Francia 2. Munich, 1974.

L'école carolingienne d'Auxerre de Murethach à Remi, 830–908. Ed. Dominique Iogna-Prat, Colette Jeudy, and Guy Lobrichon. Paris, 1991.

Effros, Bonnie. *Caring for Body and Soul: Burial and the Afterlife in the Merovingian World*. University Park, Pa., 2002.

———. *Merovingian Mortuary Archaeology and the Making of the Early Middle Ages*. Berkeley, 2003.

Elliott, Dyan. *Spiritual Marriage: Sexual Abstinence in Medieval Wedlock*. Princeton, N.J., 1993.

Evergates, Theodore. "The Chancery Archives of the Counts of Champagne: Codicology and History of the Cartulary-Registers." *Viator* 16 (1985), 159–79.

Ewig, Eugen. "Die Namengebung bei den Ältesten Franken Königen und im Merowingischen Königshaus." *Francia* 18 (1991), 21–69.

———. *Spätantikes und fränkisches Gallien*. 2 vols. Beihefte der Francia 3. Munich, 1976–79.

Fälschungen im Mittelalter. 6 vols. Schriften der MGH 33. Hanover, 1988–90.

Farmer, Sharon. *Communities of Saint Martin: Legend and Ritual in Medieval Tours.* Ithaca, N.Y., 1991.

Fassler, Margot E. *The Virgin of Chartres: Making History Through Liturgy and the Arts.* New Haven, Conn., 2010.

Felten, Franz J. *Äbte und Laienäbte im Frankenreich: Studien zum Verhältnis von Staat und Kirche im früheren Mittelalter.* Stuttgart, 1980.

Femmes et pouvoirs des femmes à Byzance et en Occident (VIe–XIe siècles). Ed. Stéphane Lebecq, Alain Dierkens, Régine Le Jan, and Jean-Marie Sansterre. Lille, 1999.

Fifth-Century Gaul: A Crisis of Identity? Ed. John Drinkwater and Hugh Elton. Cambridge, 1992.

Firey, Abigail. "Lawyers and Wisdom: The Use of the Bible in the Pseudo-Isidorian Forged Decretals." In *The Study of the Bible in the Carolingian Era.* Ed. Celia Chazelle and Burton Van Name Edwards. Turnhout, 2003. Pp. 189–214.

Flammarion, Hubert. "Une équipe de scribes au travail au XIIIe siècle: Le grand cartulaire du chapitre cathédral de Langres." *Archiv für Diplomatik* 28 (1982), 271–305.

Fleming, Robin. *Domesday Book and the Law: Society and Legal Custom in Early Medieval England.* Cambridge, 1998.

Fossier, Robert. *Polyptyques et censiers.* Typologie des sources du moyen âge occidental 28. Turnhout, 1978.

Fouracre, Paul. *The Age of Charles Martel.* Harlow, Eng., 2000.

———. "Merovingian History and Merovingian Hagiography." *Past and Present* 127 (1990), 3–38.

———. "Observations on the Outgrowth of Pippinid Influence in the 'Regnum Francorum' After the Battle of Tertry (687–715)." *Medieval Prosopography* 5/2 (1984), 1–31.

Fouracre, Paul, and Richard A. Gerberding. *Late Merovingian France: History and Hagiography, 640–720.* Manchester, 1996.

Frankland: The Franks and the World of the Early Middle Ages. Ed. Paul Fouracre and David Ganz. Manchester, 2008.

Freed, John B. "Reflections on the Medieval German Nobility." *American Historical Review* 91 (1986), 553–75.

Freeman, Ann. "Carolingian Orthodoxy and the Fate of the *Libri Carolini*." *Viator* 16 (1985), 65–108.

Fuhrmann, Horst. *Einfluß und Verbreitung der pseudoisidorischen Fälschungen.* 3 vols. Schriften der MGH 24. Stuttgart, 1972–74.

Gabriele, Matthew. *An Empire of Memory: The Legend of Charlemagne, the Franks, and Jerusalem Before the First Crusade.* Oxford, 2011.

Garipzanov, Ildar H. "The Image of Authority in Carolingian Coinage: The Image of a Ruler and Roman Imperial Tradition." *Early Medieval Europe* 8 (1999), 197–218.

———. *The Symbolic Language of Authority in the Carolingian World (c. 751–877).* Leiden, 2008.

Gauthier, Nancy, and Jean-Charles Picard, eds. *Topographie chrétienne des cités de la Gaule des origines au milieu du VIIIe siècle.* Vol. 8. *Province ecclésiastique de Sens (Lugdunensis Senonia).* Paris, 1992.

Geary, Patrick J. *Aristocracy in Provence: The Rhône Basin at the Dawn of the Carolingian Age.* Philadelphia, 1985.

——. *Before France and Germany: The Creation and Transformation of the Merovingian World.* Oxford, 1988.

——. *Furta Sacra: Thefts of Relics in the Central Middle Ages.* Princeton, N.J., 1978.

——. *Living with the Dead in the Middle Ages.* Ithaca, N.Y., 1994.

——. *The Myth of Nations: The Medieval Origins of Europe.* Princeton, N.J., 2002.

——. *Phantoms of Remembrance: Memory and Oblivion at the End of the First Millennium.* Princeton, N.J., 1994.

Gender in the Early Medieval World: East and West, 300–900. Ed. Leslie Brubaker and Julia M. H. Smith. Cambridge, 2004.

Genicot, Léopold. "*Discordiae concordantium*: Sur l'intérêt des textes hagiographiques." *Académie royale de Belgique, Bulletin de la classe des lettres et des sciences morales et politiques* 51 (1965), 65–75.

"The Gentle Voices of Teachers": Aspects of Learning in the Carolingian Era. Ed. Richard E. Sullivan. Columbus, Ohio, 1995.

George, Judith M. *Venantius Fortunatus: A Latin Poet in Merovingian Gaul.* Oxford, 1992.

Gerberding, Richard A. *The Rise of the Carolingians and the "Liber historiae Francorum."* Oxford, 1987.

Glenn, Jason. *Politics and History in the Tenth Century: The Work and World of Richer of Reims.* Cambridge, 2004.

Glöckner, K. "Lorsch und Lothringen, Robertiner und Capetinger." *Zeitschrift für die Geschichte des Oberrheins* 89 (1937), 301–54.

Goetz, Hans-Werner. "Serfdom and the Beginnings of a 'Seigneurial System' in the Carolingian Period: A Survey of the Evidence." *Early Medieval Europe* 2 (1993), 29–51.

Goffart, Walter. *The Le Mans Forgeries.* Cambridge, Mass., 1966.

——. *The Narrators of Barbarian History (AD 550–800): Jordanes, Gregory of Tours, Bede, and Paul the Deacon.* Princeton, N.J., 1988.

——. "Paul the Deacon's *Gesta episcoporum Mettensium* and the Early Design of Charlemagne's Succession." *Traditio* 42 (1986), 59–93.

——. *Rome's Fall and After.* London, 1989.

Goldberg, Eric J. "Louis the Pious and the Hunt." *Speculum* 88 (2013), 613–43.

Le grand domaine aux époques mérovingienne et carolingienne/Die Grundherrschaft im frühen Mittelalter. Ed. Adriaan Verhulst. Ghent, 1985.

Griffe, Elie. *La Gaule chrétienne à l'époque romaine.* Rev. ed. 3 vols. Paris, 1964–66.

Guerriers et moines: Conversion et sainteté aristocratiques dans l'Occident médiéval (IXe–XIIe siècle). Ed. Michel Lauwers. Antibes, 2002.

Guyotjeannin, Olivier. "*Penuria scriptorum*: Le mythe de l'anarchie documentaire dans la France du nord (Xe–première moitié du XIe siècle)." *Bibliothèque de l'Ecole des chartes* 155 (1997), 11–44.

Hack, Achim Thomas. *Codex Carolinus: Päpstliche Epistolographie im 8. Jahrhundert.* 2 vols. Päpste und Papstum 35. Stuttgart, 2006–7.

Hägermann, Dieter. "Eine Grundherrschaft des 13. Jh. im Spiegel des Frühmittelalters: Caesarius von Prüm und seine kommentierte Abschrift des Urbars von 893." *Rheinische Vierteljahrsblätter* 45 (1981), 1–34.

L'hagiographie du haut moyen âge du Gaule du nord. Ed. Martin Heinzelmann. Stuttgart, 2001.

Halfond, Gregory I. *The Archaeology of Frankish Church Councils, AD 511–768.* Leiden, 2010.

Halsall, Guy. *Barbarian Migrations and the Roman West, 376–568.* Cambridge, 2007.

———. *Settlement and Social Organization: The Merovingian Region of Metz.* Cambridge, 1995.

Hamerow, Helena. *Early Medieval Settlements: The Archaeology of Rural Communities in North-West Europe, 400–900.* Oxford, 2002.

Hammer, Carl L. "'Pipinus Rex': Pippin's Plot of 792 and Bavaria." *Traditio* 63 (2008), 235–76.

Hannig, Jurgen. *Consensus Fidelium: Frühfeudale Interpretationen des Verhältnisses von Königtum und Adel am Beispiel des Frankenreiches.* Stuttgart, 1982.

Harmand, Jacques. *Alesia: Une campagne césarienne.* Paris, 1969.

Hartmann, Martina. "*Pater incertus?* Zu den Vätern des Gegenkönigs Chlothar IV. (717–718) und des letzten Merowingerkönigs Childerich III. (743–751)." *Deutsches Archiv für Erforschung des Mittelalters* 58 (2002), 1–15.

Head, Thomas. *Hagiography and the Cult of Saints: The Diocese of Orléans, 800–1200.* Cambridge, 1990.

Healy, Patrick. *The Chronicle of Hugh of Flavigny: Reform and the Investiture Contest in the Late Eleventh Century.* Aldershot, Eng., 2006.

Heffernan, Thomas J. *Sacred Biography: Saints and Their Biographers in the Middle Ages.* Oxford, 1988.

Heidrich, Ingrid. "Titular und Urkunden der arnulfingischen Hausmeier." *Archiv für Diplomatik* 11/12 (1965/66), 71–279.

Heinzelmann, Martin. *Gregory of Tours: History and Society in the Sixth Century.* Trans. Christopher Carroll. Cambridge, 2001.

Heinzelmann, Martin, and Joseph-Claude Poulin. *Les vies anciennes de Sainte Geneviève de Paris: Etudes critiques.* Paris, 1986.

Helvétius, Anne-Marie. *Abbayes, évêques et laïques: Une politique du pouvoir en Hainaut au moyen âge (VIIe–XIe siècle).* Brussels, 1994.

Hen, Yitzhak. *Culture and Religion in Merovingian Gaul, A.D. 481–751.* Leiden, 1995.

———. *Roman Barbarians: The Royal Court and Culture in the Early Medieval West.* New York, 2007.

Henrion, Fabrice. "L'ancienne église Saint-Pèlerin d'Auxerre (Yonne)." *Bulletin du centre d'études médiévales d'Auxerre* 15 (2011). http://cem.revues.org/index12106.html. Accessed September 29, 2011.

Herrick, Samantha Kahn. *Imagining the Sacred Past: Hagiography and Power in Early Normandy.* Cambridge, Mass., 2007.

Heuclin, Jean. *Aux origines monastiques de la Gaule du Nord: Ermites et reclus du Ve au XIe siècle.* Lille, 1988.

———. *Hommes de Dieu et fonctionnaires du roi en Gaule du Nord du Ve au IXe siècle.* Villeneuve-d'Ascq, 1998.

Hobsbawm, Eric. "Inventing Traditions." In *The Invention of Tradition.* Ed. Eric Hobsbawm and Terence Ranger. Cambridge, 1983. Pp. 1–14.

Hodges, Richard, and David Whitehouse. *Mohammed, Charlemagne and the Origins of Europe.* Ithaca, N.Y., 1983.

Hummer, Hans J. *Politics and Power in Early Medieval Europe: Alsace and the Frankish Realm, 600–1000.* Cambridge, 2005.

Humour, History and Politics in Late Antiquity and the Early Middle Ages. Ed. Guy Halsall. Cambridge, 2002.

Innes, Matthew. *State and Society in the Early Middle Ages: The Middle Rhine Valley, 400–1000.* Cambridge, 2000.

The Invention of Saintliness. Ed. Anneke B. Mulder-Bakker. New York, 2002.

James, Edward. *The Franks.* Oxford, 1988.

Janin, Pierre. "Heiric d'Auxerre et les Gesta pontificum Autissiodorensium." *Francia* 4 (1976), 89–105.

Jarnut, Jörg. *Agiolfingerstudien: Untersuchungen zur Geschichte einer adligen Familie im 6. und 7. Jahrhundert.* Stuttgart, 1986.

———. "Chlodwig und Chlothar: Anmerkungen zu den Namen zweier Sohne Karls des Grossen." *Francia* 12 (1984), 645–51.

Jasper, Detlev, and Horst Fuhrmann. *Papal Letters in the Early Middle Ages.* Trans. Steven Rowan and Timothy Reuter. Washington, D.C., 2001.

Jobert, Philippe. *La notion de donation: Convergences, 630–750.* Paris, 1977.

Joch, Waltraud. *Legitimität und Integration: Untersuchungen zu den Anfängen Karl Martells.* Husum, Germany, 1999.

Jones, A. H. M., and J. R. Martindale. *The Prosopography of the Later Roman Empire.* 3 vols. Cambridge, 1971–92.

Kaiser, Reinhold. *Bischofsherrschaft zwischen Königtum und Fürstenmacht.* Bonn, 1981.

Karl der Grosse: Lebenswerk und Nachleben. Ed. Wolfgang Braunfels. 5 vols. Düsseldorf, 1965–68.

Karl Martell in seiner Zeit. Ed. Jörg Jarnut, Ulrich Nonn, and Michael Richter. Beihefte der Francia 37. Sigmaringen, 1994.

Kasten, Brigitte. *Königssöhne und Königsherrschaft: Untersuchungen zur Teilhabe am Reich in der Merowinger- und Karolingerzeit.* Schriften der MGH 44. Hanover, 1997.

Kéry, Lotte. *Canonical Collections of the Early Middle Ages (ca. 400–1140): A Bibliographical Guide to the Manuscripts and Literature.* Washington, D.C., 1999.

King, Peter. *Western Monasticism: A History of the Monastic Movement in the Latin Church.* Kalamazoo, Mich., 1999.

Kitchen, John. *Saints' Lives and the Rhetoric of Gender: Male and Female in Merovingian Hagiography*. Oxford, 1998.

Klingshirn, William E. *Caesarius of Arles: Life, Testament, Letters*. Liverpool, 1994

———. *Caesarius of Arles: The Making of a Christian Community in Late Antique Gaul*. Cambridge, 1994.

Kloster Fulda in der Welt der Karolinger und Ottonen. Ed. Gangolf Schrimpf. Frankfurt, 1996.

Kölzer, Theo. *Merowingerstudien*. 2 vols. MGH Studien und Texte 21, 26. Hanover, 1998–99.

Kosto, Adam J. "The *Liber feudorum maior* of the Counts of Barcelona: The Cartulary as an Expression of Power." *Journal of Medieval History* 27 (2001), 1–22.

Koziol, Geoffrey. *The Politics of Memory and Identity in Carolingian Royal Diplomas: The West Frankish Kingdoms (840–987)*. Turnhout, 2012.

Kuefler, Mathew. *The Making and Unmaking of a Saint: Hagiography and Memory in the Cult of Gerald of Aurillac*. Philadelphia, 2014.

Landes, Richard. *Relics, Apocalypse, and the Deceits of History: Ademar of Chabannes, 989–1034*. Cambridge, Mass., 1995.

Langres et ses évêques, VIIIe–XIe siècles: Aux origines d'une seigneurie ecclésiastique. Langres, 1986.

Lawo, Mathias. *Studien zu Hugo von Flavigny*. Schriften der MGH 61. Hanover, 2010.

Le Jan, Régine. "À la recherche des élites rurales du début du VIIIe siècle: Le 'notaire' alsacien Chrodoin." *Revue du Nord* 86 (2004), 485–98.

———. *Famille et pouvoir dans le monde franc (VIIe–Xe siècle): Essai d'anthropologie sociale*. Paris, 1995.

———. *Femmes, pouvoir et société dans le haut Moyen Age*. Paris, 2001.

Le Maître, Philippe. "L'oeuvre d'Aldric du Mans et sa signification (832–857)." *Francia* 8 (1980), 43–64.

Levison, Wilhelm. "Bischof Germanus von Auxerre und die Quellen zu seiner Geschichte." *Neues Archiv* 29 (1904), 95–175.

Leyser, Conrad. "The Temptations of Cult: Roman Martyr Piety in the Age of Gregory the Great." *Early Medieval Europe* 9 (2000), 289–307.

Lifshitz, Felice. *The Name of the Saint: The Martyrology of Jerome and Access to the Sacred in Francia, 627–827*. Notre Dame, 2006.

———. *The Norman Conquest of Pious Neustria: Historiographic Discourse and Saintly Relics, 684–1090*. Toronto, 1995.

Little, Lester K. *Benedictine Maledictions: Ritual Cursing in Romanesque France*. Ithaca, N.Y., 1993.

———. *Religious Poverty and the Profit Economy in Medieval Europe*. Ithaca, N.Y., 1978.

Lobbedey, Uwe. "Carolingian Royal Palaces: The State of Research from an Architectural Historian's Viewpoint." In *Court Culture in the Early Middle Ages*. Ed. Catherine Cubitt. Turnhout, 2003. Pp. 129–54.

Local Saints and Local Churches in the Medieval West. Ed. Alan Thacker and Richard Sharpe. Oxford, 2002.

The Long Eighth Century. Ed. Inge Lyse Hansen and Chris Wickham. Leiden, 2000.

The Long Morning of Medieval Europe: New Directions in Early Medieval Studies. Ed. Jennifer R. Davis and Michael McCormick. Aldershot, Eng., 2008.

Lot, Ferdinand. *The End of the Ancient World and the Beginnings of the Middle Ages*. Trans. Philip Leon and Mariette Leon. New York, 1931.

———. "Note sur la date du polyptyque de Montierender." *Le moyen âge* 35 (1924), 107–17.

Louis, René. *Girart, comte de Vienne (. . . 819–877), et ses fondations monastiques*. Auxerre, 1946.

Lowe, E. A. *Codices Latini antiquiores*. Vol. 6, *France*. Oxford, 1953.

Lusse, Jackie. "Le monachisme en Champagne des origines au XIIIe siècle." In *La Champagne bénédictine*. Travaux de l'Académie nationale de Reims 160. Reims, 1981. Pp. 24–78.

MacLean, Simon. "The Carolingian Response to the Revolt of Boso, 879–887." *Early Medieval Europe* 10 (2001), 21–48.

———. *Kingship and Politics in the Late Ninth Century: Charles the Fat and the End of the Carolingian Empire*. Cambridge, 2003.

MacMullen, Ramsay. *Christianizing the Roman Empire (A.D. 100–400)*. New Haven, Conn., 1984.

Madignier, Jacques. *Diocèse d'Autun*. Fasti ecclesiae Gallicanae 12. Turnhout, 2010.

Marilier, Jean. "Les privilèges épiscopaux de l'église de Losne." *Mémoires de la Société pour l'histoire du droit et des institutions des anciens pays bourguignons* 24 (1963), 247–68.

———. "Le scriptorium de l'abbaye de Flavigny au VIIIe siècle." *Annales de Bourgogne* 55 (1983), 30–33.

Markus, R. A. *The End of Ancient Christianity*. Cambridge, 1990.

———. *Gregory the Great and His World*. Cambridge, 1997.

Les martyrs de Lyon (177). Colloques internationales du Centre national de la recherche scientifique 575. Paris, 1978.

Mathisen, Ralph W. *Ecclesiastical Factionalism and Religious Controversy in Fifth-Century Gaul*. Washington, D.C., 1989.

———. *Roman Aristocrats in Barbarian Gaul: Strategies for Survival in an Age of Transition*. Austin, Tex., 1993.

McCormick, Michael. *Eternal Victory: Triumphal Rulership in Late Antiquity, Byzantium, and the Early Medieval West*. Cambridge, 1986.

———. *Origins of the European Economy: Communications and Commerce, A.D. 300–900*. Cambridge, 2001.

McGurk, Patrick. "The Oldest Manuscripts of the Latin Bible." In *The Early Medieval Bible*. Ed. Richard Gameson. Cambridge, 1994.

McKitterick, Rosamond. *The Carolingians and the Written Word*. Cambridge, 1989.

———. *Charlemagne: The Formation of a European Identity*. Cambridge, 2008.

———. *The Frankish Kingdoms Under the Carolingians, 751–987*. London, 1983.

———. *The Frankish Kings and Culture in the Early Middle Ages*. Aldershot, Eng., 1995.

————. *History and Memory in the Carolingian World*. Cambridge, 2004.

————. "Paul the Deacon and the Franks." *Early Medieval Europe* 8 (1999), 319–39.

————. *Perceptions of the Past in the Early Middle Ages*. Notre Dame, Ind., 2006.

Medieval Concepts of the Past: Ritual, Memory, Historiography. Ed. Gerd Althoff, Johannes Fried, and Patrick J. Geary. Cambridge, 2002.

The Medieval Nobility. Ed. and trans. Timothy Reuter. Amsterdam, 1978.

Medieval Transformations: Texts, Power, and Gifts in Context. Ed. Esther Cohen and Mayke B. de Jong. Leiden, 2001.

Le métier d'historien au moyen âge: Etudes sur l'historiographie médiévale. Ed. Bernard Guenée. Paris, 1977.

Les moines du Der, 673–1790. Ed. Patrick Corbet. Langres, 2000.

Le monde carolingien: Bilan, perspectives, champs de recherches. Ed. Wojciech Falkowski and Yves Sassier. Turnhout, 2009.

Monks and Nuns, Saints and Outcasts: Religion in Medieval Society. Ed. Sharon Farmer and Barbara H. Rosenwein. Ithaca, N.Y., 2000.

Morelle, Laurent. "Les 'actes de précaire,' instruments de transferts patrimoniaux (France du nord et de l'est, VIIIe–XIe siècle)." *Mélanges de l'Ecole française de Rome: Moyen âge, temps modernes* 111 (1999), 607–47.

————. "Examen de trois privilèges pontificaux du XIe siècle en faveur de Montier-en-Der." *Les cahiers haut-marnais* 161 (1985), 22–42.

Morimoto, Yoshiki. "Etat et perspectives des recherches sur les polyptyques carolingiens." *Annales de l'Est* 40 (1988), 99–149.

————. *Etudes sur l'économie rurale du haut Moyen Age: Historiographie, régime domanial, polyptyques carolingiens*. Brussels, 2008.

Morrison, Karl F. *Tradition and Authority in the Western Church, 300–1149*. Princeton, N.J., 1969.

Morrissey, Robert. *Charlemagne and France: A Thousand Years of Mythology*. Trans. Catherine Tihanyi. Notre Dame, Ind., 2003.

Moss, Candida. *The Myth of Persecution: How Early Christians Invented a Story of Martyrdom*. New York, 2013.

Mouillebouche, Hervé. "Un autre mythe historiographique: Le sac d'Autun par les Sarracins." *Annales de Bourgogne* 82 (2010), 5–36.

Nascita dell'Europa ed Europa carolingia: Un'equazione da verificare. Settimane di studio del Centro italiano di studi sull'alto medioevo 27. 2 vols. Spoleto, 1981.

Nees, Lawrence. *The Gundohinus Gospels*. Medieval Academy Books 95. Cambridge, Mass., 1987.

Negotiating Secular and Ecclesiastical Power. Ed. Henk Teunis, Andrew Wareham, and Arnoud-Jan A. Bijsterveld. Turnhout, 1999.

Nelson, Janet L. *Charles the Bald*. London, 1992.

————. *The Frankish World, 750–900*. London, 1996.

————. *Politics and Ritual in Early Medieval Europe*. London, 1986.

La Neustrie: Les pays au nord de la Loire de 650 à 850. Ed. Hartmut Atsma. 2 vols. Beihefte der Francia 16. Sigmaringen, 1989.

The New Cambridge Medieval History. Vol. 1. Ed. Paul Fouracre. Cambridge, 2005.

The New Cambridge Medieval History. Vol. 2. Ed. Rosamond McKitterick. Cambridge, 1995.

The New Cambridge Medieval History. Vol. 3. Ed. Timothy Reuter. Cambridge, 1999.

Noble, Thomas F. X. *Images, Iconoclasm, and the Carolingians.* Philadelphia, 2009.

Nobles and Nobility in Medieval Europe: Concepts, Origins, Transformations. Ed. Anne J. Duggan. Woodbridge, Eng., 2000.

Noizet, Hélène. "Le centre canonial de Saint-Martin de Tours et ses domaines péripheriques en val de Loire (IXe–Xe siècles)." *Annales de Bretagne et des pays de l'Ouest* 109 (2002), 9–33.

Nonn, Ulrich. "Erminethrud: Eine vornehme Neustrische Dame um 700." *Historisches Jahrbuch* 102 (1982), 135–43.

———. "Merowingische Testamente: Studien zum Fortleben einer römischen Urkundenform im Frankenreich." *Archiv für Diplomatik* 18 (1972), 1–129.

Offergeld, Thilo. *Reges pueri: Das Königtum Minderjähriger im frühen Mittelalter.* Schriften der MGH 50. Hanover, 2001.

Onomastique et parenté dans l'Occident médiéval. Ed. K. S. B. Keats-Rohan and C. Settipani. Oxford, 2000.

Pancartes monastiques des XIe et XIIe siècles. Ed. M. Parisse, P. Pégeot, and B.-M. Tock. Turnhout, 1998.

Paradigms and Methods in Early Medieval Studies. Ed. Celia Chazelle and Felice Lifshitz. New York, 2007.

Parisse, Michel. "L'abbaye de Gorze dans le contexte politique et religieux lorraine à l'époque de Jean de Vandières (900–974)." In *L'abbaye de Gorze au Xe siècle.* Ed. Michel Parisse and Gerhard Oexle. Nancy, 1993. Pp. 51–90.

———. "Ecriture et réécriture des chartes: Les pancartes aux XIe et XIIe siècles." *Bibliothèque de l'Ecole des chartes* 155 (1997), 247–65.

Paxton, Frederick S. *Christianizing Death: The Creation of a Ritual Process in Early Medieval Europe.* Ithaca, N.Y., 1990.

———. "Power and the Power to Heal: The Cult of St. Sigismund of Burgundy." *Early Medieval Europe* 2 (1993), 95–110.

Pays de Loire et Aquitaine de Robert le Fort aux premiers Capétiens. Ed. Olivier Guillot and Robert Favreau. Poitiers, 1997.

Picard, Jean-Charles. *Evêques, saints et cités en Italie et en Gaule: Etudes d'archéologie et d'histoire.* Rome, 1998.

Poeck, Dietrich W. *Cluniacensis Ecclesia: Der cluniacensische Klosterverband (10.–12. Jahrhundert).* Munich, 1998.

Pokorny, Rudolf. "Ein übersehenes Diplom Karls des Kahlen und der 'verloren' *Liber vetus* von Saint-Pierre-le-Vif/Sens." *Archiv für Diplomatik* 30 (1984), 51–65.

Prinz, Friedrich. *Frühes Mönchtum in Frankreich.* Munich, 1965.

Property and Power in the Early Middle Ages. Ed. Wendy Davies and Paul Fouracre. Cambridge, 1995.

Quantin, Maximilien. *Dictionnaire topographique du département de l'Yonne*. Paris, 1862.

Raaijmakers, Janneke. *The Making of the Monastic Community of Fulda, c. 744–c. 900*. Cambridge, 2012.

Rapp, Claudia. *Holy Bishops in Late Antiquity: The Nature of Christian Leadership in an Age of Transition*. Berkeley, 2005.

Réal, Isabelle. *Vies de saints, vie de famille: Représentation et système de la parenté dans le royaume mérovingien (481–751)*. Turnhout, 2001.

Religion, Culture, and Society in the Early Middle Ages: Studies in Honor of Richard E. Sullivan. Ed. Thomas F. X. Noble and John J. Contreni. Studies in Medieval Culture 23. Kalamazoo, Mich., 1987.

Remensnyder, Amy G. *Remembering Kings Past: Monastic Foundation Legends in Medieval Southern France*. Ithaca, N.Y., 1995.

Renard, Etienne. "Genèse et manipulations d'un polyptyque carolingien: Montier-en-Der, IXe–XIe siècles." *Le moyen âge* 110 (2004), 55–77.

———. "Lectures et relectures d'un polyptyque carolingien (Saint-Bertin, 844–859)." *Revue d'histoire ecclésiastique* 94 (1999), 373–435.

Retour aux sources: Textes, études et documents d'histoire médiévale offerts à Michel Parisse. Paris, 2004.

Reuter, Timothy. *Germany in the Early Middle Ages, 800–1050*. Harlow, Eng., 1991.

Richard, Louis. *Le polyptyque de Montier-en-Der*. St.-Dizier, 1999.

Riché, Pierre. *Les Carolingiens: Une famille qui fit l'Europe*. Paris, 1983.

Rio, Alice. *Legal Practice and the Written Word in the Early Middle Ages: Frankish Formulae, c. 500–1000*. Cambridge, 2009.

Rituals of Power from Late Antiquity to the Early Middle Ages. Ed. Frans Theuws and Janet L. Nelson. Leiden, 2000.

Rosé, Isabelle. *Construire une société seigneuriale: Itinéraire et ecclésiologie de l'abbé Odon de Cluny (fin du IXe–milieu du Xe siècle)*. Turnhout, 2008.

Rosenwein, Barbara H. *Emotional Communities in the Early Middle Ages*. Ithaca, N.Y., 2006.

———. *Negotiating Space: Power, Restraint, and Privileges of Immunity in Early Medieval Europe*. Ithaca, N.Y., 1999.

———. *Rhinoceros Bound: Cluny in the Tenth Century*. Philadelphia, 1982.

———. *To Be the Neighbor of Saint Peter: The Social Meaning of Cluny's Property, 909–1049*. Ithaca, N.Y., 1989.

Roserot, Alphonse. *Dictionnaire topographique du département de la Côte-d'Or*. Paris, 1924.

———. *Dictionnaire topographique du département de la Haute-Marne*. Paris, 1903.

La royauté et les élites dans l'Europe carolingienne (début IXe siècle aux environs de 920). Ed. Régine Le Jan. Lille, 1998.

Sackur, Ernst. *Die Cluniacenser in ihrer kirchlichen und allgemeinschichtlichen Wirksamkeit bis zur Mitte des elften Jahrhunderts*. Vol. 1. Halle an der Salle, 1892; rpt. Darmstadt, 1965.

Sághy, Marianne. "*Scinditur in partes populus*: Pope Damasus and the Martyrs of Rome." *Early Medieval Europe* 9 (2000), 273–87.

Saint-Germain d'Auxerre: Intellectuels et artistes dans l'Europe carolingienne, IXe–XIe siècles. Auxerre, 1990.

Saint Germain d'Auxerre et son temps. Ed. Société des sciences historiques et naturelles de l'Yonne. Auxerre, 1950.

Sassier, Yves. "Quelques remarques sur les diplômes d'immunité octroyés par les Carolingiens à l'abbaye de Saint-Germain d'Auxerre." *Bibliothèque de l'Ecole des chartes* 139 (1981), 37–54.

———. *Recherches sur le pouvoir comtal en Auxerrois du Xe au début du XIIIe siècle.* Auxerre, 1980.

Sato, Shoichi. "The Merovingian Account Documents of Tours: Form and Function." *Early Medieval Europe* 9 (2000), 143–61.

Scharf, Ralf. "Germanus von Auxerre: Chronologie seiner Vita." *Francia* 18/1 (1991), 1–19.

Semmler, Josef. "Bonifatius, die Karolinger und 'die Franken.'" In *Mönchtum—Kirche—Herrschaft, 750–1000.* Ed. Dieter R. Bauer, Rudolf Hiestand, Brigitte Kasten, and Sönke Lorenz. Sigmaringen, 1998. Pp. 3–49.

———. *Der Dynastiewechsel von 751 und die fränkische Königssalbung.* Düsseldorf, 2003.

———. "Zur pippinidisch-karolingischen Sukzessionskrise, 714–723." *Deutsches Archiv für Erforschung des Mittelalters* 33 (1977), 1–36.

Settipani, Christian. *La préhistoire des Capétiens, 481–987.* Villeneuve d'Ascq, 1993.

The Settlement of Disputes in Early Medieval Europe. Ed. Wendy Davies and Paul Fouracre. Cambridge, 1986.

The Sixth Century: Production, Distribution and Demand. Ed. Richard Hodges and William Bowden. Leiden, 1998.

Smith, Julia M. H. "Early Medieval Hagiography in the Late Twentieth Century." *Early Medieval Europe* 1 (1992), 69–76.

———. *Europe After Rome: A New Cultural History, 500–1000.* Oxford, 2005.

Society and Culture in Late Antique Gaul: Revisiting the Sources. Ed. Ralph W. Mathisen and Danuta Shanzer. Burlington, Vt., 2001.

Sot, Michel. *Gesta episcoporum, gesta abbatum.* Typologie des sources du moyen âge occidental 37. Turnhout, 1981.

———. *Un historien et son église: Flodoard de Reims.* Paris, 1993.

———. "Rhétorique et technique dans les préfaces des *gesta episcoporum* (IXe–XIIe s.)." *Cahiers de civilisation médiévale* 28 (1985), 181–200.

Soultrait, Georges de. *Dictionnaire topographique du département de la Nièvre.* Paris, 1865.

Spaces of the Living and the Dead: An Archaeological Dialogue. Ed. Catherine E. Karkov, Kelley M. Wickham-Crowley, and Bailey K. Young. Oxford, 1999.

Spencer, Mark. "Dating the Baptism of Clovis." *Early Medieval Europe* 3 (1994), 97–116.

Spiegel, Gabrielle M. "History, Historicism, and the Social Logic of the Text in the Middle Ages." *Speculum* 65 (1990), 59–86.

———. *The Past as Text: The Theory and Practice of Medieval Historiography.* Baltimore, 1997.

Stoclet, Alain J. "La 'Clausula de unctione Pippini regis': Mises au point et nouvelles hypothèses." *Francia* 8 (1980), 1–42.

Stone, Rachel. *Morality and Masculinity in the Carolingian Empire.* Cambridge, 2012.

Studien und Vorarbeiten zur Geschichte des grossfränkischen und frühdeutschen Adels. Ed. Gerd Tellenbach. Freiburg, 1957.

Sullivan, Richard E. "The Carolingian Age: Reflections on Its Place in the History of the Middle Ages." *Speculum* 64 (1989), 267–306.

Tellenbach, Gerd. "Die geistigen und politischen Grundlagen der Karolingischen Thronfolge." *Frühmittelalterliche Studien* 13 (1979), 184–302.

———. *Königtum und Stamme in der Werdezeit des deutschen Reiches.* Weimar, 1939.

Thompson, E. A. *Saint Germanus of Auxerre and the End of Roman Britain.* Woodbridge, Eng., 1984.

Tischler, Matthias M. *Einharts "Vita Karoli": Studien zur Entstehung, Überlieferung und Rezeption.* 2 vols. Schriften der MGH 48. Hanover, 2001.

Tock, Benoît-Michel. "Les mutations de vocabulaire latin des chartes au XIe siècle." *Bibliothèque de l'Ecole des chartes* 155 (1997), 119–48.

Topographies of Power in the Early Middle Ages. Ed. Mayke de Jong and Frans Theuws. Leiden, 2001.

Towns and Their Territories Between Late Antiquity and the Early Middle Ages. Ed. G. P. Brogiolo, N. Gauthier, and N. Christie. Leiden, 2000.

Tremp, Ernst. *Studien zu den Gesta Hludowici imperatoris des Trierer Chorbischofs Thegan.* Schriften der MGH 32. Hanover, 1988.

Ugé, Karine. *Creating the Monastic Past in Medieval Flanders.* York, 2005.

Ullman, Walter. *The Growth of Papal Government in the Middle Ages.* 2nd ed. London, 1962.

The Uses of the Past in the Early Middle Ages. Ed. Yitzhak Hen and Matthew Innes. Cambridge, 2000.

Van Dam, Raymond. "Images of Saint Martin in Late Roman and Early Merovingian Gaul." *Viator* 19 (1988), 1–27.

———. *Leadership and Community in Late Antique Gaul.* Berkeley, 1985.

———. *Saints and Their Miracles in Late Antique Gaul.* Princeton, N.J., 1993.

Van Egmond, Wolfert S. *Conversing with the Saints: Communication in Pre-Carolingian Hagiography from Auxerre.* Trans. Betsy van der Hoek. Turnhout, 2006.

Van Houts, Elisabeth. *Memory and Gender in Medieval Europe, 900–1200.* Toronto, 1999.

Venarde, Bruce L. *Women's Monasticism and Medieval Society: Nunneries in France and England, 890–1215.* Ithaca, N.Y., 1997.

Verhulst, Adriaan. *The Carolingian Economy.* Cambridge, 2002.

Voyage litteraire de deux réligieux Bénédictins de la congrégation de Saint Maur. Vol. 1. Paris, 1717.

Wallace-Hadrill, J. M. *The Frankish Church.* Oxford, 1983; rpt. 2001.

———. *The Long-Haired Kings and Other Studies in Frankish History.* London, 1962.

Wemple, Suzanne Fonay. *Women in Frankish Society: Marriage and the Cloister, 500 to 900.* Philadelphia, 1981.

Werner, Karl Ferdinand. "Liens de parenté et noms de personne: Un problème historique et méthodologique." In *Famille et parenté dans l'Occident médiéval.* Ed. Georges Duby and Jacques Le Goff. Rome, 1977.

————. *Vom Frankenreich zur Entfaltung Deutschlands und Frankreichs*. Sigmaringen, 1984.

White, Stephen D. *Custom, Kinship, and Gifts to Saints: The "Laudatio Parentum" in Western France, 1050–1150*. Chapel Hill, 1988.

Wickham, Chris. *Framing the Early Middle Ages: Europe and the Mediterranean, 400–800*. Oxford, 2005.

Wickstrom, John B. *The Life and Miracles of Saint Maurus: Disciple of Benedict, Apostle to France*. Collegeville, Minn., 2008.

Williams, Schafer. "Pseudo-Isidore from the Manuscripts." *Catholic Historical Review* 53 (1967), 58–66.

Wilsdorf, Christian. "Les Etichonides aux temps carolingiens et ottoniens." *Bulletin philologique et historique du Comité des travaux historiques et scientifiques* (1964), 1–33.

Wood, Ian. "Administration, Law, and Culture in Merovingian Gaul." In *From Roman Provinces to Medieval Kingdoms: Rewriting Histories*. Ed. Thomas F. X. Noble. New York, 2006. Pp. 358–75.

————. "The Governing Class of the Gibichung and Early Merovingian Kingdoms." In *Der frühmittelalterliche Staat—europäische Perspektiven*. Ed. Walter Pohl and Veronika Wieser. Vienna, 2008. Pp. 11–22.

————. *The Merovingian Kingdoms, 450–751*. Harlow, Eng., 1994.

————. "Saint-Wandrille and Its Hagiography." In *Church and Chronicle in the Middle Ages: Essays Presented to John Taylor*. Ed. Ian Wood and G. A. Loud. London, 1991. Pp. 1–14.

Wood, Susan. *The Proprietary Church in the Medieval West*. Oxford, 2006.

The World of Gregory of Tours. Ed. Kathleen Mitchell and Ian Wood. Leiden, 2002.

Index

Aachen, 90, 138–39, 141
Abbo, founder of Novalesa, 177
Adalgar, bishop of Autun, 85, 240, 325 n.17
Adalgisel-Grimo, 115
Adela of Pfalz, 103
"Admonitio generalis" (789), 88, 93, 138
Agano, bishop of Chartres, 47
Agaune. *See* St.-Maurice of Agaune
Alberic of Trois-Fontaines, 38
Alcuin, 89, 126, 144, 159
Aldric, bishop of Le Mans, 67–69, 75, 141–42, 171
Alise-Ste.-Reine, 48, 164, 177
Alsace, 143, 170, 173, 183, 188, 190
Amalgarius, duke, 25, 183
Ambrose, saint, 219–20, 226
Annales regni Francorum, 96–97
Annals of Metz. *See* Metz, annalist of
Anselm of St.-Remy, 1
Aquitaine, 76, 92–93, 129, 144, 172
Arnulf, bishop of Metz, 118, 182; in the Carolingian family tree, 112–16, 123, 148, 253 n.1
Arnulfings, xiii, 112. *See also* Carolingian kings
"Astronomer," 92, 98, 122, 143
Audoin, bishop of Rouen, 51, 202, 209, 222–23
Augustine, saint, 210, 219
Aunarius, bishop of Auxerre, 177, 222, 226
Aurelian, emperor, 45, 214–15, 217, 222–23
Autun, 49, 76, 85, 166, 225. *See also* Notre-Dame of Autun; St.-Martin of Autun; St.-Symphorien of Autun
Auxerre, 45, 51, 177, 220–22; cartulary of, 23, 27, 35; churches of, 245–49; *Gesta* of, 22, 245; martyrology of, 225–27. *See also* St.-Germain of Auxerre; St.-Julien of Auxerre
Aymo, count of Auxois, 162

Baio and Cylinia, donors, 158
Balthildis, queen, 44, 102, 200–201, 203, 209; and the "senior basilicas," 139–40, 200, 237, 247

Basina, queen, 102
Benedict, saint, 65, 138
Benedictine Rule, 44, 138, 194, 203–4
Benedict of Aniane, 138
Benedictus *levita,* 83–84
Bercharius, first abbot of Montier-en-Der, 24–25, 177, 239
Bertrada, queen, 97, 110, 119, 148
Bertram, bishop of Le Mans, 176–77
Betto, bishop of Langres, 19, 25, 129
Bèze, monastery, 1, 42–43, 129, 150, 183; cartulary-chronicle, 15, 39, 166, 202; foundation, 25, 201–2, 238
bigamy, 119
bishops: and the Pseudo-Isidorian decretals, 77–83; relations with monasteries, 50–52. *See also names of individual dioceses*
Bobbio, monastery, 208
Boniface, missionary, 83, 127, 170, 172; and Carloman, 133–34, 170; and Charles Martel, 130–31
Boso, count and king (879–887), 57, 109–10, 172, 242, 247
Brunhildis, queen, 108, 207, 236
Bruno, bishop of Langres, 43
Burgundian martyrs, 199, 215–17
Burgundofaro, bishop of Meaux, 209

Caesarius of Arles, 133, 195, 198–99, 217, 229
Caesarius of Prüm, 58–60
Cancor, founder of Lorsch, 173, 188
Capetians. *See* Robertian dynasty
"Capitulare de villis," 53, 138
Carilef, saint, 68–72
Carloman, king of the Franks (768–771), 120–21, 123–24
Carloman, mayor of the palace, 120–21, 124, 133–36, 144, 170

Carolingian kings: and the church, 126–51, 169–74, 230; cousins of, 122; creating an image of, 87–105, 229–30; dynasty of, 97–98, 106–25, 180, 229–30; family tree, 107; ties to the Merovingians, 122–24

Carthage, council of (525), 210

cartularies, 9–37; as administrative records, 32–33; and chronicles, 39–40; composition of, 22–26; and forgeries, 16–17; organization, 27–31; origins, 11–16, 53; and original charters, 34–36; and pancartes, 20–21; purposes, 31–34; uses, 36–37; and the written word, 18–20

cathedrals, relations with monasteries, 50–52. *See also names of individual dioceses*

Chalcedon, council of (451), 72, 76, 194–96, 210

Châlons-sur-Marne, 9, 22, 26, 30, 209. *See also* Warin, cantor of Châlons

Chalon-sur-Saône, 38, 42, 138, 195. *See also* St.-Marcel-lès-Chalon

Charlemagne, king and emperor (768–814), 17, 35, 48, 124, 158; as Christian leader, 87–89; and the *Codex carolinus*, 11; and the church, 80, 136–38, 142–45; dynasty of, 106–25; in forged documents, 63–64, 83; as Frankish leader, 91–93; as Hebrew king, 82, 93–94; and polyptyques, 53–54; as Roman emperor, 89–91

Charles Martel, 104, 114, 126; and the battle of Poitiers, 129–30; and bishops, 75; and church property, 128–31, 149; legitimacy of, 118–19; as mayor of the palace, 110, 124; and the Merovingians, 109; and the popes, 97

Charles the Bald, king and emperor (840–877), 43, 54, 60, 76, 82; charters of, 9, 17, 55–56, 166; and the church, 139; and Le Mans, 68, 73–75, 77, 85, 103; and the Vivien Bible, 92–94

Charlieu, monastery, 172, 242–43

Charters, in cartularies, 18–20, 22–26, 34–36. *See also* cartularies; Merovingian-era charters

Chartres, 23, 31. *See also* Paul of Chartres

Chelles, nunnery, 169, 200

Childebert I, king (511–558), 69–74

Childebert III, "the Adopted," 108–9, 282 n.9, 283 n.11

Childebert IV, king (694–711), 74, 104, 132

Childeric II, king (662–675), 24–25, 42, 146, 183

Childeric III, king (743–751), 48, 91; deposition of, 95–96

Chilperic I, king (561–584), 74, 132, 154, 206–7

Chilperic II, king (715–721), 189

Chrodegang, bishop of Metz, 172–73, 188

chroniclers. *See* Fredegar; Gregory of Tours;

Hugh of Flavigny; Paul of Chartres; Paul the Deacon; St.-Pierre-le-Vif, chronicle of

chronicles, 38–50; and cartularies, 39–40

Cistercian order, 15, 21, 43

Cîteaux, monastery, 15

Clairvaux, monastery, 15

"Clausula de Pippino," 95–97

Clothar I, king (511–561), 198

Clothar II, king (584–629), 25, 74, 103, 108, 133, 190; his wives, 148, 182

Clothar III, king (657–673), 44, 74, 101, 190, 201–2

Chlothar IV, king (717–719), 109

Clovis I, king (481–511), 41, 102–4, 123; baptism, 51, 97, 123, 148, 195

Clovis II, king (639–657), 74, 102, 146, 200

Clovis III, king (691–694), 74, 189

Cluny, monastery, 33, 166; cartularies of, 14–15, 23, 31, 35; foundation of, 42, 76, 172, 243; immunity of, 76, 209; priories of, 42–43, 243

Codex Carolinus, 11–12, 88, 96, 98

Cologne, 12, 223

Columbanus (d. 615), 41, 127, 203, 317 n.60; and exemptions, 209, 211; and the Merovingian kings, 108, 195, 207. *See also* Luxeuil

Compiègne, council of (757), 173

Constantine, emperor, 89–90

Constantius of Lyon, 216

Corbie, monastery, 122, 200, 209

Corbigny, monastery, 48, 172, 242

Dagobert I, king (623–639), 101, 146, 154, 182, 190, 211; and St.-Denis, 12, 17, 148–50

Dagobert II, king (676–679), 109

Dagobert III, king (711–715), 104, 119

deposition of Childeric III (751), 95–99, 108

Dijon, 13–14, 51. *See also* St.-Bénigne

Domesday Book, 54

Donation of Constantine, 66, 81

Drogo, duke, 111, 114, 118, 132, 155

dynasty, creation of, 106–27, 179–81, 190–92

Ebersheim, monastery, 183

Echternach, monastery, 106, 141, 173–74; foundation, 141, 170, 172, 178, 202

Effincourt, 57

Eigenkirchen, 143

Einhard, 188; creation of a Carolingian dynasty, 110–13, 121–23; as Carolingian publicist, 87, 91–92; and the Merovingian dynasty, 91, 96–100, 107

Elias, bishop of Chartres, 47
Emmo, bishop of Sens, 209
Erchinoald, 146
Erminethrudis, 178
Ermoldus Nigellus, 90
Etichonids, 132, 181–85
Eucharius, bishop of Orléans, 131
exemptions, 140–42, 173, 208–12. *See also* immunities

families in the early Middle Ages, 176–92; transformations of, 179–81
Faremoutier, monastery, 200
Ferrières, monastery, 139, 144, 237. *See also* Lupus of Ferrières
Flavigny, monastery, 240; in association of prayers, 172; cartulary of, 14–15, 37, 48, 139, 144, 165; chronicle of, 39–40, 47–50; eighth-century mutations, 156–64; formulary of, 157, 159–62; foundation, 41–42, 48, 157, 171, 202–3, 231; gospel of, 159; immunity of, 76. *See also* Hugh of Flavigny; Wideradus
Fleury (St.-Benoît-sur-Loire), monastery, 65
Fontenay, monastery, 15, 27
Fontenelle (St.-Wandrille), monastery, 111, 127, 138, 200, 203–4; and the Carolingians, 115, 145–48; charters of, 12–13, 154; and the Robertians, 189–90
forgery, 2–3, 16, 24, 33–34, 63–86; at Le Mans, 67–77; at Moûtier-St.-Jean, 198; and Pseudo-Isidore, 77–83; at St.-Denis, 16–17; and the written word, 64–66
forgetting the Merovingians, 99–103
formularies, 136–37, 141, 154–55, 157, 159–62, 168–69, 211
Fosses, monastery, 143, 167
foundation charters, 24–25, 27–29, 40–41, 194, 197–203
Franks, image of, 91–93
Fredegar, chronicler, 101–2, 112, 114–15, 180, 182, 207; continuations of, 95, 97, 114, 119, 129, 182; and the Franks, 91; and Hildebrand, 95, 158; inspiration for later chronicles, 47, 148; and the Merovingian kings, 107–8, 199–200
Fredegundis, queen, 208
Fulda, monastery, 11–12, 34, 156, 170, 172
Fulrad, 97, 177

Gauzlin, bishop of Le Mans, 72–73
Geary, Patrick, 3–4
Genovefa, saint, 195, 214

Germanus, bishop of Auxerre, 51, 196, 214, 216, 220–23
Gesta, 4, 44, 48, 54; of Auxerre, 22, 245–49; of Fontenelle, 145–48; of Le Mans, 65, 67, 69, 141
gesta municipalia, 157
Ghent, 12–13
Girard of Roussillon, founder of Vézelay, 40, 76, 241
Glanfeuil, monastery, 65
Goffart, Walter, 3
Gorze, monastery, 172–73
Grandval, monstery, 132, 183
Gregory, bishop of Langres, 43, 217, 224
Gregory I, pope (590–604), 38, 222
Gregory VII, pope (1073–1085), 80
Gregory of Tours, 71, 221–22, 224–25, 231; family of, 179, 217, 224; inspiration for later chronicles, 47; and the Merovingian kings, 91–93, 100–102, 132–33, 154, 205–7; and Radegund, 198
Grigny, 177
Grimoald I, 118, 136; coup of, 108–9, 282 n.9
Grimoald II, mayor of the palace, 111, 118–19
Guntram, king (561–592), 43, 74, 93, 108, 132, 205; and St.-Marcel, 196, 199–200, 211

Hadrian I, pope (772–795), 98, 138, 159
Hautvillers, monastery, 209
Henry, count of Bar, 26
Henry, count of Champagne, 26
Heraclius, papal legate, 35–36
Hildebrand, 95, 111, 158
Hincmar, archbishop of Reims, 82–83, 85, 139, 149
Homblières, monastery, 27–28, 33
Honau, monastery, 183
Honorius I, pope (625–638), 208
Hrabanus Maurus, abbot of Fulda, 11, 34
Hucbertus, 144, 235
Hugh, abbot of Cluny, 33
Hugh "the Abbot," 143
Hugh of Flavigny, 14, 41–42, 47–50
Hugh of Tours, 138–39, 181, 184

immunities, 74–77, 140, 208. *See also* exemptions
Ingelheim, 90
intercessory prayer, 204–5
Investiture Controversy, 49, 80
Irmina, 154, 178, 202

Isaac, bishop of Langres, 43
Isidore of Seville, 77, 142

Jerome, son of Charles Martel, 114–15
Jonas of Bobbio, 207
Jouarre, nunnery, 200
Judith, queen, 139
Jumièges, monastery, 111, 145, 147–48, 200, 203

"Karolus magnus et Leo papa," 87–88

La Bussière, monastery, 21
lacuna in monastic history, 165–71
La Ferté, monastery, 20
Langres, 28, 35–36, 43; bishops of, 48, 51, 76, 174; cartulary of, 15, 26, 32–35. *See also* Betto, bishop of Langres; Gregory, bishop of Langres
lay abbots, 142–45, 185–86
Le Mans: bishops of, 70, 133, 135, 137, 141–44, 171; forgeries of, 65–77, 103
Leo IX, pope (1049–1054), 1
Lérins, monastery, 157, 195, 198, 209, 211
Liber Historiae Francorum, 102, 108, 119, 148, 182, 208
Liber Pontificalis, 81, 97
Libri memoriales, 29, 34, 205
Limoges, 51
literacy in the Merovingian era, 153–56
literate mode, 18–20
Liutfred, saint, 104
Lobbes, monastery, 54
Longué, monastery, 15, 28
Lorsch, monastery, 11, 156, 174; foundation, 173, 188
Losne, 42
Louis the Pious, emperor (814–840), 23, 76, 90, 92–93, 98, 122–24, 159; and bishops, 19, 65, 144–45; and *dona,* 139–40; and the Le Mans forgeries, 70, 72–73, 75, 171; and monasteries, 138–41, 165–67, 169
Lupus of Ferrières, 139
Lupus of Troyes, 214
Luxeuil, monastery, 44, 157, 195, 200, 207–9, 211. *See also* Columbanus
Lyon, 35–36, 130, 199, 225; martyrs of, 214, 217, 221–22

Mabillon, Jean, 14, 35
Mâcon, 18, 35
manorialism, 56, 61, 153, 167

Marcellus, saint, 199–200, 217. *See also* St.-Marcel-lès-Chalon
Marcigny, nunnery, 15, 31
Marculf, 141, 154, 159–60, 211–12. *See also* formularies
Marmoutier, monastery, 51, 54, 140, 185, 200; cartularies, 28; foundation, 69, 194. *See also* Martin, saint
Marseille, 136
Martial, saint, 50, 185–86
Martin, saint, 54, 69, 72, 194, 214, 217
Martyrs, 199, 214–18, 221–22; martyrologies, 225–27
Maurus, saint, 65
Melun, monastery, 139, 236
memory, creative, 1–4, 40–43, 190–93, 197, 213; and the Carolingian dynasty, 87, 106, 122–25; and the dead, 228–29; and forgery, 2–3, 63; historiography, 3–4; and the Merovingian dynasty, 103–4, 122–24; and record-keeping, 22, 32
Merovech, 71, 205–6
Merovingian-era charters, 63–64, 153–56; at Le Mans, 71–75; reworked, 24–25, 29–30; at St.-Denis, 16–17. *See also* papyrus
Merovingian kings: and the church, 126–28, 132, 140–43, 205–8; deposition of, 95–99; dynasty, 180; family tree, 101; forgotten deliberately, 99–103; as Franks, 91–92; images of, 98–104; remembered, 103–5; as Roman rulers, 90–91, 102. *See also names of individual kings*
Metz: annalist of, 96, 99, 112, 117–21; bishops of, 115–16, 143. *See also* Arnulf, bishop of Metz
"Mirrors for Princes," 103
Molesme, monastery, 15
Molosmes, monastery, 241
monasteries: in Burgundy and Champagne, 233–44; and the Carolingians, 126–51, 171–74; and cathedrals, 50–52; in the early Middle Ages, 193–212; foundations, 41–42, 197–203; and the Merovingians, 126–28, 198, 205–8. *See also names of individual monasteries*
Montiéramey, monastery, 241
Montier-en-Der, monastery, 128, 166–67, 209; cartularies, 15–16, 22–23, 30, 37; forged documents from, 16; foundation, 24–25, 177, 239; polyptyque, 54–58, 60
Montier-la-Celle, monastery, 28, 239
Moûtier-St.-Jean (Reomaus), monastery, 139, 144, 196, 233–34; foundation, 198

Murbach, monastery, 137, 143, 184
mutations of the year 1000, 61–62, 152

Nesle, monastery, 139, 240
Nevers, 40, 242
Nicholas I, pope (858–867), 73–74
Nicaea, Council of (787), 89
Nivard, bishop of Reims, 24
notaries, 13, 156–58, 160, 170–71
Notker the Stammerer, 80, 82, 142
Notre-Dame of Autun, nunnery, 236
Novalesa, monastery, 177

Odila, saint, 181–83
Odorannus of St.-Pierre-le-Vif, 39

pancartes, 20–21
papyrus, 16–17, 24, 62, 64, 74, 155–56
Paray-le-Monial, monastery, 244
Paris, Council of (614), 42
Paternus, saint, 203–4
Paul of Chartres, 23, 31–32, 39, 46–47, 56–58, 60, 150
Paul the Deacon, 96, 106, 173; dynasty constructed by, 112–17, 123
Pelagius II, pope (579–590), 226
Philip I, king (1060–1108), 50
Pippin I, 112, 117–18, 182
Pippin of Herstal, 126, 136, 141, 155; family, 112–15, 117–19, 145–47; and the battle of Tertry, 99
Pippin the Short, king (751–768), 23, 42, 48, 116, 138, 141; anointing, 93, 95, 97; deposition of the Merovingians, 95–99, 109, 117; and Le Mans, 72–74, 135
Pirenne thesis, 152
Poitiers, 71, 198; battle of, 129–30
polyptyques, 53–62; fiscal aspects, 56; in the high Middle Ages, 58–62; in the ninth century, 53–58
Pontigny, monastery, 15–16, 22
Popes: authority of, 16–17, 78–83; and the Carolingians, 88–89, 91, 95–97; and the *Codex carolinus,* 11–12, 88; and the *Libri Carolini,* 88–89; papal bulls, 16, 22, 28; and the Pseudo-Isidorian decretals, 77–83. *See also names of individual popes*
Poulangy, nunnery, 239
Pouthières, monastery, 42, 76, 172, 242
poverty and property, 203–5
precarial grants, 60, 70, 133–37
Prüm, monastery, 54, 58–60, 170, 172

Pseudo-Isidorian decretals, 17, 66, 77–83
Puellemontier, nunnery, 240

Radegund, queen, 154, 198
realm, division of, 124
Rebais, monastery, 208–9, 211
Redon, monastery, 27
relics, 218–26
Remigius, bishop of Reims, 51
Reims, 24–25, 51, 114, 123; Council of (1049), 1
Reomaus. *See* Moûtier-St.-Jean
Rhineland monasteries, 11–14, 169
Richer, 185
Robert, bishop of Le Mans, 68, 73
Robert II, king (996–1031), 42, 186
Robertian dynasty, 185–90; family tree, 186
Robert the Strong, 185–88
Romanus, bishop of Rouen, 51
Rothgar, count, 135
Rouen, 51, 74–75, 121, 146–47, 219, 222–23
royal grants and privileges, 19, 28, 34, 66, 75, 85, 129, 185–86; for new monastic foundations, 24–25, 157, 198. *See also* exemptions; forgery at Le Mans; immunities

St.-Aignan of Orléans, monastery, 140, 200
St.-Andoche of Saulieu, 177, 240
St.-André of Vienne, monastery, 199
St.-Bénigne of Dijon, monastery, 49, 144, 166, 172, 234; and the bishops of Langres, 51; cartulary of, 14; chronicle of, 39; foundation of, 41, 43, 196
St.-Bertin, monastery, 5, 12–13, 54, 60
St.-Calais, monastery, 67–72, 141
St.-Denis, monastery, 85, 97, 132, 140, 178, 190, 200; cartulary of, 16–17; and King Dagobert, 12–13, 17, 148–50; forgery at, 16–17; formulary of, 159; papyrus from, 16, 155–56; privilege for, 208–9
St.-Dizier, 57
Ste.-Colombe of Sens, 209, 238
St.-Etienne of Dijon, house of canons, 13, 15, 240
St.-Etienne of Nevers, monastery, 238
St.-Gall, monastery, 12, 27, 34–35, 161, 171, 174
St.-Georges of Couches, 239
St.-Germain-des-Prés, monastery, 54–55, 325 n.12
St.-Germain of Auxerre, monastery, 51, 140, 143, 200, 221; cartulary, 15, 27–28; foundation, 246–47
St.-Jean of Sens, nunnery, 234

St.-Julien of Auxerre, nunnery, 25–26, 143, 184, 236, 248
St.-Loup of Troyes, monastery, 144, 237
St.-Marcel-lès-Chalon, monastery, 15, 33–35, 144, 166, 209, 211–12; foundation, 196, 199–200, 235
St.-Marien of Auxerre, monastery, 196, 233, 246
St.-Martial, monastery, 51
St.-Martin of Autun, monastery, 172, 236
St.-Martin of Nevers, house of canons, 242
St.-Martin of Tours, monastery, 53, 60, 144, 155, 167, 186, 205–6. *See also* Marmoutier
St.-Maur-des-Fossés, monastery, 54
St.-Maurice of Agaune, 157, 195, 199–200, 209, 211–12
St.-Médard of Soissons, monastery, 140, 200
St.-Mesmin of Micy, monastery, 103–4
St.-Michel of Tonnerre, monastery, 243
St.-Ouen, monastery, 51
St.-Père of Chartres, monastery, 23, 31–32, 39, 47, 54, 58, 150. *See also* Paul of Chartres
St.-Pierre-le-Vif, monastery, 51, 140, 200, 237; cartulary, 13–14; chronicle of, 38–41, 43–46, 169; privileges for, 209–10; relics at, 168
St.-Pierre of Chalon, monastery, 172, 241
St.-Pierre of Châlons, monastery, 244
St.-Remi of Reims, monastery, 51, 54, 60
St.-Remi of Sens, monastery, 234
St.-Rigaud, monastery, 18
St.-Sauveur/Notre-Dame of Nevers, monastery, 242
St.-Seine, monastery, 15, 139, 172, 196, 235
St.-Serge of Angers, monastery, 15, 37
Sts.-Géosmes, monastery, 241
St.-Symphorien of Autun, monastery, 172, 196, 215, 235
St.-Urbain of Châlons, monastery, 242
St.-Vanne, monastery, 47, 51
St.-Victor of Marseille, monastery, 54
St.-Vivant of Vergy, monastery, 243
St.-Wandrille. *See* Fontenelle
saints: competition for, 50–52; discovery of, 220, 222–25; lives of, 4, 231–32; multiplication of, 214–18. *See also names of individual saints*
Sancho and Beata, saints, 45
Saracen attacks on monasteries, 19, 129, 150, 167
sarcophagi, 229
seals, 18, 21, 23, 32–33, 36
Sens, 13, 43–46, 51, 168–69, 209. *See also* Ste.-Colombe of Sens; St.-Jean of Sens; St.-Pierre-le-Vif

serfs, 55–61
settlement patterns, 163–64, 167–68
Sidonius Apollonaris, 204, 215–16
Sigibert I, king (561–575), 208
Sigibert III, king (632–656), 108, 136
Simon of Clefmont, 26
Simon of Sexfontaines, 26
Stavelot-Malmedy, monastery, 136
Stephen, saint, 214, 219
Stephen II, pope (752–757), 17, 97–98
Sulpicius Severus, 214–19
Symphorien, saint, 215–17
synods, 133–36, 144

Tertry, battle of (687), 99, 280 n.68
testaments, 154, 157, 160–64, 176–78
Thegan, 184
Theodebert II, king (596–612), 71
Theoderic I, king (511–533), 74
Theoderic II, king (596–613), 42, 108, 207, 211
Theoderic III, king (673–691), 24–25, 74, 103, 132, 147, 183
Theoderic IV, king (721–737), 48, 109, 157, 162, 184
Theodulf, bishop of Orléans, 89, 104
Theuchildis, *regina*, 41, 168, 237
Theuley, monastery, 15
Tonnerre, 44–45, 243
Tournus, monastery, 241
Tours. *See* Gregory of Tours; Marmoutier; St.-Martin of Tours
Turibius, bishop of Le Mans, 69–70
Tussonval, monastery, 132, 155, 209

Urban I, pope (222–230), 79

Valence, council of, 211
Venantius Fortunatus, 71, 153–54, 203, 207, 217–18
Verberie, Council of (863), 68, 72–74
Verdun, 47–49, 51, 115
Vézelay, monastery, 15, 40, 42, 76, 172, 241
Victricius, bishop of Rouen, 219, 226
Vikings, 45–47, 75, 127–28, 150, 164, 201; and lost records, 13, 19
Vivien Bible, 92–94
Vultrogoda, queen, 69

Wala, abbot of Corbie, 122
Waldalenus, first abbot of Bèze, 201–2

Wandregesil, saint, 115, 145–46
Warin, cantor of Châlons-sur-Marne, 9, 11, 15, 22, 26, 29, 31
Wickham, Chris, 152–53, 179
Wideradus, founder of Flavigny, 48, 157–58, 163–66, 177, 202–3
William, abbot of St.-Bénigne, 43
Willibrord, missionary, 126, 141, 172, 202

Williswinda, 173, 188. *See also* Cancor; Lorsch
Wissembourg, monastery, 11, 54–55, 138–39, 170, 184
witnesses, 32, 160–61
written word, 18–20, 64–66, 68, 83, 85, 153–56

Zacharias, pope (741–752), 17, 83, 96–97

Acknowledgments

The first draft of this book was written at the Institute for Advanced Study (IAS) in Princeton, and revisions were made there on a return visit. Like many before me I found the IAS a Promised Land for scholars, composed of tranquil woods and meadows, plenty of books and a helpful staff ready to locate even more books, excellent food, stimulating colleagues, and a great deal of quiet time for thinking and writing. I was lucky to be part of two wonderful groups of medievalists, and my ideas greatly benefited from conversations with Caroline Bynum, Giles Constable, Stephen Bensch, Celia Chazelle, William Connell, Robin Fleming, Katherine French, Sharon Gerstel, James Grier, Elisabeth Mégier, Marcus Plested, and Karl Ubl. I am deeply grateful to the Institute both for a Membership and for the opportunity to return as a Visitor. My stays there were made possible by faculty improvement leaves from the University of Akron.

Jerry Singerman of the University of Pennsylvania Press has been wonderfully positive and supportive and found me two excellent readers in Alice Rio and Amy Remensnyder, who both helped shape the book's final version. Some of my ideas first developed during many conversations with Aline Hornaday, who was working on Merovingian saints long before I was. Gordon Thompson created an excellent map from my rough sketch. I would also like to acknowledge Felice Lifshitz, who may have set the North American record for volume of reader's comments on this book's first draft. Although I have not always agreed with her, I very much appreciate her generosity to a colleague working her way back from the twelfth century into the Merovingian period.

Preliminary versions of some of my ideas have been presented over the years at the International Medieval Congress in Kalamazoo and at the meetings of the Medieval Academy of America, the Midwest Medieval History Conference, the Ohio Academy of History, and the Delaware Valley Medieval Association. I first started thinking seriously about cartularies as a form of memory when invited to give a paper at the meetings of the Commission internationale de diplomatique—meetings held at the Institute for Advanced Study. Other portions of this book received their first public airings in the Medieval Seminar and in the School of Historical Studies series of presentations, both at the IAS, and in papers delivered to the medieval studies groups at the Ohio State University, Cleveland State University, and Hiram College. I thank everyone whose comments made me clarify what I really wanted to say, whether they found my work convincing or not, and all those who shared their own ideas and scholarship. Unless otherwise indicated, all translations are my own.

This book is dedicated to my mother, Harriet Ann Beckwith Brittain. My first "big" book, over twenty-five years ago, was dedicated to my father, and a dedication to her is long overdue. She has spent her adult life encouraging and supporting the academics in our family, and she always thought that going to France was an excellent idea.